Other Books and Series by Jeff Bowen

Applications for Enrollment of Chickasaw Newborn Act of 1905 Volumes I thru VII

Cherokee Intermarried White 1906 Volume I, II, III, IV & V

Visit our website at **www.nativestudy.com** to learn more about these and other books and series by Jeff Bowen

CHEROKEE INTERMARRIED WHITE 1906 VOLUME VI

TRANSCRIBED BY
JEFF BOWEN

NATIVE STUDY
Gallipolis, Ohio
USA

Other Books and Series by Jeff Bowen

Turtle Mountain Reservation Chippewa Indians 1932 Census with Births & Deaths, 1924-1932

Chickasaw By Blood Enrollment Cards 1898-1914 Volume I thru V

Cherokee Descendants East An Index to the Guion Miller Applications Volume I
Cherokee Descendants West An Index to the Guion Miller Applications Volume II (A-M)
Cherokee Descendants West An Index to the Guion Miller Applications Volume III (N-Z)

Applications for Enrollment of Seminole Newborn Freedmen, Act of 1905

Eastern Cherokee Census, Cherokee, North Carolina, 1915-1922, Taken by Agent James E. Henderson   Volume I (1915-1916)
Volume II (1917-1918)
Volume III (1919-1920)
Volume IV (1921-1922)

Complete Delaware Roll of 1898

Eastern Cherokee Census, Cherokee, North Carolina, 1923-1929, Taken by Agent James E. Henderson   Volume I (1923-1924)
Volume II (1925-1926)
Volume III (1927-1929)

Applications for Enrollment of Seminole Newborn Act of 1905 Volumes I & II

North Carolina Eastern Cherokee Indian Census 1898-1899, 1904, 1906, 1909-1912, 1914 Revised and Expanded Edition

1932 Hopi and Navajo Native American Census with Birth & Death Rolls (1925-1931) Volume 1 - Hopi
1932 Hopi and Navajo Native American Census with Birth & Death Rolls (1930-1932) Volume 2 - Navajo

Western Navajo Reservation Navajo, Hopi and Paiute 1933 Census with Birth & Death Rolls 1925-1933

Cherokee Citizenship Commission Dockets 1880-1884 and 1887-1889 Volumes I thru V

Other Books and Series by Jeff Bowen

1901-1907 Native American Census Seneca, Eastern Shawnee, Miami, Modoc, Ottawa, Peoria, Quapaw, and Wyandotte Indians (Under Seneca School, Indian Territory)

1932 Census of The Standing Rock Sioux Reservation with Births And Deaths 1924-1932

Census of The Blackfeet, Montana, 1897- 1901 Expanded Edition

Eastern Cherokee by Blood, 1906-1910, Volumes I thru XIII

Choctaw of Mississippi Indian Census 1929-1932 with Births and Deaths 1924-1931   Volume I
Choctaw of Mississippi Indian Census 1933, 1934 & 1937, Supplemental Rolls to 1934 & 1935 with Births and Deaths 1932-1938, and Marriages 1936-1938 Volume II

Eastern Cherokee Census Cherokee, North Carolina 1930-1939 Census 1930-1931 with Births And Deaths 1924-1931 Taken By Agent L. W. Page Volume I
Eastern Cherokee Census Cherokee, North Carolina 1930-1939 Census 1932-1933 with Births And Deaths 1930-1932 Taken By Agent R. L. Spalsbury   Volume II
Eastern Cherokee Census Cherokee, North Carolina 1930-1939 Census 1934-1937 with Births and Deaths 1925-1938 and Marriages 1936 & 1938 Taken by Agents R. L. Spalsbury And Harold W. Foght Volume III

Seminole of Florida Indian Census, 1930-1940 with Birth and Death Records, 1930-1938

Texas Cherokees 1820-1839 A Document For Litigation 1921

Choctaw By Blood Enrollment Cards 1898-1914 Volumes I thru XVII

Starr Roll 1894 (Cherokee Payment Rolls) Districts: Canadian, Cooweescoowee, and Delaware Volume One
Starr Roll 1894 (Cherokee Payment Rolls) Districts: Flint, Going Snake, and Illinois   Volume Two
Starr Roll 1894 (Cherokee Payment Rolls) Districts: Saline, Sequoyah, and Tahlequah; Including Orphan Roll   Volume Three

Cherokee Intruder Cases Dockets of Hearings 1901-1909 Volumes I & II

Indian Wills, 1911-1921 Records of the Bureau of Indian Affairs Books One thru Seven;
 Native American Wills & Probate Records 1911-1921

Copyright © 2014
by Jeff Bowen

ALL RIGHTS RESERVED
No part of this publication may be reproduced
or used in any form or manner whatsoever
without previous written permission from the
copyright holder or publisher.

Originally published:
Baltimore, Maryland
2014

Reprinted by:

Native Study LLC
Gallipolis, OH
www.nativestudy.com
2020

Library of Congress Control Number: 2020917307

ISBN: 978-1-64968-075-4

Made in the United States of America.

This series is dedicated to
Jerry Bowen
the Brave and the Strong.

DEPARTMENT OF THE INTERIOR
Commissioner to the Five Civilized Tribes
Muskogee, Indian Territory, March 9, 1907.

NOTICE IS HEREBY GIVEN that the undersigned, the Commissioner to the Five Civilized Tribes, has been designated by the Secretary of the Interior, as the official to make and approve appraisals of the value of improvements upon land in the Cherokee Nation which were made prior to November 5, 1906, by white persons who intermarried with Cherokee citizens prior to December 16, 1895, and who have the right under the Act of Congress approved March 2, 1907 (Public 180), to sell improvements.

NOTICE IS FURTHER GIVEN that former claimants to citizenship by intermarriage who have made permanent and valuable improvements on lands of the Cherokee Nation and who claim the right to sell the same under and by virtue of said Act of Congress of March 2, 1907 (Public 180), must appear before the Commissioner to the Five Civilized Tribes prior to April 1, 1907, and designate the land upon which are located the improvements which they claim the right to sell by virtue of said Act; and if any such intermarried citizen shall fail to appear before the Commissioner to the Five Civilized Tribes prior to April 1, 1907, it will be considered that he makes no claim to the benefits conferred by said Act. Such appearance and designation of improvements must be made before the Commissioner at his office in Muskogee, Indian Territory, at any time between Monday, March 11th, 1907, and Saturday, March 30th, 1907, inclusive, or at any of the following named places between the dates named at which places the Commissioner will have a representative to receive said designations and hear testimony relative thereto:

Bartlesville, Ind. Ter., Monday March 18th, 1907, to Saturday March 23rd, 1907, inclusive.
Tulsa, Ind. Ter., Monday March 25th, 1907, to Saturday March 30th, 1907, inclusive.
Claremore, Ind. Ter., Monday March 18th, 1907, to Saturday March 23rd, 1907, inclusive.
Nowata, Ind. Ter., Monday March 25th, 1907, to Saturday March 30th, 1907, inclusive.
Vinita, Ind. Ter., Monday March 18th, 1907, to Saturday March 23rd, 1907, inclusive.
Pryor Creek, Ind. Ter., Monday March 25th, 1907, to Saturday March 30th, 1907, inclusive.
Tahlequah, Ind. Ter., Monday March 18, 1907, to Saturday March 23rd, 1907, inclusive.
Sallisaw, Ind. Ter., Monday March 25th, 1907, to Saturday March 30th, 1907, inclusive.

Designations must be made in person by the intermarried white claimant, or in case proper proof is made that he is physically unable to appear, by some adult member of his immediate family, or in case proper proof is made of the fact that the intermarried white claimant is physically unable to appear and has no adult member of his immediate family, by a person holding a properly executed power of attorney; provided, that in every case the designation must be made by a party familiar with the character, ownership, location and value of the improvements to be designated. At the time of said designation the testimony of any competent person will be taken by the Commissioner as to the location, character and value of said improvements.

No former intermarried white claimant will be permitted to designate improvements upon more land than he would have been entitled to take in allotment had he for himself had he been admitted to citizenship. If any intermarried white claimant has made a tentative selection of a full allotment he will not be allowed to designate improvements upon other land.

NOTICE IS FURTHER GIVEN that if any citizen of the Cherokee Nation entitled to select an allotment shall claim that the improvements on land tentatively selected by a former intermarried white claimant, or held by him, do not belong to said intermarried white claimant, or makes any adverse claim to said improvements, or to the right of the intermarried white claimant to sell said improvements under the Act approved March 2, 1907 (Public 180), said citizen must appear before the Commissioner to the Five Civilized Tribes either at Muskogee, Indian Territory, prior to April 1, 1907, or at one of the places above designated and within the dates above designated and make formal complaint before the Commissioner to the Five Civilized Tribes of his contention. At Muskogee, Indian Territory, between March 11th and March 30th, 1907, inclusive, and at the other places herein named during the hearings at said places as herein fixed, plats will be open for inspection showing the location of tentative allotments made by former claimants to citizenship by intermarriage and all other land on which such claimants claim improvements, so far as indicated by the records of this office.

All persons interested should take careful note of the limitation of time herein provided for, within which designations and complaints may be made, and that they must be made by appearance before the Commissioner.

TAMS BIXBY,
Commissioner.

This particular notice concerns the appraisals of improvements on properties held by Cherokee intermarried whites. You would have found notices like this throughout the Nation to bring in people to finalize the allotment question, of who belonged and who did not.

E.C.M.

Cherokee 58.

DEPARTMENT OF THE INTERIOR,
COMMISSIONER TO THE FIVE CIVILIZED TRIBES.

In the matter of the application for the enrollment of ALBERTIN HAMPTON as a citizen by intermarriage of the Cherokee Nation.

D E C I S I O N

THE RECORDS OF THIS OFFICE SHOW: That at Fairland, Indian Territory, July 9, 1900, Albertin Hampton appeared before the Commission to the Five Civilized Tribes, and made application for the enrollment of himself as a citizen by intermarriage, and for the enrollment of his wife, Jane E. Hampton, et al. as citizens by blood of the Cherokee Nation. The application for the enrollment of the said Jane E. Hampton et al. as citizens by blood of the Cherokee Nation has been heretofore disposed of, and their rights to enrollment will not be considered in this decision. Further proceedings in the matter of said application were had at Muskogee, Indian Territory, September 3, 1902, October 14, 1902, and January 2, 1907.

THE EVIDENCE IN THIS CASE SHOWS: That the applicant herein, Albertin Hampton, a white man, was married, in accordance with Cherokee law, January 20, 1874, to his wife, Jane E. Hampton, nee Thomas, who was at the time of said marriage a recognized citizen by blood of the Cherokee Nation, and whose name appears on the approved partial roll of citizens by blood of the Cherokee Nation, opposite No. 195; that since said marriage the said Albertin Hampton and Jane E. Hampton have resided together as husband and wife, and have continuously lived in the Cherokee Nation. Said Albertin Hampton is identified on the Cherokee authenticated tribal roll of 1880, and the Cherokee census roll of 1896, as "Bert Hampton", an intermarried citizen of the Cherokee Nation.

IT IS, THEREFORE, ORDERED AND ADJUDGED: That in accordance with the decision of the Supreme Court of the United States, dated November 5, 1906, in the case of Daniel Red Bird et al. vs. the United States,

E.C.M.   - 2 -   Cherokee 58.

under the provisions of Section twenty-one, of the Act of Congress approved June 28, 1898 (30 Stat., 495), Albertin Hampton is entitled to enrollment as a citizen by intermarriage of the Cherokee Nation, and his application for enrollment as such is accordingly granted.

                                              _____
                                                  Commissioner.

Dated at Muskogee, Indian Territory,
this JAN 18 1907

The above is an accepted decision of the Commissioner to the Five Civilized Tribes. The Attorney for the Cherokee Nation had fifteen days after the date of Commissioner's decision in which to protest.

Cherokee
58.

W. W. HASTINGS, ATTORNEY
H. H. VANCE, SECRETARY

OFFICE OF

Attorney for the Cherokee Nation,

MUSKOGEE, I.T. January 18, 1907.

The Commissioner to the Five Civilized Tribes,

Muskogee, Indian Territory.

Sir:

Receipt is acknowledged of the testimony and of your decision enrolling Albertin Hampton, as a citizen by intermarriage of the Cherokee Nation. Time for protesting said decision is waived and I consent that said person may be placed upon the schedule immediately.

Yours very truly,

W. W. Hastings

Attorney for Cherokee Nation.

The above is a notice of the Attorney waiving the time for protesting the Commissioner's decision (on the two previous pages) concerning Albertin Hampton's application and consenting to place the applicant upon schedule immediately.

INTRODUCTION

The *Cherokee Intermarried White*, National Archive film M-1301, Rolls 305-307, are found under the heading of Applications for Enrollment of the Commission to the Five Civilized Tribes. The genealogical value of this series concerning the relationships between many Cherokee tribesman and their marriages among another race is very important and virtually a treasure trove of information long sought after. While on the other hand what these cases are really about are the efforts of many to attain Cherokee land allotments. Referenced from the Supreme Court Decision, Cherokee Intermarriage Cases – 203 U.S. 76 (1906).

This collection of Intermarried claims involves two hundred and eighty-eight separate cases with a variety of scenarios from the divorced to the widowed to the deserving to the deceptive. During these times there were many that wanted what was rightfully only the Cherokees. You will see each case will be headed by the title from the first folder as an example: *Intermarried White I, Trans from Cher. 34*, the transfer number is the Dawes Commission number from the claimants spouse.

These cases are fascinating because of the generational bloodlines that can be verified by documentation rather than just word of mouth. From Kent Carter's book, *The Dawes Commission*, "The tribe also, continued to oppose the enrollment of whites who had married into the Cherokee tribe. That controversy dragged through the U.S. Court of Claims and then the Supreme Court, which finally ruled in favor of the tribe on November 05, 1906. The court upheld the Cherokee citizenship laws that denied rights to any white who had married into the tribe after November 1, 1877. It also upheld an 1839 law which stated that anyone who moved out of the nation lost their citizenship unless they were readmitted. The applications of 3,341 persons were rejected as a result of this ruling, and the allotment clerks were forced to undo a great deal of their work. With the issue finally settled by the courts, the commission was able to send the first schedule of Cherokees by intermarriage, containing fifty-five names, to the secretary of interior on June 10, 1907. Eventually only 286 people were enrolled as intermarried whites----far fewer than the number put on the rolls of the Choctaw and Chickasaw tribes, which had much more liberal laws on rights based on marriage." [1]

---

[1] The Dawes Commission and the Allotment of the Five Civilized Tribes, 1893-1914 by Kent Carter, pg. 121

In Cohen's Handbook of Federal Indian Law he states, "In the *Cherokee Intermarriage Cases,* the Supreme Court considered the claims of certain white persons, intermarried with Cherokee Indians, who wanted to participate in the common property of the Cherokee Nation. Such persons were permitted by tribal law to be tribal citizens with limited rights in tribal property. The tribe had also provided for the revocation of citizenship rights of a white person who intermarried with a Cherokee if the Cherokee spouse were abandoned or if a widower or widow married a non-Cherokee. The Court found that the Cherokee Nation had authority to qualify the rights of citizenship which it offered to its "naturalized citizens. Such tribal action defeated the claims of the plaintiffs:

> The laws and usages of the Cherokees, their earliest history, the fundamental principles of their national policy, their constitution and statutes, all show that citizenship rested on blood or marriage; that the man who would assert citizenship must establish marriage; that when marriage ceased (with a special reservation in favor of widows or widowers) citizenship ceased; that when an intermarried white married a person having no rights of Cherokee citizenship by blood it was conclusive evidence that the tie which bound him to the Cherokee people was severed and the very basis of his citizenship obliterated."[2]

An important footnote that Cohen published within his pages for the above paragraph also needs to be studied. He noted, "Under Cherokee law white persons intermarrying with Cherokees before 1875 were tribal citizens for most purposes, including allotment of tribal land, but had no interest in tribal funds except those funds derived from tribal lands. A Cherokee law that became effective in 1875 provided that whites marrying Cherokees had no rights to tribal property but could obtain full citizenship by the payment of $500 to the tribe. In 1877 the tribe provided that no intermarried citizen could obtain any rights to tribal land or funds."[3]

During many years of study this author has found cases that should have been been accepted, especially with the particular documentation presented. All in all the outcome of the decision made should have rendered a different result. Also there have been many that numb the mind as to how they their cases were even considered. The years have given many the hopes that their ancestors were one of those that had a decent claim and an honest consideration. Like any time in history there are political struggles

---

[2] Felix S. Cohen's Handbook of FEDERAL INDIAN LAW 1982 ED. pgs 20-21.
[3] Felix S. Cohen's Handbook of FEDERAL INDIAN LAW 1982 ED. pg 21 footnote16.

and the human factor that points out man is not perfect. These pages were transcribed with the wish that another person somewhere along the line will find their relation from the past and give them the answers long hoped for.

Jeff Bowen
Gallipolis, Ohio
NativeStudy.com

Cher IW 166

Cherokee Intermarried White 1906
Volume VI

◇◇◇◇◇

E.C.M.

DEPARTMENT OF THE INTERIOR,

COMMISSIONER TO THE FIVE CIVILIZED TRIBES.

In the matter of the application for the enrollment of

ELVIRA B. DANNENBERG

As a citizen by intermarriage of the Cherokee Nation.

CHEROKEE NO. 10065.

◇◇◇◇◇

State Hospital for Insane
No. 2
Superintendent's Office

St Joseph, Mo   June 12, 1902   *190*

TO WHOM IT MAY CONCERN

I here by state that Mrs. Elvira Danenburg[sic] of Andrew County, Missouri, was admitted to this Institution June 6, 1878. She has been an inmate of this Institution since that date. She has Chronic Mania. She is very badly disturbed, destructive, and generally troublesome. I do not think that she will ever be any better mentally. Her general health is very good.

C R Woodson
Superintendent.

◇◇◇◇◇

Cherokee Intermarried White 1906
Volume VI

R.
Cher

Department of the Interior,
Commission to the Five Civilized Tribes,
Muskogee, I. T., June 24, 1902.

In the matter of the application of JOHN C. DANNENBERG, for the enrollment of his mother as a citizen by intermarriage of the Cherokee Nation.

JOHN C. DANNENBERG, being duly sworn and examined by the Commission, testified as follows:

Q What is your name ?   A John C. Dannenberg.
Q Is Tahlequah your post office address ?   A Yes sir.
Q Do you make application for the enrollment of your mother ?   A Yes sir.
Q What is the name of your mother ?   A Elvira B. Dannenberg.
Q About how old is she ?   A I suppose she must be 48.
Q Is she a Cherokee by blood ?   A No sir.
Q What was her father's name ?   A Doctor Vestal is all I can tell you. I know her mother's full name.
Q What was her mother's full name.[sic]   A Mary J. Vestal.
Q Her parents are both dead ?   A No sir, her mother is still living, her father is dead.

By Mr. Hastings: What is your father's name ?
A Richard M. Dannenberg.
Q Was he ever married but the one time ?   A He has been married twice.
Q Was your mother ?   A No sir, my mother has only been married once.
Q Her marriage to your father was her only marriage ?   A Yes sir.

--1880 roll, page 361, # 430, Flint District, E. B. Dannenberg;

By the Commission: When was your mother married to your father Mr. Dannenberg ?   A In 1873 I believe.
Q How long did they continue to live together as man and wife ?
A Well, I was born in 1874, and I think it must have been about in 1878.
Q Have they separated ?   A Yes sir.
Q Where has your mother been since that time ?
A She has been in an asylum at St. Joe, Missouri.
Q Has she been there since her separation from your father ?
A I think so, I haven't seen her.

The Commission: There is offered in evidence by the applicant a certificate from C. R. Woodson, Superintendent of the State Hospital for the Insane, St. Joe,

Cherokee Intermarried White 1906
Volume VI

Missouri, June 12, 1902, relative to the mental condition of Mrs. Elvira Dannenberg. The same is filed herewith and made a part of the record.

Q To the best of your knowledge your mother separated from your father about 1878 ?
A Yes sir.

--The following note appears opposite the name of the applicant on the 1880 roll: "In State of Missouri--insane".

John C. Dannenberg applies for the enrollment of his mother as a citizen by intermarriage of the Cherokee Nation. His mother is duly identified on the roll of 1880 as an adopted white.
It appears from the evidence in this case that about the year 1878, she separated from her husband, and that she has been confined in an insane asylum at St. Joe, Missouri, since. Final judgment as to her case will be suspended and her name placed upon a doubtful card pending final consideration and judgment by the Commission.

E. C. Bagwell, on oath states that as stenographer to the Commission to the Five Civilized Tribes, he correctly recorded the testimony and proceedings had in the above entitled cause, and that the foregoing is an accurate transcript of his stenographic notes thereof.

E.C. Bagwell

Subscribed and sworn to before me this June 28, 1902.

PG Reuter
Notary Public.

◇◇◇◇◇

Statement of Applicant Taken Under Oath.

CHEROKEE BY BLOOD AND ADOPTION.

Date **June 25th, 1902**   ~~1900.~~

Name
District .... Year .... Page .... No. ....
Citizen by blood .... Mother's citizenship ....
Intermarried citizen ....
Married under what law .... Date of marriage ....
License .... Certificate ....

48
Wife's name   **Elvira B. Dannenberg**
District   **Flint**   Year **1880**   Page **861**   No. ~~543~~ **430**
Citizen by blood   **No**   Mother's citizenship   **Vestal - d- w**
Intermarried citizen **Yes**   **Mary J " - l - w**
Married under what law .... Date of marriage ....
License .... Certificate ....

3

Cherokee Intermarried White 1906
Volume VI

Names of Children:

	Dist.	Year	Page	No.	Age
	Dist.	Year	Page	No.	Age
Doubtful	Year	Page	No.	Age	
	Dist.	Year	Page	No.	Age
	Dist.	Year	Page	No.	Age

On 1880 roll as E.B. Dannenberg.

J.C. Dannenberg - Agent

Cher D 1347
Supp'l

Department of the Interior,
Commission to the Five Civilized Tribes,
Muskogee, I. T., October 13, 1902.

In the matter of the application of ELVIRA B. DANNENBERG, for the enrollment of herself as a citizen by intermarriage of the Cherokee Nation:

JOHN C. DANNENBERG, called as a witness, being duly sworn and examined by the Commission, testified as follows:

Q What is your name ?   A John C. Dannenberg.
Q What is your age ?   A Twenty eight.
Q What is your post office ?   A Tahlequah, I. T.
Q Are you acquainted with Elvira B. Dannenberg ?   A Yes sir.
Q She is an applicant before this Commission for enrollment as a citizen by intermarriage of the Cherokee Nation ?   A Yes sir.
Q What relation are you to her ?   A She is my mother.
Q Where is she at present ?   A In the State Hospital for the Insane, St. Joseph, Missouri.
Q How long has she been there Mr. Dannenberg ?
A I presume about twenty three or four years.
Q What was the name of her husband ?   A Richard M. Dannenberg.
Q He is a citizen by blood of the Cherokee Nation ?
A He is.
Q Were your mother and Richard M. Dannenberg separated before she was placed in the Hospital at St. Joe ?   A No sir.
Q Where were the living at the time she became insane ?
A Flint, Indian Territory.
Q In the Cherokee Nation ?   A Yes sir.

Cherokee Intermarried White 1906
Volume VI

Q Was she taken from the Cherokee Nation up to St. Joe, Missouri, when she went insane ? A Yes sir.
Q And she has been in the asylum ever since ? A Ever since.
Q She has never married any other man except your father Richard M. Dannenberg ? A No sir.
Q Did your father get a divorce from her when she went insane ? A I don't know.
Q You know that so far as your mother is concerned she had never married any other man up to the first day of September, 1902 ? A Oh no sir.
Q Do you know what her condition is at this time ?
A Yes sir, the physician in charge advises me that her case is hopeless.

E. C. Bagwell, on oath states that, as stenographer to the Commission to the Five Civilized Tribes, he correctly recorded the testimony and proceedings had in the above entitled cause, and that the foregoing is an accurate transcript of his stenographic notes thereof.

E.C. Bagwell

Subscribed and sworn to before me this October 23, 1902.

BC Jones
Notary Public.

◇◇◇◇◇

Cherokee D-1347.

DEPARTMENT OF THE INTERIOR,
COMMISSION TO THE FIVE CIVILIZED TRIBES.
---o---

In the matter of the application for the enrollment of Elvira B. Dannenberg as a citizen by intermarriage of the Cherokee Nation.

II II II II II II II II

D E C I S I O N.

--:o:--

The record in this case shows that on June 25, 1902, John C. Dannenberg appeared before the Commission at Muskogee, Indian Territory, and made application for the enrollment of his mother, Elvira B. Dannenberg, as a citizen by intermarriage of the

Cherokee Intermarried White 1906
Volume VI

Cherokee Nation. Further proceedings in the matter of said application were had at Muskogee, Indian Territory, on October 13, 1902.

The evidence shows that the said Elvira B. Dannenberg was lawfully married to Richard M. Dannenberg, a Cherokee citizen by blood, about the year 1873, and they lived together in the Cherokee Nation until about 1878, at which time she became insane and was taken to the State Hospital for Insane at St. Joseph, Missouri, and that she has been an inmate of said institution since June 6, 1878. The said Elvira B. Dannenberg is identified on the Cherokee Authenticated Tribal Roll of 1880.

The evidence further shows that the said Elvira B. Dannenberg, on the date of this application, had been continuously confined since 1878 at the State Hospital for Insane at St. Joseph, Missouri, and that she had never been divorced from her said husband, Richard M. Dannenberg, and was, therefore, his lawful wife on September 1, 1902.

It is not considered that the absence of the applicant from the Cherokee Nation and Indian Territory, under the conditions states, has worked a forfeiture of her citizenship, and it is considered by the Commission that Elvira B. Dannenberg should be enrolled as a citizen by intermarriage of the Cherokee Nation, in accordance with the provisions of Section twenty-one of the Act of Congress approved June 28, 1898, (30 Stats., 495), and it is so ordered.

COMMISSION TO THE FIVE CIVILIZED TRIBES.

Tams Bixby
Chairman.

TB Needles
Commissioner.

C. R. Breckinridge
Commissioner.

Dated at Muskogee, Indian Territory,
this   DEC 10 1902

Cherokee Intermarried White 1906
Volume VI

Cherokee
No. 10065

DEPARTMENT OF THE INTERIOR
COMMISSIONER TO THE FIVE CIVILIZED TRIBES
Muakogee[sic], Indian Territory

January 4, 1907

In the matter of the application for the enrollment of Elvira B. Dannenberg as a citizen by intermarriage of the Cherokee Nation.

John C. Dannenberg, representing the applicant, being duly sworn, testified as follows:

Q What is your name? A John C. Dannenberg.
Q How old are you? A My next brithday[sic], 33.
Q What is your postoffice address? A Tahlequah
Q Do you know Elvira B. Dannenberg? A Yes sir
Q What relation are you to Elvira B. Dannenberg? A I am her son
Q You appear here today in behalf of her application for enrollment as a citizen by intermarriage of the Cherokee Nation? A I do.
Q Through whom does Elvira B. Dannenberg claim her right to enrollment as a citizen by marriage of the Cherokee Nation?
A Through my father, Richard M. Dannenberg.
Q When was Richard M. Dannenberg and your mother married?
A April 9, 1873.
Q Where were they married, if you know? A They were married in Buchanan County, state of Missouri.
Q Have you any documentary evidence of their marriage? A I have. I have the certificate of the minister who performed the ceremony
Q Do you desire to offer this in evidence? A I do. I also wish to introduce my father to prove that B. M. Denenberge mentioned in this certificate and Richard M. Dannenberg are one and the same person.

Certificate of Marriage of B.M. Denenberge and Miss E. B. Vestal filed herewith and made a part of the record in this case.

Witness excused.

Richard M. Dannenberg being called as a witness in behalf of the applicant testified as follows:

Q What is your name? A Richard M. Dannenberg.
Q How old are you Mr. Dannenberg? A 56 next birthday.
Q What is your postoffice address? A Tahlequah.

Cherokee Intermarried White 1906
Volume VI

Q Are you the husband of Elvira B. Dannenberg? A Yes sir
Q When was you married to Elvira B. Dannenberg? A April 9, 1873
Q Are you the identical person mentioned in the certificate filed here by her son who is mentioned in said certificate as B. M. Denenberge? A Yes sir
Q How long did you live with Elvira B. Dannenberg after you married her?
A Five years
Q Was she a recognized citizen of the Cherokee Nation at the time you married her?
A Yes sir.
Q Where did you live with her? A I lived in the Cherokee Nation.
Q Moved to the Cherokee Nation immediately after your marriage?
A I was born and raised in the Cherokee Nation, moved there immediately after my marriage with Elvira B. Dannenberg
Q Is Elvira B. Dannenberg living at this time? A That I don't know, I suppose she is.
Q When was the last time you saw her? A About 26 years ago, I con't[sic] remember the exact date.
Q Where was she at that time? A She was in Missouri.

Witness excused

The applicant is identified on the 1880 Cherokee roll, Flint District, opposite No. 430. Her husband through whom she claims right to enrollment is identified on said roll in said district opposite No. 429. He is also identified on the final roll of citizens by blood of the Cherokee Nation opposite No. 17102.

Gertrude Hanna, being duly sworn, states that as stenographer to the Commissioner to the Five Civilized Tribes she reported the proceedings had in the above numbered case on January 4, 1907 and that the above and foregoing is a true and correct transcript of her stenographic notes thereof stenographic notes taken therein.

Gertrude Hanna

Subscribed and sworn to before me this 5 day of January, 1907.

Chas E Webster
Notary Public.

Cherokee Intermarried White 1906
Volume VI

HARTFORD FIRE INSURANCE CO.
INCORPORATED 1810.
LOSSES PAID $72,000,000.00.
RESIDENT AGENT

Office of
J.C. Dannenberg,
Insurance

Tahlequah, I.T.   Oct. 15th. 1902.

The Commission to the Five Civilized Tribes,
    Muscogee[sic], Indian Territory.
Gentlemen:--

  In re Mrs. Elvira Danneberg[sic], applicant for enrollment as a Cherokee citizen by intermarriage.

  I appeared before the Commission on the 18th instant to make further statement with reference to this case. In reply to a question, "Was your father divorced from your mother," I believe my reply was, "I do not know." This is not correct and I make this statement to correct it. My father was not divorced from my mother and I would respectfully request that this letter be filed with my statement if possible.

      Very respectfully,

      J.C. Dannenberg

◇◇◇◇◇

Denenberge   To   Vestal

State of Missouri ⎱
County of Buchanan ⎰ ss   I hereby certify that I joined in Marriage on the 9th day of April, 1873 Mr. B. M. Denenberge and Miss E. B. Vestal of the County aforesaid.

  Given under my hand this 9th day of April, 1873.
          Elder T. R. Ferguson
Filed for record April 12th, 1873.
          Thomas Kelly   Recorder

Cherokee Intermarried White 1906
Volume VI

STATE OF MISSOURI, ⎫
⎬ ss
COUNTY OF BUCHANAN, ⎭   I, JOSEPH N. KARNES, Recorder of Deeds, within and for the County and State aforesaid, do hereby certify that the above and foregoing instrument of writing is a true and correct copy of the Record of the Marriage of Mr. B. M. Denenberge and Miss E. B. Vestal as recorded in book "C" at page 428 of the Marriage Records of Buchanan County.

       IN TESTIMONY WHEREOF, I have hereunto set my hand and affixed my official seal at my office in ST. JOSEPH, MO, this 29th day of December 1906.

                                                Joseph N. Karnes   Recorder.
                                                                        of Deeds.

◇◇◇◇◇

E C M   Cherokee 10065.

DEPARTMENT OF THE INTERIOR,

COMMISSIONER TO THE FIVE CIVILIZED TRIBES.

      In the matter of the application for the enrollment of ELVIRA B. DANNENBERG as a citizen by intermarriage of the Cherokee Nation.

D E C I S I O N

      THE RECORDS OF THIS OFFICE SHOW: That on June 25, 1902, application was received by the Commission to the Five Civilized Tribes for the enrollment of Elvira B. Dannenberg as a citizen by intermarriage of the Cherokee Nation. Further proceedings in the matter of said application were had at Muskogee, Indian Territory October 13th, 1902 and January 4th, 1907.

      THE EVIDENCE IN THIS CASE SHOWS: That the applicant herein, Elvira B. Dannenberg, a white woman, married on April 9th, 1873 one Richard M. Dannenberg, who was at the time of said marriage a recognized citizen by blood of the Cherokee Nation and who is identified on the Cherokee authenticated tribal roll of 1880, Flint District, page 361, No. 429 as a native Cherokee. It is further shown that from the time of said marriage on April 9th, 1873 until June 6th, 1878 the said Richard M. Dannenberg and Elvira B. Dannenberg resided together as husband and wife and continuously lived in the Cherokee Nation; that on June 6th, 1878 the said Elvira B. Dannenberg was sent to the State Hospital for the Insane at St. Joseph, Missouri; that since her reception into said institution the said Elvira B. Dannenberg has remained hopelessly insane and continued a patient therein; that said Richard M. Dannenberg and Elvira B. Dannenberg have not

Cherokee Intermarried White 1906
Volume VI

been divorced nor has the said Richard M. Dannenberg remarried since April 9th, 1873. Said applicant is identified on the Cherokee authenticated tribal roll of 1880 as an intermarried citizen of the Cherokee Nation.

IT IS, THEREFORE, ORDERED AND ADJUDGED: That in accordance with the decision of the Supreme Court of the United States, dated November 5th, 1906, in the cases of Daniel Red Bird, et al. vs. the United States, Nos. 125, 126, 127 and 128, under the provision of Section Twenty-one of the Act of Congress approved June 28th, 1898 (30 Stats., 495), to enrollment as a citizen by intermarriage of the Cherokee Nation, and her application for enrollment as such is accordingly granted.

Tams Bixby
Commissioner.

Dated at Muskogee, Indian Territory,
this   JAN 30 1907

◇◇◇◇◇

Cherokee 10065

DEPARTMENT OF THE INTERIOR,

COMMISSIONER TO THE FIVE CIVILIZED TRIBES.

In the matter of the application for the enrollment of Elvira B. Dannenberg, as a citizen by intermarriage of the Cherokee Nation.

--:--

SUPPLEMENTAL DECISION.

The records of this office show that on June 25, 1902, application was received by the Commission to the Five Civilized Tribes for the enrollment of Elvira B. Dannenberg as a citizen by intermarriage of the Cherokee Nation. Further proceedings in the matter of said application were had at Muskogee, Indian Territory, October 13, 1902, and January 4, 1907.

The Commissioner to the Five Civilized Tribes in his decision dated January 30, 1907, granted the application for the enrollment of said Elvira B. Dannenberg as a citizen by intermarriage of the Cherokee Nation.

The records further show that on December 10, 1902, the Commission to the Five Civilized Tribes rendered its decision granting the application for the enrollment of said applicant as a citizen by intermarriage of the Cherokee Nation, a fact not mentioned by the Commissioner in his decision dated January 30, 1907.

It is therefore ordered and adjudged that the decision of the Commission to the Five Civilized Tribes dated December 10, 1902, granting the application for the enrollment of Elvira B. Dannenberg as a citizen by intermarriage of the Cherokee Nation,

Cherokee Intermarried White 1906
Volume VI

be, by this supplemental decision, affirmed, and the Commissioner's decision dated January 30, 1907, granting said applicant the right to enrollment as a citizen by intermarriage of the Cherokee Nation, be also affirmed.

              Tams Bixby
              Commissioner.

Dated at Muskogee, Indian Territory,
this   February 1, 1907.

October 3rd, 1902

J. C. Dannenberg,
  Tahlequah, I. T.

Dear Sir:-

  Yours of the 27th ult. at hand. Enclosed find certificate as to Mrs. Dannenberg condition etc.

  Mrs. Elvira Dannenberg of Andrew County, Missouri has been an inmate of this institution continuously during my incumbency as Superintendent since August 11th, 1890. and that the said Mistress Dannenberg was an inmate at the time I took charge of said institution. She has not married during this period of time.

              Respectfully,
              CR Woodson
              Superintendent.

Cherokee Intermarried White 1906
Volume VI

COPY   Cherokee D 1347.

Muskogee, Indian Territory, December 20, 1902.

W. W. Hastings,
    Attorney for the Cherokee Nation,
        Muskogee, Indian Territory.

Dear Sir:

    There is herewith enclosed a copy of the decision of the Commission to the Five Civilized Tribes, dated December 10, 1902, granting the application of John C. Dannenberg for the enrollment of his mother, Elvira B. Dannenberg, as a citizen by intermarriage of the Cherokee Nation.

    You are hereby advised that you will be allowed fifteen days from date hereof in which to file such protest as you desire to make against the action of the Commission in this case, a copy of which protest you will be required to serve upon the applicant. If you fail to file protest within the time allowed, this decision will be considered final.

                Respectfully,

                            Tams Bixby

Enclosure H. No. 418.   Acting Chairman.

◇◇◇◇◇

                                   Cherokee D-1347
COPY

Muskogee, Indian Territory, January 14, 1903.

John C. Dannenberg,
    Tahlequah, Indian Territory.

Dear Sir:-

    There is herewith enclosed a copy of the decision of the Commission to the Five Civilized Tribes, dated December 10, 1902, granting your application for the enrollment of your mother, Elvira B. Dannenberg, as a citizen by intermarriage of the Cherokee Nation.

                Respectfully,

                            Tams Bixby
                          Acting Chairman.

Enc. M-240
Register.

◇◇◇◇◇

Cherokee Intermarried White 1906
Volume VI

~~Cherokee Freed~~.
C. 10065

Muskogee, Indian Territory, November 19, 1906.

J. C. Dannenberg,
    Tahlequah, Indian Territory.

Dear Sir:

    Replying to your letter of November 12, 1906, you are advised that as this office has not been officially advised of the decision of the United States Supreme Court in the case involving the question of the right of intermarried white persons to enrollment as citizens of the Cherokee Nation, it can give you no information at this time as to whether or not your mother, Elvira B. Dannenberg, is entitled to enrollment as a citizen by intermarriage of the Cherokee Nation, and h application for enrollment as such is accordingly granted., or whether the record in her case is complete.

    On receipt of official notice of the Court's decision, intermarried white cases will receive prompt consideration of this office.

                    Respectfully,

S.W.   Commissioner.

◇◇◇◇◇

Cherokee
10065

Muskogee, Indian Territory, December 27, 1906.

J. C. Dannenberg,
    Tahlequah, Indian Territory.

Dear Sir:

    November 6, 1906, the United States Supreme Court held that white persons who intermarried with Cherokee citizens according to Cherokee law prior to November 1, 1875, are entitled to enrollment and allotments of land as citizens of the Cherokee Nation.

    You are advised that to properly determine the right of your mother, Elvira B. Dannenberg, to enrollment as a citizen by intermarriage of the Cherokee Nation, it will be necessary for you to appear before the Commissioner for the purpose of giving testimony as to the date of her marriage and whether or not her husband, by reason of her marriage to whom she claims the right to enrollment as a citizen by intermarriage of the Cherokee Nation, was a recognized Cherokee citizen at the time of her marriage to him.

Cherokee Intermarried White 1906
Volume VI

You are therefore directed to appear before the Commissioner at Muskogee, Indian Territory, at 9 o'clock A. M., on Saturday, January 5, 1907, and give testimony as above indicated.

Respectfully,

GHL   Acting Commissioner.

◇◇◇◇◇

Cherokee 10065

Muskogee, Indian Territory, January 30, 1907.

W. W. Hastings,
    Attorney for the Cherokee Nation,
        Muskogee, Indian Territory.

Dear Sir:

There is enclosed herewith copy of the decision of the Commissioner to the Five Civilized Tribes, dated January 30, 1907, granting the application for the enrollment of Elvira B. Dannenberg as a citizen by intermarriage of the Cherokee Nation.

Respectfully,

Enc I-39   Commissioner.

RPI

◇◇◇◇◇

Cherokee 10065

Muskogee, Indian Territory, January 30, 1907.

The Commissioner to the Five Civilized Tribes,
    Muskogee, Indian Territory.

Sir:

Receipt is acknowledged of the testimony and of your decision enrolling Elvira B. Dannenberg as a citizen by intermarriage of the Cherokee Nation. Time for protesting said decision is waived and I consent that said person may be placed upon the schedule immediately.

Respectfully,
W. W. Hastings
Attorney for the Cherokee Nation.

◇◇◇◇◇

Cherokee Intermarried White 1906
Volume VI

Cherokee 10065

Muskogee, Indian Territory, January 30, 1907.

J. C. Dannenberg,
    Tahlequah, Indian Territory.

Dear Sir:

    There is enclosed herewith copy of the decision of the Commissioner to the Five Civilized Tribes, dated January 30, 1907, granting the application for the enrollment of your mother, Elvira B. Dannenberg, as a citizen by intermarriage of the Cherokee Nation.

    You will be advised when your mother's name has been placed upon a schedule of citizens of the Cherokee Nation and approved by the Secretary of the Interior.

                              Respectfully,

Enc I-40   Commissioner.

RPI

◇◇◇◇◇

Cherokee 10065

Muskogee, Indian Territory, February 1, 1907.

W. W. Hastings,
    Attorney for the Cherokee Nation,
        Muskogee, Indian Territory.

Dear Sir:

    There is enclosed herewith a copy of supplemental decision of the Commissioner to the Five Civilized Tribes, dated February 1, 1907, granting the application for the enrollment of Elvira B. Dannenberg as a citizen by intermarriage of the Cherokee Nation.

                              Respectfully,

Encl. H-92   Commissioner.
JMH

◇◇◇◇◇

Cherokee Intermarried White 1906
Volume VI

Cherokee 10065

Muskogee, Indian Territory, February 1, 1907.

J. C. Dannenberg,
    Tahlequah, Indian Territory.

Dear Sir:

    There is enclosed herewith a copy of the supplemental decision of the Commissioner to the Five Civilized Tribes, dated February 1, 1907, granting the application for the enrollment of your mother, Elvira B. Dannenberg, as a citizen by intermarriage of the Cherokee Nation.

    You will be advised when your mother's name has been placed upon a schedule of citizens of the Cherokee Nation and approved by the Secretary of the Interior.

                      Respectfully,

Encl. H-93
JMH
                                    Commissioner.

Cher IW 167

◇◇◇◇◇

CFB

DEPARTMENT OF THE INTERIOR,

COMMISSIONER TO THE FIVE CIVILIZED TRIBES.

In the matter of the application for the enrollment of

JOHN W. BREEDLOVE

as a citizen by intermarriage of the Cherokee Nation.

CHEROKEE 1471

◇◇◇◇◇

Cherokee Intermarried White 1906
Volume VI

Department of the Interior,
Commission to the Five Civilized Tribes,
Muldrow, I.T., August 15, 1900.

In the matter of the application of John W. Breedlove for the enrollment of himself, wife and children as Cherokee citizens, beig[sic] sworn and examined[sic] by Commissioner Breckinridge he testifies as follows:

Q What is your full name? A John W. Breedlove.
Q What is your age? A Forty-eight years old.
Q What is your post-office? A Muldrow.
Q What is your district? A Sequoyah.
Q For whom do you apply for enrollment? A Myself, my wife and children.
Q How many children under age? A Six living.
Q Do you apply for yourself as a Cherokee by blood? A No sir, I am an adopted citizen.
Q What is your wife's name? A Carrie W.
Q How old is she? A She is forty-two.
Q When were you married? A In 1875.
Q Your wife is upon the roll of 1880? A Yes sir.
Q Has she lived in the Cherokee Nation ever since 1880? A Yes sir, and continuously; she has been out with the children at school recently.
Q Did she go out for the purpose of making a home, or simply for school purposes?
A No sir, for school purposes.
Q Has your principal home and place of residence ben all the time since 1880 in the Cherokee Nation? A Yes sir, I have never been out.
Q You are on the roll of 1880 are you? A Yes sir.
Q You have made your home continuously in the Cherokee Nation since 1880[sic]
A Yes sir.
Q You and your wife have lived together ever since 1880? A Since 1875.
Q Give me the names of your children an[sic] the ages? A William O., eighteen years old; John C., sixteen years old; Cassie, fourteen years old; Wharton, twelve years old; Walton D., ten years old; Charles W., one and one-half years old.
Q These are all living at this time? A Yes sir.
1880 roll, page 686 #215 John W. Breedlove, Sequoyah District.
1880 roll, page 686 #216 Carrie W. Breedlove, Sequoyah District.
1896 roll, page 1054 #171 Carrie W. Breedlove, Sequoyah District.
1896 roll, page 1111 #17 John W. Breedlove, Sequoyah District.
1896 roll, page 1054 #173 William O. Breedlove, Sequoyah District.
1896 roll, page 1054 #174 John C. Breedlove, Sequoyah District.
1896 roll, page 1054 #175 Cassie Breedlove, Sequoyah District.
1896 roll, page 1054 #176 Wharton Breedlove, Sequoyah District.
1896 roll, page 1054 #177 Walton D. Breedlove, Sequoyah District.

Com'r Breckinridge: The wife of this applicant is identified on the roll of 1880 as a Cherokee by blood; he is identified on the roll of 1880 as a Cherokee by adoption; they are both identified on the roll of 1896; five of their children, William O., John C., Cassie,

Cherokee Intermarried White 1906
Volume VI

Wharton and Walton D., are identified on the roll of 1896; now the applicant will be listed at this time for enrollment as a Cherokee by adoption, and his wife and these five children will be listed at this time for enrollment as Cherokees by blood; the youngest child, Charles W. is too young to be upon any roll of the Cherokee Nation; now certificate of the birth of this child is duly made out and attested and supplied to this Commission then this child Charles W. Breedlove will also be enrolled as a Cherokee by blood.

M.D. Green, being first duly sworn, states that as stenographer to the Commission to the Five Civilized Tribes he reported the foregoing case and that the above and foregoing is a full true and complete transcript of his stenographic notes.

MD Green

Subscribed and sworn to before me this 23 day of August 1900.

TB Needles
Commissioner.

◇◇◇◇◇

Cherokee 1471.

Department of the Interior,
Commission to the Five Civilized Tribes,
Muskogee, I. T., October 9, 1902.

In the matter of the application of John W. Breedlove for the enrollment of himself as a citizen by intermarriage, and for the enrollment of his wife, Carrie W., and children, William O., John C., Cassie, Wharton, Walton D. and Charles W. Breedlove, as citizens by blood of the Cherokee Nation.
James W. Breedlove, being sworn and examined by the Commission, testified as follows:
Q What is your name, age and postoffice? A James W. Breedlove; I am twentyf-ive[sic] years old, live at Muldrow, I. T.
Q Are you acquainted with John W. Breedlove who is an applicant before this Commission as an intermarried citizen of the Cherokee Nation? A Yes sir, I am.
Q Is he any relation of yours? A He is my father.
Q Where does John W. Breedlove live? A He lives at Muldrow, Indian Territory; he has a temporary residence I might say at Fort Smith where his children are going to school. His family stays down there in the winter, in school season, and attend school at Fort Smith.
Q Has John W. Breedlove and his wife, Carrie, lived together ever since 1880 as husband and wife? A Yes sir.
Q They never have been separated? A No sir.
Q They were living together on the first day of September, 1902, as husband and wife? A Yes sir.
Q You say they have a temporary residence in Fort Smith? A Yes sir.

Cherokee Intermarried White 1906
Volume VI

Q When did they go to Fort Smith? A I think it must have been in '99 or 1900. I think it was in '99; I am not positive, I am making a rough guess.
Q When they went to Fort Smith did all the family go, did the mother and father and all the younger children? A Yes sir.
Q Do they keep house there in Fort Smith? A Yes sir.
Q Now was 1899 or 1900 the first time they went to Fort Smith? A Yes sir.
Q They never have been to Fort Smith prior to that time to live? A No sir.
Q And as I understand you do they go over there in the fall of every year and stay during the school term? A They come back to our home in the territory during the summer months.
Q Where is that? One and a half miles from Muldrow, Indian Territory our old home place.
Q Who still owns that? A My father.
Q Does your mother and father and all the children come up there in the summer? A Yes sir.
Q Do they stay out on the farm? A Yes sir, they stay out on the farm and some time they stay in town where my father's office is.
Q What business is your father in at Muldrow? A He is in the long distance telephone business.
Q This home place you speak of, while they are away what is done with the house while they are away? A We have some tenants live in the back yard; they take care of the property, servants there that oversee the property there etc.
Q Don't anybody occupy the main house proper while they are away? A Yes sir, I think they do.
Q When they come back in the summer time do they go out and keep house or simply board along with the renters; or live in town? A I don't know that they make anything like a permanent residence out of it, no more than to spend the summer months out there.
Q Isn't it a fact since your father has taken his family to Fort Smith in '99, isn't that the only place he has kept house since he went there? A Yes sir.
Q He never kept house anywhere else except in Fort Smith since he took his family there in '99? A Yes sir.
Q Since then he has kept his property here and has it rented out? A No sir, no more than to bring the family up in the summer months and they stay there on the farm.
J. C. Starr: Did your father live at Fort Smith any time before 1899? A Not that I know of; not since I have been born; if he ever did I don't know anything of it.
Commission: Where did he live before he went to Fort Smith? A On this farm at Muldrow. He has lived there ever since I was born, I was born right there.

 This testimony will be filed as supplemental in the matter of the application of John W. Breedlove et al. In case further testimony will be required the applicant will be notified to appear.

 The undersigned, being duly sworn, states that as stenographer to the Commission to the Five Civilized Tribes he correctly recorded the testimony and proceedings in this

Cherokee Intermarried White 1906
Volume VI

case, and that the foregoing is a true and complete transcript of his stenographic notes thereof.

E.G. Rothenberger

Subscribed and sworn to before me this 6th day of November, 1902.

BC Jones
Notary Public.

◇◇◇◇◇

Cherokee 1471.

Department of the Interior,
Commission to the Five Civilized Tribes,
Muskogee, I. T., December 10, 1902.

In the matter of the application of John W. Breedlove for the enrollment of himself as a citizen by intermarriage, and for the enrollment of his wife, Carrie W. and children, William O., John C., Cassie, Wharton, Walton D. and Charles W. Breedlove, as citizens by blood of the Cherokee Nation: he being sworn and examined by the Commission, testified as follows:

Q What is your name? A John W. Breedlove.
Q What is your age at this time? A Fifty years old.
Q What is your postoffice? A Muldrow.
Q You are an applicant for enrollment as an intermarried citizen are you of the Cherokee Nation? A Yes sir.
Q What is your wife's name? A Carrie W. Bruton was her name.
Q Is she a recognized citizen by blood of the Cherokee Nation? A Yes sir.
Q When were you married to your wife, Carrie? A August 25, 1875.
Q You are on the roll of 1880 with her as her husband are you? A Yes sir.
Q Have you ever been married to any other woman besides your wife, Carrie W. Bruton? A No sir.
Q She is the only wife you have ever had is she? A Yes sir.
Q Has she ever been married to any other man? A No sir.
Q You were the only husband she ever had? A Yes sir.
Q Have you lived in the Cherokee Nation continuously from 1880 up until the present time? A Yes sir.
Q Where has your family been for the last two years? A My family has been in Fort Smith.
Q When did your family first go to Fort Smith? A They moved to Fort Smith August 12, 1898.
Q Are they keeping house there, Mr. Breedlove? A Yes sir, they went there to get the children in school. She stayes[sic] there and I stay in the territory.
Q Do you go over there to see her? A Yes sir.
Q How often do you go there? A Once and twice a week.

Cherokee Intermarried White 1906
Volume VI

Q Do you run a house in the City of Fort Smith do you not? A Yes sir, I have a house there.
Q House furnished? A Yes sir.
Q You are not separated from your wife? A No sir.
Q You and she were living together on the first day of September, 1902? A Yes sir.
Q But you claim your residence in the territory and she resides in Arkansas is that it?
A Yes sir, my business is over in the territory; I always stay here and sometimes run home at night.
Q How do you fix the date when your family first went to Fort Smith? A I have been in the territory - I have twelve children, and was at one place all the time, and a man nearly always remembers when he leaves a home like that; I was there for over twenty years.
Q Your family lived right there all the time until they went to Fort Smith in '98?
A Yes sir, in '98.
Q They never moved away from the farm before that? A No sir, we never had but two places where we resided; that was there and in the house at Fort Smith.
Q Your wife has not been on this side to keep house since she went to Fort Smith? A She comes up in summer to camp and fish and hunt with the children - fishing. She has never kept house on this side.
Q She kept house always in Fort Smith? A Yes sir; I have a hotel built on the place where I am and they come there and stay part of the time during vacations and then they go back to school.
Q Give me the date of when your wife and family went to Fort Smith, Arkansas the first time they moved over there? A August 12, 1898.
Q And your wife with the children have kept house there in Fort Smith ever since up until now have they? A Yes sir.
Q And you go over there once and twice a week to see them? A Yes sir.
Q How far is your place in the Cherokee Nation from Fort Smith? A It is ten miles.
Q When you go over to see them you usually stay all night do you not? A Yes sir.
Q How long is the longest time you ever spent at any one time in Fort Smith since you have been over there? A Not longer than one or two days; I don't believe I stayed over two days.
Q And your children, Mr. Breedlove, attend the public schools in Fort Smith or private schools? A They attend - some of them attend the public schools and some private schools. I have two boys that are grown, that are both back in the territory; they come just as soon as they could leave schooling and came out here and stayed with me.
Q You pay taxes on your property in Fort Smith don't you? A Yes sir, I pay taxes on it.
Q Have you ever voted in any of the municipal elections in Fort Smith? A NO sir.
Q Did you ever vote in any of the state or county elections? A No sir.
Q Have you ever paid poll tax in Fort Smith? A No sir. I want to say that before I moved my family to town I talked to McKennon and he said it would be perfectly right; he said if your home is there for the purpose of education you have a right to go there on business and attend to anything.

The undersigned, being duly sworn, states that as stenographer to the Commission to the Five Civilized Tribes he correctly recorded the testimony and proceedings in this

Cherokee Intermarried White 1906
Volume VI

case, and that the foregoing is a true and complete transcript of his stenographic notes thereof.

E.G. Rothenberger

Subscribed and sworn to before me this 10th day of December, 1902.

BC Jones
Notary Public.

◇◇◇◇◇

Cherokee 1471.

DEPARTMENT OF THE INTERIOR,
COMMISSION TO THE FIVE CIVILIZED TRIBES.
Muskogee, Indian Territory, January 3, 1907.

In the Matter of the Application for the Enrollment of John W. Breedlove as a citizen by intermarriage of the Cherokee Nation.

Carrie W. Breedlove being first sworn by John E. Tidwell, Notary Public, testified as follows:

Q What is your name?
A Carrie W. Breedlove.
Q What is your age?
A 48.
Q What is your post office address?
A Muldrow, Indian Territory.
Q Are you a citizen by blood of the Cherokee Nation?
A I am.
Q Your name appears on the Tribal Roll as such, does it?
A Yes sir.
Q Are you married?
A I am a widow.
Q What was the name of your husband.
A John W. Breedlove.
Q When did he die?
A May 18, 1904.
Q You appear here to-day for the purpose of giving testimony relative to his right to enrollment as a citizen by intermarriage of the Cherokee Nation, do you?
A Yes sir.
Q He was not a Cherokee by blood?
A No sir.
Q His claim to the right to enrollment is ased[sic] upon his marriage to you?
A Yes.
Q When were you married to your husband?
A 1875.

23

Cherokee Intermarried White 1906
Volume VI

Q   Where were you living at the time you married him?
A   Near a small place called Cottonwood, before Muldrow was in existence, in the Cherokee Nation.
Q   Was he living in the Cherokee Nation at that time?
A   Yes; had been for a number of years.
Q   Was he ever married prior to his marriage to you?
A   If he was, I never knew of it.
Q   You never were married before you married him?
A   No.
Q   From the date of your marriage, did you and he continuously live together as husband and wife until the time of his death in 1904?
A   We did.
Q   And lived continuously in the Cherokee Nation?
A   For about seven years we lived in Fort Smith, Arkansas, for the benefit of the schools, or I did rather; Mr. Breedlove stayed at Muldrow.
Q   That was temporary absence?
A   Yes sir; for the benefit of the schools.
Q   You considered the Cherokee Nation your home all the time you were living in Fort Smith?
A   Yes sir.
Q   You had property here and a home here?
A   Yes sir; and I neglected to say that it was September, '75 that we were married.
Q   When John W. Breedlove married you, did he secure the license in due form?
A   He did.
Q   And you were married in accordance with the laws of the Cherokee Nation?
A   Yes sir; and you have our certificate with the Clerk's seal on it, filed here with the Dawes' Commission, I suppose. I gave it to my husband to file.
Q   He filed it with the Commission to the Five Civilized Tribes?
A   Yes sir; before his death.

The applicant, John W. Breedlove, is identified on Cherokee authenticated Tribal Roll of 1880, Sequoyah District, No. 215. His wife, Carrie W. Breedlove, is included in approved partial roll of citizens by blood of the Cherokee Nation, opposite No. 4006.

Q   In what district were you living at the time you were married?
A   We have always lived in Sequoyah District.

The undersigned being first duly sworn states that as stenographer to the Commission to the Five Civilized Tribes, she correctly recorded the testimony taken in this case and that the foregoing is a full, true and correct transcript of her stenographic notes thereof.

Myrtle Hill

Cherokee Intermarried White 1906
Volume VI

Subscribed and sworn to before me this the 4th day of January, 1907.

B.P. Rasmus
Notary Public.

◇◇◇◇◇

CERTIFIED COPY.

Cherokee Nation.)
Seqouya[sic] District.)

    John W. Breedlove, a white man and a citizen of the United States, having this day made application for a marriage license by presenting a petition with the requisite number of signers and having also already complied with the law respecting intermarriage with white men, therefore marriage license is hereby granted to the said John W. Breedlove to marry Miss Carrie Bruton, a Cherokee Lady.

    Now, therefore, to any of the Judges of the Cherokee Nation or any regularly ordained minister of the Gospel, "Greeting". You are hereby authorized to join in the holy state of matrimony by solemnizing the rites usually observed in such cases between the above named John W. Breedlove and Miss Carrie Bruton. Given from under my hand in office on this 2nd. day of Sept., 1875.

R. R. Taylor,
Clk. Seq. Dist.

    This certifies that I, W. S. Derrick, have this day solemnized the rite of matrimony between the parties whose names are within. Witness my hand this the 10th of Sept. 1875.

W. S. Derrick,
Ordained Minister of the Gospel.

    Recorded in the office of the Dist. Clerk of Seq. Dist. this 2nd. day of Oct., 1875.

R. R. Taylor,
Clk. Seq. Dist.

Cherokee Intermarried White 1906
Volume VI

I, Frances R. Lane, a stenographer to the Commissioner to the Five Civilized Tribes, hereby certify that the foregoing is a true and complete copy of a marriage license and certificate now on file in this office.

Frances R. Lane

Subscribed and sworn to before me this February 5, 1907.

Walter W. Chappell
Notary Public.

◇◇◇◇◇

C.F.B. Cherokee 1471

DEPARTMENT OF THE INTERIOR,

COMMISSIONER TO THE FIVE CIVILIZED TRIBES.

In the matter of the application for the enrollment of John W. Breedlove as a citizen by intermarriage of the Cherokee Nation.

D E C I S I O N

THE RECORDS OF THIS OFFICE SHOW: That at Muldrow, Indian Territory, August 15, 1900, application was received by the Commission to the Five Civilized Tribes, for the enrollment of John W. Breedlove as a citizen by intermarriage of the Cherokee Nation. Further proceedings in the matter of said application were had at Muskogee, Indian Territory, October 9, 1902, December 10, 1902, and January 3, 1907.

THE EVIDENCE IN THIS CASE SHOWS: That the applicant herein, John W. Breedlove, was married in accordance with Cherokee law, in September 1875, to his wife, Carrie W. Breedlove, who was at the time of said marriage, a recognized citizen by blood of the Cherokee Nation, who is identified on the Cherokee authenticated tribal roll of 1880, Sequoyah District, No. 216, as a native Cherokee; and whose name appears on the approved partial roll of citizens by blood of the Cherokee Nation, opposite No. 4006. It is further shown that since said marriage the said John W. and Carrie W. Breedlove have resided together as husband and wife and continuously lived in the Cherokee Nation until the death of the said John W. Breedlove, which occurred in 1904. Said applicant is duly identified on the Cherokee authenticated tribal roll of 1880, and the Cherokee census roll of 1896, as an intermarried citizen of the Cherokee Nation.

IT IS, THEREFORE, ORDERED AND ADJUDGED: That in accordance with the decision of the Supreme Court of the United States, dated November 5, 1906, in the cases of Daniel Red Bird, et al., vs. the United States, Nos. 125, 126, 127 and 128, the said applicant, John W. Breedlove, is entitled, under the provisions of Section twenty-one of the Act of Congress approved June 28, 1898 (30 Stats., 495), to enrollment as a citizen by

Cherokee Intermarried White 1906
Volume VI

intermarriage of the Cherokee Nation, and his application for enrollment as such is accordingly granted.

Tams Bixby
Commissioner.

Dated at Muskogee, Indian Territory,
this   FEB 8 1907

◇◇◇◇◇

Cherokee 1471

Muskogee, Indian Territory, December 6, 1902.

John W. Breedlove,
    Muldrow, Indian Territory.

Dear Sir:-

    You are hereby notified that the testimony given before the Commission on October 9, 1902, by James W. Breedlove, relative to your right to enrollment on September 1, 1902, as a citizen by intermarriage of the Cherokee Nation, is not considered sufficient by the Commission, and before your application for enrollment will be complete, it will be necessary for you to appear in person and give further testimony in your case.

Respectfully,

Acting Chairman.

◇◇◇◇◇

Cherokee
1471

Muskogee, Indian Territory, December 27, 1906.

Carrie W. Breedlove,
    Muldrow, Indian Territory.

Dear Madam:

    November 6, 1906, the United States Supreme Court held that white persons who intermarried with Cherokee citizens according to Cherokee law prior to November 1, 1875, are entitled to enrollment and allotments of land as citizens of the Cherokee Nation.

    You are advised that to properly determine your deceased husband's right to enrollment as a citizen by intermarriage of the Cherokee Nation, it will be necessary for

Cherokee Intermarried White 1906
Volume VI

you to appear before the Commissioner for the purpose of giving testimony as to the date of his marriage and whether or not his wife, by reason of his marriage to whom he claims the right to enrollment as a citizen by intermarriage of the Cherokee Nation, was a recognized Cherokee citizen at the time of his marriage to her, and whether or not he was married to her in accordance with Cherokee laws.

You are, therefore, directed to appear before the Commissioner at Muskogee, Indian Territory, at 9 o'clock A. M., on Thursday, January 3, 1907, and give testimony as above indicated.

Respectfully,

J.M.H.   Acting Commissioner.

◇◇◇◇◇

Cherokee 1471

Muskogee, Indian Territory, February 8, 1907.

W. W. Hastings,
    Attorney for the Cherokee Nation,
        Muskogee, Indian Territory.

Dear Sir:

There is enclosed herewith a copy of the decision of the Commissioner to the Five Civilized Tribes, dated February 8, 1907, granting the application for the enrollment of John W. Breedlove as a citizen by intermarriage of the Cherokee Nation.

Respectfully,

Encl. H-1   Commissioner.
JMH

◇◇◇◇◇

Cherokee 1471

Muskogee, Indian Territory, February 8, 1907.

The Commissioner to the Five Civilized Tribes,
    Muskogee, Indian Territory.

Sir:

Receipt is acknowledged of the testimony and of your decision enrolling John W. Breedlove as a citizen by intermarriage of the Cherokee Nation. Time for protesting said

Cherokee Intermarried White 1906
Volume VI

decision is waived and I consent that said person may be placed upon the schedule immediately.

>   Respectfully,
>   W. W. Hastings
>   Attorney for Cherokee Nation.

◇◇◇◇◇

Cherokee 1471

> Muskogee, Indian Territory, February 8, 1907.

Carrie W. Breedlove,
    Muldrow, Indian Territory.

Dear Madam:

    There is enclosed herewith a copy of the decision of the Commissioner to the Five Civilized Tribes, dated February 8, 1907, granting the application for the enrollment, as a citizen by intermarriage of the Cherokee Nation, of your deceased husband, John W. Breedlove.

    You will be advised when the name of your said husband has been placed upon a schedule of citizens of the Cherokee Nation and approved by the Secretary of the Interior.

> Respectfully,

Encl. H-2   Commissioner.
JMH

◇◇◇◇◇

Cherokee
I.W. 167.

> Muskogee, Indian Territory, April 16, 1907.

Carrie W. Breedlove,
    Muldrow, Indian Territory.

Dear Madam:

    Your marriage license and certificate filed in connection with your application for enrollment as a citizen by intermarriage of the Cherokee Nation is returned to you herewith, copies of the same being retained in the files of this office.

> Respectfully,

Encl. W-7   Commissioner.
S.W.

Cherokee Intermarried White 1906
Volume VI

Cher IW 168

◇◇◇◇◇

C.E.W.

DEPARTMENT OF THE INTERIOR,

COMMISSIONER TO THE FIVE CIVILIZED TRIBES.

In the matter of the application for the enrollment of

HARVY LINDSY

as a citizen by intermarriage of the Cherokee Nation.

Cherokee 2250.

◇◇◇◇◇

Department of the Interior,
Commission to the Five Civilized Tribes,
Fort Gibson, I.T., August 30, 1900.

In the matter of the application of Harvey Lindsay for the enrollment of himself as a Cherokee by intermarriage and his wife as a Cherokee by blood: being sworn and examined by Commissioner Needles, he testified as follows:

Q What is your name? A Harvey Lindsay.
Q What is your age? A 75.
Q What is your post office address? Z[sic] Texana[sic], I. T.
Q Are you a recognized citizen of the Cherokee Nation? A I am.
Q By blood? A No, sir, by adoption.
Q Who do you want to enroll? A Well, myself and my wife is all.
Q What district do you live in? A Canadian.
Q How long have you been a resident of the Cherokee Nation? A I came here in the fall of 1869, but I was married January 1, 1873.
Q Have you been living here ever since? A Yes, sir.
Q Your father and mother non citizens? A Yes, sir, non citizens.
Q What is the name of your wife? A Elizabeth Jane.
Q What is the name of her father? A I don't know.
Q What is the name of her mother? A Margaret Eiffert.
Q She living? A Yes, sir.
Q What is your wife's age? A She is about 65.

30

Cherokee Intermarried White 1906
Volume VI

Q Has she lived in the Cherokee Nation continuously for the last ten or fifteen year? A Yes, sir.
(On 1880 roll, page 32, No. 862, Harry Lindsay, Canadian district. Elizabeth Jane Lindsat[sic] on 1880 roll, page 32, No. 863, Bettie Lindsay Canadian district. Harvey Lindsay on 1896 roll, page 89, No. 161, Harvey Lindsay, Canadian district. Elizabeth Jane Lindsay on 1896 roll, page 44, No. 1194, Bettie J. Lindsay, Canadian district.)

The name of Harvey Lindsay appears upon the authenticated roll of 1880 as Harry Lindsay and upon the census roll of 1896 as Harvey Lindsay, and the name of his wife appears upon the authenticated roll of 1880 as Bettie Lindsay and upon the census roll of 1896 as Bettie J. Lindsay. They being fully identified according to page and number of the roll as indicated in the testimony and having made satisfactory proof as to their residence, said Harvey Linsday[sic] and his wife, Elizabeth Jane, will be duly listed for enrollment by this Commission, he as a Cherokee citizen by intermarriage and she as a Cherokee citizen by blood.

----------0----------

Bruce C Jones, being duly sworn, says that as stenographer to the Commission to the Five Civilized Tribes he correctly recorded the proceedings and testimony in the above case, and the foregoing is a true and complete transcript of his stenographic notes thereof.

Bruce C. Jones

Sworn to and subscribed before me this the 6th day of September, 1900.

TB Needles
Commissioner.

◇◇◇◇◇

Cherokee 2250.

DEPARTMENT OF THE INTERIOR,
COMMISSION TO THE FIVE CIVILIZED TRIBES.
Muskogee, I. T., October 25, 1902.

In the matter of the application of Harvy[sic] Lindsy[sic] for the enrollment of himself as a citizen by intermarriage and for the enrollment of his wife, Elizabeth J. Lindsy, as a citizen by blood, of the Cherokee Nation.

SUPPLEMENTAL PROCEEDINGS.

HARVY LINDSY, being sworn, testified as follows:

By the Commission.

Cherokee Intermarried White 1906
Volume VI

Q What is your name, please? A Harvy Linds (e) y.
Q What is your age at this time? A I was seventy-seven the 16th day of July.
Q What's your postoffice? A Texanna.
Q Are you the same Harvey Lindsey[sic] that made application for enrollment as an intermarried citizen in August, 1900? A No, sir? Done what?
Q Are you the same Harvy Lindsey that made application for enrollment as an intermarried citizen in August, 1900? Two years ago last August? A I don't remember, I was enrolled here way back about '80, somewhere.
Q Have you ever made application to this Commission for enrollment as an intermarried citizen? A No, sir.
Q Never been before them? A No, sir.
Q Who made the application for you? A What?
Q For enrollment to this Commission? A I don't remember now.
Q Has your wife ever made application for enrollment to this Commission? A I did not know I had to make no application before I come here.
Q Somebody come here before the Commission in 1900 and made application for enrollment of Harvy Lindsey as a citizen by intermarriage, whose age at the time was given as seventy five years old, and for his wife, Elizabeth J., as a citizen by blood?
A What's the name of the wife?
Q Elizabeth J. A That's my wife's name.
Q Is that the name of your wife? A I never made no application.
Q Is that the name of your wife? A Harvy is my name and hers Elizabeth J.
Q And her age was given as sixty-five. A That ain't her age, sixty-nine.
Q Somebody evidently made application for you, didn't they? A I never made any.
Q Do you want to make application now? A Yes, sir.
Q Doctor, you have been sick a good deal in the last year? A No, I had a touch of paralysis about two months ago, but I am getting pretty well over that.
Q Getting pretty well over it? A Yes, sir, it is in the left side here.
Q What is your postoffice, two years ago? A Texanna.
Q Well, you're an applicant for enrollment as an intermarried citizen now, are you?
A Yes, sir, my wife was a Cherokee.
Q What's your wife's name? A Elizabeth Jane, we call her Bettie Jane.
Q Is she living now? A Yes, sir.
Q Is she a citizen by blood of the Cherokee Nation? A Yes, sir.
Q When were you married to her? A I was married the first day of January, '73.
Q '73? A Yes, sir.
Q Are you on the '80 roll with her? A I guess so, I was on the first roll made.
Q Were you ever married before you married her? A Yes, sir.
Q How many times had you been married before you married her? A I was married twice before.
Q Both of your wives dead? A Yes, sir.
Q Was Elizabeth Jane ever married before her marriage to you? A Yes, sir.
Q How many times? A Once.
Q Where? A In California, her husband was dead.
Q Have you and your wife, Elizabeth, lived together since '80 up to the present time?
A Yes, sir.

Cherokee Intermarried White 1906
Volume VI

Q Never been separated? A Not at all.
Q And you were living together as husband and wife on the first day of September, 1902? A Yes, sir.
Q Have you and your wife lived in the Cherokee Nation all the time since '80 up to the present time? A Yes, sir, we have.

      Retta Chick, being first duly sworn, states that, as stenographer to the Commission to the Five Civilized Tribes, she recorded the testimony and proceedings in the matter of the foregoing application, and that the above is a true and complete transcript of her stenographic notes thereof.

Retta Chick

Subscribed and sworn to before me this 28th day of November, 1902.

PG Reuter
Notary Public.

Cherokee 2250.

DEPARTMENT OF THE INTERIOR,
COMMISSION TO THE FIVE CIVILIZED TRIBES.
Muskogee, Indian Territory, January 3, 1907.

      In the Matter of the Application for the Enrollment of Harvey Lindsey as a citizen by intermarriage of the Cherokee Nation.

      Harvey Lindsey being first duly sworn by B. P. Rasmus, Notary Public, testified as follows:

Q What is your name?   A Harvey Lindsey.
Q What is your age?
A I was 81 years old the 16th day of last July.
Q What is your post office address?
A Texana[sic], Indian Territory.
Q You are an applicant for enrollment as a citizen by intermarriage of the Cherokee Nation?
A Yes sir.
Q You have no Cherokee blood?
A No sir.
Q The only right you have to enrollment as a citizen of the Cherokee Nation is by virtue of your marriage to a citizen by blood of the Cherokee Nation?
A Yes sir.
Q What is the name of the citizen through whom you claim the right to enrollment?
A Bettie Jane McCarty; her maiden name was Hanks.

Cherokee Intermarried White 1906
Volume VI

Q When were you married to her?
A 1st day of January, 1873.
Q Were you ever married prior to your marriage to her?
A Yes sir.
Q Was your former wife living or dead at the time?
A Dead.
Q Was she married prior to her marriage to you?
A No sir, my first wife wasn't.
Q When did you marry your first wife?
A In 1851.
Q What was her name?
A Martha Cowsar.
Q Was she a Cherokee by blood?
A No, she was a white woman.
Q You claim the right to enrollment through your second wife?
A Yes sir.
Q And what was the date of your marriage to her?
A 1st day of January, 1873.
Q She had been married prior to her marriage to you, had she?
A Yes sir.
Q Was her former husband living or dead?
A Dead.
Q And your former wife was dead at the time you married your second wife?
A Yes sir; had been a good many years.
Q Is your second wife living at the present time?
A Yes sir.
Q Since your marriage to your second wife, have you and she continuously lived together as husband and wife?
A We have.
Q And lived in the Cherokee Nation, have you?
A Yes sir.
Q Have you any evidence showing the marriage of yourself to your second wife?
A Yes sir.
Q Did you secure a license at that time you married your second wife?
A I did.
Q Have you that license with you?
A No sir; I don't know where it is now.
Q You secured a license in accordance with the laws of the Cherokee Nation, did you?
A Yes sir; I did.
Q Your wife, Elizabeth J. Lindsey was a recognized citizen by blood of the Cherokee Nation at the time you married her, was she?
A Yes sir.
Q In what district did you secure the license to marry your second wife?
A It was down at Webber's Falls; Canadian District.
Q How many signers did you have to have?
A I don't recollect now.

Cherokee Intermarried White 1906
Volume VI

Q You got the license though in accordance with the Cherokee laws?
A Yes sir; I did.
Q You present here a certificate of marriage showing that on the 1st day of January, 1873, one Dr. Harvey Lindsey was married to Bettie J. McCarty by Samuel Taylor. Are you the identical person mentioned in this marriage certificate as Harvey Lindsey?
A I am.
Q And your wife, Elizabeth J. Lindsey, is the identical person mentioned in this marriage certificate as Bettie J McCarty?
A Yes sir.

The applicant Harvey Lindsey is identified on the Cherokee authenticated Tribal Roll of 1880, Canadian district, No. 862. His wife, Elizabeth J. Lindsey, to whom he was married in 1873 is included in the approved partial roll of citizens by blood of the Cherokee Nation opposite No. 5842.

The undersigned being first duly sworn states that as stenographer to the Commission to the Five Civilized Tribes, she correctly recorded the testimony taken in this case and that the foregoing is a full, true and correct transcript of her stenographic notes thereof.

                                Myrtle Hill

Sworn to and subscribed before me this the 4th day of January, 1907.

                                B.P. Rasmus
                                Notary Public.

◇◇◇◇◇

(COPY)

THIS CERTIFIES THAT Dr. Harvy Lindsey & Bettie J. McCarty were solemnly united by me in the HOLD BOND OF MATRIMONY at Webbers Falls Ind. Ter. on the 1st day of January day of January[sic] in the year of our Lord One Thousand Eight Hundred and seventy three conformably to the Ordinance of God and the laws of the State.

In Presence of   Signed
Their families and   (Signed) Samuel Taylor.
friends

                      "Love One Another"

Cherokee Intermarried White 1906
Volume VI

Homer J. Councilor being first duly sworn states that as stenographer to the Commission to the Five Civilized Tribes he made the above and foregoing from the original thereof and that the same is a true and correct copy.

Homer J Councilor

Subscribed and sworn to before me this 1st day of February 1907.

Chas E Webster
Notary Public.

◇◇◇◇◇

(COPY)

Office Clerk of the Dist. Court, I
I
Canadian District C.N. I
I
January 1st 1873. I

To any Ordained Minister of the Gospel or any Acting Chairman Judge of the Cherokee Nation.

You are hereby authorized to solemnize the rites of matrimony between Dr H. Lindsey a whiteman a Citizen of the United States, and Mrs. E. J. McCartey a Cherokee Citizen he having fully complied with the law regulating intermarriage between white man and Cherokee woman.

The Oath has been administered as the law directs.

Given under my hand Officially day and date above written.

(Signed) J. L. McCorkle Clerk Dist Court Can.
Dist C. N.

The Rights of Matrimony solemnized between the within named parties by me on the 1st day of Jan 1873.

Saml U. Taylor,
Judge C. Court Can Dist.

Homer J. Councilor being frist[sic] duly sworn states that as stenographer to the Commissioner to the Five Civilized Tribes he made the above and foregoing from the original thereof and that the same is true and correct.

Homer J. Councilor

Cherokee Intermarried White 1906
Volume VI

Subscribed and sworn to before me this 1st day of February 1907.

                Chas E Webster
                Notary Public.

◇◇◇◇◇

C.E.W..   Cherokee 2250.

DEPARTMENT OF THE INTERIOR,

COMMISSIONER TO THE FIVE CIVILIZED TRIBES.

In the matter of the application for the enrollment of Harvy Lindsy as a citizen by intermarriage of the Cherokee Nation.

D E C I S I O N

THE RECORDS OF THIS OFFICE SHOW: That at Fort Gibson, Indian Territory, August 30, 1900, application was received by the Commission to the Five Civilized Tribes for the enrollment of Harvy Lindsy as a citizen by intermarriage of the Cherokee Nation. Further proceedings in the matter of said application were had at Muskogee, Indian Territory, October 25, 1902, and January 3, 1907.

THE EVIDENCE IN THIS CASE SHOWS: That the applicant herein, Harvy Lindsy, a white man was married in accordance with Cherokee law January 1, 1873, to one Elizabeth J. Lindsy, formerly McCarty, who was at the time of said marriage a recognized citizen by blood of the Cherokee Nation, who is identified upon the Cherokee authenticated tribal roll of 1880, Canadian District, page 43, No. 863, as a native Cherokee, and whose name is included in the approved partial roll of citizens by blood of the Cherokee Nation opposite No. 5842. It is further shown that from the time of said marriage the said Harvy Lindsy and Elizabeth J. Lindsy resided together as husband and wife and lived continuously in the Cherokee Nation up to and including September 1, 1902. Said applicant is identified upon the Cherokee authenticated tribal roll of 1880 and the Cherokee Census roll of 1896, as an intermarried citizen of the Cherokee Nation.

IT IS, THEREFORE, ORDERED AND ADJUDGED: That in accordance with the decision of the Supreme Court of the United States, dated November 5, 1906, in the cases of Daniel Red Bird, et al., vs. the United States, Nos. 125, 126, 127 and 128 the said applicant, Harvy Lindsy, is entitled, under the provisions of Section 21 of the Act of Congress approved June 28, 1898 (30 Stats., 495), to enrollment as a citizen by intermarriage of the Cherokee Nation and his application for enrollment as such is accordingly granted.

Cherokee Intermarried White 1906
Volume VI

Tams Bixby
Commissioner.

Dated at Muskogee, Indian Territory,
this   FEB 11 1907

◇◇◇◇◇

Cherokee 2250

Muskogee, Indian Territory, February 11, 1907.

W. W. Hastings,
    Attorney for the Cherokee Nation,
        Muskogee, Indian Territory.

Dear Sir:

There is enclosed herewith a copy of the decision of the Commissioner to the Five Civilized Tribes, dated February 11, 1907, granting the application for the enrollment of Harvy Lindsy as a citizen by intermarriage of the Cherokee Nation.

Respectfully,

Encl. H-33
JMH

Commissioner.

◇◇◇◇◇

Cherokee 2250

Muskogee, Indian Territory, February 11, 1907.

The Commissioner to the Five Civilized Tribes,
    Muskogee, Indian Territory.

Sir:

Receipt is acknowledged of the testimony and of your decision enrolling Harvy Lindsy as a citizen by intermarriage of the Cherokee Nation. Time for protesting said decision is waived, and I consent that said person may be placed upon the schedule immediately.

Respectfully,
W. W. Hastings
Attorney for Cherokee Nation.

◇◇◇◇◇

Cherokee Intermarried White 1906
Volume VI

Muskogee, Indian Territory, February 11, 1907.

Harvy Lindsy,
    Texana[sic], Indian Territory.

Dear Sir:

    There is enclosed herewith a copy of the decision of the Commissioner to the Five Civilized Tribes, dated February 11, 1907, granting the application for your enrollment as a citizen by intermarriage of the Cherokee Nation.

    You will be advised when your name has been placed upon a schedule of citizens of the Cherokee Nation and approved by the Secretary of the Interior.

Respectfully,

Encl. H-34
JMH
                                                                            Commissioner.

◇◇◇◇◇

Cherokee
I.W. 168.

Muskogee, Indian Territory, April 16, 1907.

Harvy W. Lindsy,
    Texana[sic], Indian Territory.

Dear Sir:

    Your marriage license and certificate filed in connection with your application for enrollment as a citizen by intermarriage of the Cherokee Nation is returned to you herewith, copies of the same being retained in the files of this office.

Respectfully,

Encl. W-6
S.W.
                                                                            Commissioner.

Cher IW 169

◇◇◇◇◇

Cherokee Intermarried White 1906
Volume VI

C.E.W.

DEPARTMENT OF THE INTERIOR,

COMMISSIONER TO THE FIVE CIVILIZED TRIBES.

In the matter of the application for the enrollment of

GEORGE W. WILLIAMS

as a citizen by intermarriage of the Cherokee Nation.

CHEROKEE 2832.

DEPARTMENT OF THE INTERIOR,
COMMISSION TO THE FIVE CIVILIZED TRIBES,
VINITA, I.T., SEPT/[sic] 17., 1900.

In the matter of the application of George W. Williams for enrollment of himself, wife and five children, as citizens of the Cherokee Nation, said Williams being sworn by Commissioner Breckinridge, testified as follows:

Q What is your full name? A George W. Williams.
Q Your age? A 56.
Q Your postoffice? A Afton.
Q In what district do you live? A Delaware.
Q Whom do you want to have put on the rolls? A Myself, wife and five children.
Q These children are all unmarried and living at home? A Yes.
Q Do you apply for yourself as a Cherokee by blood? A No sir, white man.
Q Your wife is a Cherokee? A A[sic] Yes.
Q Have you your marriage license and certificate? A No sir, I have not; I am on the '80 roll.
Q When were you married? A In '70, to my present wife.
Q What district were you in in '80? A Delaware.
Q Also in '96? A Yes.
Q Is your wife that you married in '70 still living and living with you? A Yes.
Q Lived with her all the time in the Cherokee Nation? A Yes.
Q Give me name of your father please? A John D. Williams.
Q White man? A Yes.
Q Dead or alive? A Dead.
Q What was the name of your mother? A Narcissa.
Q Is she dead? A Yes.

Cherokee Intermarried White 1906
Volume VI

Q Was she a shite woman? A Yes.
Q Give me, please, your wife's present name? A Malinda N.,[sic]
Q How old is she? A About 48.
Q What is your[sic] father's name? A John Countryman.
Q Cherokee or white man? A White man.
Q Dead or alive? A Dead.
Q How long has he been dead? A Died during the war.
Q What is her mother's given name? A Patsy.
Q Cherokee? A Yes.
Q Dead or alive? A dead.
Q How long has she been dead? A Died just after the war.
Q Give me names, please, of your five children under age? A Mattie L., 18 years old.
   On '96 roll, page 551, number 3375.
Q Next? A Allie B., 14 years old.
   On '96 roll, page 551, number 3376, as Ally.
Q Next? A Andrew W.M., 12 years old.
   On '96 roll, page 551, number 3377, as Watie M.
Q Next? A Charlotte C., 10 years old.
   On '96 roll, page 551, number 3378.
Q Next? A Arthur R., 8 years old.
   On '96 roll, page 551, number 3379, as Auther.
   Applicant on '80 roll, page 333, number 2816, as Geroge[sic].
   Applicant on '96 roll, page 594, number 607.
   Applicant's wife on '80 roll, page 333, number 2817, as Malind
   On '96 roll, page 551, number 3373, as Nancy M. Williams.
Q What proportion of Cherokee blood has your wife? A About 1/16.
Q These children are all alive now? A Yes.

    The applicant applies for the enrollment of himself, his wife, and five minor children. He is identified on the rolls of '80 and '96 as a Cherokee by adoption. He and his Cherokee wife have lived together in the Cherokee Nation ever since their enrollment in '80, and he will be listed now for enrollment as a Cherokee citizen by adoption. His wife is identified on the '80 and '96 rolls as a native Cherokee. She has lived in the Cherokee Nation since her enrollment in '80 and she will be listed now for enrollment as a Cherokee by blood. Their five children enumerated in the testimony are identified with their parents in '96; they are all alive at this time, and will be listed for enrollment as Cherokees by blood.

    The undersigned, being first duly sworn, states that as stenographer to the Commission to the Five Civilized Tribes, he correctly recorded the testimony and proceedings in this case, and that the foregoing is a true and complete transcript of his stenographic notes thereof.

                                                                  B McDonald

Cherokee Intermarried White 1906
Volume VI

Subscribed and sworn to before me this 19th day of September, 1900.

CR Breckinridge
Commissioner.

◇◇◇◇◇

Cherokee 2832.

Department of the Interior,
Commission to the Five Civilized Tribes,
Muskogee, I. T., October 7, 1902.

In the matter of the application of George W. Williams for the enrollment of himself as a citizen by intermarriage, and for the enrollment of his wife, Malinda N. and children, Mattie L., Allie B., Andrew W. M., Charlotte C. and Arthur R. Williams, as citizens by blood of the Cherokee Nation; he being sworn and examined by the Commission, testified as follows:

Q What is your name? A George W. Williams.
Q What is your age at this time? A Fifty-eight.
Q What is your postoffice? A Afton.
Q Are you the same George W. Williams that mad application to the Commission for enrollment as an intermarried citizen on September 27, 1900? A I don't remember the day, but I made application for enrollment before the Commission.
Q It was in September, 1900, was it? A It was either in September or October; it was at Vinita I know.
Q What is your wife's name? A Malinda N.
Q Is she living at this time? A Yes sir.
Q Is she a citizen by blood of the Cherokee Nation? A Yes, said to be.
Q When were you and she married? A We were married in September, '67 I believe.
Q Where? A In Delaware District.
Q Cherokee Nation? A Yes sir.
Q Were you ever married before you were married to this woman? A Yes sir.
Q How many times before? A Once.
Q Was your first wife a Cherokee or white woman? A A white woman.
Q Was she living or dead when you married Malinda? A Dead.
Q Had your wife, Malinda, ever been married prior to her marriage to you? A No sir.
Q You her first husband? A Yes sir.
Q She is your second wife? A Yes sir.
Q You and she married under Cherokee license, according to Cherokee law? A Yes sir.
Q Have you and your wife Malinda, lived together as husband and wife continuously from the time you were married up until the present time? A Yes sir.
Q Never been separated? A No sir.
Q And you have never been married to any other woman since your marriage to Malinda? A No sir.

Cherokee Intermarried White 1906
Volume VI

Q Have you and she lived together as husband and wife on the first day of September, 1902? A Yes sir.
Q Have you and your wife lived in the Cherokee Nation all the time since 1880 up to the present time? A Yes sir, in Delaware District.
Q These children, Mattie L., Allie B., Andrew W. M., Charlotte C. and Arthur R., your children by your wife, Malinda? A Yes sir.
Q Are these children all living at this time? A They are.
Q Have they lived in the Cherokee Nation from the time of their birth up until the present time? A Yes sir.
Q They never lived outside of the Nation? A No sir.

The undersigned, being duly sworn, states that as stenographer to the Commission to the Five Civilized Tribes he correctly recorded the testimony and proceedings in this case, and the foregoing is a true and correct transcript of his stenographic notes thereof.

E.G. Rothenberger

Subscribed and sworn to before me
this 29th day of October, 1902.

BC Jones
Notary Public.

DEPARTMENT OF THE INTERIOR,
COMMISSION TO THE FIVE CIVILIZED TRIBES.
AUXILIARY CHEROKEE LAND OFFICE.

Muskogee, Indian Territory, February 23, 1905.

In the matter of the allotment of land to Mattie L. Stoaks (nee Williams) Cherokee Card No. 2832, Approved Roll No. 7104.

Martin L. Stoaks, husband and intermarried citizen, Cherokee Card D 28, being sworn as a witness, testified as follows:

Examination by the Commission:
Q What is your name? A Martin L. Stoaks.
Q About how old are you? A 34
Q What is the name of your father? A James R. Stoaks
Q The name of your mother? A Elizabeth Stoaks
Q What is your post office? A Afton, Indian Territory.
Q Are you married? A Yes sir.
Q What is the name of your wife? A Mattie L. Stoaks
Q What was her name before you married her? A Mattie L. Williams.
Q What is the name of her father? A George W. Williams

Cherokee Intermarried White 1906
Volume VI

Q What is the name of her mother? A Malid[sic] Williams.
Q ~~When~~ and where were you married to your wife? A At Afton, I. T.
Q What day, month and year? A On the second day of June, 1901.
Q Were you married under United States License? A Yes sir.
Q Are you and your wife living together at this time? A Yes sir.
Q Do you desire to designate lands for allotment for her today? A Yes sir.
Q Are said lands suitable for an allotment? A Yes sir.
Q Are there any improvements on the land? A Yes sir.
Q Is it your home place? A Yes sir.
Q State the reasons why your wife does not make personal appearance and selection. A One reason, she went to Tahlequah and stayed a week and could not file and we found out that I could file for her by getting power of attorney and mother has not been very well so she stayed with her.
Q On account of your mother being ill she stayed at home with her? A Yes sir.
Q Have you power of attorney from your wife? A Yes sir.

    Applicant offers Power of Attorney executed by Mattie L. Stoaks dated February 16, 1905, appointing Mattie[sic] L. Stoaks her attorney for the purpose of selecting her allotment in the Cherokee Nation.

(WITNESS EXCUSED).

    Blanch Ashton upon oath states that as stenographer to the Commission to the Five Civilized Tribes she accurately recorded the testimony in the above entitled cause and that the foregoing is a correct transcript of her stenographic notes thereof.

                                                         Blanch Ashton

Subscribed and sworn to before me this the 23rd day of February, 1905.

                                                          W.S. Hawkins
                                                          Notary Public.

Cherokee Intermarried White 1906
Volume VI

Cherokee 2832.

DEPARTMENT OF THE INTERIOR,
COMMISSIONER TO THE FIVE CIVILIZED TRIBES.
MUSKOGEE?[sic] Ind. Ter., January 2, 1907.

In the matter of the application for the enrollment of George W. Williams as a citizen by intermarriage of the Cherokee Nation.

George W. William[sic] Being first duly sworn by Frances R. Lane, a Notary Public for the Western District of Indian Territory, testified as follows:

By the Commissioner:
Q What is your name? A George W. Williams.
Q How old are you? A Sixty-two.
Q What is your postoffice address? A Afton, I. T.
Q You claim to be a citizen by intermarriage of the Cherokee Nation? A Yes sir.
Q Through whom do you claim that right? A Malinda Ann Countryman.
Q When were you married to her? A The 28th day of September, 1870, I think.
Q Did you get a Cherokee tribal license? A Yes sir.
Q Have you got that license with you? A No sir.
Q Where is it? A Well, sir, I never did get it out of the office.
Q Who married you? A Eli Butler.
Q Did you present a petition to the Judge to get your license? A I did.
Q How many signers did you have on it? A I have forgotten what the law was--six or seven.
Q Were you ever married before you married Malinda A. Countryman? A Yes sir.
Q Who was your first wife? A She was a Thomas.
Q Was she a citizen or non-citizen? A Non-citizen.
Q Was she living at the time of your marriage to Malinda Ann Countryman? A No sir.
Q Was Malinda Ann Countryman ever married before her marriage to you? A No sir.
Q Have you lived together in the Cherokee Nation continuously, as husband and wife ever since your marriage in 1870? A Yes sir.
Q What district were you married in? A Delaware District.

Witness excused.

Frances R. Lane upon oath states that as stenographer to the commissioner[sic] to the Five Civilized Tribes she reported the testimony in the above entitled cause and that the above and foregoing is an accurate transcript of her stenographic notes thereof.

Frances R. Lane

Subscribed and sworn to before me this January 4, 1907.

Edward Merrick
Notary Public.

Cherokee Intermarried White 1906
Volume VI

Cherokee 2832

SUPPLEMENTAL STATEMENT of records.

An examination of Book S of the marriage records of the Cherokee Nation, Delaware District, in the back part, opposite No. 55, shows that a certificate was issued to George W. Williams, the applicant herein, to marry Malinda Countryman, on the 26th day of September, 1870, and the same was issued by T. J. McGhee, the Clerk of Delaware District, said certificate reading as follows: "This is to certify by me that George W. Williams, a white man was licens[sic] to marry Malinda Countryman, a female Cherokee, on the 26th day of September, 1870, and this licens executed and returned Sept. 26, 1870, being under according to act passed by National council being dated October 15, 1855, in regard to white men marrying with this nation.
T. J. McGhee, Clerk Delaware Dist., C. N."

C.E.W.   Cherokee 2832.

DEPARTMENT OF THE INTERIOR,

COMMISSIONER TO THE FIVE CIVILIZED TRIBES.

In the matter of the application for the enrollment of GEORGE W. WILLIAMS as a citizen by intermarriage of the Cherokee Nation.

D E C I S I O N

THE RECORDS OF THIS OFFICE SHOW: That at Vinita, Indian Territory, September 17, 1900, application was received by the Commission to the Five Civilized Tribes for the enrollment of George W. Williams, as a citizen by intermarriage of the Cherokee Nation. Further proceedings in the matter of said application were had at Muskogee, Indian Territory, October 7, 1902, February 23, 1905 and January 2, 1907.

THE EVIDENCE IN THIS CASE SHOWS: That the applicant herein, George W. Williams, a white man, was married in accordance with Cherokee law September 26, 1870, to one, Malinda N. Williams, nee Countryman, who was at the time of said marriage a citizen by blood of the Cherokee Nation, who is identified on the Cherokee authenticated tribal roll of 1880, Delaware District, page 333, No. 2817, as a native Cherokee, and whose name is included in the approved partial roll of citizens by blood of the Cherokee Nation, opposite No. 7103. It is further shown that from the time of said

Cherokee Intermarried White 1906
Volume VI

marriage the said George W. and Malinda N[sic] Williams have resided together as husband and wife, and have continuously lived in the Cherokee Nation. Said applicant is identified on the Cherokee authenticated tribal roll of 1880, and the Cherokee census roll of 1896, as an intermarried citizen of the Cherokee Nation.

IT IS, THEREFORE, ORDERED AND ADJUDGED: That in accordance with the decision of the Supreme Court of the United States, dated November 5, 1906, in the cases of Daniel Red Bird, et al., vs. the United States, Nos. 125, 126, 127 and 128 the said applicant, George W. Williams, is entitled under the provisions of Section 21, of the Act of Congress approved June 28, 1898 (30 Stats., 495), to enrollment as a citizen by intermarriage of the Cherokee Nation and his application for enrollment as such is accordingly granted.

Tams Bixby
Commissioner.

Dated at Muskogee, Indian Territory,
this   FEB 8 1907

◇◇◇◇◇

Cherokee 2832

Muskogee, Indian Territory, February 8, 1907.

W. W. Hastings,
Attorney for the Cherokee Nation,
Muskogee, Indian Territory.

Dear Sir:

There is enclosed herewith a copy of the decision of the Commissioner to the Five Civilized Tribes, dated February 8, 1907, granting the application for the enrollment of George W. Williams as a citizen by intermarriage of the Cherokee Nation.

Respectfully,

Encl. H-15
JMH

Commissioner.

◇◇◇◇◇

Cherokee Intermarried White 1906
Volume VI

Cherokee 2832

Muskogee, Indian Territory, February 8, 1907.

The Commissioner to the Five Civilized Tribes,
    Muskogee, Indian Territory.

Sir:

    Receipt is acknowledged of the testimony and of your decision enrolling George W. Williams as a citizen by intermarriage of the Cherokee Nation. Time for protesting said decision is waived and I consent that said person may be placed upon the schedule immediately.

                        Respectfully,
                                W. W. Hastings
                                Attorney for Cherokee Nation.

◇◇◇◇◇

Cherokee 2832

Muskogee, Indian Territory, February 8, 1907.

George W. Williams,
    Afton, Indian Territory.

Dear Sir:

    There is enclosed herewith a copy of the decision of the Commissioner to the Five Civilized Tribes, dated February 8, 1907, granting your application for enrollment as a citizen by intermarriage of the Cherokee Nation.

    You will be advised when your name has been placed upon a schedule of citizens of the Cherokee Nation and approved by the Secretary of the Interior.

                        Respectfully,

Encl. H-16   Commissioner.
JMH

Cher IW 170

Cherokee Intermarried White 1906
Volume VI

COPY

DEPARTMENT OF THE INTERIOR,
COMMISSION TO THE FIVE CIVILIZED TRIBES,
VINITA, I.T., SEPTEMBER 17, 1900.

In the matter of the application of Stacy Eliza Perry for the enrollment of herself and children as citizens of the Cherokee Nation; said Perry being sworn by Commissioner C. R. Breckinridge, testified as follows:

Q What is your full name? A Stacy Eliza Perry.
Q How old are you? A 46.
Q What is your post office? A Vinita.
Q In what district do you live? A Cooweescoowee now.
Q For whom do you apply for enrollment? A Myself and children.
Q How many children? A Four that are under age.
Q These four all alive at this time are they? A Yes, sir.
Q Do you apply for yourself as a Cherokee by blood? A No, sir.
Q As an adopted white? A Yes, sir.
Q When were you married? A In 1872.
Q Is your husband living now? A No, sir, dead.
Q What was his name? A Eliver[sic] V. Perry
Q Cherokee or white man? A Cherokee.
Q How long since he died? A About a year.
Q Did you and he live together from the time of your marriage until his death? A Yes, sir.
Q And did you live all the time in the Cherokee Nation? A Yes, sir.
Q You have never married since his death? A No, sir.
Q In what district were you enrolled in 1880? A Delaware.
Q What district were you enrolled in 1896? A Delaware.
Q You have made your home steadily in the Cherokee Nation since 1880? A Yes, sir.
Q Give me the name of your father? A H. G. Bursom.
Q Is he dead or alive? A Dead.
Q The name of your mother? A Rebecca Bursom.
Q Dead or alive? A Alive.
Q Now give me the names of these children, the four? A Earnest Bursom Perry.
Q How old is that child? A 19
Q The next child? A Effie D.
Q How old is she? A 17.
Q The next child? A Myrtle.
Q How old is that child? A 13.
Q The next child? A Oliver H.
Q How old is he? A Ten.

Cherokee Intermarried White 1906
Volume VI

J. L. BAUGH, Representative of the Cherokee Nation:

Q You said awhile ago your post office was at Vinita, where is your regular post office?
A I live at Vinita now.
Q Where have you been living? A Delaware. We lived there 26 years, but I just moved over here to school our children.
Q You have not lived anywhere else except the Cherokee Nation? A No, sir.

        1880 enrollment; page 297, #1963, Eliza Perry, Delaware.
        1896 enrollment; page 585, #400, Eliza A. Perry,   "
        1896 enrollment; page 517, #2444, Earnest V[sic]. Perry,   "
        1896 enrollment; page 517, #2445, Ella D. Perry,   "
        1896 enrollment; page 517, #2446, Merthe Perry,   "
        1896 enrollment; page 517, #2447, Oliver H. Perry,   "

    Com'r Breckinridge:--The applicant applies for the enrollment of herself and four children: Her husband is dead. She is identified on the rolls of 1880 and 1896 as a Cherokee by adoption. She has never re-married since the death of her husband. She has lived in the Cherokee Nation ever since her enrollment in 1880 and she will be listed now for enrollment as a Cherokee by adoption. Her four children, enumerated in the testimony are identified with her on the roll of 1896. They are all living at this time, and they will be listed for enrollment as Cherokees by blood.

---oooOOOooo---

    J. O. Rosson, being first duly sworn, states that as stenographer to the Commission to the Five Civilized Tribes, he correctly recorded the testimony and proceedings in this case, and the foregoing is a true and complete transcript of his stenographic notes thereof.

                                                  J. O. Rosson

Subscribed and sworn to before me this 19th day of September, 1900.

                                                        T.B. Needles
                                                        Commissioner.

Endorsement

        DEPARTMENT OF THE INTERIOR
COMMISSION TO THE FIVE CIVILIZED TRIBES
                 FILED
            SEP 20, 1900
                    Tams Bixby, Acting Chairman.

Cherokee Intermarried White 1906
Volume VI

Cherokee 2861.

Department of the Interior,
Commission to the Five Civilized Tribes,
Muskogee, I. T., October 21, 1902.

In the matter of the application of Stacy E. Perry for the enrollment of herself as a citizen by intermarriage, and for the enrollment of her children, Earnest B., Effie D., Myrtle and Oliver H. Perry, as citizens by blood of the Cherokee Nation; she being sworn and examined by the Commission, testified as follows:

Q What is your name? A Stacy E. Perry.
Q How old are you? A Forty-nine.
Q What is your postoffice? A Vinita.
Q Are you a white woman? A Yes sir.
Q Is your name on the roll of 1880 as an adopted white citizen? A Yes sir.
Q What was your husband's name in 1880? A Oliver B. Perry.
Q Is he living now? A No sir.
Q Is he the husband through whom you claim your citizenship? A Yes sir.
Q When did he die? A Four years ago.
Q Did you live with your husband in the Cherokee Nation from 1880 up until the time he died? A Yes sir.
Q Never were separated? A No sir.
Q How many children have you? A I have six.
Q Four living at home with you? A Yes sir, four with me.
Q You have had no deaths in your family in the past two and a half years? A No sir.
Q You are still a widow? A Yes sir.
Q Haven't married again? A No sir.
Q Has your home been in the Cherokee Nation since 1880? A Yes sir.
Q Haven't lived anywhere else have you? A No sir.

The undersigned, being duly sworn, states that as stenographer to the Commission to the Five Civilized Tribes he correctly recorded the testimony and proceedings in this case, and the foregoing is a true and correct transcript of his stenographic notes thereof.

E.G. Rothenberger

Subscribed and sworn to before me this 20th day of November, 1902.

BC Jones
Notary Public.

Copy.

Cherokee Intermarried White 1906
Volume VI

◇◇◇◇◇◇

(The testimony above of October 21, 1902, given again.)

◇◇◇◇◇◇

(There are two pages for this applicant that are completely illegible.)

◇◇◇◇◇◇

(The below was handwritten on the microfilm.)

Georgia
Catoosa County

        I J C Hix ordinary of said county, do hereby certify that the forgoing[sic] page is a true copy of the record in my office, as appears of record in Book A page 173 of the Marriage record
Witness my hand and seal of office this 18" day of January 1907

                J C Hix Ordinary
                and Exofficio Clerk

◇◇◇◇◇◇

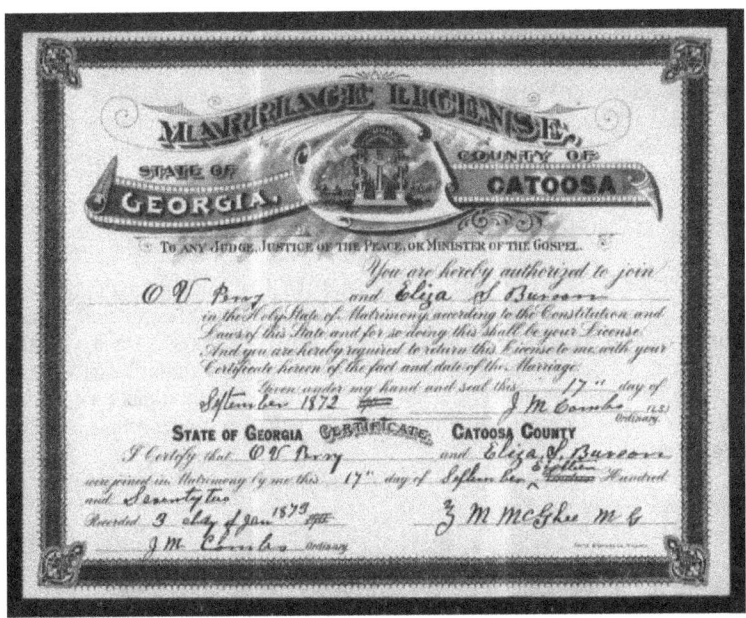

Cherokee Intermarried White 1906
Volume VI

◇◇◇◇◇

E C M

Cherokee 2861.

DEPARTMENT OF THE INTERIOR,

COMMISSIONER TO THE FIVE CIVILIZED TRIBES.

In the matter of the application for the enrollment of STACY E. PERRY as a citizen by intermarriage of the Cherokee Nation.

D E C I S I O N

THE RECORDS OF THIS OFFICE SHOW: That at Vinita, Indian Territory, September 17, 1900, application was received by the Commission to the Five Civilized Tribes for the enrollment of Stacy E. Perry as a citizen by intermarriage of the Cherokee Nation. Further proceedings in the matter of said application were had at Muskogee, Indian Territory, October 21, 1902 and January 30, 1907.

THE EVIDENCE IN THIS CASE SHOWS: That the applicant herein, Stacy E. Perry, a white woman, married in the State of Georgia in 1872 one Oliver V. Perry, who is identified on the Cherokee authenticated tribal roll of 1880, Delaware District opposite No. 1962, as a native Cherokee marked "Dead"; that on December 16, 1870 the said Oliver V. Perry was admitted to citizenship by the National Council of the Cherokee Nation as one of the children of Susan J. Perry; that from the time of said marriage until the death of said Oliver V. Perry, which occurred in 1898, the said Oliver V. Perry and Stacy E. Perry resided together as husband and wife and continuously lived in the Cherokee Nation; that since the death of said Oliver V. Perry the said Stacy E. Perry has remained unmarried and continuously lived in the Cherokee Nation. Said applicant is identified on the Cherokee authenticated tribal roll of 1880 and the Cherokee census roll of 1896 as an intermarried citizen of the Cherokee Nation.

IT IS, THEREFORE, ORDERED AND ADJUDGED: That in accordance with the decision of the Supreme Court of the United States, dated November 5, 1906, in the cases of Daniel Red Bird, et al. vs. the United States, Nos. 125, 126, 127 and 128, the said applicant, Stacy E. Perry, is entitled, under the provisions of Section Twenty-one of the Act of Congress approved June 28, 1898 (30 Stats. 495), to enrollment as a citizen by intermarriage of the Cherokee Nation, and her application for enrollment as such is accordingly granted.

Tams Bixby   Commissioner.

Dated at Muskogee, Indian Territory,
this   FEB 9 1907

◇◇◇◇◇

Cherokee Intermarried White 1906
Volume VI

Cherokee 2861

Muskogee, Indian Territory, February 9, 1907

Stacy E. Perry,
    Vinita, Indian Territory.

Dear Madam:

    There is enclosed herewith copy of the decision of the Commissioner to the Five Civilized Tribes, dated February 9, 1907, granting the application for your enrollment as a citizen by intermarriage of the Cherokee Nation.

    You will be advised when your name has been placed upon a schedule of citizens of the Cherokee Nation and approved by the Secretary of the Interior.

                  Respectfully,

Enc I-49   Commissioner.

RPI

◇◇◇◇◇

N.
Cherokee 2861

Muskogee, Indian Territory, February 9, 1907.

W. W. Hastings,
    Attorney for the Cherokee Nation,
        Muskogee, Indian Territory.

Dear Sir:

    There is enclosed herewith copy of the decision of the Commissioner to the Five Civilized Tribes, dated February 9, 1907, granting the application for the enrollment of Stacy E. Perry as a citizen by intermarriage of the Cherokee Nation.

                    Respectfully,

                    Commissioner.

Enc I-49
RPI

◇◇◇◇◇

Cherokee Intermarried White 1906
Volume VI

Muskogee, Indian Territory, February 20, 1907

DIRECT

SPECIAL

The Honorable,
The Secretary of the Interior.

Sir:

February 13, 1907, the Commissioner transmitted a schedule of intermarried white citizens of the Cherokee Nation, Nos. 167 to 179, inclusive, found to be entitled to enrollment as Cherokee citizens. On said schedule, opposite No. 170, appears the name of Stacy E. Perry. February 9, 1907 the Commissioner rendered a decision holding that said Stacy E. Perry was married to a recognized citizen by blood of the Cherokee Nation, prior to November 1, 1875, and in accordance with the decision of the Supreme Court of the United States of November 5, 1906, in the case of Daniel Red Bird et al., vs. the United States, said applicant was entitled to enrollment as a citizen by intermarriage of the Cherokee Nation. A copy of the Commissioner's decision was furnished the attorney for the Cherokee Nation in a letter of February 9, 1907, addressed to the Commissioner, said attorney advised that he did not protest against the enrollment of this person as a citizen by intermarriage of the Cherokee Nation.

Stacy E Perry claims the right to enrollment as a citizen of the Cherokee Nation by reason of her marriage in 1872, to one Oliver V. Perry, a Cherokee Indian by blood. The Commissioner found in his decision that said Oliver V. Perry was admitted to citizenship by the National Council of the Cherokee Nation, as one of the children of Susan J. Perry, on December 16, 1870.

The attorney for the Cherokee Nation has this day called the Commissioner's attention to the Docket of the Cherokee commission on citizenship known as the Chambers Court, in which is found a judgment of said Court admitting said Oliver V. Perry, as O. V. Perry, to citizenship in the Cherokee Nation, on June 20, 1879 the case being Number 290 on Page 132 of said Docket.

The applicant in testifying in this case on January 30, 1907, testified that she was married to Mr. Perry in Georgia, in 1872, that immediately after said marriage she and her husband removed from the State of Georgia to the Cherokee Nation and that her

Cherokee Intermarried White 1906
Volume VI

husband was then admitted to citizenship, saying, "well he was admitted after he arrived here, admitted at once; part of the family was already here and had been admitted before we arrived." She also testified that her husband was a son of Susan J. Perry.

It would appear from the record evidence found since the applicant was placed upon the schedule, as already recited, that the applicant's husband was not admitted to citizenship immediately upon his arrival in the Cherokee Nation, nor until June 20 1879. In the Commissioner's decision of February 9, 1907, it was assumed that the admission of Susan J. Perry and her children in 1870 included the admission of the applicant, but the record of the judgment of the Chambers Court of June 20, 1879, taken in connection with the testimony of the applicant herself, that her husband was admitted after their arrival in the nation in 1872, and that part of his family were already in the nation at that time and had been admitted seems to make it clear that the applicant's husband was never admitted to citizenship until 1879.

This being so, the applicant, Stacy E. Perry, was not married to a recognized citizen by blood of the Cherokee Nation prior to November 1, 1875, and is, therefore, not entitled to enrollment as a citizen by intermarriage of the Cherokee Nation

The Commissioner's decision in this case, together with the record of proceedings had therein, and the letter of the attorney for the Cherokee Nation waiving protest against her enrollment, is enclosed herewith, and it is respectfully recommended that the Department strike the name of this applicant from said schedule and that her application for enrollment as a citizen by intermarriage of the Cherokee Nation be denied.

Respectfully,

Commissioner.

Encl. B-26.

Cherokee Intermarried White 1906
Volume VI

REFER IN REPLY TO THE FOLLOWING:
I.W. Cherokee
170

DEPARTMENT OF THE INTERIOR,
COMMISSIONER TO THE FIVE CIVILIZED TRIBES.

Muskogee, Indian Territory, May 25, 1907.

Stacy E. Perry,
    Vinita, Indian Territory.

Dear Madam:

    You are hereby advised that on May 13, 1907, the Secretary of the Interior denied a motion filed by the Attorney for the Cherokee Nation, for a review of its decision authorizing your enrollment as a citizen by intermarriage of the Cherokee Nation.

    For your information, there is enclosed herewith a copy of Departmental decision referred to.

                  Respectfully,

                  Tams Bixby Commissioner.

Encl. C-12
LMC

◇◇◇◇◇

(The letter below does not belong with the current applicant.)

Cherokee
253 et al.

Muskogee, Indian Territory, May 25, 1907.

W. W. Hastings,
    Attorney for the Cherokee Nation,
        Muskogee, Indian Territory.

Dear Sir:

    You are hereby advised that on May 13, 1907, the Secretary of the Interior denied the motion filed by you for a review of its decision authorizing the enrollment of Jacob A. Bartles, et al., as citizens by intermarriage of the Cherokee Nation.

    For your information, there is enclosed herewith a copy of Departmental decision referred to.

Cherokee Intermarried White 1906
Volume VI

Respectfully,

Commissioner.

Encl. C-20
LMC

Cher IW 171

◇◇◇◇◇

E.C.M.

DEPARTMENT OF THE INTERIOR,

COMMISSIONER TO THE FIVE CIVILIZED TRIBES.

In the matter of the application for the enrollment of

ALFRED C. RAYMOND

As a citizen by intermarriage of the Cherokee Nation.

CHEROKEE NO. 3009.

◇◇◇◇◇

DEPARTMENT OF THE INTERIOR,
COMMISSION TO THE FIVE CIVILIZED TRIBES.
VINITA, I.T., SEPTEMBER 19, 1900.

In the matter of the application of Alfred C. Raymond for the enrollment of himself and wife as citizens of the Cherokee Nation, said Raymond being sworn by Commissioner T.B. Needles, testified as follows:

Q What is your full name? A Alfred C Raymond.
Q What is your age? MR. Raymond? A 73.
Q What is your post office address? A Vinita.
Q What district do you live in? A Cooweescoowee.
Q Are you a recognized citizen of the Cherokee Nation? A Sup-to[sic] be.
Q By blood or inter-marriage? A Inter-marriage.
Q Your father and mother are non-citizens were they? A Yes Sir.
Q What is the name of your wife? A Amanda J.
Q What was her name before you married her? A Daniel.

Cherokee Intermarried White 1906
Volume VI

Q When did you marry her? A In 1875.
Q What is the age of your wife? A 62.
Q What degree of blood does she claim? A One quarter Cherlee[sic].
Q Her father and mother living? A No, sir, dead.
Q Her father8s[sic] name? A Hiram McCrone.
Q Have you any children under 21 years of age? A No, Sir.
Q Just want to enroll yourself and wife? A Yes, Sir.
Q How long have you been a continuous resident of the Cherokee Nation?
A 33 years, I came here in 1867.
       1880 enrollment; page 160, #2299, A.C. Raymond, Cooweescoowee.
       1880 enrollment; page 160, #2300, Amanda J. Raymond,   "
       1896 enrollment; page 322, #886, Alford C. Raymond,   "
       1896 enrollment; page 242, 34031, Amanda J. Raymond,   "
Com'r Needles:
       The name of Alford C. Raymong[sic] and his wife Amanda J., appears upon the authenticated roll of 1880; he under the name of A.C., and their names also appear upon the census roll of 1896. Having made satisfactory proof as to their residence, and being duly identified according to the page and number as indicated in the testimony; said Alfred C. Raymong[sic] will be duly listed by the Commission as a Cherokee citizen by inter-marriage, and his wife, Amanda J., as a Cherokee citizen by blood.
                 ---ooOOOoo---------

       J. O. ROsson[sic], being first duly sworn, states that as stenographer to the Commission to the Five Civilized Tribes, he correctly recorded the testimony and proceedings in this case, and the foregoing is a true and correct transcript of his stenographic notes thereof.
                Signed,   J.O. Rosson.
Subscribed and sworn to before me this 21st. day of September, 1900.
                signed   T.B. Needles.
                             Commissioner.

       The undersigned being duly sworn states that as stenographer to the Commission to the Five Civilized Tribes, she made the above copy, and that the same is a true nd[sic] correct copy of the instrument now on file in this office.

                                     Mary Tabor Mallory

Subscribed and sworn to before me this the 19th. day of January 1907.

                                     Chas E Webster
                                     Notary Public.

Cherokee Intermarried White 1906
Volume VI

Cherokee 3009.

Department of the Interior,
Commission to the Five Civilized Tribes,
Muskogee, I. T., October 6, 1902.

In the matter of the application of Alfred C. Raymond for the enrollment of himself as a citizen by intermarriage, and for the enrollment of his wife, Amanda J. Raymond, as a citizen by blood of the Cherokee Nation.

L. B. Bell, being sworn and examined by the Commission, testified as follows:

Q What is your name? A L. B. Bell, postoffice Vinita, age 64.
Q Are you acquainted with Alfred C. Raymond who is an applicant before this Commission for enrollment as an intermarried citizen of the Cherokee Nation? A Yes sir.
Q How long have you known him? A I guess 28 or 30 years intimately.
Q Do you know his wife? A His present wife, yes sir, Amanda J.
Q She is a Cherokee by blood? A She is a Cherokee by blood.
Q Were Alfred C. Raymond and his wife married prior to 1880? A I couldn't tell you that now for a fact.
Q They are both on the 1880 roll? A Yes, I believe they were.
Q Has Alfred C. Raymond and his wife, Amanda J., lived together as husband and wife since 1880 up until the present time? A Yes sir, and are living together to-day.
Q They have never been separated since 1880? A Never have been separated since their marriage.
Q Living together on the first day of September, 1902, as husband and wife? A Yes sir.
Q Have they lived in the Cherokee Nation since 1880 up until the present time? A Yes sir.

The undersigned, being duly sworn, states that as stenographer to the Commission to the Five Civilized Tribes he correctly recorded the testimony and proceedings in this case, and that the foregoing is a true and correct transcript of his stenographic notes thereof.

E.G. Rothenberger

Subscribed and sworn to before me this 27th day of October, 1902.

BC Jones
Notary Public.

◇◇◇◇◇

Cherokee Intermarried White 1906
Volume VI

Cher
Supp'l to # 3009

Department of the Interior,
Commission to the Five Civilized Tribes,
Muskogee, I. T., October 16, 1902.

In the matter of the application of ALFRED C. RAYMOND, for the enrollment of himself as a citizen by intermarriage, and his wife, AMANDA RAYMOND, ad a citizen by blood, of the Cherokee Nation.

ALFRED C. RAYMOND, being duly sworn and examined by the Commission, testified as follows:

Q   What is your name ?   A   Alfred C. Raymond.
Q   How old are you ?   A   Seventy five.
Q   What is your post office ?   A   Vinita.
Q   Are you a white man ?   A   I am.
Q   Is your name on the roll of 1880 as an adopted white citizen ?
A   It is.
Q   What is your wife's name ?   A   Amanda J.
Q   Was she your wife in 1880 ?   A   She was.
Q   Is she the wife through whom you claim your citizenship ?
A   She is not.
Q   She is your second wife is she ?   A   Yes sir, my second wife.
Q   When were you married to your first wife ?   A   In about 1868.
Q   When did she die ?   A   I think in 1871.
Q   Then you married your present wife before 1880 ?
A   Married her; we was married in 1875.
Q   Have you and your wife Amanda J. been living together ever since 1880 ?
A   We have.
Q   You have never been separated ?   A   Never. Been parted but a few days at a time.
Q   Have you been living and making your home in the Cherokee Nation for the past twenty years ?   A   Been in here for thirty years.
Q   You have never lived anywhere else ?   A   No sir.

E. C. Bagwell, on oath states that, as stenographer to the Commission to the Five Civilized Tribes, he correctly recorded the testimony and proceedings had in the above entitled cause, and that the foregoing is an accurate transcript of his stenographic notes thereof.

E.C.Bagwell

Cherokee Intermarried White 1906
Volume VI

Subscribed and sworn to before me this November 19, 1902.

             BC Jones
             Notary Public.

◇◇◇◇◇

LGD

             Cherokee 3009.

DEPARTMENT OF THE INTERIOR,
COMMISSIONER TO THE FIVE CIVILIZED TRIBES.

Muskogee, Indian Territory, January 3, 1907.

  In the matter of the application for the enrollment of ALFRED C. RAYMOND, as a citizen by intermarriage of the Cherokee Nation.

  Alfred C. Raymond, being first duly sworn by B. P. Rasmus, a Notary Public, testified as follows:

Q What is your name? A Alfred C. Raymond.
Q How old are you? A 79 this year.
Q What is your post office address? A Vinita, I. T.
Q Do you claim to be an intermarried citizen of the Cherokee Nation? [sic] I do.
Q Through whom do you claim your intermarried rights?
A Through my wife, Minerva Russell.
Q When were you married to her? A On Saturday, the 29th day of February, 1868.
Q Where were you married? A Fort Gibson.
Q Were you married under the Cherokee law? A I was.
Q Did you have a license? A I did.
Q Have you a copy with you? A I have not.
Q Where is your license? A I dont[sic] know. The form of it was: You got a petition with seven signers; went to the District Clerk; after you went through a certain form of declaring allegiance to the Cherokee Nation and paying a fee, he issued you a license, and the preacher that married you certified on that license that he married you and the time, and he returned that to the clerk.
Q Was that what was done with your license? A I suppose so. I never saw it after the preacher took it from me.
Q What preacher married you? A You have got me -- I cant[sic] tell you. He is a licensed preacher in Fort Gibson and was so considered, but I cant[sic] tell you his name.
Q Were you ever married before you married your Cherokee wife? A I was.

Cherokee Intermarried White 1906
Volume VI

Q   What was the name of your first wife?   A   Flora Granis.
Q   Was she living or dead at the time you married your last wife?
A   She died in Buffalo, New York, before I ever saw this western country.
Q   How long did you live with your Cherokee wife?   A   She died in 1871.
Q   You lived with her up to 1871, did you?
A   Yes, from February, 1868, to   1871.
Q   Then did you remarry after her death?   A   Yes, in 1875.
Q   Whom did you marry after her death?   A   I married Amanda Daniels.
Q   Was she a citizen of the Cherokee Nation?   A   Yes sir.
Q   Did you marry her according to the Cherokee law?   A   Yes.
Q   Have you a license.[sic]   A   I have at home.
Q   Where did you get the license when you were married to Amanda Daniels?
A   Last marriage I did not get any license. They did not require a license, but I have got a certificate.
Q   What time in 1875 were you married to her?   A   The 20th of April.
Q   Are you still living with Amanda Daniels?   A   Yes sir.
Q   Have you lived in the Cherokee Nation continuously from 1875 up to the present time?   A   I have never been out of here more than a week or month unless my wife was with me.
Q   Never lived anywhere else?   A   No sir.
Q   Was Amanda Daniels ever married before she married you?   A   She was.
Q   What was the name of her first husband?   A   Jonathan Mall.
Q   Was he living or dead at the time you married Amanda Daniels?   A   Dead.
Q   Did she ever have any other husband besides Mall?
A   Yes, she married Tom Daniels.
Q   You are her third husband?   A   Yes.
Q   Was Daniels living or dead at the time you married her?   A   He was dead.

The applicant is identified on the 1880 Cherokee roll, Cooweescoowee District, opposite No. 2299. His present wife is identified on said roll for said district opposite No. 2300. She is also identified on the final roll of citizens by blood of the Cherokee Nation opposite No. 7479.

Q   What was the name of your first Cherokee wife's father and mother?   A   Petitt.
Q   Is either one living?   A   No, both dead.
Q   Did your first Cherokee wife have any brothers or sisters?
A   Yes, Frank Petitt and Bill Petitt.
Q   Are they living?   A   Frank Petitt lives at Edna, Kansas. Bill Petitt died years ago.
Q   Is Frank Petitt a full brother of your Cherokee wife?   A   Yes.
Q   Was your wife's brother known by any other name?   A   No.
Q   Where did you get your license in the Canadian District.
A   We crossed the river and went over on the mountain to his house -- the clerk didn't have an office.

Cherokee Intermarried White 1906
Volume VI

Q   Was your brother-in-law, Frank Petitt, ever married?   A   I dont[sic] know.
Q   When was the last time you saw Frank Petitt?   A   Last summer.
Q   How old a man is Frank Petitt?   A   That's guesswork.
Q   About how old?   A   In the seventies.
Q   What was the name of the father of your first Cherokee wife?
A   I dont[sic] know.

      The records of this office show that one Frank Petitt, whose postoffice is Edna, Kansas, is 71 years of age, is enrolled opposite No. 28796 upon the final roll of citizens by blood of the Cherokee Nation. Said Frank Petitt also appears to have been enrolled upon the 1880 Cherokee roll, Illinois District, opposite No. 1440-A.
      The applicant testifies that his first Cherokee wife was named Petitt, and had a brother by the name of Frank Petitt, whose present postoffice address if ~~Petitt~~, Kansas.   Edna

Witness excused.

      James M. Keys, being first duly sworn by B. P. Rasmus, a notary public, testified as follows:

Q   What is your name?   A   James M. Keys.
Q   How old are you?   A   63 years old.
Q   What is your postoffice address?   A   Pryor Creek, I. T.
Q   Are you a citizen by blood of the Cherokee Nation?   A   Yes sir.
Q   Are you acquainted with Alfred C. Raymond?   A   Yes.
Q   Were you acquainted with his Cherokee wife?   A   Yes.
Q   What was her name?   A   Minerva Petitt.
Q   Do you know when Alfred C. Raymond and Minerva Petitt were married?
A   In 1868 or 1869.
Q   Were they married according to the Cherokee law?   A   Yes.
Q   Was Minerva Petitt a citizen by blood of the Cherokee Nation?   A   Yes.
Q   Did you know any other members of her family?   A   Yes.
Q   Were they considered citizens of the Cherokee Nation?   A   They were.
Q   Do you know their names?   A   Frank Petitt and Bill Petitt were her brothers.
Q   Do you know anything about the third marriage of Alfred C. Raymond - to Amanda Daniels?   A   Yes, she is his present wife.
Q   Do you know when they were married?   A   Yes.
Q   Were they married under the Cherokee law?   A   I do not know.
Q   Was she a citizen of the Cherokee Nation?   A   Yes.

Witness excused.

Cherokee Intermarried White 1906
Volume VI

R. W. Lindsay, being first duly sworn by B. P. Rasmus, a notary public, testified as follows:

Q   What is your name?   A   R. W. Lindsay.
Q   What is your age?   A   74 years old.
Q   What is your postoffice address?   A   Choteau, I. T.
Q   Are you a citizen of the Cherokee Nation?   A   Yes, a citizen by intermarriage.
Q   Are you acquainted with Alfred C. Raymond?   A   Yes.
Q   Did you know his wife, Amanda Petit[sic]?   A   Yes.
Q   Did you know of their marriage?   A   Yes. When I first knew them they were living together as man and wife and so considered by the community.
Q   Were they married according to the Cherokee law?
A   I dont[sic] know, but he was recognized as a citizen and voted, and they were always strict about voting.
Q   When did he first vote?   A   About 1869.
Q   Do you know whether he voted prior to 1875?   A   Not of certain knowledge.
Q   Did he hold property in the Cherokee Nation?   A   Yes.
Q   Do you know anything about his marriage to his present wife?   A   Yes.
Q   Do you know whether they were married according to the Cherokee law.
A   Only from inference.

Witness excused.

The undersigned, being first duly sworn, on oath states that as stenographer to the Commissioner to the Five Civilized Tribes, she reported the above proceedings, and that the same is a true and correct transcript of her stenographic notes thereof.

Demie T. Stubblefield

Subscribed and sworn to before me this, January 4, 1907.

Edward Merrick
Notary Public.

Cherokee Intermarried White 1906
Volume VI

E C M

Cherokee 3009.

DEPARTMENT OF THE INTERIOR,

COMMISSIONER TO THE FIVE CIVILIZED TRIBES.

In the matter of the application for the enrollment of ALFRED C. RAYMOND as a citizen by intermarriage of the Cherokee Nation.

_D_E_C_I_S_I_O_N_

THE RECORDS OF THIS OFFICE SHOW: That at Vinita, Indian Territory, September 19th, 1900 application was received by the Commission to the Five Civilized Tribes for the enrollment of Alfred C. Raymond as a citizen by intermarriage of the Cherokee Nation. Further proceedings in the matter of said application were had at Muskogee, Indian Territory, October 6th, 1902, October 16th, 1902 and January 3rd, 1907.

THE EVIDENCE IN THIS CASE SHOWS: That the applicant herein, Alfred C. Raymond, a white man, was married in accordance with Cherokee law February 29th, 1868 to one Minerva Raymond, nee Russell, since deceased, who was at the time of said marriage a recognized citizen by blood of the Cherokee Nation. It is further shown that from the time of said marriage until the death of said Minerva Raymond, which occurred in 1871, the said Alfred C. Raymond and Minerva Raymond resided together as husband and wife and continuously lived in the Cherokee Nation; that from the time of the death of the said Minerva Raymond until his remarriage on April 20th, 1875, the said Alfred C. Raymond remained unmarried and continuously lived in the Cherokee Nation. It is also shown that on April 20th, 1875 said Alfred C. Raymond was married in accordance with Cherokee law to his present wife, Amanda J. Raymond, nee McCrary, who was at the time of said marriage a recognized citizen by blood of the Cherokee Nation, who is identified on the Cherokee authenticated tribal roll of 1880, Cooweescoowee District No. 2300 as a native Cherokee. It is further shown that from the time of said marriage the said Alfred C. Raymond and Amanda J. Raymond resided together as husband and wife and continuously lived in the Cherokee Nation up to and including September 1st, 1902. Said applicant is identified on the Cherokee authenticated tribal roll of 1880 and the Cherokee census roll of 1896 as an intermarried citizen of the Cherokee Nation.

IT IS, THEREFORE, ORDERED AND ADJUDGED: That in accordance with the decision of the Supreme Court of the United States dated November 5th, 1906 in the cases of Daniel Red Bird et al. vs. the United States, Nos. 125, 126, 127 and 128, the said applicant, Alfred C. Raymond is entitled, under the provisions of Section Twenty-one of the Act of Congress approved June 28th, 1898 (30 Stats. 495), to enrollment as a citizen

Cherokee Intermarried White 1906
Volume VI

by intermarriage of the Cherokee Nation and his application for enrollment as such is accordingly granted.

Tams Bixby
Commissioner.

Dated at Muskogee, Indian Territory,
this   FEB 8 1907

◇◇◇◇◇

Cherokee 3009

Muskogee, Indian Territory, February 8, 1907.

W. W. Hastings,
    Attorney for the Cherokee Nation,
        Muskogee, Indian Territory.

Dear Sir:

There is enclosed herewith a copy of the decision of the Commissioner to the Five Civilized Tribes, dated February 8, 1907, granting the application for the enrollment of Alfred C. Raymond as a citizen by intermarriage of the Cherokee Nation.

Respectfully,

Encl. H-13
JMH

Commissioner.

◇◇◇◇◇

Cherokee 3009

Muskogee, Indian Territory, February 8, 1907.

The Commissioner to the Five Civilized Tribes,
    Muskogee, Indian Territory.

Sir:

Receipt is acknowledged of the testimony and of your decision enrolling Alfred C. Raymond as a citizen by intermarriage of the Cherokee Nation. Time for protesting said decision is waived, and I consent that said person may be placed upon the schedule immediately.

Respectfully,
W. W. Hastings
Attorney for Cherokee Nation.

◇◇◇◇◇

Cherokee Intermarried White 1906
Volume VI

Cherokee 3009

Muskogee, Indian Territory, February 8, 1907.

Alfred C Raymond,
    Vinita, Indian Territory.

Dear Sir:

There is enclosed herewith a copy of the decision of the Commissioner to the Five Civilized Tribes, dated February 4, 1907, granting the application for your enrollment as a citizen by intermarriage of the Cherokee Nation.

You will be advised when your name has been placed upon a schedule of citizens of the Cherokee Nation and approved by the Secretary of the Interior.

Respectfully,

Encl. H-14
JMH

Commissioner.

Cher IW 172

◇◇◇◇◇

E.C.M.

DEPARTMENT OF THE INTERIOR,

COMMISSIONER TO THE FIVE CIVILIZED TRIBES.

In the matter of the application for the enrollment of

MARGARET M. WOODALL

As a citizen by intermarriage of the Cherokee Nation.

CHEROKEE NO. 3559.

◇◇◇◇◇

Cherokee Intermarried White 1906
Volume VI

DEPARTMENT OF THE INTERIOR,
COMMISSION TO THE FIVE CIVILIZED TRIBES,
VINITA, I.T., SEPTEMBER 26, 1900.

In the matter of the application of John P. Woodall for the enrollment of himself and wife as citizens of the Cherokee Nation; said Woodall being sworn by Commissioner C. R. Breckinridge, testified as follows:

Q Give me your full name, please? A John P. Woodall.
Q How old are you? A 59
Q What is your post office? A Vinita.
Q In what district do you live? A Delaware.
Q Who is it you want to have put on the roll? A Myself and wife.
Q You apply as a Cherokee by blood? A Yes, sir.
Q What proportion of Cherokee blood do you claim? A I do not know exactly, I guess about fourth.
Q Your wife Cherokee or white woman? A White woman.
Q How long have you lived in the Cherokee Nation? A I was out 9 years in '57.
Q Wat[sic] district were you enrolled from in 1880? A Saline.
Q In 1896 what district? A Saline.
Q What is your wife's name? A Maver M.
Q How old is she? A She is 58.
Q When did you marry her? A I think it was in 1872.
Q You lived together ever since your marriage? A Yes, sir.
Q And lived all the time in the Cherokee Nation? A Yes, sir.
Q What is the name of her father? A Sanders., I do not know his given name.
Q Is he dead or alive? A Dead.
Q Her mother's name? A Elizabeth.
Q Dead or alive? A Both dead.

    1880 enrollment; page 678, #1326, J. P. Woodall, Saline.
    1880 enrollment; page 678, #1327, M. M. Woodall, Saline.
    1896 enrollment; page 554, #3462, John P. Woodall, Delaware.
    1896 enrollment; page 593, #579, M. (Maud) Woodall, Delaware.

Com'r Breckinridge:--The applicant applies for the enrollment of himself and wife: He is identified on the rolls of 1880 and 1896 as a native Cherokee. He has lived in the Cherokee Nation all his life, except a few years about 1860, and he will be listed nor[sic] for enrollment as a Cherokee by blood. His wife is identified with him on the rolls of 1880 and 1896, as an adopted white. She has lived with him in the Cherokee Nation ever since their marriage in 1872, and she will be listed now for enrollment as a Cherokee by adoption.

---oooOOOooo---

    J. O. Rosson, being first duly sworn, states that as stenographer to the Commission to the Five Civilized Tribes, he correctly recordec[sic] the testimony and proceedings in

Cherokee Intermarried White 1906
Volume VI

this case, and the foregoing is a true and complete transcript of his stenographic notes thereof.

J.O. Rosson

Subscribed and sworn to before me this 29th day of September, 1900.

C. R. Breckinridge

Commissioner.

◇◇◇◇◇

JOR.
Cher. 3559.

Department of the Interior.
Commission to the Five Civilized Tribes.
Tahlequah, I. T., October 17, 1902.

SUPPLEMENTAL TESTIMONY in the matter of the application for the enrollment of MAVER M. WOODALL as a citizen by intermarriage of the Cherokee Nation.

MAVER M. WOODALL, being first duly sworn, and being examined, testified as follows:

BY COMMISSION: What is your name? A Margaret Maver Woodall, but they put it down wrong, they put the Maver first. I don't know why Mr. Woodall put it that way. The Margaret comes first, but it is all the same, that is all the name. I guess when he first enrolled me on the 1880 roll they must have enrolled me that way.
Q Your correct name is Margaret Maver Woodall? A Yes sir.
Q How old are you? A *(No answer given.)*
Q What is your post office address? A Big Cabin, Indian Territory.
Q You are a white woman, are you? A Yes sir.
Q Application has been made to this Commission for your enrollment as a citizen by intermarriage of the Cherokee Nation? A Yes sir.
Q What is the name of your husband? A John Peter Woodall.
Q Is he living? A Yes sir.
Q Is he a Cherokee by blood? A Yes sir.
Q Do you claim your right to enrollment by reason of your marriage to him? A Yes sir.
Q When were you and he married? A Married the 1st day of January, 1873.
Q At the time application was made for your enrollment, did you make satisfactory proof of your marriage to him? A Yes sir.
Q Does your name appear upon the 1880 roll? A Yes sir.
Q Were you ever married before you married him? A Yes sir.
Q What was the name of your first husband? A Eneas Ridge.
Q Is he living? A No sir.
Q Was he living when you married your present husband? A No sir.

Cherokee Intermarried White 1906
Volume VI

Q Is that the only time you were ever married before you married your present husband?
A No sir, married once before.
Q What was the name of your next husband? A Samuel Cecil.
Q Is he living? A No sir.
Q Was he living when you married your present husband? A No sir.
Q Was he ever married before, your present husband? A No sir.
Q You are his first wife, and he is your third husband? A Yes sir.
Q Have you and he lived together continuously since you were married? A Yes sir.
Q Were you living together on the 1st day of September, 1902? A Yes sir.
Q You have never been separated at all? A No sir.
Q Have you resied[sic] in the Cherokee Nation continuously since you and he were married? A Yes sir.
Q Has he also? A Yes sir.
Q You have no minor children, you say? A No sir, I have no minor children.

This testimony will be filed with and made a part of the record in the matter of the application for the enrollment of Maver M. Woodall as a citizen by intermarriage of the Cherokee Nation, Cherokee straight card field No. 3559.

Wm. Hutchinson, being first duly sworn, states that as stenographer to the Commission to the Five Civilized Tribes he correctly recorded the testimony and proceedings in this case, and the foregoing is a true and complete transcript of the stenographic notes thereof.

Wm Hutchinson

Subscribed and sworn to before me this 27th day of October, 1902.

John O Rosson
Notary Public.

◇◇◇◇◇

F.R. Cherokee 3559.
DEPARTMENT OF THE INTERIOR,
COMMISSIONER TO THE FIVE CIVILIZED TRIBES.
Muskogee, I. T., January 28, 1907.

In the matter of the application for the enrollment of Margaret M. Woodall as a citizen by intermarriage of the Cherokee Nation.

John P. Woodall being first duly sworn by Frances R. Lane, a Notary Public for the Western District of Indian Territory, testified as follows:

By the Commissioner:
Q What is your name? A John P. Woodall.
Q Your age? A Sixty-six.
Q And your postoffice address? A Big Cabin, I. T.

Cherokee Intermarried White 1906
Volume VI

Q You appear here for the purpose of giving testimony relative to the right to enrollment of Margaret M. Woodall, a citizen by intermarriage of the Cherokee Nation? A Yes sir.
Q Is Margaret M. Woodall your wife? A Yes sir.
Q Is she living at this time? A Yes sir.
Q Is she unable to come here? A She has been; she might come down but she is not well enough.
Q You are a citizen of the Cherokee Nation by blood? A Yes sir.
Q When were you married to Margaret M. Woodall? A In 1873.
Q Where were you married to her? A I was married in Delaware district.
Q Who performed the marriage ceremony? A My brother did.
Q Is your brother a minister? A No, he was district judge at that time.
Q At the time you married Margaret M. Woodall, were you a recognized citizen of the Cherokee Nation? A Yes sir.
Q From the time of your marriage to Margaret M. Woodall on down to the present time, you have resided together as husband and wife and lived continuously in the Cherokee Nation? A Yes sir.
Q Had you been married before you married Margaret M. Woodall? A Yes sir.
Q How many times had you ben[sic] married? A Only once.
Q What was the name of your first wife? A Her name was Mary Thorn.
Q Was Mary Thorn living at the time you married Margaret Woodall? A No, she was dead.
Q Was Margaret M. Woodall married before she married you? A Yes sir.
Q How many times had she been married? A She had been married before me, I think twice.
Q Were either of her first husbands living at the time you married her? A Well, I can't say positively because I didn't know the men at all; might be living. They might have been living.
Q She had separated from her first and second husbands? A The second one.
Q But she never secured any divorce as far as you know? A All I know about that is what she told me herself.
Q What did she tell you? A She said she was divorced.
Q The name[sic] from whom she was divorced, was he a Cherokee citizen or was he a white man? A I reckon he was a white man. I didn't know him at all.
Q How long had she been living in Delaware District at the time you married her? A Well, I was gone then, and I was out one time nine years and I went back and been there ever since, that is, in the country.
Q Did you ever leave the Cherokee Nation for any length of time--move out of it? A Only one time when I was a young fellow I went to California and staid, and came back in 1866.
Q When you returned were you readmitted to citizenship? A Yes sir.
Q In what year were you readmitted? A I don't remember that exactly. I couldn't say; it was not very long; might have ben[sic] in 1867.
Q But it was prior to the time of your marriage to Margaret M. Woodall, was it? A Yes sir.
Q Were you admitted by the council? A Yes, by the Council; that is, the whole family was admitted at one time.

Cherokee Intermarried White 1906
Volume VI

Q Since that time you never moved out of the Cherokee Nation? A No, I have lived right here.
Q Do you know where it was--in what state, Margaret M. Woodall secured the divorce from her second husband? A No, I don't.
Q Where did she live before she came to the Cherokee Nation? A She lived at Springfield, Missouri, and in Virginia awhile I believe--that's just what she said.
Q You never made any effort to get any copy of the decree of the court granting her a divorce? A No sir.
Q You have no reason to think that she was not divorced from that man at the time you married her? A No, I think they was divorced.
Q And you don't know whether he was dead at the time she married you? A No, I couldn't say; he might have been living because I don't know him at all.
Q I believe you said that her first husband was dead at the time she married you?
A Yes sir.
Witness excused.

William C. Woodall, being first duly sworn by Frances R. Lane, a Notary Public for the Western District of Indian Territory, testified as follows:

By the Commissioner:
Q What is your name? A William C. Woodall.
Q Your age? A Seventy-one and a half.
Q And your postoffice address? A Vinita, I. T.
Q Your[sic] are a brother of John F. Woodall, are you? A Yes sir.
Q Did you know his wife, Margaret M. Woodall? A Yes sir.
Q When were they married? A In 1873 I expect.
Q Who performed the marriage ceremony? A I did.
Q At that time what office of the Cherokee nation[sic] did you hold? A Judge of the district court of Delaware District.
Q They were lawfully married in accordance with the Cherokee laws at the time?
A Yes sir.
Q They have resided together as husband and wife and continuously lived in the Cherokee Nation from that time until the present time? A Yes sur[sic].
Q How do you fix the date of 1873 as being the date of their marriage? A I was judge in 1872, and it was along about the last of that year or the first of the other year, I can't tell which, I married them.
Q How long did you remain judge? A I was elected for two years, but I didn't serve the full term.
Q At the time you performed the marriage ceremony was your brother a recognized citizen of the Cherokee Nation? A Yes sir.
Q Had he never been married before that had he? A Yes, been married once.
Q Was his first wife living at the time he married Margaret M. Woodall?
A No, she was dead.
Q Do you know whether or not Margaret M. Woodall had been married before she married John P. Woodall? A She was widow Ridge at the time I married them; that was the name she went by.

Cherokee Intermarried White 1906
Volume VI

Q It was you understanding that she had been divorced from that husband? A I don't know nothing about that.

    The applicant, Margaret M. Woodall is identified on the Cherokee authenticated tribal roll of 1880, Saline District, No. 1327.

    The husband of the applicant, John P. Woodall, is identified on the Cherokee authenticated tribal roll of 1880, Saline District, No. 1326, and is included in the approved partial roll of citizens by blood of the Cherokee Nation, opposite No. 8672.

    The applicant and her husband are also identified on the Cherokee Census Roll of 1896, Delaware District, opposite No. 579 and No. 3462, respectively.

    John P. Woodall Recalled, testified as follows:

By the Commissioner:
Q From yiur[sic] testimony awhile ago I understood that your wife was probably divorced from her husband in Springfield, Mo. Is that your understanding? A Well sir, I don't know; I can't state for certain.
Q Did you ever hear her say whether she secured a divorce, or whether he secured a divorce? A No, I don't remember that, either.
Q Did you ever make any effort to secure a copy of the decree granting the divorce? A No sir.
Q Is your wife able to come here at this time and testify in this case? A Not hardly; she is poorly; she is getting kind of old.
Q Has she been away from her home in the last year? A No, not outside the nation she hasn't been.
Q Has she been able to make any tripe this last year? A She comes down to Adair; and once in awhile she goes to Tahlequah. Adair is only 8 miles.
Q Don't you think she could come down here this week sometime and give some testimony as to that divorce from this husband? A Well, it may be she could.

Frances R. Lane upon oath states that as stenographer to the Commissioner to the Five Civilized Tribes she reported the testimony in the above entitled cause and that the foregoing is an accurate transcript of her stenographic notes thereof.

                                                  Frances R. Lane

Subscribed and sworn to before me this January 28, 1907.

                                                        Edward Merrick
                                                          Notary Public.

Cherokee Intermarried White 1906
Volume VI

.18th Day. Greene Circuit Court, Saturday, May 28th, 1870.

Mavor Cecil, :
               :
   vs   :Final decree of divorce.
               :
S. W. Cecil, :

    Now at this day come the Plff and this cause coming on to be heard and being submitted to the Court the Court from an examination of the same doth find that the defendant has been duly notified of the commencement of this sir by a writ of summons and copy of the petition served on him for at least fifteen days before the commencement of the present term of this Court and the Court further find from an examination of the petition, answer and from the evidence of the Plff and defendant that the Plaintiff is the innocent and injured party. It is therefore considered adjudged and decreed by the Court that the said Mavor Cecil be divorced from the bonds of matrimony by her contracted with the said Samuel W. Cecil and that the bonds of matrimony be annulled on the part of said Plaintiff and that the plaintiff have and recover of and from defendant her cost of suit, for which execution may issue.

State of Missouri, :
                 : ss
County of Greene. :

    I, T. A. Nicholson, Clerk of the Circuit Court within and for the County and State aforesaid do hereby certify that the above and foregoing is a full, true and complete copy of the decree of divorce in the case wherein Mavor Cecil is plaintiff and S. W. Cecil is defendant as fully as the same appears of record in my office.
                 In testimony whereof I have hereunto set my hand as Clerk of the Circuit Court and affixed the seal hereto. Done at my office in the City of Springfield, Missouri, this 1st day of February, A. D. 1907.

                                 T.A. Nicholson
                                          Circuit Clerk.

Cherokee Intermarried White 1906
Volume VI

E.C.M.

Cherokee 3559.

DEPARTMENT OF THE INTERIOR,

COMMISSIONER TO THE FIVE CIVILIZED TRIBES.

In the matter of the application for the enrollment of Margaret M. Woodall as a citizen by intermarriage of the Cherokee Nation.

D E C I S I O N

THE RECORDS OF THIS OFFICE SHOW: That on September 26, 1900, application was received by the Commission to the Five Civilized Tribes for the enrollment of Margaret M. Woodall as a citizen by intermarriage of the Cherokee Nation. Further proceedings in the matter of said application were had at Tahlequah, Indian Territory, September 17, 1902, and at Muskogee, Indian Territory, January 28, 1907.

THE EVIDENCE IN THIS CASE SHOWS: That the applicant herein, Margaret M. Woodall, a white woman, married January 1, 1873, one John P. Woodall, who is identified on the Cherokee authenticated tribal roll of 1880, Saline District, No. 1326, as a native Cherokee, and whose name is included in the approved partial roll of citizens by blood of the Cherokee Nation opposite No. 8672. It is further shown that from the time of said marriage the said John P. Woodall and Margaret M. Woodall resided together as husband and wife and continuously lived in the Cherokee Nation up to and including September 1, 1902. Said applicant is identified on the Cherokee authenticated tribal roll of 1880, and the Cherokee census roll of 1896, as an intermarried citizen of the Cherokee Nation.

IT IS, THEREFORE, ORDERED AND ADJUDGED: That in accordance with the decision of the Supreme Court of the United States, dated November 5, 1906, in the cases of Daniel Red Bird, et al., vs. the United States, Nos. 125, 126, 127 and 128, the said applicant, Margaret M. Woodall is entitled, under the provisions of Section twenty-one of the Act of Congress approved June 28, 1898 (30 Stats. 495), to enrollment as a citizen by intermarriage of the Cherokee Nation, and her application for enrollment as such is accordingly granted.

Tams Bixby
Commissioner.

Dated at Muskogee, Indian Territory,
this   FEB 8 1907

Cherokee Intermarried White 1906
Volume VI

Cherokee 3559

Muskogee, Indian Territory, February 8, 1907.

W. W. Hastings,
    Attorney for the Cherokee Nation,
        Muskogee, Indian Territory.

Dear Sir:

    There is enclosed herewith a copy of the decision of the Commissioner to the Five Civilized Tribes, dated February 8, 1907, granting the application for the enrollment of Margaret M. Woodall as a citizen by intermarriage of the Cherokee Nation.

        Respectfully,

Encl. H-3
JMH
        Commissioner.

◇◇◇◇◇

Cherokee 3559

Muskogee, Indian Territory, February 8, 1907.

The Commissioner to the Five Civilized Tribes,
    Muskogee, Indian Territory.

Sir:

    Receipt is acknowledged of the testimony and of your decision enrolling Margaret M. Woodall as a citizen by intermarriage of the Cherokee Nation. Time for protesting said decision is waived, and I consent that said person may be placed upon the schedule immediately.

        Respectfully,
        W. W. Hastings
        Attorney for Cherokee Nation.

◇◇◇◇◇

Cherokee Intermarried White 1906
Volume VI

Cherokee 3559

Muskogee, Indian Territory, February 8, 1907.

Margaret M. Woodall,
    Vinita, Indian Territory.

Dear Madam:

    There is enclosed herewith a copy of the decision of the Commissioner to the Five Civilized Tribes, dated February 8, 1907, granting the application for your enrollment as a citizen by intermarriage of the Cherokee Nation.

    You will be advised when your name has been placed upon a schedule of citizens of the Cherokee Nation and approved by the Secretary of the Interior.

                            Respectfully,

Encl. H-4   Commissioner.
JMH

Cher IW 173

◇◇◇◇◇

                                                                     C.E.W.

DEPARTMENT OF THE INTERIOR,

COMMISSIONER TO THE FIVE CIVILIZED TRIBES.

In the matter of the application for the enrollment of

GEORGE W. MITCHELL

as a citizen by intermarriage of the Cherokee Nation.

CHEROKEE 4041

◇◇◇◇◇

Cherokee Intermarried White 1906
Volume VI

DEPARTMENT OF THE INTERIOR,
COMMISSION TO THE FIVE CIVILIZED TRIBES,
VINITA, I.T., OCTOBER 3d, 1900.

In the matter of the application of George W. Mitchell for the enrollment of himself, wife and children as citizens of the Cherokee Nation; said Mitchell being sworn by Commission T. B. Needles, testified as follows:

Q What is your name? A George W. Mitchell.
Q What is your age, Mr. Mitchell,[sic] [sic] 48.
Q What is your post office address? A Vinita.
Q Are you a recognized citizen of the Cherokee Nation? A Yes, sir
Q By blood or intermarriage? A Intermarriage.
Q For whom do you apply? A Myself, wife and family.
Q What is the name of your wife? A Martha J.
Q What was her name before you married her? A Horn.
Q What is her age? A 38.
Q Have you a certificate of marriage? A No, sir, I am on the 1880 roll. I was married in 1872.
Q What is[sic] the name[sic] of your children? A My oldest Savola L.
Q How old is she? A 19.
Q What is the name of the next one? A Claud S.
Q How old is he? A 17.
Q Next one? A Lee R.
Q How old is Lee R.? A 12.
Q Name of the next one? A Joseph F.
Q How old is Joseph F.? A He is eight.
Q Next one? A Clay A.
Q How old is Clay A? A Six.
Q Next one? A Beulah W.
Q What is her age? A Four.
Q What is the name of the next one? A George W., Jr.
Q How old is George W.? A One.
    1880 enrollment; page 287, #1711, George Mitchell, Delaware.
Q She is on the roll a some other name? A She is with her step-father, J. C. Cleveland
    1880 enrollment; page 763, #843, Martha L. Horn, Delaware.
    1896 enrollment; page 316, #692, George W. Mitchell, Cooweescoowee.
    (3326)
    1896 enrollment; page 217, #326, Mattie J. Mitchell, Cooweescoowee.
    1896 enrollment; page 217, #3329, Sivolie[sic] Mitchell, "
    1896 enrollment; page 217, #3331, Lee R.   "   "
    1896 enrollment; page 217, #3332, Joseph F.   "   "
    1896 enrollment; page 217, #3333, Clay A.   "   "
    1896 enrollment; page 216, #3334, Bulah V.[sic] "   "
Q These children all alive and living with you, Mr. Mitchell? A Yes, sir.
Q You were married before you marriage[sic] your present[sic] wife? A Yes, sir.

Cherokee Intermarried White 1906
Volume VI

Q What was that wife's name? A Susan.
Q Living? A No, sir.
Q Was she a Cherokee citizen by blood? A Yes, sir
Q Did you live with her until her death? A Yes, sir.
Q After wards[sic] married Mattie Horn another Cherokee citizen by blood? A Yes sir.
Q Have you lived with her ever since your marriage? A Yes, sir.

      Com'r Needles:--The name of George W. Mitchell appears upon the authenticated roll of 1880 as an intermarried white. He avers that he was married to his present wife, Martha J. Horn, in the year 1896, and the name of his wife Martha J. Horn is found upon the authenticated roll of 1880 as Martha L. Horn, and upon the roll of 1896 as Mattie J. Mitchell. The applicant's name appears upon the roll of 1880 as George Mitchell. The names of his children, Savola L., Claud S., Lee R., Joseph F., Clay A., and Beulah B., appears upon the census roll of 1896, and he makes satisfactory proof as to the birth of the youngest child, George W., Jr., whose names[sic] does not appear on the roll of 1896. They all being duly identified according to the page and number of the rolls as indicated in the testimony, and having made satisfactory proof as to their residence, the said George W. Mitchell will be duly listed for enrollment as a Cherokee citizen by intermarriage, and his wife Martha J. and her children as enumerated in the testimony as Cherokee citizens by blood.

---oooOOOooo---

      J. O. Rosson, being first duly sworn, states that as stenographer to the Commission to the Five Civilized Tribes, he correctly recorded the testimony and proceedings in this case, and the foregoing is a true and complete transcript of his stenographic notes thereof.

J O Rosson

Subscribed and sworn to before me this 8th day of October, 1900.

C R Breckinridge
Commissioner.

◇◇◇◇◇

Cherokee 4041.

DEPARTMENT OF THE INTERIOR,
COMMISSION TO THE FIVE CIVILIZED TRIBES.
Muskogee, I. T., October 17, 1902.

      In the matter of the application of George W. Mitchell for the enrollment of himself as a citizen by intermarriage, and for the enrollment of his wife, Martha J. Mitchell, and his eight minor children, Savola L., Claud S., Lee R., Joseph F., Clay A., Beulah V[sic]., George W., Jr., and Ross B. Mitchell, as citizens by blood, of the Cherokee Nation.

Cherokee Intermarried White 1906
Volume VI

SUPPLEMENTAL PROCEEDINGS.

GEORGE W. MITCHELL, being sworn, testified as follows:

By the Commission,

Q What is your name? A George W. Mitchell.
Q How old are you? A I am fifty-one years old.
Q What is your postoffice? A Vinita.
Q Are you a white man? A Yes, sir.
Q Does your name appear upon the roll of 1880 as an adopted white citizen? A Yes, sir.
Q What's your wife's name? A Susan C.
Q What was her name in 1880? A Susan C. Mitchell.
Q Who was Martha J. Mitchell? A That's my first wife.
Q You are talking about your first wife, Susan? What was her first name?
A Helderbrand was her name when I married her.
Q You claim your citizenship through her? A Yes, sir.
Q When did she die? A In 1884.
Q Did you live with her from '80 to '84? A Yes, sir.
Q Never separated from her during that time? A No, sir.
Q When did you marry the second time? She died in 1884? A 1883, I believe it was she died; in December, 1883.
Q What was your second wife's name? A Henry.
Q What was her first name? A Annie B.
Q Who is Martha J.? A I have been married three times.
Q How long did you live with her? A Three months.
Q You were divorced from her? A Yes, sir.
Q Who got the divorce? A We both got it; we both signed the petition.
Q When did you marry Martha J. Mitchell? A 1889.
Q You were divorced from your second wife in '85, were you? A Yes, sir; yes, '85.
Q Did you file the record of that divorce with the Commission?
A You say did I?
Q Yes. A I can get a record.

Applicant must file proof of divorce from second wife.

Q Now, is your present wife, Martha J., a Cherokee by blood? A Yes, sir.
Q How long has she lived in the Cherokee Nation? A Born and raised here.
Q Has she lived in the Cherokee Nation all her life? A Yes, sir.
Q Have you been in the Cherokee Nation ever since '80? A Yes, sir. Ever since 1871.
Q Was Martha J. ever married before? A No, sir.
Q How many children have you? A Four by my first wife, six by my last wife.
Q Ten altogether? A I reckon you have not got one on there.
Q What's your two oldest ones' names? They have enrolled themselves? A Yes, sir, Robert and Lee have enrolled themselves.
Q What's the youngest one's name? A Ross Benge is his full name.

Cherokee Intermarried White 1906
Volume VI

Q You have eight living with you? A Yes, sir, they are all living with me. My son and daughter are teaching school.

Q You have had no deaths in the last two and a half years? A No, sir.

Retta Chick, being first duly sworn, states that, as stenographer to the Commission to the Five Civilized Tribes, she recorded the testimony and proceedings in the matter of the foregoing application, and that the above is a true and complete transcript of her stenographic notes thereof.

Retta Chick

Subscribed and sworn to before me this 17th day of November, 1902.

P.G. Reuter
Notary Public.

Cherokee #4041

DEPARTMENT OF THE INTERIOR, COMMISSION TO THE FIVE CIVILIZED TRIBES, MUSKOGEE, IND. TER., DEC. 17, 1902.

In the matter of the application for the enrollment of George W. Mitchell et al. as citizens of the Cherokee Nation:

SUPPLEMENTAL STATEMENT.

An examination of the 1880 authenticated tribal roll of the Cherokee Nation shows that the mother of Savola L. Mitchell is identified thereon, at page 287, #1712, Delaware District.

It is ordered that this statement be filed with and made a part of the record of this case.

TB Needles
Commissioner.

Cherokee Intermarried White 1906
Volume VI

Cher
Supp'l to # 4041

Department of the Interior,
Commission to the Five Civilized Tribes,
Vinita, I. T., February 20, 1903.

In the matter of the application of GEORGE W. MITCHELL, for the enrollment of himself, as a citizen by intermarriage, and his wife, MARTHA J. MITCHELL, and his children, SAVOLA L., CLAUD S., LEE R., JOSEPH F., CLAY A., BEULAH V., GEORGE W. JR. and ROSS B. MITCHELL, as citizens by blood, of the Cherokee Nation.

GEORGE W. MITCHELL, being first duly sworn, and examined, testified as follows:

Examined by the Commission:

Q State your name ?   A George W. Mitchell.
Q How old are You ?   A I am fifty years old.
Q What is your post office ?   A My nearest post office is Woodley, but Vinita is my post office.
Q You are a white man, are you ?   A Yes sir.
Q Claiming as an intermarried citizen ?   A Yes sir.
Q Is your name on the roll of 1880 ?   A Yes sir.
Q What was your wife's name at that time ?   A Susan Mitchell.
Q Was she a Cherokee by blood ?   A Yes sir.
Q She is the wife through whom you claim citizenship ?   A Yes sir.
Q You were married to her prior to 1880 ?   A Yes sir.
Q How many children did you have by Susan ?   A Four.
Q Your wife's name was Susan C. Mitchell ?   A Yes sir.
Q What is the name of your oldest child ?   A Robert L.
Q He is of age ?   A Yes sir.
Q He has enrolled himself ?   A Yes sir.
Q What is the name of the next one ?   A Levia L.
Q She enrolled herself ?   A Yes sir.
Q What is the name of the oldest child you enrolled ?
A Savola L., she has become of age since then.
Q Is she married ?   A No sir.
Q What is the name of the next one ?   A Claud S.
Q Susan is his mother ?   A Yes sir.
Q What is the name of the next one ?   A That's all by that first woman, but I have six by my last one.
Q Susan is the mother of Claud ?   A Yes sir. Claud, I reckon, is the only one I can't file for.

Cherokee Intermarried White 1906
Volume VI

Q You have how many by your second wife ?   A Six, Lee, Joseph, Clay, Beulah George and Ross.
Q They are your children by whom ? A Martha J. Horn.
Q That's your second wife ? A Yes sir.
Q When did your first wife Susan die ?   A My first wife in--well I can't tell that question; I just came up these steps, I have been sick about three weeks; she died in 1884.
Q Did you live with her from the time you married her up until the time she died ? A Yes sir.
Q Never were separated in all that time ? A No sir.
Q When did you marry your present wife Martha ? A I married her in 1886.
Q She is your second wife ? A No sir, I was married between these.
Q Who did you marry after the death of your wife Susan ? A Annie B. Henry.
Q Was she a Cherokee by blood ? A Yes sir. We never had any children.
Q Was she on the 1880 roll ? A No sir; yes sir I believe she was on the 1880 roll, I believe she was, she was from Alabama here.
Q Was she admitted ? A Yes sir.
Q When ? A She must have been admitted about 1880, I guess.
Q Admitted by the Cherokee Commission ? A By the Cherokee Council.
Q When did she come to the Cherokee Nation ? A She come to the Nation in about 1882 I think; no, in 1881.
Q And resided in the Cherokee Nation up until the time you married her ? A Yes sir.
Q How long did you live with her ? A Lived with her about four months.
Q Did she die ? A No sir, we separated.
Q Your first wife was dead was she ? A Yes sir. We separated and we was divorced by act of the Nation Council.
Q When ? A In 1886.
Q Now, have you made proof of that divorce before the Commission ? A Yes sir.
Q And after that divorce you married your present wife Martha ? A Yes sir.
Q Is she on the 1880 roll ? A Yes sir, all these women were Cherokees by blood.
Q Have you and Martha been living together ever since you were married ? A Yes sir.
Q Are all these children for whom you make application living at this time ? A Yes sir.
Q Have you resided in the Cherokee Nation ever since 1880 ? A Ever since 1874.
Q Never been out ? A No sir, only out and back, its[sic] been my home ever since.
Q Did you have any children by Annie ? A No sir.
Q You say she was admitted by the Council in 1880 ? A Yes sir.
Q Did you offer in evidence a copy of that act of Council ? A No sir, I didn't offer any as to her admission, she lives in this country yet, and has been a citizen ever since.
Q What is her name now ? A Well sir, I don't know, I know she married, but I don't know what her name is; she's up about Collinsville I think, but I can't say what her name is.
Q Was she admitted under the name of Henry ?

Cherokee Intermarried White 1906
Volume VI

By the Commission: It appears from an examination of the record in Cherokee # 5448, that applicant's second wife, Annie B. Henry, who is now the wife of Hiram R. Snyder, was admitted to citizenship in the Cherokee Nation on September 22, 1883.

Q Now, Mr. Mitchell, when did you say you married Annie B. Henry ? A In 1884.
Q Do you know if she is now the wife of Hiram R. Snyder ? A Yes sir, I heard she married a man named Snyder, she was always been quite a distance from me.
Q Do you know if she is now living with her husband near Chelsea ?
A She is living somewhere west of here.

E. C. Bagwell, on oath states that, as stenographer to the Commission to the Five Civilized Tribes, he correctly recorded the testimony and proceedings had in the above entitled cause, and that the foregoing is an accurate transcript of his stenographic notes thereof.

E.C. Bagwell

Subscribed and sworn to before me this March 24, 1903.

Samuel Foreman
Notary Public.

◇◇◇◇◇

Cherokee No. 4041.

DEPARTMENT OF THE INTERIOR,

COMMISSIONER TO THE FIVE CIVILIZED TRIBES,

MUSKOGEE, INDIAN TERRITORY, JANUARY 4, 1907.

IN THE MATTER OF THE APPLICATION for the enrollment of George W. Mitchell, as a citizen by intermarriage of the Cherokee Nation.

GEORGE W. MITCHELL, being first duly sworn by Walter W. Chappell, Notary Public in the Western District of the Indian Territory, testified as follows:

EXAMINATION

ON BEHALF OF THE COMMISSIONER:

Q What is your name, age and postoffice address?

Cherokee Intermarried White 1906
Volume VI

A George W. Mitchell; going on 55, - 54, going on 55; Blue Jacket, R. F. D. No. 1. My postoffice has been near Woodley.
Q You claim to be a citizen by intermarriage of the Cherokee Nation, do you?
A Yes sir.
Q Through whom do you claim that right? A Susan C. Hildebrand.
Q Is Susan C. Hildebrand living at the present time? A No sir.
Q When did she die? A In 1884, February 13th.
Q Was she a citizen of the Cherokee Nation?
A Yes sir, Cherokee by blood.
Q Born and raised here? A Yes sir, born and raised in Going Snake District, Cherokee Nation.
Q When were you and she married? A We was married in 1873, September 21. I haven't got any license, but it should appear on the Tahlequah book. I wrote to Tahlequah here awhile back for it. They wrote me they had sent the books all to the Dawes Commission.
Q Where were you married to her? A. Married in Going Snake District.
Q Who married you? A Baptist Minister. His name was J. Hogan. I think he is on the Baptist circuit here in this Creek country now. He might not be here, and then he might. I think my marriage appears on the Tahlequah books. That is where I got my license.
Q You secured your license in the Tahlequah District? A Yes.
Q Were with you or Susan Hildebrand married prior to your marriage in 1873?
A No sir.

Q Did you live together continuously after your marriage until her death? A Yes sir.
Q Where did you reside during that time? A In Going Snake District, we lived the first four or five years we married, we lived in the Delaware District, if it is necessary to state that. We are on the 1875 roll in the Delaware District
Q Have you married since her death? A Yes sir.
Q Is your second wife living? A Yes sir.
Q What is her name? A I am like the other man, been married twice. First woman I married her name was Anna B Henry; she was a Cherokee by blood.
Q When were you and Anna B. Henry married? A We were married in I think it was about December 1884.
Q Is your second wife living at the present time?
A Yes. She only stayed with me about five months I reckon, and we was divorced by an act of the National Council.
Q Is she living in the Cherokee Nation at the present time?
A Yes, she is living near Chelsea.
Q Has she made application for enrollment?
A Yes, she is married again.
Q Under what name did she apply? A Snyder. Q Anna H. Snyder? A Yes sir.
Q What is her present husband's name?
A I don't know his given name, but I think it is Hiram Snyder.
Q Is he living? A Yes, he was the last time I heard anything from him.

Cherokee Intermarried White 1906
Volume VI

Q Have you married since you and Anna B. Henry separated?
A Yes sir.
Q Who did you marry? A Martha J. Horne.
Q Is she living? A Yes sir.
Q What is her citizenship? A Cherokee by blood.
Q When did you marry her? A That was June 1887.
Q Did you have any children by your first wife? A Four, all grown.
Q All living? A Yes sir, - all got allotments right there by me.
Q What is the name of the youngest one?
A The youngest one of these four?
Q Yes? A Claude Stevens.
Q And the one next older, what is its name? A It is a girl, Sabola[sic] L. Mitchell. She filed for herself, she was of age.

ON BEHALF OF THE COMMISSIONER:

>The records of this office show that Claude S. and Sabola L. Mitchell, children of the applicant George W. Mitchell and Susan C. Mitchell, deceased, are included in an approved partial roll of Cherokees by blood, opposite Nos. 27688 and 27689, respectively.
>On Page No. 51, Marriage Records from 1870-1892 Tahlequah District, "appears the following "License granted George Mitchell to marry Susan Hildebrand, given September 13, 1873, ceremony performed by J. H. Hogan September 21, 1873, ordained minister.

Q Since you and your second wife separated, you say you think she married a man named Hiram Snyder? A Yes sir.
Q Do you know whether or not she had any children by him? A I think she has.
Q Do you know their names? A No sir, I don't know them.

ON BEHALF OF THE COMMISSIONER:

>The records of this office show that said Anna B. Snyder, wife of one Hiram R. Snyder, a non-citizen of the Cherokee Nation, together with four children of the said Anna B. Snyder and Hiram R. Snyder, are included in the approved partial roll of Cherokees by blood, opposite Nos. 13040 to 13044, inclusive.

Q Have you any children by your last wife? A Yes, seven. Six boys and one girl.

ON BEHALF OF THE COMMISSIONER:

>The records of this office further show that Martha J. Mitchell (nee Horne) is included in an approved partial roll of Cherokees by blood opposite No. 27687.

Cherokee Intermarried White 1906
Volume VI

The applicant George W. Mitchell is identified on the authenticated Cherokee tribal roll of 1880, Delaware District, and the Cherokee census roll of 1896, Cooweescoowee District, opposite Nos. 1711 and 692, respectively, as an intermarried white.

Q Have you lived continuously in the Cherokee Nation since your first marriage in 1873? A Yes, never lived any where else.

(Witness dismissed).

I, S. T. Wright, stenographer to the Commissioner to the Five Civilized Tribes, on oath, state that I recorded the testimony and proceedings had in the above entitled cause on January 4, 1907, and that the above and foregoing is a true and correct transcript of my stenographic notes thereof taken on said date.

S. T. Wright

Subscribed and sworn to before me this January 5th, 1907.

Edward Merrick
NOTARY PUBLIC.

◇◇◇◇◇

C.E.W.   Cherokee 4041.

DEPARTMENT OF THE INTERIOR,

COMMISSIONER TO THE FIVE CIVILIZED TRIBES.

In the matter of the application for the enrollment of GEORGE W. MITCHELL as a citizen by intermarriage of the Cherokee Nation.

D E C I S I O N

THE RECORDS OF THIS OFFICE SHOW: That at Vinita, Indian Territory, October 5, 1900, application was received by the Commission to the Five Civilized Tribes for the enrollment of George W. Mitchell as a citizen by intermarriage of the Cherokee Nation. Further proceedings in the matter of said application were had at Muskogee, Indian Territory, October 17, 1902, December 17, 1902, at Vinita, Indian Territory, February 20, 1903, and at Muskogee, Indian Territory, January 4, 1907.

THE EVIDENCE IN THIS CASE SHOWS: That the applicant herein, George W. Mitchell, a white man, was married in accordance with Cherokee law September 21, 1873, to one Susan C. Mitchell, nee Hildebrand, since deceased, who was at the time of

Cherokee Intermarried White 1906
Volume VI

said marriage a recognized citizen by blood of the Cherokee Nation, and who is identified on the Cherokee authenticated tribal roll of 1880, Delaware District, Page 287, No. 1712, as a native Cherokee; that from the time of said marriage the said George W. and Susan C. Mitchell resided together as husband and wife until her death, which occurred February 13, 1884; that subsequent to the death of the said Susan C. Mitchell said George W. Mitchell, in December, 1884, married one Anna B. Mitchell, nee Henry, who is identified on the Cherokee Orphan roll of 1880, Cooweescoowee District, Page 5, No. 30, as a native Cherokee; that from the time of said marriage the said George W. and Anna B. Mitchell resided together as husband and wife until the year 1885; that said applicant was divorced from his wife, Anna B. Mitchell, in the year 1885, by an Act of the National Council; that in June, 1887, said George W. Mitchell was married to one Martha J. Mitchell, nee Horne, who was at the time of said marriage a recognized citizen by blood of the Cherokee Nation, who is identified on the Cherokee authenticated tribal roll of 1880, Tahlequah District, Page 763, No. 843, as a native Cherokee, and whose name appears on the approved partial roll of citizens by blood of the Cherokee Nation, opposite No. 27687; that said George W. Mitchell and Martha J. Mitchell, since their marriage, have resided together as husband and wife, and have continuously lived in the Cherokee Nation; and that said George W. Mitchell has continuously lived in the Cherokee Nation since September 21, 1873. Said applicant is identified on the Cherokee authenticated tribal roll of 1880, and the Cherokee census roll of 1896, as an intermarried citizen of the Cherokee Nation.

IT IS, THEREFORE, ORDERED AND ADJUDGED: That in accordance with the decision of the Supreme Court of the United States, dated November 5, 1906, in the cases of Daniel Red Bird et al. vs. the United States, Nos. 125, 126, 127, and 128, the said applicant George W. Mitchell, is entitled, under the provisions of Section 21, of the Act of Congress approved June 28, 1898 (30 Stats., 495), to enrollment as a citizen by intermarriage of the Cherokee Nation, and his application for enrollment as such is accordingly granted.

Tams Bixby
Commissioner.

Dated at Muskogee, Indian Territory,
this   FEB 11 1907

◇◇◇◇◇

Cherokee Intermarried White 1906
Volume VI

Cherokee
4041.

Muskogee, Indian Territory, February 11, 1907.

W. W. Hastings,
    Attorney for the Cherokee Nation,
        Muskogee, Indian Territory.

Dear Sir:

    There is enclosed herewith copy of the decision of the Commissioner to the Five Civilized Tribes, dated February 11, 1907, granting the application for the enrollment of George W. Mitchell as a citizen by intermarriage of the Cherokee Nation.

        Respectfully,

Enc I-1   Commissioner.

RPI

◇◇◇◇◇

Cherokee 4041

        Muskogee, Indian Territory, February 11, 1907.

The Commissioner to the Five Civilized Tribes,
    Muskogee, Indian Territory.

Sir:

    Receipt is acknowledged of the testimony and of your decision enrolling George W. Mitchell as a citizen by intermarriage of the Cherokee Nation. Time for protesting said decision is waived and I consent that said person may be placed upon the schedule immediately.

        Respectfully,
           W. W. Hastings
           Attorney for the Cherokee Nation.

◇◇◇◇◇

Cherokee Intermarried White 1906
Volume VI

Cherokee 4041.

Muskogee, Indian Territory, February 11, 1907.

George W. Mitchell,
Blue Jacket, Indian Territory.

Dear Sir:

There is enclosed herewith copy of the decision of the Commissioner to the Five Civilized Tribes, dated February 11, 1907, granting the application for your enrollment as a citizen by intermarriage of the Cherokee Nation.

You will be advised when your name has been placed upon a schedule of citizens of the Cherokee Nation and approved by the Secretary of the Interior.

Respectfully,

Enc I-2.

Commissioner.

RPI

Cher IW 174

E.C.M.

DEPARTMENT OF THE INTERIOR,

COMMISSIONER TO THE FIVE CIVILIZED TRIBES.

In the matter of the application for the enrollment of

GEORGE W. EATON

As a citizen by intermarriage of the Cherokee Nation.

CHEROKEE NO. 4708.

Cherokee Intermarried White 1906
Volume VI

Department of the Interior,
Commission to the Five Civilized Tribes,
Claremore, I.T., October 22, 1900.

In the matter of the application of George W. Eaton for the enrollment of himself as a Cherokee citizen; being sworn and examined by Commissioner Breckinridge he testified as follows:

Q Give me your full name? A George W. Eaton.
Q How old are you? A 54
Q What is your post-office? A Claremore.
Q You live in Cooweescoowee District? A Yes sir.
Q Do you apply for the enrollment of yourself and family? A Just myself.
Q Are you a Cherokee by blood? A No sir, white man.
Q Let me see your license and certificate? A I haven't got one
Q Are you on any roll of the Cherokee Nation? A Yes sir, on all of them I guess.
Q On the roll of 1880? A Yes sir.
Q What was the name of your wife? A Nancy E. Williams.
Q She was a Cherokee, was she? A Yes sir.
Q When did she die? A 4 years ago.
Q She was living in 1880? A Yes sir.
Q You married her when? A In 1868
Q Did you live with her until she died 4 years ago? A Yes sir
Q Have you married since her death? A No sir.
1880 roll page 87 #1002 G. W. Eaton Cooweescoowee Dist, adopted White
1896 roll page 303 #341 George W. Eaton Cooweescoowee Dist.

Com'r Breckinridge: The applicant is identified on the rolls of 1880 and 1896 as an adopted white; his Cherokee wife with whom he lived in 1880 died some four years ago; he has lived in the Cherokee Nation ever since his enrollment in 1880 a[sic] he has not remarried since the death of his Cherokee wife, and he will be listed now for enrollment as a Cherokee by intermarriage.

M.D. Green, being first duly sworn, states that as stenographer to the Commission to the Five Civilized Tribes he correctly recorded the testimony and proceedings in this case and the foregoing is a true and correct transcript of his stenographic notes thereof.

MD Green

Subscribed and sworn to before me this 23 day of October 1900.

CR Breckinridge
Commissioner.

Cherokee Intermarried White 1906
Volume VI

COOWEESCOOWEE
Statement of Applicant Taken Under Oath.

CHEREOKEE BY BLOOD AND ADOPTION.

54 Date OCT 22 1900 1900.
Name ....**George W. Eaton**........**Claremore I.T.**
District ....**COOWEESCOOWEE**........ Year **1880** Page **98** No. **1002**
Citizen by blood........ **No** ....Mother's citizenship
Intermarried citizen .. **Yes**
Married under what law........................Date of marriage ... **1868**
License ....Certificate
Wife's name
District................Year........Page........No.
Citizen by blood........Mother's citizenship
Intermarried citizen
Married under what law................Date of marriage
License ....Certificate

Names of Children:
................Dist.........Year........Page........No........Age
................Dist.........Year........Page........No........Age
................Dist.........Year........Page........No........Age
................Dist.........Year........Page........No........Age
................Dist.........Year........Page........No........Age

On 1880 Roll as G.W. Eaton

◇◇◇◇◇

DEPARTMENT OF THE INTERIOR.
Commission to the Five Civilized Tribes.
Muskogee, Indian Territory, October 14th, 1902.

In the matter of the application of George W. Eaton for the enrollment of himself as a citizen by intermarriage of the Cherokee Nation.

Supplemental to #47o8[sic].

GEORGE W. EATON, being duly sworn, testified as follows:
Examination by the Commission.
Q. What is your name? A. George W. Eaton.
Q. How old are you? A. 57.
Q. What is your post office? A. Claremore.

93

Cherokee Intermarried White 1906
Volume VI

Q. Are you a white man? A. Yes, sir.
Q. You are on the eighty roll as an adopted citizen, are you? A. Yes, sir.
Q. What was your wife' name in 1880? A. Nancy Eaton.
Q. Is that the only wife you ever had? A. Yes, sir.
Q. Was she ever married before she married you? A. No, sir.
Q. Is she dead or living? A. Dead.
Q. When did she die? A. Either 5 or 6 years ago.
Q. Did you live with her in the Cherokee Nation from the time you were married until she died? A. Yes, sir.
Q. Have you married since her death? A. No, sir.
Q. Have you been living in the Cherokee Nation since 1880? A. Yes, sir.
Q. How many children have you? A. Four.
Q. Are they living at home with you? A. No, sir.
Q. They are all grown? A. They are all grown.

I I I I I I I I I I I I I I I I I I I I I I I I I I I I

Jesse O. Carr, being first duly sworn, states that as stenographer to the Commission to the Five Civilized Tribes he reported the above entitled case and that the foregoing is a true and complete transcript of his stenographic notes thereof.

Jesse O Carr

Subscribed and sworn to before me this 24th day of December, 1902.

BC Jones
Notary Public.

◇◇◇◇◇

Cherokee 4708.

DEPARTMENT OF THE INTERIOR,
COMMISSION TO THE FIVE CIVILIZED TRIBES.
Muskogee, Indian Territory, January 4, 1907.

In the Matter of the Application for the Enrollment of George W. Eaton as a citizen by intermarriage of the Cherokee Nation.

APPEARANCES:
    Applicant appears in person.
    Cherokee Nation represented by H. M. Vance, in behalf of W. W. Hastings, Attorney.

Cherokee Intermarried White 1906
Volume VI

George W. Eaton being first duly sworn by B. P. Rasmus, Notary Public, testified as follows:

ON BEHALF OF COMMISSIONER:

Q   What is your name? A   George W. Eaton.
Q   What is your age? A   61 years.
Q   What is your post office address?
A   Claremore.
Q   Are you an applicant for enrollment as a citizen by intermarriage of the Cherokee Nation?
A   Yes sir; I suppose I have been enrolled.
Q   You have no Cherokee blood?
A   No sir.
Q   Your only claim to the right for enrollment as a citizen of the Cherokee Nation is by virtue of your marriage to a citizen by blood of the Nation?
A   Yes sir.
Q   What is the name of the citizen through whom you claim the right to enrollment?
A   Her name was Nancy Elizabeth Williams.
Q   Is she living or dead?
A   Dead.
Q   When did she die?
A   September, 1896.
Q   Was she a recognized citizen of the Cherokee Nation at the time you married her?
A   Yes sir.
Q   Living in the Cherokee Nation?
A   Yes sir.
Q   What is the date of your marriage to her?
A   17th day of May, 1868.
Q   Were you married in the Cherokee Nation in accordance with Cherokee laws?
A   Yes sir.
Q   You secured a license, did you?
A   Yes sir.
Q   In what district was that license issued?
A   Goingsnake.
Q   From the date of your marriage in 1868, did you and your wife continuously reside in the Cherokee Nation until the time of her death?
A   Yes sir.
Q   And lived together continuously as husband and wife?
A   Yes sir.
Q   Since her death have you re-married?
A   No sir.
Q   You have lived continuously in the Cherokee Nation up until the present time?
A   Yes sir.

Cherokee Intermarried White 1906
Volume VI

Q Have you any evidence of a documentary character showing your marriage to your deceased wife?
A No sir.
Q You have no license or certificate?
A No sir.
Q Are there any people present who have personal knowledge of your marriage?
A There are only a few people living who were there; only two or three that I know of. Mr. Ward may be here.
Q When you made application, did you present any evidence as to your marriage?
A No. The law then required five signers, Cherokee citizens. I got up my petition and went down and got the license and turned it over to the preacher and we were married. That's the last I ever saw of it. The Dawes Commission at Claremore took that up and decided then, as I understand it, that it wasn't necessary to furnish marriage certificate or any evidence of that kind. I am on all the rolls.
Q Did you say there is a person living who was a witness to your marriage?
A Yes.
Q Is that person living in the Cherokee Nation?
A Yes; there two or three or maybe four or more.

The applicant, George W. Eaton, is identified on the Cherokee Authenticated Tribal Roll of 1880, Cooweescoowee District, 1002.

Q Were you ever married more than one time?
A No sir.
Q Was you wife ever married prior to her marriage to you?
A No sir.

T. F. Ward being first duly sworn by B. P. Rasmus, Notary Public, testified as follows:

ON BEHALF OF COMMISSIONER.

Q What is your name? A T. F. Ward.
Q How old are you? A 56 years old.
Q What is your post office? A Foyil.
Q Do you know a person in the Cherokee Nation by the name of George W. Eaton?
A Yes sir.
Q You desire to give testimony relative to his right to enrollment as a citizen of the Cherokee Nation?
A Yes sir.
Q Is George W. Eaton a married man?
A No, I don't think he is at this time.
Q He has been married?
A He has been, yes.
Q But his wife is dead?
A Yes sir.

Cherokee Intermarried White 1906
Volume VI

Q   What was his wife's name?
A   Nan Williams.
Q   Do you remember when George W. Eaton was married to his wife?
A   No, I can't tell you just the date but it was sometime before '75.
Q   Were you present at the marriage ceremony?
A   Yes sir.
Q   You saw them married?
A   I saw them married.
Q   Do you know of your own personal knowledge that George W. Eaton secured a license and complied with the laws of the Cherokee Nation relative to marriage?
A   So far as I know; the person read the license and that is as far as I know.
Q   Has it always been the understanding among those who knew the parties, that they were married in accordance with the laws of the Cherokee Nation?
A   Yes sir.
Q   You have known these parties ever since their marriage have you?
A   Yes sir.
Q   There was never any separation of any kind until the time of the death of Mrs. Eaton?
A   None that I know of.

The undersigned being first duly sworn states that as stenographer to the Commission to the Five Civilized Tribes, she correctly recorded the testimony taken in this case and that the foregoing is a full, true and correct transcript of her stenographic notes thereof.

Myrtle Hill

Subscribed and sworn to before me this the 5th day of January, 1907.

John E. Tidwell
Notary Public.

Cherokee Intermarried White 1906
Volume VI

E C W
Cherokee 4708.

DEPARTMENT OF THE INTERIOR,

COMMISSIONER TO THE FIVE CIVILIZED TRIBES.

In the matter of the application for the enrollment of GEORGE W. EATON as a citizen by intermarriage of the Cherokee Nation.

D E C I S I O N

THE RECORDS OF THIS OFFICE SHOW: That on October 22nd, 1900 application was received by the Commission to the Five Civilized Tribes for the enrollment of George W. Eaton as a citizen by intermarriage of the Cherokee Nation. Further proceedings in the matter of said application were had at Muskogee, Indian Territory, October 14th, 1902 and January 4th, 1907.

THE EVIDENCE IN THIS CASE SHOWS: That the applicant herein, George W. Eaton, a white man, was married in accordance with Cherokee law May 17th, 1868 to his wife, Nancy E. Eaton, nee Williams, since deceased, who was at the time of said marriage a recognized citizen by blood of the Cherokee Nation, who is identified on the Cherokee authenticated tribal roll of 1880, Cooweescoowee District No. 1003 as a native Cherokee. It is further shown that from the time of said marriage until the death of said Nancy E. Eaton, which occurred in September 1896, the said George W. Eaton and Nancy E. Eaton resided together as husband and wife and continuously lived in the Cherokee Nation; that since the death of said Nancy E. Eaton in September, 1896 the said George W. Eaton has remained unmarried and continuously lived in the Cherokee Nation. Said applicant is identified on the Cherokee authenticated tribal roll of 1880 and the Cherokee census roll of 1896 as an intermarried citizen of the Cherokee Nation.

IT IS, THEREFORE, ORDERED AND ADJUDGED: That in accordance with the decision of the Supreme Court of the United States, dated November 5th, 1906, in the cases of Daniel Red Bird et al. vs. the United States, Nos. 125, 126, 127, and 128, the said applicant, George W. Eaton is entitled, under the provisions of Section Twenty-one of the Act of Congress approved June 28th, 1898 (30 Stats. 495), to enrollment as a citizen by intermarriage of the Cherokee Nation, and his application for enrollment as such is accordingly granted.

Tams Bixby
Commissioner.

Dated at Muskogee, Indian Territory,
this   FEB 8 1907

Cherokee Intermarried White 1906
Volume VI

Cherokee
4708.

Muskogee, Indian Territory, December 27, 1906.

George W. Eaton,
    Claremore, Indian Territory.

Dear Sir:

    November 6, 1906, the United States Supreme Court held that white persons who intermarried with Cherokee citizens according to Cherokee law prior to November 1, 1875, are entitled to enrollment and allotments of land as citizens of the Cherokee Nation.

    You are advised that to properly determine your right to enrollment as a citizen by intermarriage of the Cherokee Nation, it will be necessary for you to appear before the Commissioner for the purpose of giving testimony as to the date of your marriage and whether or not your wife, by reason of your marriage to whom you claim the right to enrollment as a citizen of the Cherokee Nation, was a recognized citizen of the Cherokee Nation at the time of your marriage to her, and whether or not you were married to her in accordance with the Cherokee laws.

    You are therefore directed to appear before the Commissioner at Muskogee, Indian Territory, at 9 o'clock A. M., on Friday, January 4, 1907, and give testimony as above indicated.

    Respectfully,

H.J.C.   Acting Commissioner.

◇◇◇◇◇

Cherokee 4708

Muskogee, Indian Territory, February 8, 1907.

W. W. Hastings,
    Attorney for the Cherokee Nation,
        Muskogee, Indian Territory.

Dear Sir:

    There is enclosed herwith[sic] a copy of the decision of the Commissioner to the Five Civilized Tribes, dated February 8, 1907, granting the application for the enrollment of George W. Eaton as a citizen by intermarriage of the Cherokee Nation.

Cherokee Intermarried White 1906
Volume VI

Respectfully,

Commissioner.

Encl. H-9
JMH

◇◇◇◇◇

Cherokee 4708

Muskogee, Indian Territory, February 8, 1907.

The Commissioner to the Five Civilized Tribes,
Muskogee, Indian Territory.

Sir:

Receipt is acknowledged of the testimony and of your decision enrolling George W. Eaton as a citizen by intermarriage of the Cherokee Nation. Time for protesting said decision is waived and I consent that said person may be placed upon the schedule immediately.

Respectfully,
W. W. Hastings
Attorney for Cherokee Nation.

◇◇◇◇◇

Cherokee 4708

Muskogee, Indian Territory, February 8, 1907.

George W. Eaton,
Claremore, Indian Territory.

Dear Sir:

There is enclosed herewith a copy of the decision of the Commissioner to the Five Civilized Tribes, dated February 8, 1907, granting the application for your enrollment as a citizen by intermarriage of the Cherokee Nation.

You will be advised when your name has been placed upon a schedule of citizens of the Cherokee Nation and approved by the Secretary of the Interior.

Cherokee Intermarried White 1906
Volume VI

Respectfully,

Encl. H-10
JMH

Commissioner.

Cher IW 175

◇◇◇◇◇

CFB

DEPARTMENT OF THE INTERIOR,

COMMISSIONER TO THE FIVE CIVILIZED TRIBES.

In the matter of the application for the enrollment of

JOHN T. McSPADDEN

as a citizen by intermarriage of the Cherokee Nation.

CHEROKEE 5461.

◇◇◇◇◇

Department of the Interior,
Commission to the Five Civilized Tribes,
Chelsea, I. T., November 16, 1900.

In the matter of the application of John T. McSpadden for the enrollment of himself as a Cherokee by intermarriage, and his wife and five children as Cherokees by blood: being sworn and examined by Commissioner Breckinridge, he testified as follows:

Q Give me your full name? A John T. McSpadden.
Q How old are you? A 48.
Q What is your post office? A Chelsea.
Q Do you live in Cooweescoowee district? A Yes, sir.
Q Do you want to enroll yourself and family? A Yes, sir.
Q Have you a wife? A Yes, sir.
Q How many children have you? A Five.
Q Are you a Cherokee by blood? A No, sir.

Cherokee Intermarried White 1906
Volume VI

Q Is your wife a Cherokee by blood? A Yes, sir.
Q Let me see your marriage license and certificate? A (Exhibits paper.)
Q Have you got a license? A Yes, sir, I was married in 1873.
Q Then you are on the roll of 1880? A Yes, sir.
Q Have you and your wife lived together ever since you were married in 1873?
A No, sir, not all the time: I was divorced from that woman?
Q To whom were you married in 1873? A Eliza Daniel.
Q Was she a Cherokee woman? A Yes, sir.
Q Is she dead now or alive? A No, sir, she is living.
Q How long did you live with her? A Most ten years.
Q You lived with her until 1882, did you? A Yes, sir.
Q Then you were divorced from her? A Yes, sir.
Q Have you a copy of the decree of divorce? A No, sir, I haven't; it is in Delaware district.
Q Was the divorce granted to you or to your wife? A It was granted to her, I guess, she sued for the divorce.
Q What do you care to state in regard to the circumstances of that divorce; the question is, whether you abandoned your wife, or your wife abandoned you? A I suppose she abandoned me, because she married a very short time afterwards.
Q After the divorce? A Yes, sir.
Q That would have no bearing whatever on the question of whether she abandoned you or you abandoned her? A She abandoned me.
Q What do you wish to state about that? A She can't be satisfied.
Q What is the present name of your former wife? A Eliza Strout.
Q Did you first wife Eliza leave your house and home before the divorce was procured?
A Yes, sir, she went to her mother's.
Q You claim, therefore, that she abandoned you? A Yes, sir.
Q And then how did you procure that divorce; was it by her bring suit or you bringing suit, or by agreement? A It was by agreement, Hooley Bell and Jim Keys were the lawyers.
Q And you claim it was her will and desire and that you assented to having the divorce to mett[sic] her wishes? A Yes, sir.
(Reference is made to the testimony in the case Card No. 3692, the same being the application for the enrollment of Frederick W. Strout et al.)
Q Now when did you marry the second time? A In 1885.
(The applicant presents a certificate showing that he was married on the 16th day of December, 1885, to Miss Sallie C. Rogers, the ceremony being performed by the Rev. John W. McCrary. This is filed with the application.)
Q Have you ever been married except upon these two occasions? A No, sir.
Q Was your present wife ever married except to you? A No, sir.
Q Have you and she lived together ever since you married her in 1885? A Yes, sir.
Q Have you lived in the Cherokee Nation ever since 1880? A Yes, sir.
Q Your present wife is a Cherokee, is she? A Yes, sir.
Q You say you haven't got a copy of the decree of divorce from your first wife?
A No, sir.
Q Can you supply the Commission with a copy of it? A I don't know whether I can.

Cherokee Intermarried White 1906
Volume VI

Q Give me the name of the father of your present wife? A Clem V. Rogers.
Q Is he dead or alive? A He is living.
Q Give me the name of her mother? A Mary Rogers.
Q Is she living? A No, sir, she is dead.
Q Has your present wife lived in the Cherokee Nation all her life? A Yes, sir.
Q How old is she now? A 36.
Q Give me the names of your children, please? A Clem Mayes is the first, 13 years old.
Q The next child? A May, nine.
Q The next child? A Herbert Thomas, seven.
Q The next child? A Maud Irene.
Q How old is that child? A Four.
Q The next child? A Helen, one.

(John T. McSpadden on 1880 roll, page 291, No. 1841, Thomas McSpadden, Delaware district, adopted white. Sallie C. McSpadden on 1880 roll, page 161, No. 2333, Sallie Rogers, Cooweescoowee district, native Cherokee; on 1896 roll, page 208, No. 3077, Sallie McSpadden, Cooweescoowee district. John T. McSpadden on 1896 roll, page (216), No. Page 316 699, Thomas J. McSpadden, Cooweescoowee district. Clem M. McSpadden on 1896 roll, page 208, No. 3078, Cooweescoowee district. May McSpadden on 1896 roll, page 208, No. 3079, Cooweescoowee district. Herbert T. McSpadden on 1896 roll, page 208, No. 3080, Cooweescoowee district. Maud I. McSpadden on 1896 roll, page 208, No. 3081, (Illinois) district.)

(Cooweescoowee)

The applicant applies for the enrollment of himself and his wife and five children. His wife is identified on the rolls of 1880 and 1896 as a native Cherokee, she has lived in the Cherokee Nation all her life, and she will be listed for enrollment as a Cherokee by blood. Of the five children, the first four named in the testimony are identified with their parents on the roll of 1896, they are all living, and will be listed for enrollment as Cherokees by blood. When a certificate of the birth of the youngest child is filed with the Commission, this child also will be listed for enrollment as a Cherokee by blood. The applicant has been married twice. He is identified under his first marriage on the roll of 1880 as an intermarried white, he being a white man. In 1882 he was divorced from his first wife, said divorce being by mutual consent, and it appears to have been without detriment to the applicant's rights to citizenship. In 1885 he married his present wife, also a Cherokee by blood, and he has lived with her in the Cherokee Nation ever since their marriage. He has lived in the Cherokee Nation ever since his enrollment in 1880. He is identified on the roll of 1896, and he will now be listed for enrollment as a Cherokee by intermarriage.

-------o-------

Bruce C. Jones, being duly sworn, says that as stenographer to the Commission to the Five Civilized Tribes he correctly recorded the proceedings and testimony in the above case, and the foregoing is a true and complete transcript of his stenographic notes thereof.

Bruce C Jones

Cherokee Intermarried White 1906
Volume VI

Sworn to and subscribed before me this the 16th of November, 1900.

          C R Breckinridge
                Commissioner.

◇◇◇◇◇

Cher
Supp'l to # 5461

        Department of the Interior,
     Commission to the Five Civilized Tribes,
       Muskogee, I. T., October 24, 1902.

   In the matter of the application of JOHN T. McSPADDEN, for the enrollment of himself as a citizen by intermarriage, and his wife, SALLIE C. McSPADDEN, and his children, CLEM M., MAY, HERBERT T., Maud I., HELEN and PAULINE McSPADDEN, as citizens by blood, of the Cherokee Nation.

   JOHN T. McSPADDEN, being duly sworn and examined by the Commission, testified as follows:

Q What is your name ? A John T. McSpadden.
Q How old are you ? A Fifty.
Q What is your post office address ? A Chelsea.
Q Are you a white man ? A Yes sir.
Q Is your name on the roll of 1880 as an adopted white citizen ? A Yes sir.
Q What was your wife's name in 1880 ? A Sallie C.
Q Is that your present wife ? A Yes sir.
Q Was she your wife in 1880 ? A No sir.
Q Who was your wife in 1880 ? A E. A. Daniels.
Q E. A. Daniels is the wife through whom you are claiming your citizenship ?
A Yes sir.
Q Was she on the roll of 1880 with you ? A Yes sir.
Q Is your wife E. A. Daniels dead or alive ? A She's living.
Q Have you been separated from her ? A Yes sir.
Q When did you separate ? A In 1883.
Q Did you live with her from 1880 up to 1883 ? A Yes sir.
Q What was the cause of your separation ?
A She liked another man better.
Q And went off with him ? A Yes sir.
Q Where were you living at the time you were separated ? A Vinita.
Q How long had you been married to your wife ? A Since 1873.
Q Ten years ? A Yes sir, ten years.
Q What was you occupation at that time ?
A I was a blacksmith, then, and living at Vinita.
Q Did you provide for that wife within your means properly ? A Oh yes sir.

Cherokee Intermarried White 1906
Volume VI

Q Always a kind and indulgent husband, were you ?   A   Yes sir.
Q Did you give her any cause to leave your home ?   A   I thought not.
Q Did she ever tell you why she left you ?
A She said she preferred going with this other man.
Q What was his name ?   A   F. W. Strout.
Q Was he a white man ?   A   Yes sir.
Q Well, did she go off with him ?   A   Yes sir, she went to Texas; she went to her mother's after she left me, and then went to Texas.
Q With this man Strout ?   A   Yes sir.
Q How soon after the separation ?   A   It must have been about two weeks after the divorce.
Q You were divorced from her ?   A   Yes sir.
Q In what court ?   A   In the Cherokee Court ?
A No sir, not in any court, the Cherokee council passed a law providing that all marriages were civil contracts; and Mr. Bales was my lawyer, and Keyes was hers, and Thompson was deputy clerk.
Q You had no divorce in the courts ?   A   No sir. They just appointed those three arbitrators under the Cherokee law.
Q That was the only kind of a divorce that you had, by these arbitrators ?
A Yes sir.
Q These arbitrators decided that you were no longer husband and wife ?   A   Yes sir.
Q You accepted that decree ?   A   Yes sir.
Q How long after that before you married Sallie ?   A   About two years.
Q Is Sallie C., a Cherokee by blood ?   A   Yes sir.
Q How long has she been living in the Cherokee Nation ?   A   All her life
Q You didn't marry Sallie under a Cherokee license ?   A   No sir.
Q You were married as a citizen of the Cherokee Nation ?   A   Yes sir.
Q Have you been living with your wife Sallie C., since you married her ?   A   Yes sir.
Q You have been living in the Cherokee Nation ever since 1880 ?   A   Yes sir.
Q Did you have any children by your first wife ?   A   No sir, we had one or two but they died when they were infants.
Q How many children have you by your wife Sallie C ?   A   Six.
Q Are they all living ?   A   Yes sir.
Q Been living in the Cherokee Nation all their lives, have they ?   A   Yes sir.

E. G. Bagwell, on oath states that, as stenographer to the Commission to the Five Civilized Tribes, he correctly recorded the testimony and proceedings had in the above entitled cause, and that the foregoing is an accurate transcript of his stenographic notes thereof.

E.C. Bagwell

Cherokee Intermarried White 1906
Volume VI

Subscribed and sworn to before me this December 13, 1902.

BC Jones
Notary Public.

Cherokee 5461.

DEPARTMENT OF THE INTERIOR,
COMMISSIONER TO THE FIVE CIVILIZED TRIBES.
Muskogee, I. T., January 4, 1907.

In the matter of the application for the enrollment of JOHN T. McSPADDEN, as a citizen by intermarriage of the Cherokee Nation.

John T. McSpadden, being first duly sworn by B. P. Rasmus, testified as follows:

By the Commissioner:
Q What is your name? A John T. McSpadden.
Q How old are you? A Fifty-four.
Q What is your postoffice address? A Chelsea, I. T.
Q Are you an applicant for enrollment as a citizen by intermarriage of the Cherokee Nation? A Yes sir.
Q You have no Cherokee blood? A No sir.
Q Your only claim to the right to enrollment is by virtue of your marriage to a citizen by blood of the Cherokee Nation? A Yes sir.
Q What is the name of the citizen through whom you claim your right? A Eliza A. Daniels, was her maiden name.
Q Is she living or dead? A Living.
Q Was she a recognized citizen of the Cherokee Nation at the time you married her? A Yes sir.
Q When did you marry her? A In July, 1873.
Q Was she living in the Cherokee country at that time? A Yes
Q Was she your first wife? A Yes sir.
Q Were you her firsy[sic] husband? A Yes sir.
Q Did you marry her in accordance with the laws of the Cherokee nation[sic]? A Yes sir.
Q Secured a license did you? A Yes sir.
Q In what district was that license issued? A Tahlequah District.
Q Since you marriage to her have you and she lived together continuously in the Cherokee Nation, and lived together as husband and wife? A Yes, up to 1883.
Q You lived together as husband and wife up until 1883? A Yes sir.
Q Did you separate then? A Yes sir.
Q Did she leave you or did you leave her? A She left me and went to her mothers[sic], and lived there 2 or 3 weeks, and then we arbitrated our divorce. We did not go to the courts but just simply had witnesses and divided up our property.

Cherokee Intermarried White 1906
Volume VI

Q You made a division of your property and separated? A Yes.
Q What was the cause of your wife leaving you? Do you know.[sic]
A Well, her present husband was boarding at out[sic] house, and he went to Texas, and she went to Texas after we were divorced and married him.
Q She left you then of her own free will? A Yes sir.
Q And you did not leave her? A No sir.
Q You didn't force her to leave you? A No. I did not.
Q Do you have any reason to believe that you were in any way responsible for her leaving you? A No, I think not. I did everything I could to reconcile [sic] her.
Q But you were not successful? A No sir.
Q Have you remarried since you and she parted? A Yes sir.
Q Is your present wife living? A Yes sir.
Q What was her name? A Sallie C. Rogers.
Q She is a Cherokee by blood is she? A Yes sir
Q When did you marry her? A In December, 1885.
Q Since your marriage to Sallie C. McSpadden, have you and she continuously lived together as husband and wife up to the present time? A Yes sir.
Q Have you resided continuously in the Cherokee Nation since your marriage to your first wife? A Yes sir.
Q Have you any evidence of a documentary character showing your marriage to your first wife? A No, the record is all I can refer to.
Q You have no marriage license and certificate to present at this time? A No sir.
 The applicant John T. McSpadden is identified on the Cherokee authenticated tribal roll, 1880, Delaware District, opposite No. 1841.

By the Cherokee Nation.
Q What is the name at the present time of the wife from whom you were divorced?
A Eliza A. Strout.
Q Where does she live? A Vinita, I. T.
 The original martiage[sic] records of Tahlequah District, Book C., which is in the possession of this office, shows the following entry: No. 56 "License granted John T. McSpadden, to marry a Cherokee, Eliza A. Daniel. Ceremony solemnized by James Ketchum, July 31, 1873.

Q As I understand you there was no divorce granted from your first wife? You and she got together in the presence of witnesses and arbitrated? A Yes sir.
Q You divided the property and decided in the presence of these witnesses to dissolve this marriage? A Yes sir.
Q Was this contract of divorced reduced to writing? A Yes.
Q Did you sign it? A Yes sir.
Q Did you wife sign it? A Yes sir.
Q Have you a copy of that contract? A No sir.
Q Who were some of the witness[sic] present when that contract was made?
A Hooley Bell,
Q Hooley Bell was one of the witnesses? A Yes sir.

Cherokee Intermarried White 1906
Volume VI

Q Can you give me that[sic] names of any others? A No, not anyone that is here. James Keys was also present and Joe L. Thompson who was deputy clerk of court of Delaware District. He was there.
Q This contract was satisfactory to both parties? A Yes sir.
Witness excused.

Edward B. Frazier, being first duly sworn by Frances R. Lane, a Notary Public for the Western District of Indian Territory, testified as follows:

By the Commissioner:
Q What is your name? A Edward B. Frazier.
Q How old are you? A Fifty-seven.
Q What is your postoffice address? A Vinita, I. T.
Q Do you desire to give testimony as to the right of enrollment of John T. McSpadden as a citizen by intermarriage of the Cherokee Nation? A Yes, I am willing to tell what I know. I know the circumstances.
Q You are acquainted with James T. McSpadden? A Yes, and know his first and second wives.
Q What was his first wife's name? A Eliza Daniels.
Q You were acquainted with her before she was married to John T. McSpadden?
A Yes, and know his first and second wives.
Q Do you know when she and John T. McSpadden separated?
A About 1883 or 1884, somewhere along there.
Q Were you present at the time they separated? A I was present when she got in the cars[sic] and left him. When she went south and left him.
Q Do you know why she left him? A No sir.
Q You never heard her give any reason for leaving him? A No, I heard a friend of hers say that she was going to Texas and marry that man Strout.
Q Did you know this man Strout? A I never saw him until that time.
Q It is your understanding is it that she went to Texas and married this man? A Yes sir.
Q Do you know whether or not there was any divorce or agreement separating John T. McSpadden from his wife, Eliza? Q[sic] Mr. McSpadden told me, and so did his friends, that he gave her the greater part of his property. He gave her a house and lot and some money when they separated. I think $1000 in money and a house and lot if I aint[sic] mistaken, which was more than have[sic] of his estate at that time.
Q Is it your understanding that he left her or she left him? A She left him. I heard him say that he would just as soon die as see that woman go and marry this man. Heard him say it right when the cars started off. He was an intimate friend of mine. We had been a great deal together; had been there 7 or 8 years together, and we were very intimate, and that was the very expression he used as she took that train south.

Witness excused.

Cherokee Intermarried White 1906
Volume VI

Frances R. Lane upon oath states that as stenographer to the Commissioner to the Five Civilized Tribes she reported the testimony in the above entitled cause and that the foregoing is an accurate transcript of her shorthand notes thereof.

Frances R Lane

Subscribed and sworn to before me this 5th day of January, 1907

Edward Merrick
Notary Public.

◇◇◇◇◇

C.F.B.   Cherokee 5461.

DEPARTMENT OF THE INTERIOR,

COMMISSIONER TO THE FIVE CIVILIZED TRIBES.

In the matter of the application for the enrollment of JOHN T. McSPADDEN as a citizen by intermarriage of the Cherokee Nation.

D E C I S I O N

THE RECORDS OF THIS OFFICE SHOW: That at Chelsea, Indian Territory, November 16, 1900, application was received by the Commission to the Five Civilized Tribes for the enrollment of John T. McSpadden as a citizen by intermarriage of the Cherokee Nation. Further proceedings in the matter of said application were had at Muskogee, Indian Territory, October 24, 1902, and January 4, 1907.

THE EVIDENCE IN THIS CASE SHOWS: That the applicant herein, John T. McSpadden, was married in accordance with Cherokee law July 31, 1873, to one Eliza A. Daniels, a recognized citizen by blood of the Cherokee Nation, and who is identified on the Cherokee authenticated tribal roll of 1880, Tahlequah District, No. 1842, as a native Cherokee; that the said John T. and Eliza A. McSpadden resided together as husband and wife in the Cherokee Nation until the year 1883, when said Eliza A. McSpadden left her said husband without other cause than an apparent dislike for him, and that they have since lived separate and apart; that in the year 1885 the said John T. McSpadden married one Sallie C. Rogers, who was at the time of said marriage a recognized citizen by blood of the Cherokee Nation, who is identified on the Cherokee authenticated tribal roll of 1880, Cooweescoowee District, No. 2333, as a native Cherokee, and whose name appears on the approved partial roll of citizens by blood of the Cherokee Nation, opposite No. 3071. It is further shown that since said marriage the said John T. and Sallie C. McSpadden have resided together as husband and wife, and have continuously lived in

Cherokee Intermarried White 1906
Volume VI

the Cherokee Nation. Said applicant is duly identified on the Cherokee authenticated tribal roll of 1880, and the Cherokee census roll of 1896, as an intermarried citizen of the Cherokee Nation.

In view of the foregoing, it is considered that, following the ruling of the Department in the case of Andrew Brimmer (I.T.D. 3299-01), the right to citizenship in the Cherokee Nation acquired by said John T. McSpadden by virtue of his marriage to Eliza A. Daniels July 31, 1873, has not been forfeited or lost.

IT IS, THEREFORE, ORDERED AND ADJUDGED: That in accordance with the decision of the Supreme Court of the United States, dated November 5, 1906, in the cases of Daniel Red Bird et al. vs. the United States, Nos. 125, 126, 127, and 128, the said applicant, John T. McSpadden, is entitled, under the provisions of Section 21, of the Act of Congress approved June 28, 1898 (30 Stats., 495), to enrollment as a citizen by intermarriage of the Cherokee Nation, and his application for enrollment as such is accordingly granted.

Tams Bixby
Commissioner.

Dated at Muskogee, Indian Territory,
this   FEB 8 1907

◇◇◇◇◇

Cherokee 5461

Muskogee, Indian Territory, February 8, 1907.

W. W. Hastings,
    Attorney for the Cherokee Nation,
        Muskogee, Indian Territory.

Dear Sir:

    There is enclosed herewith a copy of the decision of the Commissioner to the Five Civilized Tribes, dated February 8, 1907, granting the application for the enrollment of John T. McSpadden as a citizen by intermarriage of the Cherokee Nation.

Respectfully,

Encl. H-7   Commissioner.
JMH

◇◇◇◇◇

Cherokee Intermarried White 1906
Volume VI

Cherokee 5461

Muskogee, Indian Territory, February 8, 1907.

The Commissioner to the Five Civilized Tribes,
Muskogee, Indian Territory.

Sir:

Receipt is acknowledged of the testimony and of your decision enrolling John T. McSpadden as a citizen by intermarriage of the Cherokee Nation. Time for protesting said decision is waived, and I consent that said person may be placed upon the schedule immediately.

Respectfully,
W. W. Hastings
Attorney for Cherokee Nation.

◇◇◇◇◇

Cherokee 5461

Muskogee, Indian Territory, February 8, 1907.

John T. McSpadden,
Chelsea, Indian Territory.

Dear Sir:

There is enclosed herewith a copy of the decision of the Commissioner to the Five Civilized Tribes, dated February 8, 1907, granting the application for your enrollment as a citizen by intermarriage of the Cherokee Nation.

You will be advised when your name has been placed upon a schedule of citizens of the Cherokee Nation and approved by the Secretary of the Interior.

Respectfully,

Commissioner.

Encl. H-8
JMH

Cher IW 176

◇◇◇◇◇

Cherokee Intermarried White 1906
Volume VI

C.E.W.

DEPARTMENT OF THE INTERIOR,

COMMISSIONER TO THE FIVE CIVILIZED TRIBES.

In the matter of the application for the enrollment of

FREDERICK W. GULAGER

as a citizen by intermarriage of the Cherokee Nation.

Cherokee 5982.

Department of the Interior,
Commission to the Five Civilized Tribes,
Tahlequah, I. T. December, 3rd 1900.

In the matter of the application of Martha L. Gulager for the enrollment of herself, husband and three children as Cherokee citizens. She being sworn before Commissioner Breckinridge testified as follows

Q What is your name? A. Martha L. Gulager
Q How old are you? [sic] 55.
Q What is your post office? A. Eureka, I. T.
Q Are you living in Tahlequah district? A. Yes sir.
Q Who is it that you want to have enrolled? A. Myself, husabnd[sic] and three children.
Q Are you a Cherokee by blood? A. Yes sir.
Q What is your husband? A. A white man
Q How long have you lived in the Cherokee Nation? A. All my life.
Q Give me the name of your father? A. Nartin[sic] Schrimpscher[sic].
Q Is he dead or alive? A. Dead.
Q Give me the name of your mother? A. Elizabeth
Q Is she dead or alive? A. Dead
Q Have you ever been married more than once? A. Only once.
Q When were you married to your husband? A. In 1869.
Q Has he lived with you ever since you were married to him? A. Yes sir.
Q Give me your husbands[sic] full name? A. Frederick W. Gulager
Q How old is your husband? A. About 56.
Q Give me the names of your children? A. Mary E. Q How old? A. 20

Cherokee Intermarried White 1906
Volume VI

Q Next child? A. Henry G.   Q How old? A. 17.
Q Next child? A. John D.   Q How old? A. 13.
Q Are these children all living at this time? A. Yes sir.

1880 roll, page 761, No. 800, Martha L. Gulegar[sic], Tahlequah.
1880	761	799	F. W. Gulegar	"
1880	762	806	Mary E. Gulegar	"
1896	1174	1195	Martha L. Gulager	"
1896	1280	85	Frederric[sic] W. Gulager	"
1896	1174	1198	Mary E. Gulager	"
1896	1174	1199	Henry G. Gulegar[sic]	"
1896	1174	1200	John D. Gulegar,	"

The applicant applied for the enrollment of herself, husband and 3 children. She is identified on the roll of 1880 and also on the roll of 1896 as a native Cherokee. She has lived in the Cherokee Nation all her life and she will be listed now for enrollment as a Cherokee by blood. She and her husband were married in 1869, they have lived together ever since. He is a white man. He is identified on the roll of 1880 and 1896, and he will be listed now for enrollment as a Cherokee by inter-marriage. The oldest child of the three named in the application, Mary E. is identified on the 1880 and 1896 rolls. She is still a minor, is living and will be listed for enrollment as a Cherokee by blood. The two younger children Henry C. and John D. are identified on the 1896 roll, they are living and will be listed for enrollment a Cherokee citizens by blood.

Chas. von Weise on oath states that as stenographer to the Commission to the Five Civilized Tribes he reported in full all proceedings in the above cause and the foregoing is a full, true and correct transcript of his stenographic notes therein.

Chas. von Weise

Subscribed and sworn to before me this the 3rd of December, 1900.

C R Breckinridge

Commissioner.

◇◇◇◇◇

Cherokee 5982.

DEPARTMENT OF THE INTERIOR,
COMMISSION TO THE FIVE CIVILIZED TRIBES.
Muskogee, I. T., October 17, 1902.

In the matter of the application of Frederick W. Gulager for the enrollment of himself as a citizen by intermarriage, and for the enrollment of his wife, Martha L. Gulager, and his three minor children, Mary E., Henry G. and John D. Gulager, as citizens by blood of the Cherokee Nation.

Cherokee Intermarried White 1906
Volume VI

SUPPLEMENTAL PROCEEDINGS.

MARTHA L. GULAGER, being sworn, testified as follows:

By the Commission,

Q What is your name? A Martha Gulager.
Q Martha L., is it? A Yes, sir.
Q How old are you? A Fifty-five or six.
Q What is your postoffice? Eureka.
Q Are you a Cherokee by blood? A Yes, sir.
Q What is your husband's name? A F. W. Gulager.
Q Frederick W. Gulager, is it? A Yes, sir.
Q Is he a white man? A Yes, sir.
Q Is he on the roll of '80 as an adopted white citizen? A Yes, sir.
Q He claims his citizenship through you, does he? A Yes, sir.
Q Now, have you and your husband been living together in the Cherokee Nation since 1880? A Yes, sir.
Q Never been separated, have you? A No, sir.
Q Living together now? A Yes, sir.
Q And you have made your home in the Cherokee Nation for the past twenty-two years? A Yes, sir.
Q Never lived anywhere else, have you? A No, sir.
Q How many children have you living at home? A Four.
Q What are their names? Let me ask you this - is Mary E. living at home, Henry G., John D.; they are at home with you? A Yes, sir.
Q All living? A Yes, sir.
Q I suppose the others are old enough to enroll themselves? A Yes, sir.

Retta Chick, being first duly sworn, states that, as stenographer to the Commission to the Five Civilized Tribes, she recorded the testimony and proceedings in the matter of the foregoing application, and that the above is a true and complete transcript of her stenographic notes thereof.

Retta Chick

Subscribed and sworn to before me this 14th day of November, 1902.

PG Reuter
Notary Public.

Cherokee Intermarried White 1906
Volume VI

Cherokee No. 5982.

DEPARTMENT OF THE INTERIOR,
COMMISSIONER TO THE FIVE CIVILIZED TRIBES.

Muskogee, Indian Territory. January 7, 1907.

In the matter of the application of Frederick W. Gulager for enrollment as a citizen by intermarriage of the Cherokee Nation.

William M. Gulager appears in behalf of the applicant, and after being first duly sworn, testified as follows:

BY THE COMMISSIONER:

Q What is your name? A William M. Gulager.
Q What is your age? A 34.
Q What is your postoffice address? A Muskogee.
Q In whose behalf do you appear here today? A My father, Frederick W. Gulager.
Q Did Frederick W. Gulager claim to be a citizen by intermarriage of the Cherokee Nation? A Yes, sir.
Q Through whom did he claim such citizenship? A By marriage to my mother, Martha L. Schrimsher.
Q When were Frederick W. Gulager and Martha L. Gulager married?
A In 1869.
Q Were they married under a license of the Cherokee Nation? A Yes, sir.
Q Have you a copy of that license? A I have.

Witness presents an instrument purporting to be a certified copy of a marriage license issued on January 26, 1869, by W. P. Boudinot, Clerk of District Court, Illinois District, Cherokee Nation, authorizing the marriage of Frederick W. Gulager to a Cherokee citizen. Said instrument further purports to show that Frederick W. Gulager was married to Martha L. Schrimsher under said license by W. Morris Grimes, Chaplain United States Army. This instrument is signed by W. H. Walker, Assistant Executive Secretary of the Cherokee Nation, but does not bear the seal of said Nation. Said instrument returned to the witness in order that the seal of the Nation may be attached. When this certified copy of the marriage license has been properly sealed you can return and file the same with the records in this office.

Q Was Frederick W. Gulager married prior to his marriage to Martha L. Schrimsher?
A No, sir.
Q Was Martha L. Schrimsher married prior to her marriage to Frederick W. Gulager?
A No, sir.
Q Is Frederick W. Gulager living at this time? A He is.

Cherokee Intermarried White 1906
Volume VI

Q Why was he unable to appear here today? A He is sick in bed.
Q Is Martha L. Gulager living at this time? A She is.
Q Where do Frederick W. Gulager and Martha L. Gulager reside at the present time? A They live at Eureka, about six miles west of Tahlequah, Cherokee Nation.
Q Have Frederick W. Gulager and Martha L. Gulager lived together continuously as man and wife within the Cherokee Nation from the date of their marriage until the present time? A They have.
Q Do you know whether or not Frederick W. Gulager ever applied to any of the tribunals of the Cherokee Nation to be admitted to citizenship, that is, into the Cherokee courts or Council? A No, sir.

The name of the applicant, Frederick W. Gulager and his wife, Martha L. Gulager, appear on Cherokee Field Card No. 5982, and included in the 1880 authenticated roll of citizens of the Cherokee Nation, Tahlequah District, opposite numbers 799 and 800. The applicant's wife, Martha L. Gulager, is included in the approved partial roll of citizens of the Cherokee Nation by blood opposite No. 14296. The applicant and his wife are also included on the 1896 roll opposite numbers 85 and 1174, respectively.

WITNESS EXCUSED.

F. Elma Lane, upon oath, states that as stenographer to the Commissioner to the Five Civilized Tribes, she reported the proceedings in the above entitled cause, and that the foregoing is a true and correct transcript of her stenographic notes therein.

F. Elma Lane

Subscribed and sworn to before me this 8th day of January, 1907.

Walter W. Chappell
Notary Public.

Cherokee Intermarried White 1906
Volume VI

CERTIFIED COPY.

From the records in the possession of this office, Marriage Record. Book "A". Illinois District, Cherokee Nation appears the following entry

Jany 26, 1869.

Issued License of Marriage to F.W. Gulager to marry Martha Schrimpsher[sic].

Gulager

Schrimpsher.

- - - - - - - - - - - - - -

Clerks Office Dist. Court.   )
Illinois Dist Cherokee Nation.)

Gulager: To any regular Minister of the Gospel of an Evangelical Denomination, or Judge of a Cherokee Court to whom these may come, greeting.
Schrimpsher:
    The bearer, Frederick W. Gulager, a citizen of the United States, having obtained such a recommendation as is required by the law "Regulating intermarriages with Whitemen", and presented the Same to this office with an application for a license for marriage-- You are hereby authorized to Solemnize the rites of Matrimony between him, F.W. Gulager and the Cherokee Lady to whom he signified his desire to be wedded, according to the form and ceremony usual and practised[sic] in your Church or Office, and this shall be your warrant for so doing.
    Please afterwards, attach the requisite Certifiactef[sic], specifying the names of the parties, and return by bearer to this office for Record.

Gulager:
    Given on this Jany. 26th 1869.
        (Signed) W.P. Boudinot
        Clk. D.C. Ill Dist
Oath admisintered[sic] this Jany 26" 1869.
Schrimpsher: (Signed) W.P. Boudinot, Clk.

Fort Gibson, Cherokee Nation.
Jany 27" 1869.

"To all whom it may concern"

Cherokee Intermarried White 1906
Volume VI

I hereby certify that I, this day Soleminised[sic] the marriage of Mr. Frederick W. Gulager and Miss Martha L. Schrimpsher, under a license from the Clk of the Illinois District Court, Cherokee Nation.

(Signed) W. Morris Grimes.

Chaplain U.S. Army.

A true copy from the original.

(Singed[sic]) W. P. Boudinot.
Clk Dist Court. Ill. Dist.

Jany 29" 1869.

I Harriett E. Arbuckle, on oath swear that the above and foregoing is a true, full and correct [sic] of the original instrument now on file in the records of this office.

Harriett E Arbuckle

Subscribed and sworn to before me this 5 day of February 5, 1907.

Frances R Lane
Notary Public.

C E W

Cherokee 5982.

DEPARTMENT OF THE INTERIOR,

COMMISSIONER TO THE FIVE CIVILIZED TRIBES.

In the matter of the application for the enrollment of FREDERICK W. GULAGER as a citizen by intermarriage of the Cherokee Nation.

D E C I S I O N

THE RECORDS OF THIS OFFICE SHOW: That at Tahlequah, Indian Territory, December 3, 1900 application was received by the Commission to the Five Civilized Tribes for the enrollment of Frederick W. Gulager as a citizen by intermarriage of the Cherokee Nation. Further proceedings in the matter of said application were had at Muskogee, Indian Territory, October 17, 1902 and January 7, 1907.

Cherokee Intermarried White 1906
Volume VI

THE EVIDENCE IN THIS CASE SHOWS: That the applicant herein, Frederick W. Gulager, a white man, was married in accordance with Cherokee law January 29, 1869 to one Martha L. Gulager, nee Schrimpsher, who was at the time of said marriage a recognized citizen by blood of the Cherokee Nation, who is identified on the Cherokee authenticated tribal roll of 1880, Tahlequah District, Page 761 No. 800, as a native Cherokee, and whose name is included on the approved partial roll of citizens by blood of the Cherokee Nation opposite No. 14296; that since said marriage the said Frederick W. Gulager and Martha L. Gulager have resided together as husband and wife and continuously lived in the Cherokee Nation up to and including September 1, 1902. Said applicant is identified on the Cherokee authenticated tribal roll of 1880 and the Cherokee census roll of 1896 as an intermarried citizen of the Cherokee Nation.

IT IS, THEREFORE, ORDERED AND ADJUDGED: That in accordance with the decision of the Supreme Court of the United States, dated November 5, 1906, in the cases of Daniel Red Bird et al. vs. the United States, Nos. 125, 126, 127, and 128, the said applicant, Frederick W. Gulager, is entitled, under the provisions of Section Twenty-one of the Act of Congress approved June 28, 1898 (30 Stats. 495), to enrollment as a citizen by intermarriage of the Cherokee Nation, and his application for enrollment as such is accordingly granted.

Tams Bixby
Commissioner.

Dated at Muskogee, Indian Territory,
this   FEB 12 1907

◇◇◇◇◇

Cherokee 5982

Muskogee, Indian Territory, February 12, 1907.

W. W. Hastings,
    Attorney for the Cherokee Nation,
        Muskogee, Indian Territory.

Dear Sir:

    There is enclosed herewith copy of the decision of the Commissioner to the Five Civilized Tribes, dated February 12, 1907, granting the application for the enrollment of Frederick W. Gulager as a citizen by intermarriage of the Cherokee Nation.

Respectfully,

Enc I-3   Commissioner.

RPI

◇◇◇◇◇

Cherokee Intermarried White 1906
Volume VI

Cherokee 5982

Muskogee, Indian Territory, February 12, 1907

The Commissioner to the Five Civilized Tribes,
Muskogee, Indian Territory.

Sir:

Receipt is acknowledged of the testimony and of your decision enrolling Frederick W. Gulager as a citizen by intermarriage of the Cherokee Nation. Time for protesting said decision is waived and I consent that said person may be placed upon the schedule immediately.

Respectfully,
W. W. Hastings
Attorney for the Cherokee Nation.

◇◇◇◇◇

Cherokee 5982

Muskogee, Indian Territory, February 12, 1907

Frederick W. Gulager,
Eureka, Indian Territory.

Dear Sir:

There is enclosed herewith copy of the decision of the Commissioner to the Five Civilized Tribes, dated February 12, 1907, granting the application for your enrollment as a citizen by intermarriage of the Cherokee Nation.

You will be advised when your name has been placed upon a schedule of citizens of the Cherokee Nation and approved by the Secretary of the Interior.

Respectfully,

Commissioner.

Enc I-4

RPI

Register.

Cherokee Intermarried White 1906
Volume VI

Cher IW 177

C.E.W.

DEPARTMENT OF THE INTERIOR,

COMMISSIONER TO THE FIVE CIVILIZED TRIBES.

In the matter of the application for the enrollment of

SARAH PHILLIPS

as a citizen by intermarriage of the Cherokee Nation.

Cherokee 7240.

DEPARTMENT OF THE INTERIOR.
COMMISSION TO THE FIVE CIVILIZED TRIBES.
MUSKOGEE, I.T., FEBUARY[sic] 7th, 1901.

IN THE MATTER OF THE APPLICATION OF Henry P. Phillips for the enrollment of himself, wife and children as citizens of the Cherokee Nation, and the said Phillips being sworn and examined by Commissioner, C. R. Breckinridge, testified as follows:

Q Give me your full name? A Henry P. Phillips.
Q How old are you? A About fifty two years old.
Q What is your Postoffice? A Texanna.
Q In what district do you live? A Canadian District.
Q Do you wnt[sic] to enroll yourself and family? A Yes sir.
Q Have you a wife? A Yes sir.
Q How many children have you? A Three children.
Q Are these children all under twenty one years of age?
A There is two of them that is.
Q Are they unmarried? A Yes sir.
Q Are you a Cherokee by blood? A Yes sir.
Q Is your wife a Cherokee by blood? A No sir.
Q A white woman? A Yes sir.
Q How long have you lived in the Cherokee Nation?
A I was born in the Cherokee Nation and have lived in the Cherokee Nation since 1868; was away time of the war and came back in '68.

Cherokee Intermarried White 1906
Volume VI

Q Give me the name of your father? A Elijah Phillips.
Q Is he dead? A Yes sir.
Q Give me the name of your mother? A Sidney Phillips.
Q Is she dead? A Yes sir.
Q Give me the name of your wife? A Sarah.
Q How old is she? A Right close to fifty four.
Q When were you and she married? A In '68.
Q Have you lived together ever since you were married? A Yes sir.
Q And all the time in the Cherokee Nation? A Yes sir.
Q What was her name before you married her?
A Her name was Henderson.
Q Give me the names of these three children? A Elmer Lee.
Q How old is he? A Twenty four.
Q The next child? A Roxie E.
Q How old is that child? A She's fifteen.
Q The next child? A Henry C.
Q How old is he? A Twelve years old.
Q Are these children all living now? A Yes sir.

Elmer L. Phillips, being sworn and examined by Commissioner, C. R. Breckinridge, testified as follows:
Q Give me your full name? A Elmer L. Phillips.
Q How old are you? A Twenty four.
Q You are the son of Henry Phillips here? A Yes sir.
Q Your mother's name is Sarah? A Yes sir.
Q Are you living with your father? A Yes sir.
Q Have you lived in the Cherokee Nation all your life? A Yes sir.

APPLICANT, HENRY P. PHILLIPS, RECALLED:
Q Do you go by the name of Dock Phillips? A Yes sir.
Q In what district were you in 1880? A I was born in Goingsnake.

(1880 Authenticated Roll of citizens of the Cherokee Nation examined, and on Page 461 thereof, number 1299 appears the name of the applicant, as "Dock Phillipps[sic]", Goingsnake District. Applicant's wife's name found on same Roll, Page 461, number 1300, Sarah Philips[sic], Goingsnake District. Applicant's son's name found on same Roll, Page 461, Number 1304, as "Elmo Philipps[sic], Goingsnake District)

(1896 Census Roll of citizens of the Cherokee Nation examined, and on Page 87 thereof appears the name of applicant, as Henry P. Phillips, Canadian District) -- (1896 Census Roll examined, and on page 91 thereof Number 217 appears the name of applicant's wife, as Sarah Phillips, Canadian District)
(1896 Census Roll examined and on Page 57 thereof appears the names of applicant's children as follows: Number 1542, Elmer D. Phillips; Number

Cherokee Intermarried White 1906
Volume VI

1543, Roxie Phillips,; Number 1544, Henry C. Phillips, all of Canadian District)

Com'r. C. R. Breckinridge: The applicant applies for the enrollment of himself, his wife and three children, one of whom is twenty four years of age, but who appears in the course of the examination. The applicant is identified on the rolls of 1880 and 1896 as a native Cherokee; he has lived in the Cherokee Nation all his life except an absence incident to the Civil War, and he will now be listed for enrollment as a Cherokee by blood.

His wife is a white woman; He states that they were married in 1868 and have lived together and in the Cherokee Nation ever since that time: She is identified with him on the rolls of 1880 and 1896 as an adopted Cherokee, and she will be listed for enrollment as a Cherokee by adoption.

The oldest child, Elmer L. Phillips, who appears in the course of the examination, is of age; is identified on the rolls of 1880 and 1896 as a native Cherokee; he has lived in the Cherokee Nation all his life, and he will be listed for enrollment as a Cherokee by blood.

The two younger children, Roxie E. and Henry C. Phillips are duly identified on the roll of 1896; they are living; and will be listed for enrollment as Cherokees by blood.

The undersigned, being sworn, states that as stenographer to the Commission to the Five Civilized Tribes, he correctly recorded the testimony and proceedings in this case, and the foregoing is a true and correct transcript of his stenographic notes thereof.

R R Cravens

Subscribed and sworn to before me this to before me this 8th day of Febuary[sic], A. D., 1901.

C R Breckinridge
COMMISSIONER.

Cher # 7240

Department of the Interior,
Commission to the Five Civilized Tribes,
Muskogee, I. T., October 13, 1902.

In the matter of the application of HENRY P. PHILLIPS, for the enrollment of himself and his children, ELMER L., ROXIE E. and HENRY C. PHILLIPS, as citizens by blood of the Cherokee Nation; and his wife Sarah Phillips as a citizen by intermarriage of the Cherokee Nation.

Cherokee Intermarried White 1906
Volume VI

SARAH PHILLIPS, called as a witness, being duly sworn and examined by the Commission, testified as follows:

Q What is your name ?   A Sarah Phillips.
Q What is your age at this time ?   A Fifty six.
Q What is your post office ?   A Texana[sic].
Q What is your husband's name ?   A Henry P. Phillips.
Q Are you the same Sarah Phillips for whom application was made in February, 1900, for enrollment as an intermarried citizen of the Cherokee Nation ?
A Yes sir.
Q Your age was give[sic] at the time of the application as sixty four, is that a mistake ?
A Yes sir, that's a mistake.
Q It should have been fifty four instead of sixty four ?   A Yes sir.
Q Is your husband living now ?   A No sir.
Q Was he a Cherokee by blood ?   A Yes sir.
Q When did he die ?   A Last May was a year ago.
Q When were you and he married ?
A I don't know whether I can tell when.
Q Was it before or after 1880 ?   A It was before 1880.
Q Well did you and your husband Henry P. Phillips live together as husband and wife from 1880 up until his death ?   A Yes sir.
Q You were never separated ?   A No sir.
Q You never married since his death ?   A No sir.
Q You were still a widow and single on the first day of September, 1902 ?   A Yes sir.
Q Have you lived in the Cherokee Nation all the time since 1880 up to the present time?
A Yes sir.
Q Are these children, Elmer L., Roxie E., and Henry C., your children by your husband Henry P. Phillips ?   A Yes sir.
Q Are these children living at this time ?   A Yes sir.
Q Have they lived in the Cherokee Nation all their lives ?   A Yes sir.
Q Your oldest son Elmer L., is of age isn't he ?   A Yes sir.
Q Where is he ?   A He is living at home at Texana[sic].
Q Why did he not appear himself and make application ?   Was he sick at the time ?
A I don't remember, he had a spell of sickness, but I don't remember whether it was at that time or not.
Q It was a year ago last February ?
A Well, he had a spell of sickness somewheres[sic] along then.

E. C. Bagwell, on oath states that, as stenographer to the Commission to the Five Civilized Tribes, he correctly recorded the testimony and proceedings had in the above entitled cause, and that the foregoing is an accurate transcript of his stenographic notes thereof.

E.C.Bagwell

Cherokee Intermarried White 1906
Volume VI

Subscribed and sworn to before me this October 21, 1902.

BC Jones
Notary Public.

CHEROKEE-7240:

DEPARTMENT OF THE INTERIOR,
COMMISSIONER TO THE FIVE CIVILIZED TRIBES.
Muskogee, Indian Territory, January 4, 1907.

In the matter of making proof of the marriage of Sarah Phillips to her Cherokee husband, prior to November 1, 1875.

Sarah Phillips, being sworn by W. W. Chappell, a Notary Public, testified as follows:

COMMISSIONER:

Q. What is your name?   A.   Sarah Phillips.
Q. What is your age?   A.   61.
Q. What is your post office address?   A.   Catoosa.
Q. Do you claim citizenship by intermarriage in the Cherokee Nation[sic]?
    A.   Yes sir.
Q. Through whom do you claim such citizenship?   A.   My husband, Henry P. Phillips.
Q. Is Henry P. Phillips living now?   A.   No sir.
Q. When did he die?   A.   5 years ago last May.
Q. What was his citizenship?   A.   He was a Cherokee by blood.
Q. When were you married to him?   A.   In '67.
Q. What month?   A.   October.
Q. Where were you married?   A.   In Arkansas.
Q   Were you married under a license issued by the State of Arkansas[sic]?
    A.   There were no licenses issued at that time.
Q. Have you any documentary evidence covering the marriage -- any papers or anything showing the marriage?   A.   No sir, I have no papers.
Q. When did you remove to the Cherokee Nation?   A.   3 days after we were married.

Cherokee Intermarried White 1906
Volume VI

Q. Did you live together as man and wife from the time of your removal to the Cherokee Nation until the death of your husband?
A. Yes sir.
Q. Was your husband recognized on the rolls of the Cherokee Nation?
A. Yes sir.
Q. Do you know which rolls?   A.   No sir, I don't remember.

Q. Were you married prior to your marriage to Henry P. Phillips?
A. No sir.
Q. Was Henry P. Phillips ever married before he married you?   A.   No sir.
Q. You say you lived together continuously as man and wife in the Cherokee Nation from 1867 until his death?   A.   Yes sir.
Q. By whom were you married?   A.   A preacher.
Q. There were no license issued, you say?   A.   No sir.
Q. There were no papers given to you or your husband at the time of the marriage, by the preacher?   A No sir.
Q. Have you married since the death of Henry P. Phillips?   A.   No sir.

(Commissioner -- Sarah A. Phillips appears upon the 1880 roll opposite No. 1300, Going Snake District. The records of this office show that Henry P. Phillips, applicant's husband, was on the 1880 roll opposite No. 1299, Going Snake District, and that he died prior to September 1, 1902, an order of dismissal was entered March 31, 1905; death affidavit was approved October 13, 1902. The of the applicant also appears upon the 1896 Census Roll, opposite No. 217, Canadian District.)

Q. Is there any one here who was present at your marriage to Henry P. PHillips[sic]?
A. No sir, I don't think there is.
Q. Are any of the witness to that marriage living now?   A.   Yes sir.
Q. Who are they?   A.   One is Frank Phillips, my brother-in-law.
Q. Where does he reside?   A.   In Canadian District, near Checotah.

Witness excused.

Eula Jeanes Branson, being sworn, states that she correctly reported the proceedings had in the above and foregoing on the 4th. day of January, 1907.

Eula Jeanes Branson

Subscribed and sworn to before me this 4th. day of January, 1907.

Edward Merrick
Notary Public.

Cherokee Intermarried White 1906
Volume VI

F.R. Cherokee Field Card No. 7240.

DEPARTMENT OF THE INTERIOR,
COMMISSIONER TO THE FIVE CIVILIZED TRIBES.
MUSKOGEE, I. T., JANUARY 5, 1907.

SUPPLEMENTAL TESTIMONY in the matter of the application for the enrollment of Sarah Phillips as a citizen by intermarriage of the Cherokee Nation.

APPEARANCES: J. Frank Phillips appears on behalf of applicant.

J. FRANK PHILLIPS, being first duly sworn by Walter W. Chappell, Notary Public, testified as follows:

ON BEHALF OF THE COMMISSIONER:

Q What is your name? A J. Frank Phillips.
Q What is your age? A 54.
Q What is your post office address? A Texanna.
Q Are you a citizen by blood of the Cherokee Nation? A Yes sir.
Q Do you know Sarah Phillips? A Yes sir.
Q Are you related to her? A Yes sir.
Q What relation? A She is my sister-in-law, my brother's widow.
Q What is the name of your brother? A Henry P. Phillips.
Q When was she married to Henry P. Phillips? A In '67.
Q Where was she married to Henry P. Phillips? A In Cook County, Arkansas.
Q Was her marriage to him under a license of the State of Arkansas. A Yes sir.
Q Do you know who issued that license? A No sir, I dont[sic].
Q Do you know who married them? A I dont[sic] remember his name; I know the man.
Q You were present at the marriage ceremony, were you? A Yes sir, but I was just a boy.
Q Do you know what became of that marriage license? A No sir.
Q Do you know whether or not it was filed for record? A No sir.
Q Have you ever endeavored to secure a certified copy of it?
    A No sir.
Q Do you know when Henry P. Phillips and his wife, Sarah Phillips, removed to the Cherokee Nation? A Yes sir.
Q When? A It was in '67.
Q Following their marriage? A Yes sir.
Q How soon after their marriage? A Well sir, I dont[sic] know just exactly; it was somewhere about two weeks.
Q Where did they locate in the Cherokee Nation? A Going Snake District.
Q Is Henry P. Phillips living? A No sir.
Q When did he die? A 5 years ago.

Cherokee Intermarried White 1906
Volume VI

Q Did Henry P. Phillips and his wife, Sarah Phillips, live together as husband and wife continuously from the time of their removal to the Cherokee Nation until the time of his death?
A Yes sir.
Q Was Sarah Phillips ever married prior to her marriage to Henry P. Phillips? A No sir.
Q Was Henry P. Phillips ever married prior to his marriage to Sarah Phillips?
A No sir.
Q Do you know whether or not, when Henry P. Phillips and his wife, Sarah Phillips, removed to the Cherokee Nation they were again married, in accordance with Cherokee tribal laws? A No sir, I know they wasn't.
Q Has Sarah Phillips married since the death of her husband, Henry P. Phillips?
A No sir.

"As this marriage was under a license of the State of Arkansas, you should endeavor to secure and file with the Commissioner to the Five Civilized Tribes a certified copy of such license."

WILLIAM B. BECK, being first duly sworn by Walter W. Chappell, Notary Public, testified as follows:

ON BEHALF OF THE COMMISSIONER:

Q What is your name? A William B. Beck.
Q What is your age? A 59.
Q What is your post office address? A Fawn.
Q Do you know Sarah Phillips? A Yes sir.
Q Are you related to her? A No sir, only by marriage; her husband and my wife were cousins.
Q Do you know that she married Henry P. Phillips? A No sir, not of my own personal knowledge; of course I heard it.
Q You were not present at their marriage? A No sir.

M. J. BECK, being first duly sworn by Walter W. Chappell, Notary Public, testified as follows:

Q What is your name? A M. J. Beck.
Q You are the wife of William B. Beck, who has just appeared on the stand, are you?
A Yes sir.
Q Are you related to Sarah Phillips? A Nothing, only just by marriage.
Q You know that she was married to Henry P. Phillips? A Well, I dont[sic] know that she was, but he brought her down the day after their marriage to my uncle's, Henry P. Phillips' father's house.
Q When was that? A In '67.
Q Do you know where they were married? A Yes sir, in Cook County, Arkansas.
Q Do you know who performed the ceremony? A A man by the name of Barber was the man that they said performed it.

Cherokee Intermarried White 1906
Volume VI

Q Upon the removal of Henry P. Phillips and his wife, Sarah Phillips, to the Cherokee Nation in 1867, were they remarried, in accordance with the Cherokee laws? A Not that I know of.

Q Did they live together continuously as man and wife, within the Cherokee Nation, from the time of their removal to such Nation in 1867 until the death of Henry P. Phillips? A Yes sir.

Q They were held out in the community as man and wife? A Yes sir.

The undersigned, being first duly sworn, states that as stenographer to the Commission to the Five Civilized Tribes, she correctly reported the above and foregoing testimony, and that the same is a full, true and correct transcript of her stenographic notes thereof.

Sarah Waters

Subscribed and sworn to before me this 5th day of January, 1907.

John E. Tidwell
Notary Public.

◇◇◇◇◇

Cherokee 7240.

DEPARTMENT OF THE INTERIOR,

COMMISSIONER TO THE FIVE CIVILIZED TRIBES.

In the matter of the application for the enrollment of SARAH PHILLIPS as a citizen by intermarriage of the Cherokee Nation.

D E C I S I O N

THE RECORDS OF THIS OFFICE SHOW: That at Muskogee, Indian Territory, February 7, 1901, application was received by the Commission to the Five Civilized Tribes for the enrollment of Sarah Phillips as a citizen by intermarriage of the Cherokee Nation. Further proceedings were had in the matter of said application at Muskogee, Indian Territory, October 13, 1902, and January 4 and 5, 1907.

THE EVIDENCE IN THIS CASE SHOWS: That the applicant herein, Sarah Phillips, a white woman, was married in accordance with Cherokee law in the year 1867, to one Henry P. Phillips, who was at the time of said marriage a recognized citizen by blood of the Cherokee Nation, and who is identified upon the Cherokee authenticated

Cherokee Intermarried White 1906
Volume VI

tribal roll of 1880, Going Snake District, page 461, number 1299, as a native Cherokee; that said Sarah Phillips, and Henry P. Phillips resided together as husband and wife and continuously lived in the Cherokee Nation until his death which occurred in May 1900; that said Sarah Phillips has not married since the death of said Henry P. Phillips and continuously lived in the Cherokee Nation. Applicant is identified upon the Cherokee authenticated tribal roll of 1880, and the Cherokee Census roll of 1896 as an intermarried citizen of the Cherokee Nation.

IT IS, THEREFORE, ORDERED AND ADJUDGED: That in accordance with the decision of the Supreme Court of the United States, dated November 5, 1906, in the cases of Daniel Red Bird, et al., vs. the United States, Nos. 125, 126, 127, and 128, the said applicant, Sarah Phillips, is entitled, under the provisions of Section 21 of the Act of Congress approved June 28, 1898 (30 Stats., 495), to enrollment as a citizen by intermarriage of the Cherokee Nation, and her application for enrollment as such is accordingly granted.

Tams Bixby
Commissioner.

Dated at Muskogee, Indian Territory,
this FEB 8 1907

◇◇◇◇◇

Cherokee 7240

Muskogee, Indian Territory, February 8, 1907.

W. W. Hastings,
Attorney for the Cherokee Nation,
Muskogee, Indian Territory.

Dear Sir:

There is enclosed herewith a copy of the decision of the Commissioner to the Five Civilized Tribes, dated February 8, 1907, granting the application for the enrollment of Sarah Phillips as a citizen by intermarriage of the Cherokee Nation.

Respectfully,

Commissioner.

Encl. H-11
JMH

◇◇◇◇◇

Cherokee Intermarried White 1906
Volume VI

Cherokee 7240

Muskogee, Indian Territory, February 8, 1907.

The Commissioner to the Five Civilized Tribes,
Muskogee, Indian Territory.

Sir:

Receipt is acknowledged of the testimony and of your decision enrolling Sarah Phillips as a citizen by intermarriage of the Cherokee Nation. Time for protesting said decision is waived and I consent that said person may be placed upon the schedule immediately.

Respectfully,
W. W. Hastings
Attorney for Cherokee Nation.

◇◇◇◇◇

Cherokee 7240

Muskogee, Indian Territory, February 8, 1907.

Sarah Phillips,
Texanna, Indian Territory.

Dear Madam:

There is enclosed herewith a copy of the decision of the Commissioner to the Five Civilized Tribes, dated February 8, 1907, granting your application for enrollment as a citizen by intermarriage of the Cherokee Nation.

You will be advised when your name has been placed upon a schedule of citizens of the Cherokee Nation and approved by the Secretary of the Interior.

Respectfully,

Encl. H-12
JMH

Commissioner.

Cher IW 178

Cherokee Intermarried White 1906
Volume VI

C.E.W.

DEPARTMENT OF THE INTERIOR,

COMMISSIONER TO THE FIVE CIVILIZED TRIBES.

In the matter of the application for the enrollment of

NOAH WHISSENHUNT[sic]

as a citizen by intermarriage of the Cherokee Nation.

Cherokee 7368.

◇◇◇◇◇

DEPARTMENT OF THE INTERIOR,
COMMISSION TO THE FIVE CIVILIZED TRIBES,
MUSKOGEE, I.T., FEBRUARY 26th, 1901.

In the matter of the application of Nancy J. Whisenhunt for the enrollment of herself, husband and child as citizens of the Cherokee Nation; said Whisenhunt being sworn and examined by Commissioner Needles, testified as follows:

Q What is your name? A Nancy J. Whisenhunt.
Q How old are you? A I am 64.
Q What is your post office address? A Texana[sic].
Q What district do you live in? A Canadian.
Q Are you a recognized citizen of the Cherokee Nation? A Yes, sir.
Q By blood? A Yes, sir.
Q Who do you want to enroll? A My youngest son, my husband, will you allow me to enroll him.[sic]
Q Why is not he here? A He was not able to come here; his name is Noah Whisenhunt.
Q White man is he? A Yes, sir.
Q How old is he? A He is 67.
Q Is his post office Texana? A Yes, sir.
Q What is the name of your child you wish to enroll? A Frederick.
Q How old is he? A 17.
Q When were you and Noah Whisenhunt married? A Been so long I have forgotten it.
Q You were married before 1880? A Yes, sir, I have been married 42 years.

Tribal Rolls of the Cherokee Nation examined and applicants' names found thereon as follows:
1880 Authenticated Roll; page 486, #1862, Noah Whisenhunt, Going Snake district.

Cherokee Intermarried White 1906
Volume VI

1880 Authenticated Roll; page 486 #1863, Nancy Whisenhunt, Going Snake district.
1896 Census Roll; page 94, #306, Noah Whisenhunt, Canadian district.
1896 Census Roll; page 79, #2188, Nancy Whisenhunt, Canadian district.
1896 Census Roll; page 79, #2192, Fred Whisenhunt, Canadian district.

Q How long have you lived in the Cherokee Nation? A Well it has been; I staid in the Cherokee Nation until I was 12 years old and I went away and staid until I was grown and come back and have been here ever since.
Q Have you and Mr. Whisenhunt been living together ever since you married?
A Yes, sir.
Q Is Frederick alive and living with you? A Yes, sir.

Com'r Needles:--The name of Nancy J Whisenhunt appears upon the authenticated of 1880 as Nancy Whisenhunt. The name of her husband, Noah Whisenhunt, appears upon the authenticated roll of 1880 as an intermarried white. Their names also appear upon the census Roll of 1896. The name of her child, Frederick, is found upon the census roll of 1896. They are duly identified and make satisfactory proof as to residence, consequently Nancy J. Whisenhunt and her son, Frederick, will be duly listed for enrollment as Cherokee citizens, by blood and her husband, Noah Whisenhunt, as a Cherokee citizen by intermarriage.

---oooOOOooo---

J. O. Rosson, being first duly sworn, states that as stenographer to the Commission to the Five Civilized Tribes, he correctly recorded the testimony and proceedings in this case, and the foregoing is a true and complete transcript of his stenographic notes thereof.

J.O. Rosson

Subscribed and sworn to before me this 26th day of February 1901.

TB Needles
Commissioner.

Cherokee Intermarried White 1906
Volume VI

DEPARTMENT OF THE INTERIOR.
Commission to the Five Civilized Tribes.
Muskogee, Indian Territory, October 10th, 1902.

In the matter of the application of Noah Whisenhunt for the enrollment of himself as a citizen by intermarriage of the Cherokee Nation and for the enrollment of his wife, Nancy J. Whisenhunt, and his son, Frederick Whisenhunt, as citizens by blood of the Cherokee Nation.

Supplemental to 37368.

NOAH WHISENHUNT, being duly sworn, testified as follows:-
Examination by the Commission.
Q. What is your name, please? A. Noah Whisenhunt.
Q. What is your post office address? A. Texanna.
Q. What is your age at this time? A. I will be 68 the 27th day of the coming month.
Q. Are you the same Noah Whisenhunt who applied to this Commission for enrollment as an intermarried citizen in February, 1901? A. Yes, sir.
Q. What is your wife's name? A. Nancy.
Q. Is she living? A. Yes, sir.
Q. Is she a citizen by blood of the Cherokee Nation? A. Yes, sir.
Q. When were you married to your wife Nancy? A Why, we was married about the 28th day of December, 1850, in Arkansas.
Q. In the state of Arkansas? A. Yes, sir.
Q. When did you come, then, to the Territory--Cherokee Nation? A. We come in '67. I lived in the states until '67.
Q. Then you came in '67? A. Yes, sir.
Q. Did you ever marry your wife under a Cherokee license? A. Yes, sir; about '72, I think. I ain't positive, but I think in '72.
Q. Were you ever married before you married this wife? A. Yes, sir; once.
Q. To a white woman? A. Yes, sir.
Q. Was that white woman dead? A. Oh, yes.
Q. Was Nancy ever married before she married you? A. No, sir.
Q. You are Nancy's first husband? A. Yes, sir.
Q. She is your second wife? A Yes, sir.
Q. Have you and your wife Nancy J. lived together all the time as husband and wife since 1880 up to the present time? A. We have.
Q. Never been separated? A. No, sir.
Q. You have never married any other woman since 1880, have you? A. No, sir.
Q. Were you living together as husband and wife on the first of September, 1902? A. Yes, sir.

Cherokee Intermarried White 1906
Volume VI

Q. Have you and your wife Nancy lived together in the Cherokee Nation from 1880 up to the present time?   A. We have.
Q. Is this Frederick your son by your wife Nancy?   A. Yes, sir.
Q. Is he living at this time?   A. Yes, sir.
Q. Has he lived in the Cherokee Nation all his life?   A. Yes, sir.
Q. Never lived out of the Nation?   A. Never has.

Jesse O. Carr, being first duly sworn, states that as stenographer to the Commission to the Five Civilized Tribes he reported the above entitled case and that the foregoing is a true and complete transcript of his stenographic notes thereof.

Jesse O. Carr

Subscribed and sworn to before me this 18th day of December, 1902.

PG Reuter
Notary Public.

F.R.   Cherokee 7368.

DEPARTMENT OF THE INTERIOR,
COMMISSIONER TO THE FIVE CIVILIZED TRIBES.
Muskogee, I. T., January 14, 1907.

In the matter of the application for the enrollment of Noah Whisenhunt as a citizen by intermarriage of the Cherokee Nation.

Noah Whisenhunt, being first duly sworn by B. P. Rasmus, a Notary Public for the Western District of Indian Territory, testified as follows:

By the Commissioner:
Q What is your name?   A Noah Whisenhunt.
Q How old are you?   A Seventy-three.
Q What is your postoffice address?   A Oolagah, I. T.
Q You are a white man, not possessed of any Indian blood?
A No, not that I know of.
Q You claim the right to enrollment by virtue of your intermarriage in the Cherokee Nation?   A Yes sir.
Q Through whom do you claim that right?   A Nancy J. Philips[sic].
Q Was she a recognized citizen by blood of the Cherokee Nation at the time you married her?   A Yes sir.
Q When were you married to Nancy J. Whisenhunt?   A I was married twice.
Q When were you married the first time to her?   A I was married the 28th day of December, 1859.

Cherokee Intermarried White 1906
Volume VI

Q Where were you married to her in 1859? A In Arkansas, Polk County.
Q When did you remove to the Cherokee nation[sic]? A Moved in 1867
Q Upon your removal to the Cherokee Nation were you remarried in accordance with the laws of the Cherokee nation[sic]? A I was, I have got my Cherokee license.
Q Was that your license that you obtained in the Cherokee nation, this second marriage? A Yes sir.
Q What district? A Going Snake District.
Q Who issued the license? A Judge Thornton.
Q Whp[sic] performed the marriage ceremony, that is, under the Cherokee license? A Judge Thornton.
Q When was this marriage under the Cherokee law? In what year
A To the best of my knowledge--I couldn't say for sure, but it was in 1872 I am most sure; it was not later than that.
Q Were you ever married prior to the time of your marriage to Nancy J. Whisenhunt? A Yes sir.
Q Who was your first wife? A She was a Howell.
Q Was she living at the time you married Nancy J. Whisenhunt? A No sir.
Q Were you Nancy J. Whisenhunt's first husband, or has she been married prior to the time she married you? A I was her first husband.
Q Have you a copy of the license or any documentary evidence showing your marriage to Nancy J. Whisenhunt in 1872 under Cherokee license? A I have filed it with the Dawes Commission. This Commission has got it somewhere.
Q Was it the original license or a copy that you filed? A It was the original license; it was the same one I got from the clerk. His name was to them and the dates, and everything.
Q About when was that turned over to the Commission? A It was in 1896 sometime.
Q Where was the Commission in session when you delivered that license to them? A I declare, I have forgot. I believe it was a Vinita but I don't know; I sent them to the Commission.
Q You didn't deliver them in person? A No sir.
Q You sent them by mail? A Yes sir.
   The records of this office show that on September 10, 1896, there was filed by Noah Whisenhunt, original marriage license authorizing his marriage to Nancy philips[sic], which marriage license appears to have been issued May 2, 1870 by John Thornton, Clerk of the District Court, Going Snake District, Cherokee Nation,[sic] Said license is filed with and made a part of the record in this case.
Q Is Nancy J. Whisenhunt living at this time? A She is; -was this morning.
Q Have you and Nancy J. Whisenhunt lived together as husband and wife from the time of your marriage up to the present time? A We have, every day.
Q You have resided continuously in the Cherokee Nation? A Yes.
Q Since your marriage to Nancy J. Whisenhunt in 1870, have you been recognized on the rolls of the Cherokee Nation as an intermarried citizen? A Yes sir.
Q You have voted at the elections have you? A Yes, voted in all the elections, and sat on juries.

Cherokee Intermarried White 1906
Volume VI

The applicant is identified on the Cherokee authenticate tribal roll of 1880, Going Snake District, opposite No. 1862.
The applicant's wife, Nancy J. Whisenhunt, is identified on said roll opposite No. 1863, and is also included in the approved partial roll of citizens of the Cherokee Nation opposite No. 17486.

Witness excused.

William B. Beck, being first dulu[sic] sworn, testified as follows:
Q What is your name? A William B. Beck
Q What is your age" A 1858.
Q What is your postoffice address? A Fawn, I. T.
Q You appears[sic] here for the purpose of giving testimony relative to the application for the enrollment of Noah Whisenhunt as a citizen of the Cherokee Nation? A Yes sir.
Q How long have you known Noah Whisenhunt? A I have known him since I suppose 1860-61.
Q Did you know his wife? A Yes, I knew her.
Q Noah Whisenhunt and Nancy J. Whisenhunt have lived together as husband and wife and resided continuously in the Cherokee nation[sic] from the time of their marriage until the present time, have they? A Yes sir.

Witness excused.

Frances R. Lane upon oath states that as stenographer to the commissioner[sic] to the Five Civilized Tribes she reported the testimony in the above entitled cause and that the foregoing is an accurate transcript of her stenographic notes thereof.

Frances R Lane

Subscribed and sworn to before me this January 16, 1907.

Edward Merrick
Notary Public.

Cherokee Intermarried White 1906
Volume VI

(The Marriage License below typed as given.)

Cherokee Nation
Going Snake Dist.

To all whom it may concern be it known that authority is hereby granted to any of the Judges of any of the Courts of in the Cherokee Nation and all ministers of all Evangelical denominations having the care of souls are hereby authorized and empowered to solemnise the of matrimony according to the ceremonies usually observed and performed in such cases between Mr. Noah Whisenhunt and Miss Nancy J. Whisenhunt formerly Miss Nancy Philips a Cherokee sitison he the said Noah Whisenhunt having complied with the Law in such cases this given from under my hand in office this the 2nd day of May 1870.

John Thornton Clk Dist Court
G. S. Dist. C. N.

The undersigned being first duly sworn, states that as stenographer to the Commission to the Five Civilized Tribes, she made the above copy and that same is a true and correct copy of the original marriage license in[sic] file in this office.

Myrtle Hill

Subscribed and sworn to before me this the 5th day of February, 1907.

Chas E Webster
Notary Public.

Cherokee Intermarried White 1906
Volume VI

Cherokee 7368

DEPARTMENT OF THE INTERIOR,

COMMISSIONER TO THE FIVE CIVILIZED TRIBES.

In the matter of the application for the enrollment of NOAH WHISENHUNT as a citizen by intermarriage of the Cherokee Nation.

D E C I S I O N.

THE RECORDS OF THIS OFFICE SHOW: That at Muskogee, Indian Territory, February 26, 1901, application was received by the Commission to the Five Civilized Tribes for the enrollment of Noah Whisenhunt as a citizen by intermarriage of the Cherokee Nation. Further proceedings were had in the matter of said application at Muskogee, Indian Territory, October 10, 1902, and January 14, 1907.

THE EVIDENCE IN THIS CASE SHOWS: That the applicant herein, Noah Whisenhunt, a white man, was married in accordance with Cherokee law in the year 1872, to one Nancy J. Whisenhunt, nee Phillips, who at the time of said marriage was a recognized citizen by blood of the Cherokee Nation, who is identified upon the Cherokee Authenticated tribal roll of 1880, Going Snake District, page 486, number 1863, as a native Cherokee and whose name is included in the approved partial roll of citizens by blood of the Cherokee Nation opposite number 17486; that said Noah Whisenhunt and Nancy J. Whisenhunt, have resided together as husband and wife and have lived continuously in the Cherokee Nation. Said applicant is identified upon the Cherokee authenticated tribal roll of 1880, and the Cherokee Census roll of 1896 as an intermarried citizen of the Cherokee Nation.

IT IS, THEREFORE, ORDERED AND ADJUDGED: That in accordance with the decision of the Supreme Court of the United States, dated November 5, 1906, in the cases of Daniel Red Bird, et al., vs. the United States, Nos. 125, 126, 127, and 128, the said applicant, Noah Whisenhunt, is entitled, under the provisions of Section twenty-one of the Act of Congress approved June 28, 1898 (30 Stats. 495), to enrollment as a citizen by intermarriage of the Cherokee Nation, and his application for enrollment as such is accordingly granted.

Tams Bixby
Commissioner.

Dated at Muskogee, Indian Territory,
this   FEB 11 1907

Cherokee Intermarried White 1906
Volume VI

Cherokee 7368

Muskogee, Indian Territory, February 11, 1907.

W. W. Hastings,
  Attorney for the Cherokee Nation,
    Muskogee, Indian Territory.

Dear Sir:

There is enclosed herewith a copy of the decision of the Commissioner to the Five Civilized Tribes, dated February 11, 1907, granting the application for the enrollment of Noah Whisenhunt as a citizen by intermarriage of the Cherokee Nation.

Respectfully,

Encl. H-36
JMH

Commissioner.

◇◇◇◇◇

Cherokee 7368

Muskogee, Indian Territory, February 11, 1907.

The Commissioner to the Five Civilized Tribes,
  Muskogee, Indian Territory.

Sir:

Receipt is acknowledged of the testimony and of your decision enrolling Noah Whisenhunt as a citizen by intermarriage of the Cherokee Nation. Time for protesting said decision is waived, and I consent that said person may be placed upon the schedule immediately.

Respectfully,
W. W. Hastings
Attorney for Cherokee Nation.

◇◇◇◇◇

Cherokee Intermarried White 1906
Volume VI

Cherokee 7368

Muskogee, Indian Territory, February 11, 1907.

Noah Whisenhunt,
    Oologah, Indian Territory.

Dear Sir:

    There is enclosed herewith a copy of the decision of the Commissioner to the Five Civilized Tribes, dated February 11, 1907, granting your application for enrollment as a citizen by intermarriage of the Cherokee Nation.

    You will be advised when your name has been placed upon a schedule of citizens of the Cherokee Nation and approved by the Secretary of the Interior.

    Respectfully,

Encl. H-35
JMH
                            Commissioner.

Cher IW 179

◇◇◇◇◇

E.C.M.

DEPARTMENT OF THE INTERIOR,

COMMISSIONER TO THE FIVE CIVILIZED TRIBES.

In the matter of the application for the enrollment of

GEORGE ZUFALL

As a citizen by intermarriage of the Cherokee Nation.

CHEROKEE NO. 10194.

◇◇◇◇◇

Cherokee Intermarried White 1906
Volume VI

Department of the Interior.
Commission to the Five Civilized Tribes.
Muskogee, I. T., January 15, 1901.

In the matter of the application of Maggie Zufall for the enrollment of herself, husband and children as Cherokee citizens; she being sworn and examined by the Commission, testified as follows:

Q What is your name? A Maggie Zufall.
Q What is your age? A 46.
Q What is your postoffice address? A Muskogee.
Q For whom do you make application; anyone besdies[sic] yourself?
A My husband, and me, and children.
Q How many children? A Six.
Q Are you a Cherokee by blood? A Yes sir.
Q What degree of Cherokee blood do you claim? A I don't know; a quarter, I guess.
Q How long have you lived here in the Creek Nation? A We have been here off and on for about 26 years. Our home is in the Cherokee Nation, but our business is here.
Q What is the name of your father ? A Jack Cobb.
Q Is he living? A No, he's dead.
Q Was he a Cherokee? A No, he was a white man.
Q What is the name of your mother? A Lucy Victory.
Q Is your mother living? A No sir.
Q Was she a Cherokee? A Yes sir.
Q What district were you enrolled in twenty years ago? A Canadian district.
Q Were you enrolled in the same district in 1896? A Yes sir.
Q Is your husband a white man? A Yes, he's german[sic].
Q When were you married to him? A Married in '73.
Q Were you ever married before you married him? A No sir.
Q Was he? A No sir.
Q You have lived together continuously since that time? A Yes sir.
Q What is the name of the oldest child under 21 and unmarried?
A Pearl E.
Q How old is she? A 21.
Q The next child? A Oscar O.
Q How old is he A He's 19.
Q The next child? A Maggie.
Q How old is she? A She's 17.
Q The next child? A Benjamin H.
Q How old is he? A He's 13.
Q Next child? A Grace A.
Q How old is she? A She's 10.
Q The next child? A Herbert, 8.
Q These children are all alive and living with you at the present time? A Yes sir.
Q Any of these children born in the Cherokee Nation? A No sir.
Q All born here in the Creek Nation? A Yes sir.

Cherokee Intermarried White 1906
Volume VI

Q Do you own any property in the Cherokee Nation? A Yes, we got two farms in the Cherokee Nation.
Q Do you derive any rents from those farms? A Yes sir.
Q You have property in the Creek Nation? A No sir, only our home.
Q Did you draw money from the Creek tribe of Indians? A No sir.
Q Have you drawn from the Cherokees? A Yes sir.
Q Were you, or your husband ever admitted to citizenship here in the Cherokee Nation? A No, we never was out to be readmitted. We always lived up to the laws, and always had property and paid our tax in the Cherokee Nation.
Q You know whether or not you were enrolled in 1880? A No, because we wasn't over there at the time, I guess is the reason. They never came out of the Nation.
Q Did you apply for enrollment at that time? A No, we didn't know anything about it. They never notified us; we are on all the rest of the roll except that roll.
Q Did you draw strip money in 1894? A Yes sir.

Commission- The roll of 1880 examined and names of applicants not found.

1896 roll; page 83, #2312, Maggie Zufall, Canadian district.
1896 roll; page 95, #322, George Zufall, Canadian district.
        83, #2315, Pearl Zufall,   "   "
        83, #2316, Otto   "   "   "
        83, #2317, Maggie " Jr. "   "
        83, #2318, Benjaimin[sic] "   "   "
        83, #2319, Grace   "   "   "
        83, #2320, Herbert   "   "   "

Q Did I understand you to say that for the past 26 years, you have been making your home continuously here in the Creek Nation?
A No, we lived down there part of the time, and here part of the time. My husband's business is here.
Q How long has it been since you actually resided in the Cherokee Nation; since you have been over there to live? A Been off and on there all the time.
Q You maintain a home over there? A We got a home there, and a home here. We have a house where our place of business is. We never been anywhere but there. We sometimes spend the summer there and sometime the winter here.
Q You stated that neither you, nor your husband, ever applied for readmission to citizenship? A No sir.
Q Were you born in the Cherokee Nation? A No sir, I was born in Georgia.
Q When did you come to the Cherokee Nation? A Since I was three years old.
Q And since that time you lived here continuously? A Yes sir.
Q Have you any evidence of your marriage to your husband? A We can only furnish witnesses. We don't know anything about the licenses; they say they were never turned in. We supposed it was on record, and found it wasn't.

Cherokee Intermarried White 1906
Volume VI

Commission-

The applicant applied for the enrollment of herself and six children as citizens by blood of the Cherokee Nation, and for the enrollment of her husband as a citizen by intermarriage of the Cherokee Nation. She avers that she came to the Cherokee Nation when three years of age, and has been living here continuously since that time. She is not identified upon the authenticated roll of 1880. She was living in the Creek Nation at that time and didn't apply to the Cherokee tribal authorities for enrollment in the year 1880. She is identified upon the Census roll of 1896 as a native Cherokee. She avers that she was married in the year 1873 to her present husband, and they have been living together continuously since that time, and neither of them had ever been previously married. Her husband is identified with her on the Census roll of 1896 as an adopted white. The six children enumerated in the testimony are identified with their mother on the Census roll of 1896 as native Cherokees. For the reason that neither the applicant nor her husband are identified on the authenticated roll of 1880, and for the further reason that they have been during the past 26 years, residing the greater part of the time in the Creek Nation, they will be listed for enrollment as citizens by blood upon what is known as a doubtful card, and the husband, George Zufall, will be listed for enrollment as a citizen by intermarriage.

E.G. Rothenberger, being duly sworn, states that as stenographer to the Commission to the Five Civilized Tribes, he reported in full the testimony and proceedings in the above case, and that the foregoing is a full, true and correct transcript of his stenographic notes in said case.

              E.G. Rothenberger

Subscribed and sworn to before me this 16th day of January, 1901.

              TB Needles
              Commissioner.

◇◇◇◇◇

Department of the Interior.
Commission to the Five Civilized Tribes.
Muskogee, I. T., January 16, 1901.

In the matter of the application of George Zufall for enrollment as a Cherokee citizen; he being sworn and examined by Commissioner C. R. Breckinridge, testified as follows:

Q Give me your full name. A George Zufall.
Q How old are you? A 24.
Q What is your postoffice? A Muskogee.
Q Are you a citizen of the Cherokee Nation? A Yes sir.
Q In what district do you claim citizenship? A Canadian.
Q Do you live in Canadian? A I have up until last year.

Cherokee Intermarried White 1906
Volume VI

Q You have been living since that time in Muskogee? A I lived here with I was 10 years old, then I went to the Cherokee Nation until the last years.
Q What are you doing in Muskogee? A I am a blacksmith.
Q Who is it you want to have enrolled; just yourself? A Yes sir.
Q You are a Cherokee by blood, are you? A Yes sir.
Q Were you born in the Cherokee Nation? A No sir, in the Creek Nation, this place.
Q How much of your life have you spent in the Cherokee Nation? A About 12 years I guess.
Q That is, 12 years up to about a year ago? A Yes sir.
Q What is the name of your father? A George Zufall.
Q Is he dead? A No sir, he's living.
Q Is he a Cherokee or white man? A No, he's german[sic].
Q Your mother? A She's a Cherokee.
Q What is her name A Maggie.
Q Is she dead? A No sir, she's alive.
Q Is your mother a native of the Cherokee Nation? A Yes sir.
Q Where is she living now? A In Muskogee.
Q How long has she lived in Muskogee? A I don't know, she was born here:- nearly all her life, I guess.
Q Have you drawn money as a Cherokee? A Yes sir.
Q Have you ever drawn money as a Creek? A No sir.
Q Have you ever voted as a Cherokee? A Yes sir.
Q Have you ever voted as a Creek? A No sir.
Q You are working here now in a blacksmith shop, are you? A Yes sir.
Q You are a single man, are you? A Yes sir.
Q Have you any interests in the Cherokee Nation? A Yes sir, we have a farm over there; two of them.
Q They belong to your father? A Yes sir.
Q You have interest in that property as a child? A That's all.
1896 roll: page 83, #2314, George Zufall, Canadian district.
1896 roll: page 83, #2312, Maggie Zufall, Canadian district.

Commissioner Breckinridge-
　　　The applicant is identified on the roll of 1896 as a native Cherokee. He is not identified on the roll of 1880, and states that he was born in the Creek Nation and lived in the Creek Nation until some twelve years ago, since which time he has lived in the Cherokee Nation to within about one year ago, since which time he has lived at Muskogee, in the Creek Nation. He is now 24 years of age. He states that he has drawn money as a Cherokee, and never drew money as a Creek, and that he has voted as a Cherokee citizen, but never has voted as a Creek citizen. He also states that his mother is a native Cherokee. She is not identified on the roll of 1880, but is identified on the roll of 1896. She made application for herself and other members of her family on the 15th of the present month, and reference is made to her case for further particulars in regard to this family. The applicant will now be listed for enrollment as a Cherokee by blood, but upon a doubtful card, for the further consideration of his case, and the decision when finally rendered will be made known to him at his present postoffice address.

Cherokee Intermarried White 1906
Volume VI

E.G. Rothenberger, being duly sworn, states that as stenographer to the Commission to the Five Civilized Tribes, he reported in full the testimony and proceedings in the above case, and that the foregoing is a full, true and correct transcript of his stenographic notes in said case.

E.G. Rothenberger

Subscribed and sworn to before me this 17th day of January, 1901.

TB Needles
Commissioner.

Department of the Interior,
Commission to the Five Civilized Tribes,
Muskogee, IT, March 18, 1902.

SUPPLEMENTAL in the matter of the enrollment of GEORGE ZUFALL, JR., as a citizen of the Cherokee Nation:

    Commission It is directed that a copy of the testimony had in the matter of the application of the applicant's mother, Maggie Zufall, Cherokee card No. D. 1041, heard this 18th day of March, 1902, be filed with and made part of the record in this case.

---oooOOOooo---

I?[sic] J. O. Rosson, do hereby certify that as stenographer to the Commission to the Five Civilized Tribes I correctly recorded the proceedings had this day in above application, and that the foregoing is a true and complete transcript of my stenographic notes thereof.

JO Rosson

Cherokee Intermarried White 1906
Volume VI

No 1088

Department of the Interior,
Commission to the Five Civilized Tribes.
Muskogee, I. T. February 11, 1901.

In the matter of the application of Lewis E. Zufall for the enrollment of himself, wife and children as Vherokee[sic] citizens; he being sworn and examined by Commissioner C. R. Breckinridge, testified as follows:

Q Give me your full name? A Lewis E. Zufall.
Q How old are you? A 27 years old.
Q What is your post office? A Checotah.
Q In what district do you live? A Canadian District. Checotah is in the Creek Nation.
Q But you live in the Canadian District? A Yes sir.
Q Who do you want to enroll? A Myself and two children.
Q You have no wife? A Yes sir.
Q Dont[sic] you want to apply for her? A Yes sir, all of them.
Q Are you a Cherokee by blood? A Yes sir.
Q Is your wife a white woman? A Yes sir.
Q How long have you lived in the Cherokee Nation? A I was born and raised here in Muskogee; but always staid on my father's ranch in the Cherokee Nation until four years ago.
Q And then what? A I moved to Checotah and run a blacksmith shop.
Q You moved there four years ago? A Yes sir.
Q Have you ever voted over there in the Creek Nation? A In the Cherokee Nation.
Q Did you vote in the Creek Nation? A No sir.
Q Always considered yourself a Cherokee? A Yes sir.
Q You continued to vote in the Cherokee Nation all the time? A Yes sir.
Q Give me the name of your father? A George Zufall.
Q Is he dead? A No sir he is living.
Q Give me the name of your mother? A Margaret Cobb, before she married.
Q Is she alive? A Yes sir.
Q Are your father and mother living in the Cherokee Nation? A No sir they live here in Muskogee.
Q Give me the name of your wife? A Lena J.
Q When did you marry her? A I married in 1897 I think.
Q How old is your wife? A I think she is 24 years old.
Q What was her name when you married her? A Jones.
Q Were you ever married except to her? A No sir.
Q Was she ever married except to you? A No sir.
Q You and she lived together ever since you married? A Yes sir.
Q What are the names of your children? A Marion R. Zufall.
Q How old is that child? A Three years old last August.
Q And then your next child is Warren E? A Yes sir.
Q He was one year old last December? A Yes sir.

Cherokee Intermarried White 1906
Volume VI

    The applicant presents a certificate showing that he was married on the 4th of May, 1897, to Lena Johns, a citizen of the United States by Judge W. S. Agnew, of Canadian District. This is filed herewith.

Q Your wife's name ought to have been put in the certificate as Jones --they have it wrong have they? A Yes sir.

    The Cherokee census roll of 1896 examined and the name of the applicant is found on page 83, No 2313 as Lewis Zufall, in Canadian District.
    The authenticated roll of 1880 examined and the name of the applicant is not found thereon.

Q How comes it that you are not on the roll of 1880? I dont[sic] know hardly. I left it to my mother I guess.
Q But I dont[sic] find your father or mother on that roll? A No sir.
Q You were born in the Cherokee Nation? A I was born in Muskogee. I staid on father's ranch after I got old enough, about 21 miles from Muskogee in the Cherokee Nation.

Commissioner Breckinridge:

    The applicant applies for the enrollment of himself, his wife and two children. He states that he is a Cherokee, and that his wife is a white woman. He is identified upon the roll of 1896 as a native Cherokee but not upon the roll of 1880; nor is his father or mother identified on the roll of 1880. He states that he was born in Muskogee, in the Creek Nation, and that after he was old enough to be of use on the farm he lived on his father's farm in the Cherokee Nation until four years ago, since which time he has lived at Checotah where he follows the trade of a blacksmith. He states that he has voted at elections in the Cherokee Nation, and never at any elections in the Creek Nation. He will be listed for enrollment as a Cherokee by blood upon a doubtful card for the further consideration of his case, and reference is made to case D-1041; the same being the case of his father, and also D-1043, the case of a brother. He is shown to have married his wife in 1897, too late under the Cherokee law of December 16, 1895 to entitle her to enrollment. He states that neither was prevuously[sic] married, and that they have lived together since their marriage. The application for her enrollment is rejected. When he presents satisfactory certificates of birth of the two chiildren[sic]Marion B. and Warren E. Zufall, these children will be listed for enrollment as Cherokees by blood upon the doubtful card with their father.

    E. G. Rothenberger, being duly sworn states that as stenographer to the Commission to the Five Civilized Tribes he reported in full all the proceedings and testimony in the above case, and that the foregoing is a full and complete transcript of his stenographic notes in said case.

                                                        E. G. Rothenberger.

Cherokee Intermarried White 1906
Volume VI

Subscribed and sworn to before me this 12th day of February, 1901.
        Signed,   C. R. Breckinridge.
                                                  Commissioner.

    I, the undersigned, do certify as stenographer to the Commission to the Five Civilized Tribes, that the above and foregoing is a true and correct copy of the original transcript.

                                                Ella Mielenz

D. 1088.

                          Department of the Interior.
                 Commission to the Five Civilized Tribes,
                     Muskogee, I.T., January 28, 1902.

    In the matter of the application of Lewis E. Zufall for the enrollment of himself, wife and children as citizens of the Cherokee Nation.

    Upon a review of the testimony had in the matter of the foregoing application the applicant, in answer to a question as to the age of his wife, states that she was twenty-four years old. The enrollment card and the memorandum made when this application was taken show her age to be twenty-seven years. In an affidavit as to the birth of her child, Marion Raymond Zufall, the applicant's wife states that she is twenty-seven years of age. It is apparent that the correct age of the applicant's wife is twenty-seven years.

    It is directed that copies of this statement be filed with the testimony in the above case.

                                                TB Needles
                                                              Commissioner.

Cherokee Intermarried White 1906
Volume VI

Cherokee D-1041.

Department of the Interior,
Commission to the Five Civilized Tribes,
Muskogee, I. T., March 18, 1902.

SUPPLEMENTAL TESTIMONY AND PROCEEDINGS, in the matter of the application of George Zufall for the enrollment of himself, wife and children as Cherokee citizens.

TESTIMONY ON BEHALF OF APPLICANTS.

BY COMMISSIONER: The applicant was notified by registered letter February 27th, 1902, that his application for the enrollment of himself, wife and children as citizens of the Cherokee Nation would be taken up for final consideration by the Commission at its offices in Muskogee, Indian Territory on the 17th day of March, 1902; receipt has been acknowledged of the Commission's letter, and on this the 18th day of March, 1902, applicants appear in person, this case having been continued over from the 17th.

JOSHUA ROSS, being first duly sworn, and being examined, testified as follows:

Appearances:
Applicants in person;
W. W. Hastings, attorney for Cherokee Nation.

BY COMMISSIONER NEEDLES:
Q What is your name? A Joshua Ross.
Q What is your age? A 69 years.
Q What is your post-office? A Muskogee.
Q Please state what you may know about the citizenship of Mr. Zufall? A In 1873 I made out papers asking signers, getting signers to give citizenship to George Zufall and his wife Mrs. Zufall. And I know that they were married October, 1873. And that they have lived together as man and wife ever since. That they had made a place over in Canadian District. George Zufall's business has been here most all the time; he has lived there and has lived here. He is a blacksmith, and has raised a large family of children I know. I know that she is a Cherokee Indian, and that he was married according to Cherokee law?
Q How do you know he was married according to Cherokee law?
A Because he got the signers there and they presented it to the clerk.
Q Did you ever see the license? A No sir, I never saw the license.
Q What do you know about her citizenship? A Well I know she was a Cherokee Indian.
Q You don't know that she was ever admitted by any act of council?
A No I don't know anything about that; I got acquainted with her here in 1872 or '3, as a Cherokee Indian.

Cherokee Intermarried White 1906
Volume VI

Q Been recognized to your knowledge as a Cherokee citizen since that time? A Yes sir.
BY MR. HASTINGS:
Q Where was she living when you first knew her? A Living here in Muskogee, Indian Territory but her relatives were living near Fort Gibson.
Q That is about all you know about it? A Yes sir, that's all I know.

ANNIE ELLIOTT BEING FIRST DULY SWORN AND BEING EXAMINED TESTIFIED AS FOLLOWS:
BY COMMISSIONER NEEDLES:
Q What is your name? A Annie Elliott.
Q What is your age? A 53.
Q Where do you live? A In Muskogee.
Q You know anything about her citizenship? A She was always considered as a citizen of the Cherokee Nation, a Cherokee.
Q Are you a citizen of the Cherokee Nation yourself? A Yes sir.
Q You know anything about her marriage to Mr. Zufall? A I was present at her marriage.
Q When was that? A In 1873.
Q You know whether they had a license from the Cherokee authorities?
A Why, no sir, I know the Judge of the Canadian District married them; Judge Taylor.
Q They been living together continuously since that time as man and wife? A Yes sir.
Q You know whether Mrs. Zufall was ever admitted as a Cherokee citizen by the Cherokee authorities? A She never was out to be admitted. She has always been here; considered a Cherokee.
Q You know whether her name is on the 1880 roll or not? A I don't know, it ought to be, but she says they couldn't find it.
Q What was her maiden name? A Cobb.
BY MR. HASTINGS:
Q Where did you first know her Mrs. Elliott? A I knew her out in Canadian about Brushy Mountain, and Checotah.
Q How long before her marriage was that? A I knew her about a year before she was married; I knew the family.
Q You didn't have any personal knowledge of her before that time? A No sir.
Q Were you present at her marriage and know the Judge of the district married her?
A Yes sir.
Q Been living in Muskogee since that time? A Oh I think she lived in the Cherokee Nation a while.
Q Most of the time in Muskogee? A Yes sir; they have always had a place.
Q What is her father's name? A Cobb.
Q You know his first name? A No sir.
Q You know her mother's name? A No sir.

SIM GARLAND, being first duly sworn, and being examined, testified as follows:
BY COMMISSIONER NEEDLES:
Q What is your name? A Sim Garland.

Cherokee Intermarried White 1906
Volume VI

Q What is your age? A 48.
Q What is your post office address? A Muskogee.
Q What is your nationality? A Choctaw.
Q Do you know Maggie Zufall? A I have known her ever since 1870 I think.
Q You know anything about her Cherokee citizenship? A Well she was always considered a Cherokee ever since I knew her, she has always lived there.
Q You know her husband, George Zufall? A Yes sir, I know him.
Q You know anything about his marriage? A Yes sir.
Q What do you know? A I was at Brushy Mountain when they were married; a few minutes after that Judge Taylor told me that George Zufall handed him a license with a ten dollar bill in it.
Q Well have they lived together since that as man and wife? A Yes sir, to the best of my knowledge.
Q You know her father and mother? A No sir, I don't know them.
Q Don't know how much Cherokee blood she has? A No sir.
BY MR. HASTINGS:
Q How do you happen to remember the circumstances of the Judge saying that Mr. Zufall handed him a license with a ten dollar bill in it? A Never thought anything more about it, until Mr. Zufall asked me to come up here the other day, and I was thinking what the circumstances were.
Q You never saw the license? A No sir.
Q Nor the ten dollar bill either? A No sir, only he was talking about it, and he said he would like for a few more white men to get married.
Q Did you know the judge who issued the license? A No sir.
Q Didn't know anything about that? A No sir.
Q The clerk of the district was not there was he? A No, not that I know of.
Q You're acquaintance with this woman is dated back as far as 1870? A Yes sir.
Q You didn't know her parents? A No sir.

GEORGE ZUFALL- being first duly sworn and being examined testified as follows:
BY COMMISSIONER NEEDLES:
Q What is your name? A My name is George Zufall.
Q What is your age? A My age is 62.
Q What is your post-office? A Muskogee.
Q Are you the husband of Maggie Zufall? A Yes sir.
Q You were married to her according to the laws of the Cherokee Nation? A Yes sir.
Q Did you get out a regular marriage license? A Went down to the office and got a certificate from the clerk of the court, handed it to Mr. Judge Taylor, and got married on Brushy Mountain under Cherokee law in the Cherokee Nation. I didn't get no marriage license, why I don't know, the time I got marriage[sic] I guess I suppose they didn't get any, I don't know, our marriage license has never been on record.
Q You haven't got the license? A No sir.
Q You are a white man? A Yes sir.
Q Have you lived with your wife continuously since that time? A Yes sir.
Q You say you paid for the license? A Down to the Falls, yes sir.

Cherokee Intermarried White 1906
Volume VI

Q How much did you pay? A Two dollars; that was to the clerk of the court down at Webbers Falls.
Q Cherokee court? A Yes sir.
Q Did you get out a petition? A I got a petition, Mr. Ross there did.
Q You got out a petition? A Yes sir, had nine signers on it; Mr. Ross was one of the first ones that ever signed it.
Q You never got the license back? A No sir.
Q License didn't cost you but two dollars? A That was a certificate; I took the oath of allegiance down there and paid the clerk two dollars; that's all I paid.
Q Was that the price of a marriage license at that time; for a white man marrying a Cherokee woman, only two dollars? A I couldn't tell you about that.
Q Who did you pay the two dollars to? A To the clerk of the court, his name is McCorkle; he is living yet.
Q Who married you? A Judge Taylor.
Q You know whether your wife ever applied to the Cherokee authorities to be admitted as a Cherokee citizen or not? A I don't know; we never went out of the Nation. I know under the compact law we could live in the Creek Nation as well as the Cherokee Nation, and we have had more property in the Cherokee Nation the last twenty years than we have got in the Creek Nation.
Q Your wife was never admitted by the Cherokee authorities, that you know of? A Not that I know of. I don't know as it is necessary to be re-admitted when we never lived out of the Nation.

MAGGIE ZUFALL, being first duly sworn and being examined testified as follows:
BY COMMISSIONER NEEDLES:
Q Your name is Maggie Zufall? A Yes sir.
Q You are the applicant here? A Yes sir.

BY MR. HASTINGS:
Q Your maiden name was Cobb? A Yes sir.
Q Where were you born? A Georgia.
Q When did you come to this coujtry[sic]? A I don't know, I was 3 years old when we come here.
Q You are about 48 now? A Yes sir.
Q You came to the country then before the war? A Yes a long time I reckon.
Q You stay here during the war? A Yes. We were over in Gibson all during the war.
Q Did you live in the Cherokee Nation up until the time you were married? A Yes sir.
Q Your father's name was Jack Cobb? A Yes sir.
Q What was your mother's name? A Lucy Vickory.
Q Where did your father and mother die? A Over there about a half a mile from Fort Gibson.
Q Where were you living at the time you married Zufall? A I was living with my aunt down on the Arkansas river[sic], at Frozen Rock.
Q In Canadian District? A Yes sir.

Cherokee Intermarried White 1906
Volume VI

Q Since that time you have either lived in Muskogee or Canadian District, one or the two? A Yes sir.
Q Most of the time in Muskogee? A Yes sir.

BY COMMISSIONER NEEDLES:
Q You know the reason your name is not on the 1880 roll? A No, I really don't. We might have been not in the Nation, or maybe was sick or something, I don't know how it was.

GEORGE W. ELLIOTT, being first duly sworn and being examined testified as follows:
BY COMMISSIONER NEEDLES:
Q What is your name? A George W. Elliott.
Q What is your age? A 66.
Q What is your post office address? A Muskogee.
Q What nationality are you? A I was born in Baltimore, Maryland.
Q You are not an Indian? A No sir.
Q Do you know Maggie Zufall? A Yes sir.
Q How long have you know her? A Since 1872 anyhow, I don't know whether it was before that or not.
Q You know anything about her marriage to George Zufall? A Yes sir. I was at the wedding, and stayed all night at their house.
Q You know whether he had a Cherokee license or not? A No sir, I do not.
Q You know anything about the citizenship of Mrs. Zufall? A No sir.

MRS. MAGGIE ZUFALL, -recalled and being examined testified as follows:
BY COMMISSIONER NEEDLES:
Q Any questions you would like to ask him? A No sir, not that I know of.
Q Any other witnesses? A No, that is all we have.
Q Are you willing to submit your case to the Commission now on the testimony that has already been given? A I don't know; if I am doubtful of course I can prove up that I am an Indian, if that is what you want to know. Indian by blood and I know my mother was an Indian.
Q Did you apply in 1896 to be enrolled as a citizen; did you apply to the Commission in 1896 under the law of June 10? A I was[sic] I was enrolled wasn't I? No, I didn't apply to the Dawes Commission.
Q Fact is you have never applied to any Commission to be enrolled as a Cherokee citizen before your present application? A No sir.
Q Well if you are willing to submit the case on the testimony given the case will be ordered closed? A Well I guess that is all right, I am willing to- I can prove I am an Indian; I have relations and aunts who have got theirs.
Q You applied for your daughter Pearl when you applied for yourself[sic] A Yes sir.
Q She was 21 years of age? A Yes sir.
Q Why didn't she apply for herself? A She was not here, she was off a school and they told me it would be all right as she was under my care; it would be all right.
Q She is still unmarried? A Yes sir.

Cherokee Intermarried White 1906
Volume VI

BY COMMISSIONER NEEDLES:
Well we will give you until the 24th of this month,- that is six days,- to bring witnesses to prove your Indian citizenship?
A Yes sir, I can get them any day I want.

BY COMMISSIONER NEEDLES: Case continued until the 24th of the present month.

I, M. D. Green, do hereby certify that as stenographer to the Commission to the Five Civilized Tribes I correctly recorded the testimony and proceedings in this case and that the foregoing is a true and complete transcript of my stenographic notes thereof.

MD Green

◇◇◇◇◇

Supl.-C.D.#1041.

Department of the Interior,
Commission to the Five Civilized Tribes,
Muskogee, I. T., March 18, 1902.

SUPPLEMENTAL TESTIMONY in the matter of the enrollment of GEORGE ZUFALL, ET AL., as citizens of the Cherokee Nation, introduced on part of applicants:

The applicant was notified by regustered[sic] letter February 27, 1902, that his application for the enrollment of himself, wife and children as citizens of the Cherokee Nation would be taken up for final consideration by the Commission at its offices in Muskogee, Indian Territory, on the 17th day of March, 1902, and on said date the applicants appeared and by agreement the case was continued until the 18th day of March, 1902. The same being this day, the 18th day of March, 1902, called the applicant appears in person.

Mr. W. W. Hastings, Cherokee Representative, present.

W. S. AGNEW, being duly sworn, testified as follows on part of the applicants:

BY THE COMMISSION:

Q What is your name? A W. S. Agnes.
Q How old are you? A 59.
Q Post office address? A Muskogee.
Q Are you acquainted with the applicant in this case, George Zufall?

Cherokee Intermarried White 1906
Volume VI

A You mean the boy?
Q No, George Zufall, Sr.? A The old man?
Q Yes. A Yes, sir.
Q Are you acquainted with his wife, Margaret? A Yes, sir.
Q How long have you known her? A I knowed[sic] the family ever since '61, when they was small children, but I don't know the names apart; I have been well acquainted with them since '67.
Q Where were they living then? A In '67?
Q Yes? A In Fort Gibson.
Q How long did she continue to reside there after that? A Well, she was there a part of the time in Canadian District with an Aunt up to about the time she was grown.
Q And then where did she go? A She married Mr. Zufall and they located here in Muskogee.
Q Had she always been recognized as a Cherokee citizen? A Yes, sir.
Q Did you ever hear her right to enrollment disputed? A No, sir, never nothing more than place of residence, or something that way.
Q Do you know about when they came to the the[sic] Creek Nation to live, about what year it was? A It must have been somewhere about '75.
Q And they continued to reside here continuously up until the present time and are living here now? A Yes, they have made this their home; they own a ranch and property down in the Cherokee Nation.
Q They own property in the Cherokee Nation? A Yes, sir, he has held a ranch there and good deal of property ever since they were married.
Q They were living here when the roll of 1880 was made? A Yes, sir.
Q Do you think that is the reason their names do not appear upon that roll[sic]
A Yes, sir, that is the only reason.
Q Have they ever made their home outside of the Territory since you have known them?
A No, sir.

MARY E. AGNEW, being duly sworn, testified as follows on part of applicant:
COMMISSION:

Q What is your name? A Mary E. Agnew.
Q How old are you, Mrs. Agnew? A I will be 53 in May.
Q You are acquainted with Maggie Zufall, the wife of George Zufall? A Yes, sir.
Q How long have you know her? A Ever since she was an infant.
Q Are you related to her? A She is my sister.
Q Same father and mother? A Yes, sir.
Q Do you know whether or not she has always made her home in the Indian Territory?
A Yes, sir.
Q She has never lived outside of the Indian Territory? A No, sir.
Q Does your name appear upon the roll of 1880? A Yes, sir.
Q You were then living in the Cherokee Nation? A Yes, sir.
Q Where was your sister living at that time? A In Muskogee.
Q In the Creek Nation? A Yes, sir.
Q Did you ever hear her right to enrollment disputed until this time? A No, sir.

Cherokee Intermarried White 1906
Volume VI

Q She has always been recognized as a citizen? A Yes, sir.

Commission: The applicant and the representative of the Cherokee Nation present submit the case. The same is now deemed completed and will be reported to the Commission for final decision based upon the evidence now of record.

---oooOOOooo---

I, J. O. Rosson, do hereby certify that as stenographer to the Commission to the Five Civilized Tribes that I correctly recorded the testimony and proceedings had this day in the above application, and that the foregoing is a true and complete transcript of my stenographic notes thereof.

JO Rosson

Supl.-C.D.#1088.

Department of the Interior.
Commission to the Five Civilized Tribes,
Muskogee, I. T., March 19, 1902.

SUPPLEMENTAL in the matter of the enrollment of LEWIS E. ZUFALL, ET AL., as citizens of the Cherokee Nation:

The applicant was notified by registered letter February 28, 1902, that his application for the enrollment of himself as a citizen of the Cherokee Nation would be taken up for final consideration by the Commission at its offices in Muskogee, Indian Territory, on the 19th day of March, 1902. The applicant has this day, been called and fails to respond either in person or by attorney, and it is directed that a copy of the testimony had on the 18th day of March, 1902, in the matter of the application of the applicant's mother, Maggie Zufall, Cherokee case No. 1041, be filed with and made a part of the record in this case. This case is now deemed completed and will be reported to the Commission for final decision based upon the evidence now of record.

---oooOOOooo---

I, J. O. Rosson, do hereby certify upon my official oath as stenographer to the Commission to the Five Civilized Tribes that I correctly recorded the testimony and proceedings this day had in the above application, and that the foregoing is a true and complete transcript of my stenographic notes thereof.

JO Rosson

R.

Cherokee Intermarried White 1906
Volume VI

DEPARTMENT OF THE INTERIOR.
Commission to the Five Civilized Tribes.
Muskogee, Indian Territory, June 27th, 1902.

In the matter of the application of George Zufall, et. al., for enrollment as citizens of the Cherokee nation[sic].

Supplemental to D 1041.

J. L. McCarkle[sic], being duly sworn, testified as follows:
Examination by the Commission.

Q. What is your name? A. J. L. McCarkle.
Q. What is your post office address? A. Webbers Falls.
Q. Have you ever held any official position in the Cherokee nation[sic]?
A. Yes, sir.
Q. What.[sic] A. Clerk of the district and circuit courts.
Q. During what year were you clerk of Canadian district? A. I was clerk of Canadian district from the year 1869 to 1874.
Q During the time that you were acting as clerk of Canadian district do you remember whether or not you ever issued a license to one George Zufall authorizing him to marry Maggie Cobb? A. I do.
Q. Did he comply with the Cherokee law in procuring that marriage license? A. Fully.
Q. Do you know whether or not he was married in accordance with the license that you issued? A. I don't know.
Q. How long had you known Mr/[sic] Zufall prior to the issuing of the license? A. I had never known him before.
Q. Have you known him since that? A. Eever[sic] since.
Q. Has he always been recognized as a citizen by intermarriage since that time?
A. Yes, sir.
Q. You didn't see the ceremony of marriage performed? A. No, sir.
Q. You are positive that the license was issued to him while you were acting--while you were clerk of that district? A. Yes, sir; issued to him in September, 1873. Let me corroborate it. In running over some of my old papers that I found in my old trunk that I had stored away I found his petition. How it happened to be retained in my possession I don't know, but I turned the papers over to my successor. Some how or other that remained.
Q. You recognized this as the original petition Mr. Zufall presented when he applied for the license? A. Yes, I do. Then here is something that I---There was my commission, one dated 1869 and here is one dated 1871, from another judge that was elected.

The witness exhibits a commission showing that on the 15th day of November, 1869, he was appointed clerk of the district court of Canadian district, Cherokee nation, by J. M. Hilderbrand, Judge of the district court of Canadian district.
He also exhibits a commission showing that on the 24th day of November, 1871, he was again appointed district clerk in and for Canadian district, Cherokee

Cherokee Intermarried White 1906
Volume VI

nation by Judge Woodall, judge of the district court of Canadian district, Cherokee nation. These documents are returned to the witness.

Jesse O. Carr, being first duly sworn, states that as stenographer to the Commission to the Five Civilized Tribes he correctly reported the testimony and proceedings in this case and that the foregoing is a true and correct transcript of his stenographic notes thereof.

Jesse O. Carr

Subscribed and sworn to before me this 9 day of July, 1902.

(Seal)   P.G. Reuter
Notary Public.

◇◇◇◇◇

Supp'l to D 1041

Department of the Interior,
Commission to the Five Civilized Tribes,
Muskogee, I. T., August 28, 1902.

In the matter of the application of George Zufall, for the enrollment of himself, and his wife Maggie, and his children, Pearl E., Oscar O., Maggie, Benjamin H., Grace A., and Herbert Zufall, as citizens by blood of the Cherokee Nation.

PEARL E. ZUFALL, being duly sworn and examined by the Commission, testified as follows:

Q What is your name ?   A   Pearl Elizabeth Zufall.
Q What is your age ?   A   Twenty four.
Q What is your post office address ?   A   Muskogee, Indian Territory.
Q What district do you live in ?   A   Muskogee, in the Creek Nation.
Q What district in the Cherokee Nation do you call your home ?   A   Canadian.
Q Do you wish to make application for enrollment as a citizen of the Cherokee Nation ? A Yes sir.
Q Do you wish to include anyone else in your application ?   A   No sir.
Q Give me the name of your father ?   A   George Zufall.
Q Is he living or dead ?   A   Living.
Q Is he a Cherokee by blood ?   A   No sir.
Q Give me the name of your mother ?   A   Maggie Zufall.
Q Is she living or dead ?   A   She is living.
Q Is she a Cherokee by blood ?   A   Yes sir.
Q Have you lived all your life in the Cherokee Nation ?   A   No sir, not all my life.

Cherokee Intermarried White 1906
Volume VI

Q How long have you been living in the Creek Nation ?   A   All my life, except about-I don't know- about three years I was in the Cherokee Nation, Canadian District. I have lived partly in the Creek Nation and partly in the Cherokee Nation.
Q You have never lived anywhere except in the Creek Nation and in the Cherokee Nation ? A   No sir.
Q Are you at this time living in Muskogee, Creek Nation ?   A   Yes sir.
Q Does you name appear upon the 1880 authenticated roll of Cherokee citizens ?
A I don't think it is on the '80 roll.
Q Were you admitted by the Cherokee National Council after that date ?
A Well I don't know.

--The 1880 authenticated roll of citizens of the Cherokee Nation examined, and applicant is not identified thereon;
--The 1896 census roll of citizens of the Cherokee Nation examined, and the applicant is identified thereon at page 83, # 2315, Canadian District, as Pearl Zufall, native Cherokee.

The Commission: This testimony will be filed with and made supplemental to the record in the matter of the application for the enrollment of George Zufall, et al, Cherokee D 1041.

E. C. Bagwell, on oath states that, as stenographer to the Commission to the Five Civilized Tribes, he correctly recorded the testimony and proceedings had in the above entitled cause, and that the foregoing is an accurate transcript of his stenographic notes thereof.

E.C.Bagwell

Subscribed and sworn to before me this September 5, 1902.

BC Jones
Notary Public.

Cherokee Intermarried White 1906
Volume VI

Cher D 1041

Department of the Interior,
Commission to the Five Civilized Tribes,
Muskogee, I. T., October 2, 1902.

In the matter of the application of GEORGE ZUFALL, for the enrollment of himself as a citizen by intermarriage, and his wife MAGGIE, and his children, PEARL E., OSCAR O., MAGGIE, BENJAMIN H., GRACE A. and HERBERT ZUFALL, as citizens by blood, of the Cherokee Nation.

GEORGE ZUFALL, called as a witness, being duly sworn and examined by the Commission, testified as follows:

Q What is your name ?   A   George Zufall.
Q What is your age ?   A   Sixty three.
Q You post office ?   A   Muskogee.
Q Are you the same George Zufall who made application to this Commission for the enrollment of yourself as an intermarried citizen of the Cherokee Nation, and for your wife and children as citizens by blood, on January 15, 1901 ?   A   My wife made the application, I think.
Q You are the same George Zufall ?   A   Yes sir.
Q What is your wife's name ?   A   Margaret.
Q Do you call her Maggie ?   A   Yes sir.
Q Do you want her enrolled as Maggie or Margaret ?   A   It don't make any difference. Just make it Maggie.
Q When were you and your wife Maggie married, Mr. Zufall ?   A   We were married in 1873, in October.
Q Were you ever married before you married your wife Maggie ?   A   No sir.
Q Was she ever married prior to her marriage to you ?   A   No sir.
Q You were her first husband and she was your first wife ?   A   Yes sir.
Q Have you and she lived together continuously from the time of your marriage, as husband and wife, up to the present time ?   A   All except three months I have been in Europe.
Q Were you living together as husband and wife on September 1, 1902 ?
A Yes sir.
Q How long have you lived in the Cherokee Nation ?
A Been living here in Muskogee since 1871.
Q You have lived in the Indian Territory all the time, then, since 1880 ?
A Yes sir, never lived out.
Q Has your wife lived in the Indian Territory all the time since 1880 ?   A   Yes sir.
Q Been living in the Cherokee Nation ?   A   She went in the Cherokee Nation every summer and stayed there four or five months, but my business was here in Muskogee.\
Q Are you children, Pearl E., Oscar O., Maggie, Benjamin H., Grace A. and Herbert, all living at this time ?   A   Yes sir.

Cherokee Intermarried White 1906
Volume VI

Q And have they always lived in the Indian Territory since they were born ?
A Yes sir.
Q Never lived outside the Indian Territory ? A   No sir. Only the oldest girl I took to the old country with me in the summer.

E. C. Bagwell, on oath states that, as stenographer to the Commission to the Five Civilized Tribes, he correctly recorded the testimony and proceedings had in the above entitled cause, and that the foregoing is an accurate transcript of his stenographic notes thereof.

EC Bagwell

Subscribed and sworn to before me this October 16, 1901.

BC Jones
Notary Public.

◇◇◇◇◇

Cherokee D 1041.1043.1088.

DEPARTMENT OF THE INTERIOR,

COMMISSION TO THE FIVE CIVILIZED TRIBES.

In the matter of the application of Maggie Zufall, et al., for enrollment as citizens of the Cherokee Nation, consolidating the applications of:

Maggie Zufall, et al	Cherokee Doubtful No. 1041
George Zufall, Jr.,	" " " 1043
Lewis E. Zufall, et al.,	" " " 1088

D E C I S I O N.

The record in these cases shows that on January 15, 1901, Maggie Zufall appeared before the Commission at Muskogee, Indian Territory, and made application for the enrollment of herself and her children, Pearl E., Oscar O, Maggie, Benjamin H., Grace A. and Herbert Zufall, as citizens by blood, and for the enrollment of her husband, George Zufall, as a citizen by intermarriage of the Cherokee Nation. Further proceedings in the matter of said application were had at Muskogee, Indian Territory, on March 18, 1902, June 27, 1902, August 28, 1902, and October 2, 1902.

On January 16, 1901, George Zufall, Jr., appeared before the Commission at Muskogee, Indian Territory, and made application for the enrollment of himself as a citizen by blood of the Cherokee Nation.

Cherokee Intermarried White 1906
Volume VI

On February 11, 1901, Lewis E. Zufall appeared before the Commission at Muskogee, Indian Territory, and made application for the enrollment of himself and his minor children, Marion R. and Warren E. Zufall, as citizens by blood of the Cherokee Nation. The application also included his wife, but as she is differently classified she is not embraced in this decision.

The evidence shows that Maggie Zufall, nee Cobb, a Cherokee citizen by blood, was born in Georgia, and was brought to the Cherokee Nation by her parents about the year 1858, being at that time about three years old. It is further shown that George Zufall, a white man, married his said wife Maggie, in 1873, under a Cherokee marriage license and in accordance with the laws of the Cherokee Nation. All of the applicants herein claim citizenship by blood through Maggie Zufall, nee Cobb, with the exception of George Zufall, the husband of said Maggie Zufall, his rights being based upon said marriage.

It is further shown that Lewis E. Zufall was lawfully married in 1897, to one Lena J. Jones, and as a result of that marriage the minor children, Marion R. and Warren E. Zufall, were born. Subsequent to the application of said Lewis E. Zufall, Eva Zufall was born.

Maggie Zufall, nee Cobb, Pearl E. Zufall, George Zufall, Jr., and Lewis E. Zufall are identified on the Cherokee rolls of 1883, 1886, 1890, 1894 and 1896. Oscar O. Zufall, Maggie Zufall and Benjamin H. Zufall are identified on the Cherokee rolls of 1886, 1890, 1894 and 1896. Grace A. Zufall is identified on the Cherokee rolls of 1890, 1894 and 1896. Herbert Zufall is identified on the Cherokee rolls of 1894 and 1896. George Zufall is identified on the Cherokees rolls of 1890 and 1896, as an intermarried white person. Marion R. Zufall and Eva Zufall are duly identified by birth affidavits made a part of the record herein.

The evidence further shows that Maggie Zufall has been a continuous resident in the Indian Territory since her removal thereto, as hereinbefore shown. Her husband, George Zufall, has resided in the Indian Territory with his said wife, Maggie Zufall, continuously since his marriage to her, up to and including September 1, 1902. The other applicants have resided in said Territory all their lives. Warren E. Zufall is shown to have died February 13, 1902, as evidenced by death affidavit made a part of the record herein. It is presumed from the enrollment by the Cherokee Nation of Maggie Zufall on the various rolls of said nation, as hereinbefore shown, and the further fact that her sister Mary E. Agnew is identified on the 1880 Cherokee roll as a citizen by blood of the Cherokee Nation, that the said Maggie Zufall and her family were duly and lawfully recognized or admitted to citizenship by the tribal authorities of the Cherokee Nation subsequent to their removal to the Cherokee Nation in 1858.

It is, therefore, the opinion of this Commission that the application for the enrollment of Maggie Zufall, Pearl E. Zufall, Oscar O. Zufall, Maggie Zufall, Benjamin H. Zufall, Grace A. Zufall, Herbert Zufall, George Zufall, Jr., Lewis E. Zufall, Marion R. Zufall and Eva Zufall as citizens by blood, and George Zufall as a citizen by intermarriage of the Cherokee Nation, should be granted, in accordance with the provisions of section twenty-one of the Act of Congress approved June 28, 1898 (30 Stats., 495), and it is so ordered.

Cherokee Intermarried White 1906
Volume VI

It is further ordered by this Commission that the application for the enrollment of Warren E. Zufall as a citizen by blood of the Cherokee Nation be, and the same is, hereby dismissed.

COMMISSION TO THE FIVE CIVILIZED TRIBES.

Tams Bixby
~~Acting~~ Chairman.

TB Needles
Commissioner.

C. R. Breckinridge
Commissioner.

Dated at Muskogee, Indian Territory, this MAR -2 1903

Cherokee-10194.

DEPARTMENT OF THE INTERIOR,
COMMISSIONER TO THE FIVE CIVILIZED TRIBES.
Muskogee, Indian Territory, January 2, 1907.

In the matter of making proof of the marriage of George Zufall to his Cherokee wife, prior to November 1, 1875.

Margaret Zufall, being first duly sworn by John E. Tidwell, a Notary Public, testified as follows:

COMMISSIONER:

Q. What is your name? A. Margaret Zufall.
Q. How old are you? A. 50 years old.
Q. What is your post office address? A. Muskogee, I.T.
Q. In whose behalf are you appearing here today? A. George Zufall.
Q. Was he a claimant for rights as an intermarried citizen of the Cherokee Nation?
A. Yes sir.
Q. What was the name of his Cherokee spouse through whom he claimed rights?
A. Margaret Cobb.
Q. When were you and George Zufall married? A. In 1873.
Q. What date? A. October 22.

Cherokee Intermarried White 1906
Volume VI

Q. Where were you married? A. At Brushy Mountain.
Q. Were you married under a license from the Cherokee Nation? A. Yes sir.
Q. Have you that license? A. No, we had no license.
Q. What became of the license? A. The Judge turned them in at the Court house at Webbers Falls, Indian Territory and the Court house was burned and all the papers, before it was moved to Tahlequah.
Q. Was George Zufall ever married prior to his marriage to you? A. No sir.
Q. Were you ever married prior to your marriage to George Zufall? A. No sir.
Q. Was he a citizen of the Cherokee Nation at the time of your marriage? A. Yes sir.
Q. Is George Zufall living or dead? A. Dead.
Q. Whan[sic] did he die? A. In 1905.
Q. What date? A. January 23rd/[sic]
Q. Who married you? A. Sam Taylor, the Judge at Canadian.
Q. Have you any other witnesses that you wish to put on? A. No. I could get witnesses, but I don't know of anything else to say.
Q. You say you were married by the Judge, Sam Taylor? A. Yes sir.
Q. Did he issue the license? A. No, the license was issued by W. F. McCarkley, and he is living.
Q. Can you get him here to testify? A. Yes, by putting up for his expenses, I guess. He gave his testimony once before the Dawes Commission. We had him here once.
Q. Where were you living in 1880? A. We were on the farm I think. We lived here in Muskogee and on the farm, and I don't remember whether we were here or on the farm.
Q. You were living in the Indian Territory? A. Yes sir.
Q. Why were you not enrolled on the 1880 Roll? A. I think we were enrolled, for they said we were enrolled. The men that took the census at that time said that we were enrolled, and I don't know why we are not on the roll.
Q. Did you make application to be enrolled in 1880? A. Yes sir, we were enrolled.
Q. In 1880? A. Yes sir.
Q. Were you living in the Cherokee or Creek Nation in 1880? A. Muskogee was our home.
Q. Did you draw money in 1893 -- the Strip Money? A. Yes sir, we drew in every payment.

(Reference is here made to the testimony offered in support of George Zufall for enrollment as a citizen by intermarriage, at Muskogee, Indian Territory on March 18, 1902; August 28, 1902 and October 2, 1902. Also a certified copy of the petition filed by the applicant for Cherokee license.
The applicant's Cherokee wife is identified on the 1896 Census Roll, opposite No. 2312.)

Witness excused.

Cherokee Intermarried White 1906
Volume VI

Eula Jeanes Branson, being duly sworn, states that she correctly reported the proceedings had in the above and foregoing, on the 2nd. day of January, 1907.

Eula Jeanes Branson

Subscribed and sworn to before me this the 3rd day of January 1907.

Walter W. Chappell
Notary Public.

◇◇◇◇◇

Sir

We have the honor to say that Mr. George Zufall of the United States thus asks for License to unite in bonds of Matrimony with Miss Margaret Cobb of the Cherokee Nation.

We know him to be a man of industry and good morals. He will be a good citizen of the Cherokee Nation.

We pray that you may grant his request, and his object attained.

Yours &c[sic]

Sept 5, 1873.   Respectfully

To the Clk Dist Court,   Joshua Ross
   Canadian Dist   I. W. Bertholf
   Cherokee Nation.   J. L. L. Smith
                                      T. R. Monroe
                                      Thomas Brewer
                                      Richard Fields
                                      P N Blackstone
                                      W. B. Rogers

Muskogee, I. T., July 26, 1902.

I, H. M. Vance, as stenographer to the Commission to the Five Civilized Tribes, do hereby certify that the above is a true and correct copy of the original Petition now on file in the office of the Commission.

H.M. Vance

Cherokee Intermarried White 1906
Volume VI

Cherokee-D- 1088

OFFICE DIST JUDGE.
CANADIAN DIST C. N.

TO WHOM IT MAY CONCERN:

Know ye that I, W. S. Agnew, Judge of the District Court of Canadian district Cherokee Nation do by virtue of authority in me vested by law this day unite in the bonds of matrimony Louia Zufall, a citizen of the Cherokee Nation and Lena Zufall (nee) Johns, a citizen of the United States this the 4th day of May A.D. 1887.

W. S. Agnew, Judge.

I, the undersigned stenographer to the Commission to the Five Civilized Tribes do hereby certify that the above and foregoing is a true and correct copy of the original offered in evidence in the matter of the application for the enrollment of Lewis E. Zufall et al. as citizens of the Cherokee Nation.

Muskogee, Indian Territory,
June 5, 1902.

M S Kaufman

E C M

Cherokee 10194.

DEPARTMENT OF THE INTERIOR, C[sic]

COMMISSIONER TO THE FIVE CIVILIZED TRIBES.

In the matter of the application for the enrollment of GEORGE ZUFALL as a citizen by intermarriage of the Cherokee Nation.

D E C I S I O N .

THE RECORDS OF THIS OFFICE SHOW: That on January 15, 1901 application was received by the Commission to the Five Civilized Tribes for the enrollment of George Zufall as a citizen by intermarriage of the Cherokee Nation. Further proceedings in the matter of said application were had at Muskogee, Indian Territory, January 16, 1901, February 11, 1901, January 28, 1902, March 18, 1902, March 19, 1902, June 27, 1902, August 28, 1902, October 2, 1902 and January 2, 1907. The records further show that on March 2, 1903 the Commission to the Five Civilized Tribes rendered its decision

Cherokee Intermarried White 1906
Volume VI

herein granting the said applicant the right to enrollment as a citizen by intermarriage of the Cherokee Nation.

THE EVIDENCE IN THIS CASE SHOWS: That the applicant herein, George Zufall, a white man, was married in accordance with Cherokee law on October 22, 1873 to his wife, Maggie Zufall, nee Cobb, who was at the time of said marriage a recognized citizen by blood of the Cherokee Nation and whose name is included on the approved partial roll of citizens by blood of the Cherokee Nation, opposite No. 27910. If it further shown that from the time of said marriage the said George Zufall and Maggie Zufall resided together as husband and wife and have continuously retained their citizenship in the Cherokee Nation. Said applicant is identified on the Cherokee census roll of 1896 as an intermarried citizen of the Cherokee Nation.

IT IS, THEREFORE, ORDERED AND ADJUDGED: That in accordance with the decision of the Supreme Court of the United States, dated November 5, 1906 in the cases of Daniel Red Bird, et al. vs. the United States, Nos. 125, 126, 127, and 128, the decision rendered by the Commission to the Five Civilized Tribes March 2, 1903, granting, in accordance with the provisions of Section Twenty-one of the Act of Congress approved June 28, 1898 (30 Stats. 495),the application for the enrollment of George Zufall as a citizen by intermarriage of the Cherokee Nation, should be, and the same is, hereby affirmed.

Tams Bixby
Commissioner.

Dated at Muskogee, Indian Territory,
this   FEB 8 1907

◇◇◇◇◇

Department of the Interior.
COMMISSIONER TO THE FIVE CIVILIZED TRIBES.

In the matter of the death of   **George Zufall** a citizen of the   **Cherokee**   Nation, who formerly resided at or near   **Muskogee**, Ind. Ter., and died on the   **about - Jany 23**$^{thd[sic]}$ day of   **January**, 190**65**

AFFIDAVIT OF RELATIVE.

Indian Territory
Western District

    I, **Maggie Zufall**, on oath state that I am **50** years of age and a citizen by **blood**, of the **Cherokee** Nation; that my postoffice address is **Muskogee**, Ind. Ter.; that I am **the widow** of **George Zufall** who was a citizen, by **intermarriage**, of the **Cherokee** Nation and that said **George Zufall** died on the about 23^d day of **January**, **1905**

Cherokee Intermarried White 1906
Volume VI

Maggie Zufall

WITNESSES TO MARK:
{

Subscribed and sworn to before me this **4**th day of **November** , 1907

John E. Tidwell
Notary Public.

AFFIDAVIT OF ACQUAINTANCE.

Indian Territory
Western District }

I, **Laura Ward** , on oath state that I am **21** years of age, and a citizen by **blood** of the **Cherokee** Nation; that my postoffice address is **Muskogee** , Ind. Ter.; that I was personally acquainted with **George Zufall** who was a citizen, by **intermarriage** , of the **Cherokee** Nation; and that said **George Zufall** died on the about **23**^d day of **January** , **1905**

Mrs Laura Ward

WITNESSES TO MARK:
{

Subscribed and sworn to before me this **4**th day of **November** , 1907

John E. Tidwell
Notary Public.

◇◇◇◇◇

Cherokee 10194

Muskogee, Indian Territory, February 8, 1907.

W. W. Hastings,
    Attorney for the Cherokee Nation,
        Muskogee, Indian Territory.

Dear Sir:

    There is enclosed herewith a copy of the decision of the Commissioner to the Five Civilized Tribes, dated February 8, 1907, granting the application for the enrollment of George Zufall as a citizen by intermarriage of the Cherokee Nation.

            Respectfully,

Encl. H-5
JMH
                              Commissioner.

Cherokee Intermarried White 1906
Volume VI

Cherokee 10194

Muskogee, Indian Territory, February 8, 1907.

The Commissioner to the Five Civilized Tribes,
Muskogee, Indian Territory.

Sir:

Receipt is acknowledged of the testimony and of your decision enrolling George Zufall as a citizen by intermarriage of the Cherokee Nation. Time for protesting said decision is waived and I consent that said person may be placed upon the schedule immediately.

Respectfully,
W. W. Hastings
Attorney for Cherokee Nation.

◇◇◇◇◇

Cherokee 10194

Muskogee, Indian Territory, February 8, 1907.

Maggie Zufall,
Muskogee, Indian Territory.

Dear Sir[sic]:

There is enclosed herewith a copy of the decision of the Commissioner to the Five Civilized Tribes, dated February 8, 1907, granting the application for the enrollment, as a citizen by intermarriage of the Cherokee Nation, of your deceased husband, George Zufall.

You will be advised when your name has been placed upon a schedule of citizens of the Cherokee Nation and approved by the Secretary of the Interior.

Respectfully,

Commissioner.

Encl. H-6
JMH

◇◇◇◇◇

Cherokee Intermarried White 1906
Volume VI

Cherokee
I.W. 179.

Muskogee, Indian Territory, April 16, 1907.

Mrs. Margaret Zufall,
Muskogee, Indian Territory.

Dear Madam:

Your marriage license and certificate filed in connection with your application for enrollment as a citizen by intermarriage of the Cherokee Nation is returned to you herewith, copies of the same being retained in the files of this office.

Respectfully,

Encl. W-5
S.W.

Commissioner.

Cher IW 180

◇◇◇◇◇

E.C.M.

DEPARTMENT OF THE INTERIOR,

COMMISSIONER TO THE FIVE CIVILIZED TRIBES.

In the matter of the application for the enrollment of

MARY LAMAR

as a citizen by intermarriage of the Cherokee Nation.

CHEROKEE NO. 44.

◇◇◇◇◇

Cherokee Intermarried White 1906
Volume VI

Department of the Interior,
Commission to the Five Civilized Tribes,
Fairland, I. T., July 9th, 1900.

In the matter of the application of Mary Lamar for the enrollment of herself as an intermarried Cherokee and her children as Cherokees by blood; being sworn and examined by Commissioner Needles she testifies as follows:

Q What is your name? A Mary Lamar.
Q What is your age? A Forty-five.
Q What is your post-office address? A Fairland.
Q Where do you live? A Three miles south of Fairland.
Q How long have you lived there? A Twenty-six or seven years.
Q Where did you live before that? A Chouteau, Delaware District.
Q Are you a Cherokee? A No sir.
Q You are a white woman? A Yes sir.
Q You make application as an intermarried citizen? A Yes sir.
Q What is the name of your father? A Stanberry.
Q Is he a Cherokee citizen? A No sir.
Q Is he a white man? A Yes sir.
Q What is the name of your mother? A Jane Stanberry.
Q Is she living? A No sir.
Q Is her name on any of the rolls of the Cherokee Nation? A No sir.
Q How long have you lived in the Indian Territory? A Since 1871.
Q Have you been outside of the Indian Territory to reside within the last three years? A No sir.
Q Have you ever been enrolled by the Cherokee authorities? A Yes sir.
Q Does your name appear upon the 1880 authenticated roll? A I suppose so.
  Note: 1880 roll examined, Mary Lamar found on page 278, #1501.
Q Does your name appear upon the 1894 Strip Payment roll? A I guess not, I didn't draw any money.
Q Does your name appear upon the 1896 roll? A I think so.
Q You have been recognized by the Cherokee authorities as a citizen by marriage? A Yes sir I drew one payment.
Q Are you married now? A No sir. My husband is dead.
Q How long has he been dead? A Three years in September.
Q Under what law were you married? A Cherokee law.
Q Have you your marriage license or certificate? A No sir.
Q Have you any evidence of your marriage? A None here.
Q Where were you living at the time? A Five miles south of Chouteau Station.
Q What is your husband's name? A Frank Lamar.
Q Is his name on the authenticated roll of the Cherokee Nation? A Yes sir.
Q On the roll of 1894? A Yes sir.
Q On the roll of 1896? A Yes sir.
Q What degree of Cherokee blood did he have? A One-eighth I guess.
Q To what district did he belong? A Delaware.

Cherokee Intermarried White 1906
Volume VI

Q Did you live with your husband until he died? A Yes sir.
Q You were never separated? A No sir.
Q Have you any children under twenty-one years of age for whom you desire to make application? A Yes sir, I have seven.
Q What do you claim these children to be? A I suppose they are about one-sixteenth.
Q What was your husband? A He claimed to be one-eighth.
Q What are the names and ages of the children? A Mabel Lamar, seventeen years old. Found on page 493, #1762, Delaware District. Jessie Lamar, fifteen years old. Found on page 493, #1763, Delaware District; on 1896 roll as Jesse. Lucius, thirteen years old. Found on page 493, #1764, Delaware District. Maud, eleven years old. Found on page 493, #1765, Delaware District. Nettie, eight years old. Found on page 493, #1766, Delaware District. Mildred, six years old. Found on page 493, #1767, Delaware District. Frankie, a girl, three years old. All but last on 1896 roll.

Com'r Needles: The name of Mary Lamar being found on the 1880 authenticated roll of the citizens of the Cherokee Nation, page 278, #1501, and that of her children, Mabel, Jessie, Lucius, Maud, Nettie and Mildred, being found upon the rolls of 1894 and 1896, and applicant, being full identified as the same person enrolled as above, she is hereby enrolled by this Commission, together with her children.

M.D. Green, being first duly sworn, states that as stenographer to the Commission to the Five Civilized Tribes he reported the foregoing case, and that the above and foregoing is a full, true and complete transcript of his stenographic notes in said case.

MD Green

Subscribed and sworn to before me this 9 day of July 1900.

TB Needles
Commissioner.

POOR ORIGINAL —
BEST AVAILABLE COPY

Cherokee Intermarried White 1906
Volume VI

R.

DEPARTMENT OF THE INTERIOR.
Commission to the Five Civilized Tribes.
Muskogee, Indian Territory, October 4th, 1902.

In the matter of the application of Mary Lamar for the enrollment of herself as a citizen by intermarriage of the Cherokee Nation and for the enrollment of her children, Mabel, Jessie, Lucius, Maud, Nettie, Mildred and Frankie Lamar, as citizens by blood of the Cherokee Nation.

Supplemental to #44.

Appearances:
Henry Kiefer for Applicant.
J. C. Starr for Cherokee Nation.

HENRY KIEFER, being duly sworn, testified as follows:--
Examination by the Commission.
Q. What is your name? A. Henry Kiefer.
Q. Age, Mr. Kiefer? A. 49.
Q. What is your post office? A. Fairland.
Q. Are you acquainted with Mary Lamar, who is an applicant before this Commission for enrollment as an intermarried citizen? A. Yes, sir.
Q. How long have you known Mary Lamar? A. 17 years.
Q. Is she a citizen by blood of[sic] white woman? A. She is a white woman.
Q. What is her husband's name? A. Frank Lamar.
Q. Is he living or dead? A. He is dead.
Q. Was Frank Lamar a citizen by blood of the Cherokee Nation? A. Citizen by blood.
Q. Do you know about when Frank Lamar and Mary Lamar were married?
A. I don't know exactly the time when they was married.
Q. Were they living together as husband and wife when you first knew them?
A. Yes, sir.
Q. How long has Frank Lamar been dead? A. He has been dead now about four years, I guess.
Q. Did Mary Lamar and Frank Lamar live together from the time you knew them up to the time of his death? A. Yes, sir.
Q. They never were separated during that time? A. No, sir.
Q. Has she remarried since his death? A. No, sir.
Q. Was she still single and a widow on the first of September, 1902? A. Yes, sir.
Q. How long has Mary Lamar lived in the Cherokee Nation?
A. She has lived here ever since I knowed[sic] her.

Cherokee Intermarried White 1906
Volume VI

Q. Has she live here for the last 17 years all the time?
A. Yes, sir.
Q. Do you know these children? A. Yes, sir; I know the children; every one of them. I am their uncle.
Q. Is Mabel, Jessie, Lucius, Maud, Nettie, Mildred and Frankie, Mary Lamar's children by her husband Frank Lamar? A. Yes, sir.
Q. Are all these children living now? A Yes, sir; all living.
Q. Have they lived in the Cherokee Nation all the time since their berth[sic]?
A. Yes, sir; right there on the farm.

Jesse O. Carr, being first duly sworn, states that as stenographer to the Commission to the Five Civilized Tribes he reported the above entitled case and that the foregoing is a true and complete transcript of his stenographic notes thereof.

Jesse O. Carr

Subscribed and sworn to before me this 29th day of October, 1902.

BC Jones
Notary Public.

◇◇◇◇◇

Cher
Supp'l to # 44

Department of the Interior,
Commission to the Five Civilized Tribes,
Muskogee, I. T., October 24, 1902.

In the matter of the application of MARY LAMAR, for the enrollment of herself as a citizen by intermarriage, and her children MABEL, JESSIE, LUCIUS, MAUD, NETTIE, MILDRED and FRANKIE LAMAR, as citizens by blood, of the Cherokee Nation.

MARY LAMAR, being duly sworn and examined by the Commission, testified as follows:

Q What is your name ? A Mary Lamar.
Q How old are you ? A Forty seven.
Q What is your post office address ? A Fairland.
Q Are you a white woman ? A Yes sir.
Q Is your name on the roll of 1880 as an adopted white citizen ? A Yes sir.
Q What was the name of your husband in 1880 ? A Franklin Lamar.
Q Is he the husband through whom you are claiming your citizenship at this time ?
A Yes sir.
Q When did he die ? A Its[sic] been five years.

Cherokee Intermarried White 1906
Volume VI

Q Did you live with your husband Franklin Lamar from 1880 up till he died five years ago ? A Yes sir.
Q Never were separated ? A No sir.
Q And did you make your home in the Cherokee Nation during that time ? A Yes sir.
Q Have you been living in the Cherokee Nation since the death of your husband ? A Yes sir.
Q Have you married again ? A No sir.
Q How many children have you ? A I have got eight.
Q What is the oldest one's name ? A Jennie.
Q She is married ? A Yes sir.
Q She enrolled herself ? A Yes sir.
Q You have got seven children living at home with you ? A Yes sir.
Q And have they lived in the Cherokee Nation all their lives ?
A Yes sir, all their lives.

E. C. Bagwell, on oath states that, as stenographer to the Commission to the Five Civilized Tribes, he correctly recorded the testimony and proceedings had in the above entitled cause, and that the foregoing is an accurate transcript of his stenographic notes thereof.

EC Bagwell

Subscribed and sworn to before me this December 12, 1902.

BC Jones
Notary Public.

F.R. Cherokee 44.

DEPARTMENT OF THE INTERIOR,
COMMISSIONER TO THE FIVE CIVILIZED TRIBES.
Muskogee, I. T., January 31, 1907.

In the matter of the application for the enrollment of Mary Lamar as a citizen by intermarriage of the Cherokee Nation.

Henry Kiefer being first duly sworn by J. R.[sic] Tidwell, a Notary Public for the Western District of Indian Territory, testified as follows:

By the Commissioner:
Q What is your name? A Henry Kiefer.
Q Your age? A Fifty-four years old.
Q What is your postoffice address? A Fairland, I. T.

Cherokee Intermarried White 1906
Volume VI

Q You appear here for the purpose of giving testimony relative to the right of Mary Lamar to enrollment as a citizen by intermarriage of the Cherokee Nation? A Yes sir.
Q In what capacity do you represent Mary Lamar? A Administrator of her estate.
Q When did Mary Lamar die? A She died April 24, 1904.
Q Mary Lamat[sic] was a white woman was she? A Yes sir.
Q Not possessed of any Indian blood? A Not that I know of.
Q She claimed her right to enrollment by virtue of her marriage to a citizen of the Cherokee Nation? A Yes, Frank Lamar.
Q Do you know when she was married to Frank Lamar? A No, I do not.
Q Do you know where she was married to him? A I heard them say.
Q What is your understanding? A I heard she waa[sic] married down here at the Salk Works at Bryant's Chapel.
Q What district? A I think it is Saline district.
Q Have you any documentary evidence of that marriage?
A No, I have not except this here from Mr. Thompson what married her, because all her papers was blowed[sic] away in a cyclone and nothing was left behind to show the evidence.
Q Who performed the marriage ceremony? A J. F. Thompson.
Q Mr. Thompson lives at Tahlequah, does he? A Yes sir.
Q He could come to testify in this case could he not? A I suppose so. That's what I come down here to find out to see if its[sic] necessary for him to come. I expect we could get him.
Q How long have you know Mary Lamar? A I know her I guess for thirty years.
Q Did you know her before she was married? A No sir.
Q Do you know what her name was before she was married?
A She was called Stansberg[sic] before she was married.
Q Is it your understanding that she had never been married before she married Frank Lamar? A No, she was never married before.
Q Is it your understanding that Frank Lamar had never been married before he married Mary Lamar? A Yes, that is my understanding.
Q Did they live together as husband and wife from the time of their marriage until his death? A Yes sir.
Q All the time in the Cherokee nation[sic]? A Yes sir. I have known them on the same place for 26 or 27 years.
Q They never separated nor ever moved out of the Territory at any time, did they?
A No sir.
Q Is it your understanding that at the time they were married Frank Lamar was a recognized citizen of the Cherokee nation[sic]? A Yes sir. She was killed in a cyclone in 1894[sic] and everything was thrown to the winds and there is nothing that could be found of any of the records. Stuff was scattered two or three miles from home. That is why we have got no record except what we can get now to establish it.
Q When did Frank Lamar die? A He died 7 or 8 years ago
Q And did Mary Lamar marry after Frank Lamar died? [sic] No, she was a widow when she died. When she was killed.

Cherokee Intermarried White 1906
Volume VI

Q Is it your understanding that Mary Lamar had records showing this marriage? A That is what they say; they say the records was in the bible and they never have found them because everything was destroyed.
Q Destroyed in the cyclone? A Yes sir.
Q That was at the time Mary Lamar was killed? A Yes sir.
Q Have you got anyone here who was present at that marriage? A No sir.
Q Do you know anyone living at this time who was present at therir[sic] marriage except the minister, Mr. Thompson? A No sir.

Margaret E. Kelley being first duly sworn by J. R.[sic] Tidwell, testified as follows:
Q What is your name? A Margaret E. Kelley.
Q How old are you? A Thirty-six.
Q What is your postoffice address? A Fairland, I T.
Q You wish to testify in this case of Mary Lamar, do you? A Yes sir.
Q How long have you known Mary Lamar? A Known her all my live.
Q Are you related to Mary Lamar? A Only by marriage.
Q How were you related to Frank Lamar? A He is my uncle.
Q Since you can first remember have these people, Mary Lamar and Frank Lamar, lived together as husband and wife and lived in the Cherokee Nation until their deaths? A Yes sir.
Q Frank Lamar died some 7 or 8 years ago? Is that correct? A I don't just recollect.
Q Who died first, Frank Lamar or Mary Lamar? A Frank.
Q And then Mary Lamar was killed in a cyclone in 1904? A Yes sir.
Q Frank Lamar was recognized as a citizen of the Cherokee Nation and exercised the rights and priveleges[sic] accorded to citizens? A Yes sir.
    The applicant, Mary Lamar, is identified on the Cherokee authenticated tribal roll of 1880, Delaware District, No. 1501, and on the Cherokee census roll of 1896, Delaware District, page 580, No. 312, as an intermarried citizen of the Cherokee Nation.

Frances R. Lane upon oath states that as stenographer to the Commissioner to the Five Civilized Tribes she reported the testimony in the above entitled cause and that the foregoing is an accurate transcript of her stenographic notes thereof.

Frances R. Lane

Subscribed and sworn to before me this January 31, 1907.

Edward Merrick
Notary Public.

Cherokee Intermarried White 1906
Volume VI

F.R. Cherokee 44.

DEPARTMENT OF THE INTERIOR,
COMMISSIONER TO THE FIVE CIVILIZED TRIBES.
Muskogee, I. T., February 1, 1907.

In the matter of the application for the enrollment of Mary Lamar as a citizen by intermarriage of the Cherokee Nation.
Cherokee Nation represented by H. M. Vance.

J. F. Thompson being first duly sworn by Frances R. Lane, a Notary Public for the Western District of Indian Territory, testified as follows:
By the Commissioner:
Q What is your name? A J. F. Thompson.
Q Your age? A Nearly 66.
Q Your postoffice address? A Tahlequah, I. T.
Q You are a minister of the Gospel are you? A Yes sir.
Q How long have you been a minister of the Gospel? A Sinve[sic] about '70.
Q Where were you preaching along about the years 1870 to '75?
A I was preaching in the neighborhood of Grand River; we called it Grand River circuit at that time.
Q That was in the Cherokee nation[sic]? A Yes sir.
Q Did you know one Mary Lamar in the Cherokee Nation? A Yes sir.
Q Did you know her husband, Frank Lamar? A A[sic] Yes sir.
Q Do you remember the circumstances of their marriage? A Yes sir.
Q Were they married by you? A Yes sir.
Q When were they married? A I am not sure whether it was in August 1872 or 1873. I lost the records I have by fire, but I married them in August either 1872 or 1873. But I am impressed with the act that it was 1872.
Q How do you fix the date as being 1872? A Because at that time I was a member of the traveling connection. I joined the traveling connection in 1873, but at that time I was local preacher- what we call in the Baptist church a local preacher and I only preached at four points, and in the fall of 1873 I joined the traveling connection and traveled over the section of country embracing about forty miles up and down the river, and it was before I joined the traveling connection, that I married them.
Q Was this marriage ceremony performed under a license of the Cherokee nation[sic]?
A No, no license.
Q Mr. Lamar was a Cherokee citizen? A Yes sir.
Q This marriage ceremony was in accordance with the laws and customs of the Cherokee Nation, however? A Yes; there was no law requiring a license where a citizen married a white lady.
Q Do you remember whether or not you executed and delivered to them a certificate showing the marriage? A No, I don't think I gave them any marriage certificate.
Q Therefore, there would not be any tribal record showing it? A No, I think not.
Q Did you know them after this marriage? A Yes, I knew them intimately until '76.

Cherokee Intermarried White 1906
Volume VI

Q Well, from the time of their marriage they lived together as husband and wife and resided in the Cherokee Nation? A Yes, I know of their living together until 1897 but I never visited their neighborhood after 1898.

Q It is your understanding that they continued to reside as husband and wife? A Yes, and I met him very often; he was a member of the council.

Q At the time you married these people did you know or understand whether or not either of them had ever been married before? A I never had much acquaintance with her, but with him I knew his father and the family before, and I knew her intimately afterwards, and I never heard of anything like that.

Frances R. Lane upon oath states that as stenographer to the Commissioner to the Five Civilized Tribes she reported the testimony in the above entitled cause and that the foregoing is an accurate transcript of her stenographic notes thereof.

Frances R Lane

Subscribed and sworn to before me this February 2, 1906

Edward Merrick
Notary Public.

◇◇◇◇◇

E C M   Cherokee 44.

DEPARTMENT OF THE INTERIOR,

COMMISSIONER TO THE FIVE CIVILIZED TRIBES.

In the matter of the application for the enrollment of MARY LAMAR as a citizen by intermarriage of the Cherokee Nation.

D E C I S I O N

THE RECORDS OF THIS OFFICE SHOW: That on July 9, 1900, application was received by the Commission to the Five Civilized Tribes for the enrollment of Mary Lamar as a citizen by intermarriage of the Cherokee Nation. Further proceedings in the matter of said application were had at Muskogee, Indian Territory, October 4, 1902, October 24, 1902, January 31, 1907 and February 1, 1907.

THE EVIDENCE IN THIS CASE SHOWS: That the applicant herein, Mary Lamar, a white woman, was married about the year 1872 to one Frank Lamar, since deceased, who was at the time of said marriage a recognized citizen by blood of the Cherokee Nation, who is identified on the Cherokee authenticated tribal roll of 1880,

Cherokee Intermarried White 1906
Volume VI

Delaware District No. 1500 as a native Cherokee, marked "Dead"; that from the time of said marriage until the death of said Frank Lamar, which occurred about 1900, the said Frank Lamar and Mary Lamar resided together as husband and wife and continuously lived in the Cherokee Nation; that since the death of said Frank Lamar the said Mary Lamar has remained unmarried and continuously lived in the Cherokee Nation up to and including September 1, 1902. Said applicant is identified on the Cherokee authenticated tribal roll of 1880 and the Cherokee census roll of 1896 as an intermarried citizen of the Cherokee Nation.

  IT IS, THEREFORE, ORDERED AND ADJUDGED: That in accordance with the decision of the Supreme Court of the United States dated November 5, 1906, in the cases of Daniel Red Bird et al. vs. the United States, Nos. 125, 126, 127, and 128, the said applicant, Mary Lamar is entitled under the provisions of Section Twenty-one of the Act of Congress approved June 28, 1898 (30 Stats., 495), to enrollment as a citizen by intermarriage of the Cherokee Nation, and her application for enrollment as such is accordingly granted.

             Tams Bixby
              Commissioner.

Dated at Muskogee, Indian Territory,
this   FEB 13 1907

◇◇◇◇◇

Cherokee

  44.

            Muskogee, Indian Territory, February 13, 1907.

W. W. Hastings,
   Attorney for the Cherokee Nation,
     Muskogee, Indian Territory.

Dear Sir:

  There is enclosed herewith a copy of the decision of the Commissioner to the Five Civilized Tribes, dated February 13, 1907, granting the application for the enrollment of Mary Lamar as a citizen by intermarriage of the Cherokee Nation.

            Respectfully,

Encl. HJ-45.
  HJC   Commissioner.

◇◇◇◇◇

Cherokee Intermarried White 1906
Volume VI

Cherokee 44.

Muskogee, Indian Territory, February 13, 1907.

The Commissioner to the Five Civilized Tribes,
    Muskogee, Indian Territory.

Sir:

    Receipt is acknowledged of the testimony and of your decision enrolling Mary Lamar as a citizen by intermarriage of the Cherokee Nation. Time for protesting said decision is waived and I consent that said person may be placed upon the schedule immediately.

                  Respectfully,
                        W. W. Hastings
                        Attorney for Cherokee Nation.

◇◇◇◇◇

Cherokee
    44.

Muskogee, Indian Territory, February 13, 1907.

Mary Lamar,
    Fairland, Indian Territory.

Dear Madam:

    There is enclosed herewith a copy of the decision of the Commissioner to the Five Civilized Tribes, dated February 13, 1907, granting your application for enrollment as a citizen by intermarriage of the Cherokee Nation.

    You will be advised when your name has been placed upon a schedule of citizens of the Cherokee Nation and approved by the Secretary of the Interior.

                    Respectfully,

Encl. HJ-46.
    HJC   Commissioner.

Cher IW 181

◇◇◇◇◇

Cherokee Intermarried White 1906
Volume VI

E.C.M.

DEPARTMENT OF THE INTERIOR,

COMMISSIONER TO THE FIVE CIVILIZED TRIBES.

In the matter of the application for the enrollment of

JOHN LEMASTER

As a citizen by intermarriage of the Cherokee Nation.

CHEROKEE NO. 119.

DEPARTMENT OF THE INTERIOR.
COMMISSION TO THE FIVE CIVILIZED TRIBES.
FAIRLAND, I. T., JULY 11th, 1900.

IN THE MATTER OF THE APPLICATION OF John Leamaster[sic] et al for enrollment as citizens of the Cherokee Nation, and he being sworn by Commissioner, C. R. Breckinridge, testified as follows:

Q What is your name? A John Leamaster.
Q What is your age? A Fifty-two.
Q What is your Postoffice address? A Fairland, I. T.
Q What is your district? A Delaware.
Q How far do you live from Fairland? A Five miles.
Q How long have you lived in this District? A Nearly six years.
Q Where did you live before you were in this District? A Flint.
Q How long did you live there? A About twenty four years.
Q Have you lived during all that time in Flint and Delaware Districts? A Yes sir.
Q Never lived out of the Territory? A No sir.
Q By inter-marriage? A Yes sir.
Q Does your name appear on the 1880 authenticated roll of citizens of the Cherokee Nation? A Yes sir.
   (Roll of 1880 examined, and on Page 377 thereof, #804, appears the name of John Leamaster, Flint District.
Q Are you married? A Yes sir.
Q Do you make application now for your wife? A I can; she is here.
Q Have you children? A Yes sir.
Q How many under twenty one years of age? and unmarried? A Five.

Cherokee Intermarried White 1906
Volume VI

Applicant's wife, being called, and sworn by Commissioner, C. R. Breckinridge, testified as follows:

Q What is your name? A Narcissa Leamaster.
Q Are you the wife of John Leamaster? A Yes sir.
Q Do you claim as a Cherokee by blood? A Yes sir.
Q Have you lived with him ever since your marriage? A Yes sir.
Q Some twenty eight years ago? A Twenty eight years ago, I guess.
Q At his home and with him all the time? A Yes sir.
Q Is your name on the 1880 roll? A Yes sir.
 (Narcissa Leamaster duly identified on Page 377, #805, Roll of 1800[sic], Flint District)
Q Is your father living? A No sir.
Q Was he on the Roll of 1880? A Yes sir.
Q What was his name? A Buffington.
Q What is his full name? A Ellis Buffington, he has been dead about forty years I guess.
Q Is your mother living? A Yes sir.
Q Give me the names of your children under twenty one years of age?
A Curtis Leamaster, 18 years old.
Q Does he live with you? A Yes sir.
(Upon examining Roll of 1896, name of Curtis Leamaster appears on Page 494 thereof, #1780, Delaware District)
Q Now the next child? A Elizabeth Leamaster, 15 years old.
(Roll of 1896 consulted and on Page 494 thereof, #1781, appears the name of Eliza Leamaster.)
Q Now the next one? A Alice May Leamaster. (Roll of 1896 consulted, and on Page 494 thereof, #1782, appears the name of Alice May Leamaster, Delaware District.)
Q Next child? A Nellie.
Q Is that all the name? A Yes sir.
Q How old is she? A Eight years old.
(Roll of 1896 consulted, and on Page 494 thereof, #1783 appears the name of Nellie Leamaster)
Q Any more? A I have one that is not on any Roll.
Q This little one (indicating baby in applicant's arms)?
A Yes sir.
Q What is its name? A Jessie, eighteen months old.
(Last question on proceeding page repeated)
Q What is its name? A Jessie, eighteen months old.
Q Boy or girl? A Girl.
Q You will be furnished a certificate to fill out proving the birth of this child, signed by the Doctor or midwife attending, and you will mail the certificate, when properly filled out, to the Commission at its offices at Muskogee.

Notice by the Commission:
Mr. Leamaster, your names being found duly recorded, that of yourself and your wife on the roll of 1880, you will be entered upon the roll now being made by the Commission,

Cherokee Intermarried White 1906
Volume VI

and your children being duly identified on the Roll of 1896, they will be also entered upon this roll, except the youngest one, who will not be entered until you furnish a certificate of birth, properly filled out, to the Commission, when[sic] the youngest will also be likewise enrolled.

R. R. Cravens, being first duly sworn, states that as stenographer to the Commission to the Five Civilized Tribes, he reported the foregoing case, and that the foregoing and above is a true, full and correct transcript of his stenographic notes in said case.

R R Cravens

Sworn to and subscribed before me this 12th day of July, 1900.

Clifton R. Breckinridge
COMMISSIONER.

◇◇◇◇◇

Cherokee Card 119

DEPARTMENT OF THE INTERIOR,

COMMISSION TO THE FIVE CIVILIZED TRIBES,

Muskogee, I. T., September 3, 1902.

In the matter of the application of John Lemaster et. al. for enrollment as Cherokee citizens.

SUPPLEMENTAL STATEMENT.
o-o-o-o

An examination of the Cherokee census roll of 1896 for Delaware District shows that John Lemaster is identified thereon, at page 580, No. 316; and that Narcissa Lemaster is identified on that roll, at page 49, No. 1778.

C. R. Breckinridge
Commissioner.

◇◇◇◇◇

Cherokee Intermarried White 1906
Volume VI

Cher
Supp'l to # 119

Department of the Interior,
Commission to the Five Civilized Tribes,
Muskogee, I. T., October 24, 1902.

In the matter of the application of JOHN LEMASTER, for the enrollment of himself as a citizen by intermarriage, and his wife, NARCISSA LEMASTER, and his children, CURTIS, ELIZABETH, ALICE MAY, NELLIE and JESSIE LEMASTER, as citizens by blood, of the Cherokee Nation:

JOHN LEMASTER, being duly sworn and examined by the Commission, testified as follows:

Q You name is John Lemaster ? A Yes sir
Q How old are you ? A Fifty four years old.
Q What is your post office address ? A Fairland
Q You are a white man ? A Yes sir.
Q Is your name on the 1880 roll as an adopted white citizen ?
A Yes sir.
Q What was your wife's name ? A Narcissa Buffington.
Q Is she a Cherokee by blood ? A Yes sir.
Q Was she your wife in 1880 ? A Yes sir.
Q Is she the wife through whom you are claiming your rights of citizenship ?
A Yes sir.
Q Have you and your wife Narcissa been living together in the Cherokee Nation ever since 1880 ? A Yes sir.
Q Never lived anywhere else ? A No sir.
Q You and your wife never been separated ? A No sir.
Q How many children have you ? A Seven.
Q Two of them are old enough to enroll themselves ?
A Three of them are.
Q How many of them are living at home with you ? A Four.
Q Is Curtis married ? A No sir.
Q Is Curtis living at home with you ? A Yes sir.
Q Elizabeth, Alice May, Nellie and Jessie ? A She is dead.
Q Jessie is dead is she ? A Yes sir.
Q When did she die ? A She died a year ago last April.
Q Have you any child younger than Jessie ? A No sir.
Q You have four children living at home with you ?
A My third son stays at home part of the time.
Q What is his name ? A William.
Q How old is he ? A About twenty two.
Q Is Jessie the only member of your family who has died within the past two years ?
A Yes sir, the only one.

Cherokee Intermarried White 1906
Volume VI

E. C. Bagwell, on oath states that, as stenographer to the Commission to the Five Civilized Tribes, he correctly recorded the testimony and proceedings had in the above entitled cause, and that the foregoing is an accurate transcript of his stenographic notes thereof.

E.C.Bagwell

Subscribed and sworn to before me this December 13, 1902.

BC Jones
Notary Public.

◇◇◇◇◇

C O P Y.

Cherokee Nation)
)
Flint District) By the authority in me vested by the Law of the Cherokee Nation, I do hereby Grant License of Marriage to John Lemaster, a citizen of the United States, and a man of Good Moral character and of industrious habits, to marry Miss. Narcissa Buffington a Cherokee by Birth and a daughter of Ellie Buffington, De'cd. He (John Lemaster) having complyed[sic] with the requirements of the Law regulating intermarriage with white men. Given from under my hand in office, this the 11th day of Feby. 1871.

(Signed) James W. Adair Clk.

Dist. Ct. Flint, C.N.

License fee $5.00

I hereby certify that I solemnized the marriage of the above names John Lemaster and Narcissa Buffington according to the requirements of law.
Flint District C.N.)

(Signed) W. A. Duncan

Feby. 15, 1871)

Minister, M.E.C South.

Cherokee Intermarried White 1906
Volume VI

This certifies that the undersigned, being duly sworn, states that as stenographer to the Commission to the Five Civilized Tribes she made the above and foregoing copy and that the same is a full, true and correct copy of the original instrument now on file in this office.

Mary Tabor Mallory

Subscribed and sworn to before me this 24th of January, 1907.

Chas E Webster
Notary Public.

◇◇◇◇◇

E C M   Cherokee 119.

DEPARTMENT OF THE INTERIOR,

COMMISSIONER TO THE FIVE CIVILIZED TRIBES.

In the matter of the application for the enrollment of JOHN LEMASTER as a citizen by intermarriage of the Cherokee Nation.

D E C I S I O N

THE RECORDS OF THIS OFFICE SHOW: That on July 11th, 1900, application was received by the Commission to the Five Civilized Tribes for the enrollment of John Lemaster as a citizen by intermarriage of the Cherokee Nation. Further proceedings in the matter of said application were had at Muskogee, Indian Territory, September 3rd, 1902 and October 24th, 1902.

THE EVIDENCE IN THIS CASE SHOWS: That the applicant herein, John Lemaster, a white man, was married in accordance with Cherokee law February 15th, 1871 to his wife Narcissa Lemaster, nee Buffington, who was at the time of said marriage a recognized citizen by blood of the Cherokee Nation, who is identified on the Cherokee authenticated tribal roll of 1880, Flint District No. 805 as a native Cherokee, and whose name appears upon the approved partial roll of citizens by blood of the Cherokee Nation, opposite No. 377. It is further shown that from the time of said marriage the said John Lemaster and Narcissa Lemaster resided together as husband and wife and continuously lived in the Cherokee Nation up to and including September 1st, 1902. Said applicant is identified on the Cherokee authenticated tribal roll of 1880 and the Cherokee census roll of 1896 as an intermarried citizen of the Cherokee Nation.

IT IS, THEREFORE, ORDERED AND ADJUDGED: That in accordance with the decision of the Supreme Court of the United States, dated November 5th, 1906 in the cases of Daniel Red Bird, et al. vs. the United States, Nos. 125, 126, 127, and 128, the said applicant, John Lemaster is entitled, under the provisions of Section Twenty-one of

Cherokee Intermarried White 1906
Volume VI

the Act of Congress approved June 28th, 1898 (30 Stats. 495), to enrollment as a citizen by intermarriage of the Cherokee Nation, and his application for enrollment as such is accordingly granted.

            Tams Bixby
              Commissioner.

Dated at Muskogee, Indian Territory,
this FEB 14 1907

◇◇◇◇◇

Cherokee 119

        Muskogee, Indian Territory, February 14, 1907.

W. W. Hastings,
  Attorney for the Cherokee Nation,
    Muskogee, Indian Territory.

Dear Sir:

  There is enclosed herewith a copy of the decision of the Commissioner to the Five Civilized Tribes, dated February 14, 1907, granting the application for the enrollment of John Lemaster as a citizen by intermarriage of the Cherokee Nation.

       Respectfully,

Encl. H-28   Commissioner.
 JMH

◇◇◇◇◇

Cherokee 119

        Muskogee, Indian Territory, February 14, 1907.

The Commissioner to the Five Civilized Tribes,
  Muskogee, Indian Territory.

Sir:

  Receipt is acknowledged of the testimony and of your decision enrolling John Lemaster as a citizen by intermarriage of the Cherokee Nation. Time for protesting said decision is waived, and I consent that said person may be placed upon the schedule immediately.

       Respectfully,
         W. W. Hastings
         Attorney for Cherokee Nation.

◇◇◇◇◇

Cherokee Intermarried White 1906
Volume VI

Cherokee 119

Muskogee, Indian Territory, February 14, 1907.

Joe Lemaster,
    Fairland, Indian Territory.

Dear Sir:

    There is enclosed herewith a copy of the decision of the Commissioner to the Five Civilized Tribes, dated February 14, 1907, granting the application for the enrollment of John Lemaster as a citizen by intermarriage of the Cherokee Nation.

    You will be advised when the name of the said John Lemaster has been placed upon a schedule of citizens of the Cherokee Nation and approved by the Secretary of the Interior.

                      Respectfully,

Encl. H-29   Commissioner.
JMH

◇◇◇◇◇

Cherokee
I.W. 181

Muskogee, Indian Territory, April 16, 1907.

Joe Lemaster,
    Fairland, Indian Territory.

Dear Sir:

    Your marriage license and certificate filed in connection with your application for enrollment as a citizen by intermarriage of the Cherokee Nation is returned to you herewith, copies of the same being retained in the files of this office.

                        Respectfully,

Encl. W-12.   Commissioner.
S.W.

Cher IW 182

◇◇◇◇◇

Cherokee Intermarried White 1906
Volume VI

DEPARTMENT OF THE INTERIOR, COMMISSION TO THE FIVE CIVILIZED TRIBES, STILWELL, I.T., JULY 26, 1900.

In the matter of the application of Benjamin F. Goss et al., for enrollment as citizens of the Cherokee Nation, said Goss being duly sworn by Commissioner Needles, testified as follows:

Q What is your name? A Benjamin F. Goss.
Q Your age? A 73.
Q Your postoffice? A Stilwell.
Q Have you been recognized by the tribal authorities of the Cherokee Nation as a citizen of the Cherokee Nation? A Yes.
Q Have you been enrolled by the Cherokee Tribal authorities as a citizen of the Cherokee Nation? A Yes.
Q Where do you live? A Goingsnake district.
Q How long have you lived there? A Since '37.
Q Been living continuously in the Cherokee Nation for that length of time? A Yes.
Q Are you a Cherokee by blood? A Yes.
Q What is the name of your father? A Thomas Goss.
Q Is he living? A No sir.
Q What is your mother's name? A Mary.
Q Is she living? A No sir.

B. F. Goss on '80 roll, page 437, number 813.
On '96 roll, page 751, number 903, as Benjamin F. Goss.
On '94 roll, page 658, number 995 as Benj. F. Goss.

Q What proportion of Cherokee blood do you claim? A 1/8.
Q Are you married? A Yes.
Q Is your wife living? A Yes. I have been married twice.
Q When were you married to your last wife? A In '72.
Q What is her name? A Demaris.
Q Is she a citizen by blood? A No sir.
Q Is her name on the '80 rolls? A Yes.

On '80 roll, page 437, number 814 as Mitie.
On '96 roll, page 822, number 76.

Q Have you any children under 21? A No sir.
Q Just want to enroll yourself and wife? A Yes.

The name of Benjamin F. Goss being found upon the authenticated roll of '80 as well as the census roll of '96 and the pay-roll of '94, and his wife, Demaris' name being also found upon the authenticated roll of '80 as well as the census roll of '96, and proof being made as to their residence, he is ordered listed for enrollment as a Cherokee by blood by this Commission, and she as a citizen by intermarriage.

Brown McDonald, being duly sworn, says as Stenographer to the Commission to the Five Civilized Tribes, he reported in full the testimony of the above named witness, and that the foregoing is a full, true and correct transcript of his notes.

Cherokee Intermarried White 1906
Volume VI

Brown McDonald

Sworn to and subscribed before me this 2nd day of August, 1900, at Bunch, I.T.

TB Needles
Commissioner.

◇◇◇◇◇

JOR.
Cher. 710.

Department of the Interior.
Commission to the Five Civilized Tribes.
Tahlequah, I. T., October 21, 1902.

SUPPLEMENTAL TESTIMONY in the matter of the application for the enrollment of DEMARIS GOSS as a citizen by intermarriage of the Cherokee Nation.

DEMARIS GOSS, being first duly sworn, testified as follows:

BY COMMISSION: What is your name? A Demaris Goss.
Q How old are you? A I don't know my age exactly. About fifty-eight or -nine.
Q What is your postoffice address? A Stilwell?
Q Are you a white woman? A Yes sir.
Q Has application been made to this Commission for your enrollment as a citizen by intermarriage of the Cherokee Nation? A Yes sir.
Q What is the name of your husband? A Benjamin F. Goss.
Q Is he living? A Yes sir.
Q Is he a Cherokee by blood? A Yes sir.
Q Do you claim your right to enrollment by reason of your marriage to him? A Yes sir.
Q When were you and he married? A In 1870.
Q Does your name appear upon the roll of 1880? A Yes sir.
Q Were you ever married before you married him? A No sir.
Q Was he ever married before he married you? A Yes sir.
Q What was the name of his first wife? A Emily bean[sic].
Q Is she living? A No sir.
Q Was she living when you and he married? Z[sic] No sir.
Q Was that the only time your husband was ever married before he married you?
A Yes sir.
Q He is your first husband and you are his second wife? A Yes sir.
Q Have you and he lived together continuously since your marriage? A Yes sir.
Q Were you living together continuously since your marriage? A Yes sir.
Q Never been separated? A No sir.
Q Have you resided in the Cherokee Nation continuously since you married him?
A Yes sir.
Q Has he also? A Yes sir.

Cherokee Intermarried White 1906
Volume VI

Q Have you any minor children? A No sir.

    This testimony will be filed with and made a part of the record in the matter of the application for the enrollment of Demaris Goss as a citizen by intermarriage of the Cherokee Nation, Cherokee straight card field No. 710.

Wm. Hutchinson, being first duly sworn, states that as stenographer to the Commission to the Five Civilized Tribes he correctly recorded the testimony and proceedings in this case, and the foregoing is a true and complete transcript of the stenographic notes thereof.

Wm Hutchinson

Subscribed and sworn to before me this 8th day of November, 1902.

BC Jones
Notary Public.

◇◇◇◇◇

C. F. B.   Cherokee 710.

DEPARTMENT OF THE INTERIOR,
COMMISSION TO THE FIVE CIVILIZED TRIBES.
Muskogee, Indian Territory, January 8, 1907.

    In the Matter of the Application for the Enrollment of Demaris Goss as a citizen by intermarriage of the Cherokee Nation.

APPEARANCES: William P. Goss for Applicant.

                         Cherokee Nation represented by
                         W. W. Hastings, Attorney.

    William P. Goss being first duly sworn by John E. Tidwell, Notary Public, testified as follows:

ON BEHALF OF COMMISSIONER.

Q What is your name?   A William P. Goss.
Q What is your age?   A 33.
Q What is your post office address?
A Stillwell[sic], Indian Territory.
Q Do you appear here to-day for the purpose of giving testimony relative to the right to enrollment of Demaris Goss as a citizen by intermarriage of the Cherokee Nation?

Cherokee Intermarried White 1906
Volume VI

A Yes sir; I have an affidavit from her executed before a Notary Public, giving me power of attorney to transact business for her.
Q Are you related to her?
A Yes sir; she's my mother.
Q She claims the right to enrollment as a citizen of the Cherokee Nation?
A Yes sir.
Q What is the name of your father?
A Benjamin F. Goss.
Q Is he living or dead?
A Living.
Q He is a Cherokee by blood?
A Yes sir.
Q The only claim that your mother makes to the right to enrollment as a citizen of the Cherokee Nation is by virtue of her marriage to your father, Benjamin F. Goss?
A Yes sir.
Q Both your father and your mother are living at this time?
A Yes sir.
Q Have you any evidence of a documentary character showing the marriage of your father and mother?
A I have her affidavit here. They didn't have any marriage license or marriage certificate but I have the affidavit of a witness who saw them married.
Q You have the affidavit of your mother as to the marriage and the affidavit of a witness who was present at the marriage?
A Yes sir.
Q Why did your father or your mother not appear to-day for the purpose of giving testimony?
A They are both sick. They are old and unable to get here.
Q Is it your understanding that your father was a recognized citizen by blood of the Cherokee Nation and residing in the Cherokee Nation at the time he married your mother?
A Yes sir.
Q They have been living together as husband and wife since youc an remember?
A Yes sir.
Q Never has been any separation of any kind?
A No sir.

    The applicant, Demaris Goss, is identified on the Cherokee authenticated tribal roll of 1880, Going Snake District, No. 814. Her husband, Benjamin F. Goss, is identified on said roll at No. 813 and his name appears on the approved partial roll of citizens of the Cherokee Nation opposite No. 1988.

Q Is it your understanding that you mother was your father's first wife?
A No sir; he has been married twice.
Q Was his former wife living or dead at the time he married your mother?
A It is my understanding that she was dead.

Cherokee Intermarried White 1906
Volume VI

Q   Was your mother, to the best of your knowledge, married prior to her marriage to your father?
A   No sir; I never have heard of it if she was.

The undersigned being first duly sworn states that as stenographer to the Commission to the Five Civilized Tribes, she recorded the testimony taken in this case and that the foregoing is a full, true and correct transcript of her stenographic notes thereof.

Myrtle Hill

Subscribed and sworn to before me this the 12th day of January, 1907.

Chas E Webster
Notary Public.

◇◇◇◇◇

(The Affidavit below was originally as given on the microfilm.)

Personally appeared before me this 7 day of Jan. 1907, Phebe A. Adair of near Stilwell I.T. Northern District who says: That on July 24th 1872, I witnessed the marriage ceremony of Mr. Benj. F. Goss and Demaris Pace - by - Rev. D. M. Morris (Dec^D) at the home of D.M. Morris according to the laws of the Cherokee Nation, and that they have been living together as man and wife from that time to this. Witness my hand this 7th day of Jan 1907.

Signed Phebe A. Adair
By R.M. Adair

Sworn to and subscribed before me this 7 day of Jan 1907.

My Commission expires Nov. 21st, 1908
THIRD TERM.

Hugh M Adair
Notary Public

◇◇◇◇◇

Cherokee Intermarried White 1906
Volume VI

COPY

POWER OF ATTORNEY

KNOW ALL MEN BY THESE PRESENTS:

That I Demaris Goss of near Stilwell, Indian Territory, has made, constituted and appointed, and by these presents does make, constitute and appoint Wm. P. Goss, of near Stilwell, Indian Territory, her true and lawful attorney for her, and in her name, place and stead, to transact such business as may be necessary in the primises[sic] to file for me or anything that is required before the "Com. of the Five Civilized Tribes."-------------------- giving and granting unto her said attorney full power and authority to do and perform all and every act and thing whatsoever, requisite and necessary to be done, as fully to all intents and purposes as she might or could do, if personally present; hereby ratifying and confirming all that her said attorney shall lawfully do, or cause to be done, by virtue hereof.

In witness whereof, she has hereunto set her hand this 7th day of Jan, A. D. 1907.

Demaris Goss

Witnesses to Mark:

UNITED STATES OF AMERICA,)
    INDIAN TERRIRORY[sic],   ) SS.
Northern District.   )

Be it remembered that on this day personally appeared before me Demaris Goss to me personally known to be the person who executed the foregoing power of attorney, and being by me examined separately and apart from her said attorney W. P. Goss stated and acknowledged that she had executed said instrument as her free and voluntary act and deed, without compulsion or undue influence, and for the purposes therein mentioned and set forth.

In testimony whereof I have hereunto set my hand and affixed my Notarial Seal this 7 day of Jan A. D. 1907.

Cherokee Intermarried White 1906
Volume VI

Hugh M. Adair.
(SEAL) Notary Public.
My commission expires Nov 21 1908.

The undersigned being first duly sworn states that as stenographer to the Commissioner to the Five Civilized Tribes, he made the above and foregoing copy and that the same is a true and correct copy of the original Power of Attorney now on file in this office.

Homer J Councilor

Subscribed and sworn to before me this 19, day of January 1907.

Chas E Webster
Notary Public.

◇◇◇◇◇

Cherokee 710.

DEPARTMENT OF THE INTERIOR,
COMMISSIONER TO THE FIVE CIVILIZED TRIBES.
Muskogee, Indian Territory,
February 11, 1907.

SUPPLEMENTAL:
In the matter of the application for the enrollment of DEMARIS GOSS as a citizen by intermarriage of the Cherokee Nation.

Benjamin F. Goss, being first duly sworn by Walter W. Chapell[sic], a Notary Public, testified as follows:

ON BEHALF OF THE COMMISSIONER:

Q What is your name?
A Benjamin F. Goss.
Q Your age?
A My age is 79 and past.
Q What is your post-office address?
A Stillwell[sic], Indian Territory.

Cherokee Intermarried White 1906
Volume VI

Q You are the husband of Demaris Goss?
A Yes sir.
Q Is she an applicant before the Commission for enrollment as a citizen by intermarriage of the Cherokee Nation?
A Yes sir.
Q When were you married to Demaris Goss?
A I was married in '72.
Q Are you a citizen by blood of the Cherokee Nation?
A Yes sir.
Q Have you always lived in the Cherokee Nation?
A Only what time I was in California, that was about two years.
Q Were you born here?
A I was born in Georgia, moved here in '37 and lived here ever since.
Q After coming from Georgia to the Cherokee Nation was it necessary for you to be admitted to citizenship?
A No sir.
Q Since your marriage to Demaris Goss have you and she continuously lived in the Cherokee Nation?
A Yes sir.
Q And lived together as husband and wife all the time?
A Yes sir.
Q Were either of you ever married before?
A I was.
Q Was your first wife dead at the time of your marriage to Demaris Goss?
A She had been dead about twelve years. Died in 1860.
Q Do you remember whether Phoebe Adair was present at your marriage or not?
A Yes sir.
Q She saw you married did she?
A Yes sir.

(Witness excused)

This certifies that the undersigned, being duly sworn, states that as stenographer to the Commission to the Five Civilized Tribes she reported the proceedings had in the above entitled cause and that the above and foregoing is a full, true and correct transcript of her stenographic notes thereof.

Georgia Coberly
Stenographer.

Subscribed and sworn to before me this 12th day of February, 1907.

Walter W. Chappell
Notary Public.

Cherokee Intermarried White 1906
Volume VI

DEPARTMENT OF THE INTERIOR,
COMMISSIONER TO THE FIVE CIVILIZED TRIBES.
STILWELL, I. T., FEBRUARY 9, 1907.

In the matter of the application for the enrollment of BENJAMIN F. GOSS as a citizen by intermarriage of the Cherokee Nation.

(The questions below were originally handwritten as given on the microfilm.)

Phoeba A Adair being sworn according to law by Hugh M Adair a Notary Public, testified as follows
What is your full and proper name?   A Phoeba A Adair
How old are you?   A I am sixty seven years old
How long have you lived in the Indian Territory?   A Since 1868
Are you acquainted with Benjamin F Goss?   A Yes sir
How long have you known him?   A Since 1866
Do you know his wife?   A Yes sir her name is Damaris[sic] Goss
Is Benjamin F Goss a Cherokee by blood?   A Yes sir
Has he lived in the Territory all the time since you became acquainted with him?   A Yes sir
How long has Benjamin F Goss and his wife Damaris Goss been married?   A They were married in the year 1872
How do you know that they were married in the year 1872?   A They were married in my house in Flint District about three miles from here
Did you see them married?   A I did.
Who performed the ceremony?   A My former husband D M Morris a baptist[sic] preacher.
Can you tell the date of their marriage?   A Yes sir July 24 1872
Was that marriage ceremony solemnized in accordance with Cherokee law and under a license issued by the Cherokee Nation?   A Yes sir
(The affidavit below typed.)
Charles B. Wilson, being first duly sworn, doth depose and say that the above and foregoing are the original questions propounded by him to, and the answers returned thereto by Phoeba A. Adair the above named witness.

Charles B Wilson

Cherokee Intermarried White 1906
Volume VI

Subscribed and sworn to before me this 11th day of February, 1907.

Walter W. Chappell
Notary Public.

◇◇◇◇◇

E C M   Cherokee 1710.

DEPARTMENT OF THE INTERIOR,

COMMISSIONER TO THE FIVE CIVILIZED TRIBES.

In the matter of the application for the enrollment of DEMARIS GOSS as a citizen by intermarriage of the Cherokee Nation.

D E C I S I O N

THE RECORDS OF THIS OFFICE SHOW: That at Stillwell[sic], Indian Territory, July 26, 1900 application was received by the Commission to the Five Civilized Tribes for the enrollment of Demaris Goss as a citizen by intermarriage of the Cherokee Nation. Further proceedings in the matter of said application were had at Tahlequah, Indian Territory, October 21, 1902 and at Muskogee, Indian Territory January 8, 1907 and February 11, 1907.

THE EVIDENCE IN THIS CASE SHOWS: That the applicant herein, Demaris Goss, a white woman, was married July 24, 1872 to one Benjamin F. Goss, who was at the time of said marriage a recognized citizen by blood of the Cherokee Nation, who is identified on the Cherokee authenticated tribal roll of 1880, Going Snake District No. 813, and whose name is included on the approved partial roll of citizens by blood of the Cherokee Nation opposite No. 1988. It is further shown that from the time of said marriage the said Benjamin F. Goss and Demaris Goss resided together as husband and wife and continuously lived in the Cherokee Nation up to and including September 1, 1902. Said applicant is identified on the Cherokee authenticated tribal roll of 1880 and the Cherokee census roll of 1896 as an intermarried citizen of the Cherokee Nation.

IT IS, THEREFORE, ORDERED AND ADJUDGED: That in accordance with the decision of the Supreme Court of the United States dated November 5, 1906 in the cases of Daniel Red Bird, et al. vs. the United States, Nos. 125, 126, 127, and 128, the said applicant, Demaris Goss, is entitled, under the provisions of Section twenty-one of the Act of Congress approved June 28, 1898 (30 Stats. 495), to enrollment as a citizen by intermarriage of the Cherokee Nation, and her application for enrollment as such is accordingly granted.

Cherokee Intermarried White 1906
Volume VI

Tams Bixby
Commissioner.

Dated at Muskogee, Indian Territory,
this   FEB 15 1907

◇◇◇◇◇

Cherokee 710

Muskogee, Indian Territory, February 15, 1907.

W. W. Hastings,
    Attorney for the Cherokee Nation,
        Muskogee, Indian Territory.

Dear Sir:

There is enclosed herewith a copy of the decision of the Commissioner to the Five Civilized Tribes, dated February 15, 1907, granting the application for the enrollment of Demaris Goss as a citizen by intermarriage of the Cherokee Nation.

Respectfully,

Encl. H-4
JMH

Commissioner.

◇◇◇◇◇

Cherokee 710

Muskogee, Indian Territory, February 15, 1907.

The Commissioner to the Five Civilized Tribes,
    Muskogee, Indian Territory.

Sir:

Receipt is acknowledged of the testimony and of your decision enrolling Demaris Goss as a citizen by intermarriage of the Cherokee Nation. Time for protesting said decision is waived, and I consent that said person may be placed upon the schedule immediately.

Respectfully,
W. W. Hastings
Attorney for Cherokee Nation.

◇◇◇◇◇

Cherokee Intermarried White 1906
Volume VI

Cherokee 710

Muskogee, Indian Territory, February 15, 1907.

Demaris Goss,
    Stilwell, Indian Territory.

Dear Madam:

There is enclosed herewith a copy of the decision of the Commissioner to the Five Civilized Tribes, dated February 15, 1907, granting the application for your enrollment as a citizen by intermarriage of the Cherokee Nation.

You will be advised when your name has been placed upon a schedule of citizens of the Cherokee Nation and approved by the Secretary of the Interior.

Respectfully,

Encl. H-5   Commissioner.
JMH

Cher IW 183
Trans from Cher 1561   3-20-07

◇◇◇◇◇

E.C.M.

DEPARTMENT OF THE INTERIOR,

COMMISSIONER TO THE FIVE CIVILIZED TRIBES.

In the matter of the application for the enrollment of

SIMEON ELDRIDGE

As a citizen by intermarriage of the Cherokee Nation.

CHEROKEE NO. 1561.

◇◇◇◇◇

Cherokee Intermarried White 1906
Volume VI

Department of the Interior,
Commission to the Five Civilized Tribes,
Muldrow, I. T.?[sic] August 17, 1900.

In the matter of the application of Simeon Eldridge for the enrollment of himself, and two children as Cherokee citizens; being sworn and examined by Commissioner Breckinridge he testifies:

Q What is your full name? A Simeon Eldridge.
Q What is your age? A Forty-six.
Q What is your post-office? A Pawpaw.
Q Your district? A Sequoyah.
Q You apply to have yourself enrolled? A Yes sir.
Q Anybody else? A My two boys.
Q No wife? A No sir.
Q You apply for yourself as a Cherokee by blood? A No, I am adopted.
Q How long have you lived in the Cherokee Nation? A Twenty-six years.
Q Are you on the roll of 1880? A Yes sir, I think so.
Q When were you married? A In 1874.
Q Is your wife dead? A Yes sir.
Q When did she die? A She died last January was a year ago. It was 1899 I reckon.
Q Have you ever re-married? A No sir.
Q Did you and your wife live together from the time of your marriage until her death? A Yes sir.
Q What was your wife's name? A Nancy Jane Thornton.
Q She was your wife in 1880? A Yes sir.
Q She was a Cherokee by blood was she? A Yes sir.
Q Give me the names of your children? A Jesse, a boy, seventeen years old; William J., fifteen years old.
Q These children are both living? A Yes sir.
Q What is the name of your father? A William B. Eldridge.
Q He was a white man? A Yes sir.
Q What is the name of your mother? A Jane Guinn.
Q Was she a white woman? A Yes sir.
Q Not an Indian? A No sir, not that I know of.
Q Is your father living or dead? A Dead.
Q Your mother living or dead? A Dead.
1880 roll examined for applicant; page 695 #440 Simon Eldridge, Sequoyah District.
1880 roll examined for wife; page 694 #441 Mary J. Eldridge, Sequoyah
1896 roll page 1113 #54 Simon Eldridge, Sequoyah District.
1896 roll page 1065 #453 Nancy J. Eldridge, Sequoyah District.
1896 roll page 1065 #454 Jessie Eldrige[sic] Sequoyah District.
1896 roll page 1065 William J. Eldrige, Sequoyah District.

Com'r Breckinridge: This applicant is duly identified on the rolls of 1880 and 1896 as a Cherokee by adoption, and he will be enrolled now as a Cherokee by adoption; his

Cherokee Intermarried White 1906
Volume VI

deceased wife, is identified on both rolls of 1880 and 1896 as his wife, and their two children Jesse and William J. are identified on the roll of 1896 and these two children will now be listed for enrollment as Cherokees by blood.

M. D. Green, being first duly sworn, states that as stenographer to the Commission to the Five Civilized Tribes he reported the foregoing case and that the above and foregoing is a full true and complete transcript of his stenographic notes.

MD Green

Subscribed and sworn to before me this 24 day of Aug. 1900.

TB Needles
Commissioner.

◇◇◇◇◇

Cherokee 1861.

Department of the Interior,
Commission to the Five Civilized Tribes,
Muskogee, I. T., October 9, 1902.

In the matter of the application of Simeon Eldridge for the enrollment of himself as a citizen by intermarriage, and for the enrollment of his children, Jesse and William J. Eldridge, as citizens by blood of the Cherokee Nation; he being sworn and examined by the Commission, testified as follows:

Q What is your name?   A Simeon Eldridge.
Q How old are you?   A Forty-nine I believe.
Q What is your postoffice address?   A Pawpaw.
Q Are you the identical Simeon Eldridge who applied to this Commission in 1900 for enrollment as a citizen by intermarriage of the Cherokee Nation?   A Yes sir.
Q Are the two children for whom you then applied, Jesse and William J. both living at this time?   A Yes sir.
Q Are they living in the Cherokee Nation with you?   A Yes sir, they are.
Q You are a white man are you?   A Yes sir.
Q What is the name of your wife through whom you claim you right to enrollment?
A Nancy J. Thornton.
Q Is she living or dead?   A She is dead.
Q When did she die?   A In '99.
Q Prior to the time you applied or enrollment?   A She died in '99.
Q Have you filed your marriage license and certificate?   A I did with the Cherokee Courts.
Q Have you filed it with this Commission?   A No sir.
Q Were you married under a Cherokee license?   A Yes sir.
Q Were you ever married before you married Nancy J. Thornton?   A No sir.

Cherokee Intermarried White 1906
Volume VI

Q Was she ever married before?   A No sir.
Q You meant by that she never was married before?   A No sir, she never was married before that I know of.
Q She was a Cherokee?   A Yes sir.
Q When were you married to her?   A In '74.
Q You are on the 1880 roll are you?   A Yes sir.
Q Did you live with her continuously from the time of your marriage up until the time of her death?   A Yes sir.
Q Have you resided in the Cherokee Nation since 1880?   A Yes sir.
Q Were your two children born and raised in the Cherokee Nation?   A Yes sir.
Q Have they always made thxxx[sic] their home?   A Yes sir.
Q Are they living there now?   A Yes sir.
Q You are living in the nation at the present time are you?   A Yes sir.
Q Have you married since the death of your wife?   A No sir, I haven't.
Q You were a widower on the first day of September, 1902?   A Yes sir.
Q Are you are to-day?   A Yes sir.

The undersigned, being duly sworn, states that as stenographer to the Commission to the Five Civilized Tribes he correctly recorded the testimony and proceedings in this case, and the foregoing is a true and correct transcript of his stenographic notes thereof.

E.G. Rothenberger

Subscribed and sworn to before me this 6th day of November, 1902.

BC Jones
Notary Public.

◇◇◇◇◇

Cherokee 1561

DEPARTMENT OF THE INTERIOR
COMMISSIONER TO THE FIVE CIVILIZED TRIBES
MUSKOGEE, INDIAN TERRITORY

In the matter of the application for the enrollment of Simeon Eldridge as a citizen by intermarriage of the Cherokee Nation.

The applicant being first duly sworn by Walter W. Chappell, a Notary Public for the Western District, testified as follows:

Q What is your name?   A Simeon Eldridge.
Q Your age?   A I am 53 now.
Q Your postoffice address?   A Pawpaw, I. T.

Cherokee Intermarried White 1906
Volume VI

Q You claim to be a citizen by intermarriage of the Cherokee Nation?   A Yes sir.
Q Through whom do you claim that right?   A By my wife.
Q What was her name?   A Her name was Nancy Jane Thornton
Q Is she living?   A No sir she's dead.
Q What was her citizenship?   A She was a Cherokee by blood
Q Where was she born?   A I aint[sic] sure, I think she was born in Fort Gibson.
Q When did she die?   A She died in '99, January 9th.
Q Did she live in the Cherokee Nation from her birth to her death?   A Yes sir, I think so, she did all the time I knew her.
Q When were you and she married?   A We were married in 1874, February 10th.
Q Where were you married?   A In Shequoyah[sic] district
Q Were you married under authority of a Cherokee license?   A Yes sir.
Q Have you a certified copy of that license?   A No sir I haven't got it
Q Where was the license issued?   A Shequoyah district Cherokee Nation.
Q Had either you or your wife been married prior to your marriage in 1874?   A No sir.
Q Did you live together continuously from the time of your marriage until her death in 1899?   A Yes sir.
Q Lived in the Cherokee Nation during that time did you?   A Ye sir
Q Did you have any children by her?   A Yes sir.
Q How many?   A Six, born to us
Q How many are living at the present time?   A Three
Q How many of these are under age?   A They are all of age now.
Q What are their names?   A Emma, Jesse and Wm J. Eldridge

The names of Jesse and Wm J. Eldridge appear on Cherokee Card No. 1561 together with the applicant and are included in the approved aprtial[sic] roll of citizens by blood of the Cherokee Nation, opposite numbers 4190 and 4191 trespectively[sic].

Q Have you married since your wife's death in 1899?   A Yes sir.
Q When did you marry the second time?   A I married in 1903, November 20th.
Q Is your wife living?   A Yes sir.
Q What is her citizenship?   A She was a citizen of Arkansas
Q citizen of the United States?   A Yes sir.

The applicant is identified on the authenticated Cherokee tribal roll of 1880 and the Cherokee Census Roll of 1896 Shequoyah[sic] district opposite numbers 440 and 1113 respectively as an intermarried white.

The marriage records of Shequoyah district furnished this office by the Cherokee Nation do not cover the years prior to 1878 hence no record of the marriage license issued by the Cherokee authorities to the applicant is in the possession of this office.
Q Have you made any effort to secure a certified copy of the license issued to you by the Cherokee authorities?   A No sir I didn't know as I would be required to.

Cherokee Intermarried White 1906
Volume VI

Q You have never had a copy of that license? A I don't remember sir, I took it and had it recorded in the Clerk's office, Shequoyah district, but I lost it some way or other

Q These old records are supposed to have been sent to the Cherokee Nation authorities at Tahlequah and to have been submitted by them to this office, but this office has no record covering the year that you allege this license was issued to you. Will you make an effort to secure a certified copy of this license from the Cherokee authorities at Tahlequah?

A Yes sir, I can do that A good many people living there knew I married there and been there all the time, some here, some men here that know it

Q If you fail to secure any documentary evidence of this marriage license having been issued to you could you produce any witnesses who know that such a license was issued. A I don't now sir. The clerk is dead--I don't know who was present when it was issued. There are some parties living who signed the petition for the license. I could get them and if the records are at Tahlequah I can get their records

Q The records may possibly be there--

A I hear there are some that can't be found

Q What is your citizenship Mr. Eldridge? Are you an Indian?

A No sir, I am a white man.

Further examination will be made for the record of the license above referred to and you will be notified of the result of this examination. In the meantime you will see if you can secure a certified copy of that license from the clerk's office? A Yes sir

Witness excused.

Gertrude Hanna, being first duly sworn, states that she reported the proceedings had in the above case on January 3, 1907 and that the above and foregoing is a true and correct transcript of her stenographic notes thereof.

Gertrude Hanna

Subscribed and sworn to before me this 4th day of January, 1907.

Walter W. Chappell
Notary Public.

Cherokee Intermarried White 1906
Volume VI

F. R.	Cherokee 1561.

DEPARTMENT OF THE INTERIOR,
COMMISSIONER TO THE FIVE CIVILIZED TRIBES.
Muskogee, Indian Territory, January 22, 1907.

In the matter of the application of Simeon Eldridge for enrollment as a citizen by intermarriage of the Cherokee Nation.

SUPPLEMENTAL.

C. A. Fargo being first duly sworn testified as follows:

Q What is your name? A C. A. Fargo.
Q What is your age? A 60.
Q What is your post office address?
A Muldrow.
Q Are you acquainted with one Simeon Eldridge?
A Yes sir.
Q How long have you know him? A Since '73.
Q At the time you first knew him was he a married man?
A No sir.
Q Did you ever know one Nancy Jane Eldridge?
A Yes sir.
Q Do you know when they were married?
A Yes sir.
Q When were they married? A In '74.
Q Where?
A I think they were married at Wilson's Rock, Sequoyah District, Cherokee Nation.
Q Do you know whether or not that marriage in '74 was under a license of the Cherokee Nation?
A No, I don't know; Mr. Eldridge was staying with me at the time and he married a second cousin of mine and he brought his petition to me to sign it. The law required 10 Cherokee signers by blood. I signed the petition and my brother did.
Q Were you present at the marriage?
A No sir.
Q It was the understanding that they had been lawfully married in accordance with the Cherokee laws?
A Yes sir.
Q From that time on, they resided together as husband and wife and were recognized as such?
A Yes sir, he enjoyed the same privileges as a Cherokee citizen; had the right to vote and sit on juries.
Q You have every reason to believe that they were married under that license?
A Yes sir.

Cherokee Intermarried White 1906
Volume VI

Q They have continued to reside together as husband and wife and lived in the Cherokee Nation all the time?
A Yes sir. He lived at my house several months after he was married; then I have known them constantly up to the present time.

Rory Wilson being first duly sworn testified as follows:

Q What is your name
A Rory Wilson.
Q What is your age?
A 39.
Q What is your post office address?
A Muldrow.
Q Do you know one Simeon Eldridge?
A Yes sir.
Q How long have you known him?
A About 33 years or 32.
Q Since you were about 7 or 8 years old, then?
A Yes sir.
Q At the time you first knew him, was he an unmarried man or a married man?
A My first recollection of him, he was a married man.
Q Do you know the name of his wife?
A Nancy J. Eldridge.
Q When you first knew them did you live in the same neighborhood with them?
A Yes sir.
Q And at that time they were living together as husband and wife?
A Yes; they were married at my father's house.
Q Were you present at the marriage?
A Yes sir.
Q Do you know whether or not the marriage was under a license of the Cherokee Nation?
A No sir; I can't say.
Q What you want to testify to is that you were present and saw them married?
A Yes sir; I was there.
Q You have no reason to believe that they were not lawfully married in accordance with the laws of the Cherokee Nation at that time?
A No sir; I have not.
Q Who performed the marriage ceremony?
A I can't say; I just remember that they were married; I was small.
Q You have known them on up to the present time?
A Yes sir.
Q They have lived together as man and wife and been so regarded from that time up to the present time?
A Yes sir.
Q You remember the year in which they were married?
A Yes sir; in '74.
Q What reasons have you for thinking it was '74?
A I remember my mother died in February, '74.

Cherokee Intermarried White 1906
Volume VI

Q And you associate the two events together and know that they happened about the same time?
A Yes sir; it was just a few days before my mother's death.
Q Where were you living at the time of this marriage?
A Sequoyah District.
Q Near Wilson's Rock?
A Yes sir; at Wilson's Rock.
Q Were you related to Nancy J. Eldridge in any way?
A Yes sir; half brother.

The undersigned being first duly sworn states that as stenographer to the Commissioner to the Five Civilized Tribes, she recorded the testimony taken in this case and that the foregoing is a full, true and correct transcript of her stenographic notes thereof.

Myrtle Hill

Subscribed and sworn to before me this the 26th day of January, 1907.

John E Tidwell
Notary Public.

◇◇◇◇◇

E C M   Cherokee 1561.

DEPARTMENT OF THE INTERIOR,

COMMISSIONER TO THE FIVE CIVILIZED TRIBES.

In the matter of the application for the enrollment of SIMEON ELDRIDGE as a citizen by intermarriage of the Cherokee Nation.

D E C I S I O N

THE RECORDS OF THIS OFFICE SHOW: That at Muldrow, Indian Territory, August 17, 1900 application was received by the Commission to the Five Civilized Tribes for the enrollment of Simeon Eldridge as a citizen by intermarriage of the Cherokee Nation. Further proceedings in the matter of said application were had at Muskogee, Indian Territory, October 9, 1902, January 4, 1907 and January 22, 1907.

THE EVIDENCE IN THIS CASE SHOWS: That the applicant herein, Simeon Eldridge, a white man, was married in accordance with Cherokee law in February, 1874

Cherokee Intermarried White 1906
Volume VI

to his wife, Nancy J. Eldridge, nee Thornton, since deceased, who was at the time of said marriage a recognized citizen by blood of the Cherokee Nation, who is identified on the Cherokee authenticated tribal roll of 1880, Sequoyah district, opposite No. 441, as "Mary J. Eldridge", an adopted white, but this enrollment is clearly erroneous as said applicant appears on the Cherokee census roll of 1896 as a citizen by blood of the Cherokee Nation. Also two children of said Nancy J. Eldridge appear on said roll as Cherokees by blood. It is further shown that from the time of said marriage until the death of said Nancy J. Eldridge, which occurred in January, 1899, the said Simeon Eldridge and Nancy J. Eldridge resided together as husband and wife and continuously lived in the Cherokee Nation; that after the death of said Nancy J. Eldridge the said Simeon Eldridge remained unmarried and continuously lived in the Cherokee Nation up to and including September 1, 1902. Said applicant is identified on the Cherokee authenticated tribal roll of 1880 and the Cherokee census roll of 1896 as an intermarried citizen of the Cherokee Nation.

IT IS, THEREFORE, ORDERED AND ADJUDGED: That in accordance with the decision of the Supreme Court of the United States dated November 5, 1906 in the cases of Daniel Red Bird, et al. vs. the United States, Nos. 125, 126, 127, and 128, the said applicant, Simeon Eldridge, is entitled, under the provisions of Section Twenty-one of the Act of Congress approved June 28, 1898 (30 Stats. 495), to enrollment as a citizen by intermarriage of the Cherokee Nation, and his application for enrollment as such is accordingly granted.

Tams Bixby
Commissioner.

Dated at Muskogee, Indian Territory,
this   FEB 14 1907

◇◇◇◇◇

Cherokee 1561

Muskogee, Indian Territory, February 14, 1907.

W. W. Hastings,
    Attorney for the Cherokee Nation,
        Muskogee, Indian Territory.

Dear Sir:

     There is enclosed herewith a copy of the decision of the Commissioner to the Five Civilized Tribes, dated February 14, 1907, granting the application for the enrollment of Simeon Eldridge as a citizen by intermarriage of the Cherokee Nation.

Respectfully,

Encl. H-18   Commissioner.
JMH

◇◇◇◇◇

Cherokee Intermarried White 1906
Volume VI

Cherokee 1561

Muskogee, Indian Territory, February 14, 1907.

The Commissioner to the Five Civilized Tribes,
Muskogee, Indian Territory.

Sir:

Receipt is acknowledged of the testimony and of your decision enrolling Simeon Eldridge as a citizen by intermarriage of the Cherokee Nation. Time for protesting said decision is waived, and I consent that said person may be placed upon the schedule immediately.

Respectfully,
W. W. Hastings
Attorney for Cherokee Nation.

◇◇◇◇◇

Cherokee 1561

Muskogee, Indian Territory, February 14, 1907.

Simeon Eldridge,
Pawpaw, Indian Territory.

Dear Sir:

There is enclosed herewith a copy of the decision of the Commissioner to the Five Civilized Tribes, dated February 14, 1907, granting the application for your enrollment as a citizen by intermarriage of the Cherokee Nation.

You will be advised when your name has been placed upon a schedule of citizens of the Cherokee Nation and approved by the Secretary of the Interior.

Respectfully,

Commissioner.

Encl. H-19
JMH

Cher IW 184

Cherokee Intermarried White 1906
Volume VI

E.C.M.

DEPARTMENT OF THE INTERIOR,

COMMISSIONER TO THE FIVE CIVILIZED TRIBES.

In the matter of the application for the enrollment of

STEPHEN N. CARLILE

As a citizen by intermarriage of the Cherokee Nation.

CHEROKEE NO. 1608.

◇◇◇◇◇

DEPARTMENT OF THE INTERIOR.
COMMISSION TO THE FIVE CIVILIZED TRIBES.
FT. GIBSON, I. T., AUGUST 20th, 1900

IN THE MATTER OF THE APPLICATION OF Stephen N. Carlile for enrollment as a citizen of the Cherokee Nation, and he being sworn by Commissioner, T. B. Needles, testified as follows:

Q What is your name?   A Stephen N. Carlile.
Q What is your age?   A Sixty three the 29th of this month.
Q What is your Postoffice?   A Gritts.
Q Are you a recognized citizen of the Cherokee Nation?
A Adopted citizen.
Q What district do you live in?   A Canadian.
Q How long have you lived there?   A Since 1867.
Q Continuously?   A Yes sir.
Q For whom do you apply to be enrolled?   A Just myself /[sic]
Q Only yourself?   A Yes sir.
Q Have you no children to enroll?   A No sir.
Q What is your mother's name?   A Polly Carlile.
Q Does your name appear on the roll of 1880?   A I suppose it does.
(Applicant identified on the roll of 1880, Page 9, #239, as S.L. Carlile, Canadian District)
(On the roll of 1896, Page 86, #57, Stephen Carlile, Canadian District)

The name of Stephen N. Carlile, appearing on the authenticated roll of 1880, and the census roll of 1896, being fully identified according to the page and number of said rolls as indicated in the testimony, and having made satisfactory proof of his residence, he will be duly listed for enrollment as a citizen of the Cherokee Nation by intermarriage.

Cherokee Intermarried White 1906
Volume VI

R. R. Cravens, being sworn, states that as stenographer to the Commission to the Five Civilized Tribes, he reported the foregoing case, and that the above and foregoing is a true, full and correct transcript of his stenographic notes in said case.

R R Cravens

Sworn to and subscribed before me this twenty fourth day of August, 1900.

C R Breckinridge
COMMISSIONER.

⋄⋄⋄⋄⋄

Statement of Applicant Taken Under Oath.

CHEROKEE BY BLOOD AND ADOPTION.

(63)
Date **AUG 20 1900** 1900.
Name **Stephen N Carlile** **Gritts I.T.**
District **Canadian** Year **1880** Page **9** No. **239**
Citizen by blood _____ Mother's citizenship _____
Intermarried citizen **Yes** parents - **Thomas Carlile**
Married under what law _____ Date of marriage **Charlotte Polly** "
License _____ Certificate _____
Wife's name _____
District _____ Year _____ Page _____ No. _____
Citizen by blood _____ Mother's citizenship _____
Intermarried citizen _____
Married under what law _____ Date of marriage _____
License _____ Certificate _____

Names of Children:

	Dist.	Year	Page	No.	Age
	Dist.	Year	Page	No.	Age
	Dist.	Year	Page	No.	Age
	Dist.	Year	Page	No.	Age
	Dist.	Year	Page	No.	Age
	Dist.	Year	Page	No.	Age
	Dist.	Year	Page	No.	Age
	Dist.	Year	Page	No.	Age

#1608

⋄⋄⋄⋄⋄

Cherokee Intermarried White 1906
Volume VI

Cher # 1608

Department of the Interior,
Commission to the Five Civilized Tribes,
Muskogee, I. T., October 2, 1902.

In the matter of the application of STEPHEN N. CARLILE, for the enrollment of himself as a citizen by intermarriage of the Cherokee Nation:

STEPHEN N. CARLILE, called as a witness, being duly sworn and examined by the Commission, testified as follows:

Q What is your name ? A Stephen N. Carlile.
Q What is your post office address ? A Gritts.
Q Are you the same Stephen N. Carlile for whom application was made before this Commission in August, 1900 ? A Yes sir.
Q What was your Cherokee wife's name ? A Josephine Carlile.
Q What was her maiden name ? A Blackstone.
Q Is she living or dead ? A She's been dead fifteen years.
Q When were you and her married ?
A We were married in 1873, in April, 1873.
Q Had you ever been married prior to your marriage to Josephine ?
A Yes sir.
Q How many times ? A Twice before.
Q Were they both white women ? A No sir, my first wife was a Cherokee, and the second a white woman.
Q Were both these wives dead when you married Josephine ? A Yes sir.
Q You married your first wife under a Cherokee license ? A Yes sir.
Q Did you file your marriage license in your application ?
A I suppose the clerk of the court did.
Q Did you and your wife Josephine live together as husband and wife from the time of your marriage up to her death ? A Yes sir.
Q You were never separated ? A No sir.
Q Since your wife Josephine's death have you ever married again ? A No sir.
Q Still a widower ? A Yes sir.
Q You were a widower on the first day of September, 1902 ? A Yes sir.
Q How long have you lived in the Cherokee Nation ? A Nearly all my life, sir.
Q Have you lived in the Cherokee Nation all the time since 1880 ? A Yes sir.
Q Never lived out ? A Lived in Canadian District ever since.

E. C. Bagwell, on oath states that, as stenographer to the Commission to the Five Civilized Tribes, he correctly recorded the testimony and proceedings had in the above entitled cause, and that the foregoing is an accurate transcript of his stenographic notes thereof.

Cherokee Intermarried White 1906
Volume VI

E.C. Bagwell

Subscribed and sworn to before me this October 11, 1902.

BC Jones
Notary Public.

◇◇◇◇◇

F.R.   Cherokee 1608.

DEPARTMENT OF THE INTERIOR, COMMISSIONER TO THE FIVE CIVILIZED TRIBES.
Muskogee, I. T., January 28, 1907.

In the matter of the application for the enrollment of Stephen N. Carlisle as a citizen by intermarriage of the Cherokee Nation.

John Carlisle, being first duly sworn by Frances R. Lane, a Notary Public for the Western District of Indian Territory, testified as follows:

By the Commissioner:
Q What is your name? A John Carlisle.
Q What is yur[sic] age? A Thirty-nine years.
Q Your postoffice address? A Campbell, I. T.
Q You appear here for the purpose of giving testimony raltive[sic] to the right to enrollment of Stephen N. Carlisle as an intermarried citizen of the Cherokee Nation?
A Yes sir.
Q What relation are you to Stephen N. Carlisle? A Son.
Q Is Stephen N. Carlisle living at this time?
A No sir.
Q When did he die? A Died in February 9, 1905.
Q Stephen N. Carlisle was a white man was he? A Yes sir.
Q Not possessed of any Indian blood? A No sir.
Q His claim to the right to enrollment is by virtue of his marriage to a citizen by blood of the Cherokee nation[sic]? A Yes.
Q What is the name of the citizen through whom he claimed?
A Josephine Blackstone.
Q When was Stephen N. Carlisle married to her?
A In 1873 I think.
Q Where were they married? A Webbers Falls.
Q Were they married under a license of the Cherokee nation?
A Yes, I think so.
Q Have you any documentary evidence showing that marriage?
A No, I havn't[sic].
Q Do you understand that at the time they were married Miss Blackstone was a citizen by blood of the Cherokee nation[sic]? A Yes sir.

Cherokee Intermarried White 1906
Volume VI

Q And that from the time of their marriage they resides[sic] together as husband and wife and lived continuously in the Cherokee nation[sic]?
A Yes, until her death.
Q Where is Mrs. Carlisle at this time? A She is dead.
Q When did she die.[sic] A I declare, I don't know; about 1888 I reckon.
Q Did Stephen N. Carlisle marry again? A Yes sir.
Q Who was his second wife? A Rose Blackstone.
Q Was she a recognized citizen of the Cherokee Nation?
A No sir.
Q She was a white woman? A She was a citizen by adoption but not by blood.
Q What was she? A White woman.
Q When were they married? A They were married in 1904, about a year before my father died, and he died in February, 1905.
Q From the time of the death of Josephine Blackstone he remained unmarried until he married Rose Blackstone in 1904? A Yes sir.
Q Were Rose Blackstone and Josephine Blackstone related in any way? A Rose Blackstone was the wife of Tom Blackstone; she was sister-in-law by marriage.
Q Is it your understanding that Josephine Blackstone was never married before she married Stephen N. Carlisle?
A Yes sir.
Q Is it your understanding that Stephen N. Carlisle was never married before he married Josephine Blackstone? A Yes, he was married before.
Q Was his first wife living at the time he married Jospehine[sic] Blackstone? A No sir.
Q Have you been recognized on any of the rolls of the Cherokee Nation? A No, my mother was a white woman.
Q You are the son of Stephen N. Carlisle's second wife? A Yes, his first wife was a Cherokee; he was married the fourth time; his first wife was a Cherokee and then he married my mother, a white woman, and then he married Josephine Blackstone.
Q What was the name of his first wife? A Eliza Alexander.
Q When was she married to Stephen N. Carlisle? A I don't know; I can't tell you.
Q What was the name of his second wife? A Lottie Pettit.
Q Was Eliza Alexander a citizen of the Cherokee Nation? A Yes, I think she was; I know she was because they enrolled the children; all on the roll. Of course I don't know anything about it; it is my understanding that she was a citizen.
Q Was she dead at the time he married Lottie Pettit? A Yes.
Q What do you understand to be the date of his marriage to Lottie Pettit? A Well, I don't know.
Q Was Lottie Pettit living at the time he was married to Josephine Blackstone?
A No sir.
Q Then Stephen N. Carlisle claims his right to enrollment through Josephine Blackstone whom he married in 1873? A Yes sir.
Q Do you know in what district they were married? A Canadian.
Q How old were you at the time of his marriage to Josephine Blackstone?
A About six years old.
Q Were you present at the marriage? A No sir.
Q Is there anyone present here today, that was present at that marriage? A No sir.

Cherokee Intermarried White 1906
Volume VI

Q Do you know of anyone who was present at the marriage who is living at this time?
A Not unless it is Mrs. McMurray, her sister.
Q Could Mrs. McMurray come here to testify in this case?
A I guess so; I don't know.

  The applicant, Stephen N. Carlisle is identified on the Cherokee authenticated tribal roll of 1880, Canadian District, No. 239, and also on the Cherokee Census roll of 1896, Canadian District opposite No. 57.

  Susan Lynch, being duly sworn by Frances R. Lane, a Notary Public for the Western District of Indian Territory, testified as follows:

By the Commissioner:
Q What is your name? A Susan Lynch.
Q What is your age? A Sixty next August.
Q What is your postoffice address? A Webbers Falls, I.T.
Q Did you ever know Stephen N. Carlisle in the Cherokee Nation?
A Yes, I knew him ever since I have been in Canadian District--ever since the war.
Q Did you ever know his wife Josephine Blackstone? A Yes.
Q Do you know when they were married? A They were married in 1873, I think in April.
Q Was you present at tht[sic] marriage? A No, they were married at home, right below our house.
Q You lived in the neighborhood at that time? A Yes sir.
Q It was the understanding in that community that Stephen N. Carlisle and Josephine Blackstone were married under a license of the Cherokee Nation--lawfully married according to the laws of the Cherokee Nation? A Yes sir.
Q They resided together as husband and wife abd[sic] continuously lived in the Cherokee Nation until her death? A Yes sir.
Q When did she die? A Somewhere-- I can't say just what year it was; it several years.
Q From the time of her death did Stephen Carlisle remain unmarried until he married in 1904? A Yes sir.
Q And continued to reside in the Cherokee Nation? A Yes, rigght[sic] in the neighborhood.
Q Do you know whether or not Jospehine[sic] Blackstone was married prior to the time she married Stephen N. Carlisle? A No, she was not.
Q Mr. Carlisle, however, had been married before? A Yes, it is my understanding he had been married twice before.
Q Were either of these wives living at the time he married Josephine Blackstone?
A No, I don't think so; I never knew either of his first wives.
Q Do you know anyone who was present at the marriage of Josephine Blackstone in 1873? A No, I don't. Josephine Blackstone had a sister. I expect there is no doubt but she was right at home when she was married.
Q You don't remember any of the signers to Mr. Carlisle's petition do you? A I think a brother of mine, Jesse Foreman, signed it.
Q Where does Mr. Foreman live? A He is dead.

Cherokee Intermarried White 1906
Volume VI

Q Stephen N. Carlisle and Josephine Blackstone never separated; they lived together until her death? A No, they never separated.

Frank Vore being first duly sworn by Frances R. Lane, a Notary Public for the Western District of Indian Territory, testified as follows:

Q What is your name? A Frank Vore.
Q Your age? A Fifty-three.
Q Your postoffice address? A Webbers Falls, I. T.
Q Did you ever know Stephen N. Carlisle in the Cherokee Nation?
A Yes sir.
Q When did you first know him? A About 1867 or 68, I expect.
Q Did you ever know Josephine Blackstone? A Yes sir.
Q Do you know whether or not Stephen N. Carlisle and Josephine Blackstone were married? A No, I don't know the day of the month. But they were married before 1875, I know that.
Q How do you fix the date as being previous to 1875?
A Jesse Foreman was killed in 1875 and I know Carlisle was married before that time.
Q You were not present at that marriage? A No, I lived about a quarter of a mile from them at that time.
Q Did you understand that that marriage was under a license of the Cherokee nation[sic]? A Not for certain, but I think they were married according to the Cherokee laws at that time.
Q You have no reason to think they were not married according to the Cherokee laws?
A No sir.
Q From the time of their marriage in 1875 they held themselves out as husband and wife and continuously lived in the Cherokee Nation until the death of his wife? A Yes sir.
Q At the time of the marriage Josephine Blackstone was recognized as a citizen by blood of the Cherokee nation? A Yes sir.
Q She had not been married previous to her marriage to Stephen N. Carlisle? A No sir.
Q Stephen N. Carlisle had been married before he married Josephine Blackstone?
A Yes sir.
Q Is it your understanding that either of his first wives were living at the time of his marriage to Josephine Blackstone? A Neither one of them.
Q About what year did Josephine Carlisle die? A I can't say; must have been ten years; must have been--must have lived something like ten years until she died.
Q From the time of her death did Stephen N. Carlisle remarry until 1904? A I believe in the fall of 1903, when he marries Rose Blackstone.
Q You couldn't be mistaken as to this daye[sic] of the marriage to Rose Blackstone as much as a year could you?
Q Can you state positively that he was not married September 1, 1902? A Well, yes, I believe I could; I think 1902 Carlisle and I took a trip to California.
Q How do you fix the date of his marriage to Rose Blackstone? By what events?
A I know when he told me about it.

Cherokee Intermarried White 1906
Volume VI

Q What other events happened that caused you to fix the date as subsequent to 1902?
A I went to California with him and it was after that trip, and that trip was in 1902; but I can't remember dates.
Q You think you made the trip to California in 1902? A Yes.
Q How long did you stay there? A Staid about a month.
Q Then you returned early in the year 1903? A Yes sir.
Q And Mr. Carlisle was not married to Rose Blackstone at that time? A No sir.
Q That is your reason for fixing this date as being after September 1, 1902? A Yes sir.

Frances R. Lane upon oath states that as stenographer to the Commission to the Five Civilized Tribes she reported the testimony in the above entitled cause and that the foregoing is an accurate transcript of her stenographic notes thereof.

Frances R Lane

Subscribed and sworn to before me this January 29, 1907.

Edward Merrick
Notary Public.

◇◇◇◇◇

(The below typed as given.)

C E R T I F I E D   C O P Y .

To any Judge or ordained Minister of the Gospel, Greeting -
You are hereby authorized to solemnize the rites of Matrimony between Stephen Carlisle, a white man, Citizen of the United States and Miss Josephine Blackstone, a Cherokee, the said Stephen Carlisle having complyed with all the requirements of law in such cases made and provided. Given from under my hand officially this the 4th day of April 1873.

(Signed) I. A. Scales, Clerk
District Court,
Can. District.

I Stephen P. Hicks one of the ordained ministers of the M. E. Church South and member of the Indian Mision Confirence do hereby Cirtify that the above copel caim before me April the 6th A.D. 1873 in the Cherokee nation and was married. given under my hand this the above date.

(Signed) Stephen P. Hicks Pole
of Canadian Circuit.

Cherokee Intermarried White 1906
Volume VI

Apr. 4th, 1873.

To the District Clerk
of Canadian District

We the undersigned citizens of the Cherokee Nation do here by Certify that we are personally acquainted with Stephen Carlile[sic], a white man a citizen of the United States, and that he is of good Moral Character.

Respt --
(Signed)   C. J. Hanks
J. O. McCoy.
H. Lindsey
E. J. Harland
John Cobb
I. A. Scales
Abe Woodall

This certifies that the undersigned, being duly sworn, states that as stenographer to the Commissioner to the Five Civilized Tribes she made the above and foregoing copy and that the same is a full, true and correct copy of the original instrument now on file in this office.

Georgia Coberly

Subscribed and sworn to before me this 1st day of February, 1907.

Oliver C Hinkle
Notary Public.

◇◇◇◇◇

E C M   Cherokee 1608.

DEPARTMENT OF THE INTERIOR,

COMMISSIONER TO THE FIVE CIVILIZED TRIBES.

In the matter of the application for the enrollment of STEPHEN N. CARLILE as a citizen by intermarriage of the Cherokee Nation.

D E C I S I O N

THE RECORDS OF THIS OFFICE SHOW: That at Fort Gibson, Indian Territory, August 20, 1900, application was received by the Commission to the Five Civilized

Cherokee Intermarried White 1906
Volume VI

Tribes for the enrollment of Stephen N. Carlile as a citizen by intermarriage of the Cherokee Nation. Further proceedings in the matter of said application were had at Muskogee, Indian Territory, October 2, 1902 and January 28, 1907.

THE EVIDENCE IN THIS CASE SHOWS: That the applicant herein, Stephen N. Carlile, a white man, was married in accordance with Cherokee law April 6, 1873 to his wife, Josephine Carlile, nee Blackstone, since deceased, who was at the time of said marriage a recognized citizen by blood of the Cherokee Nation, who is identified on the Cherokee authenticated tribal roll of 1880, Canadian District No. 240 as a native Cherokee, marked "Dead". It is further shown that from the time of said marriage until the death of said Josephine Carlile, which occurred about the year 1888, the said Stephen N. Carlile and Josephine Carlile resided together as husband and wife and continuously lived in the Cherokee Nation up to and including September 1, 1902. Said applicant is identified on the Cherokee authenticated tribal roll of 1880 and the Cherokee census roll of 1896 as an intermarried citizen of the Cherokee Nation.

IT IS, THEREFORE, ORDERED AND ADJUDGED: That in accordance with the decision of the Supreme Court of the United States, dated November 5, 1906 in the cases of Daniel Red Bird et al. vs. the United States, Nos. 125, 126, 127, and 128, the said applicant, Stephen N. Carlile is entitled, under the provisions of Section Twenty-one of the Act of Congress approved June 28th, 1898 (30 Stats. 495), to enrollment as a citizen by intermarriage of the Cherokee Nation, and his application for enrollment as such is accordingly granted.

Tams Bixby
Commissioner.

Dated at Muskogee, Indian Territory,
this FEB 13 1907

◇◇◇◇◇

REFER IN REPLY TO THE FOLLOWING:
Cherokee
1608

DEPARTMENT OF THE INTERIOR,
COMMISSIONER TO THE FIVE CIVILIZED TRIBES.

Muskogee, Indian Territory, December 27, 1906.

Rosa Carlile,
    San Pedro, California.

Dear Madam:

November 6, 1906, the United States Supreme Court held that white persons who intermarried with Cherokee citizens according to Cherokee law prior to November 1, 1875, are entitled to enrollment and allotments of land as citizens of the Cherokee Nation.

Cherokee Intermarried White 1906
Volume VI

You are advised that to properly determine the right of your deceased husband, Stephen N. Carlile, to enrollment as a citizen by intermarriage of the Cherokee Nation, it will be necessary for you to appear before the Commissioner for the purpose of giving testimony as to the date of his marriage and whether or not his wife, by reason of his marriage to whom he claims the right to enrollment as a citizen by intermarriage of the Cherokee Nation, was a recognized Cherokee citizen at the time of his marriage to her, and whether or not he was married to her in accordance with Cherokee laws[sic]

You are, therefore, directed to appear before the Commissioner at Muskogee, Indian Territory, at 9 o'clock A. M., on Thursday, January 3, 1907, and give testimony as above indicated.

Respectfully,
Wm O. Beall
Acting Commissioner.

JMH

◇◇◇◇◇

Cherokee
1608.

Muskogee, Indian Territory, February 13, 1907.

W. W Hastings,
    Attorney for the Cherokee Nation,
        Muskogee, Indian Territory.

Dear Sir:

There is enclosed herewith a copy of the decision of the Commissioner to the Five Civilized Tribes, dated February 13, 1907, granting the application for the enrollment of Stephen N. Carlile, as a citizen by intermarriage of the Cherokee Nation.

Respectfully,

Encl. HJ-41.
HJC.

Commissioner.

◇◇◇◇◇

Cherokee Intermarried White 1906
Volume VI

Cherokee 1608.

Muskogee, Indian Territory, February 13, 1907.

The Commissioner to the Five Civilized Tribes,
Muskogee, Indian Territory.

Sir:

Receipt is acknowledged of the testimony and of your decision enrolling Stephen N. Carlile as a citizen by intermarriage of the Cherokee Nation. Time for protesting said decision is waived and I consent that said person may be placed upon the schedule immediately.

Respectfully,
W. W. Hastings
Attorney for Cherokee Nation.

◇◇◇◇◇

Cherokee
1608.

Muskogee, Indian Territory, February 13, 1907.

John Carlile,
Campbell, Indian Territory.

Dear Sir:

There is enclosed herewith a copy of the decision of the Commissioner to the Five Civilized Tribes, dated February 13, 1907, granting the application for the enrollment of your father as a citizen by intermarriage of the Cherokee Nation.

You will be advised when your name has been placed upon a schedule of citizens of the Cherokee Nation and approved by the Secretary of the Interior.

Respectfully,

Encl. HJ-40.
HJC.
Commissioner.

◇◇◇◇◇

Cherokee Intermarried White 1906
Volume VI

Cherokee
I.W. 184.

Muskogee, Indian Territory, April 16, 1907.

John Carlisle,
    Campbell, Indian Territory.

Dear Sir:

    Your marriage license and certificate filed in connection with your application for enrollment as a citizen by intermarriage of the Cherokee Nation is returned to you herewith, copies of the same being retained in the files of this office.

                      Respectfully,

Encl. W-4   Commissioner.
S.W.

Cher IW 185

DEPARTMENT OF THE INTERIOR,
COMMISSION TO THE FIVE CIVILIZED TRIBES,
FORT GIBSON, I. T., AUGUST 20, 1900.

    In the matter of the application of Reece Hilderbrand for the enrollment of himself, wife and children as citizens of the Cherokee Nation; said Hilderbrand being sworn by Commissioner T. B. Needles, testified as follows:

Q What is your name? A Reece Hilderbrand.
Q What is your age? A About 50.
Q What is your post office address? A Webbers Falls.
Q Are you a recognized citizen of the Cherokee Nation? A Yes, sir.
Q What district do you live in? A Canadian.
Q How long have you lived in the Cherokee Nation continuously? A All my live.
Q Whom do you apply for enrollment for? A Myself, wife and children.
Q Both your father and mother living? A No, sir, both dead.
Q Did they die before 1880? A Yes, sir.
Q What was your wife?s[sic] name? A Lydia.
Q When did you marry her? A About 27 years ago.
Q Are her father and mother non-citizens? A Yes, sir.
Q What was your wife's name before you married her? A Lydia Latta
Q Have you any children at home under 21 years of age? A Yes, five.

Cherokee Intermarried White 1906
Volume VI

Q Give me the names of those of the oldest one at home? A Lelia; 17 years old. On '96 roll, page 867, number 821.
Q The next one? A William; 13 years old. On '96 roll, page 865, #822.
Q The next child? A Thomas; 10 years old. On '96 roll, page 865, number 823.
Q The next one? A John; six years old. On '96 roll, page 865, number 824, as Johny.
Q The next child? A Annie; five years old. On '96 roll, page 865, #825.
Q Are these children alive and living with you at this time? A Yes, sir.

Applicant on '80 roll, page 24, Number 686, as R.M. Hilderbrand.
865
On '96 roll, page (869), number 819.
Applicant's wife on '80 roll, page 24, number 679.

The name of Reece Hilderbrand appears upon the authenticated roll of 1880 as R. M. Hilderbrand, and upon the 1896 roll as Reece Hilderbrand. The name of his wife, Lydia, appears upon the authenticated roll of 1880, and the names of his children, Lelia, William, Thomas, John and Annie appear upon the census roll of 1896. His wife's name is not found upon the census roll of 1896; and they having made satisfactory proof as to their residence and being duly identified on the rolls according to page and number as indicated in the testimony; said Reece Hilderbrand will be duly listed for enrollment as a Cherokee citizen by blood, and his wife, Lydia, will be duly listed for enrollment as a Cherokee citizen by intermarriage, she having been an intermarried white before 1880, and his five children as named in the testimony being duly identified on the rolls will be duly listed for enrollment by this Commission as Cherokees by blood.

The undersigned, being first duly sworn, states that as stenographer to the Commission to the Five Civilized Tribes, he correctly recorded the testimony and proceedings in this case, and that the foregoing is a true and complete transcript of his stenographic notes thereof.

Brown McDonald

Subscribed and sworn to before me this 7th day of September 1900 at Muskogee, I.T.

TB Needles
Commissioner.

◇◇◇◇◇

(There are three pages for this applicant that are completely illegible.)

◇◇◇◇◇

Cherokee Intermarried White 1906
Volume VI

C.FB.   Cherokee 1672

DEPARTMENT OF THE INTERIOR,
COMMISSIONER TO THE FIVE CIVILIZED TRIBES.
MUSKOGEE, IND. TER., JANUARY 4, 1907.

In the matter of the application for the enrollment of LYDIA HILDERBRAND as a citizen by intermarriage of the Cherokee Nation.

APPEARANCES: APPLICANT Appears in person:

CHEROKEE NATION represented by H.M. Vance, on behalf of W. W. Hastings, Attorney.

LYDIA HILDERBRAND being first duly sworn by B. P. Rasmus, a Notary Public, testified as follows:

On Behalf of Commissioner:

Q. What is your name? A. Lydia Hilderbrand.
Q. What is your age? A. I will be fifty years old the 20th of March.
Q. What is your postoffice? A. Webbers Falls.
Q. You claim the right to enrollment as a citizen by intermarriage of the Cherokee Nation? A. Yes sir.
Q. You have no Cherokee blod[sic]? A. Well, I was adopted- I was born and raised in the Cherokee Nation.
Q. But you are not a Cherokee by blood? A. No sir.
Q. The only claim you make to enrollment as a citizen of the Cherokee Nation is by virtue of your marriage to a citizen by blood of the Cherokee Nation, is it? A. Yes sir.
Q. What is the name of the citizen through whom you claim the right to enrollment?
A. That would be my man, wouldn't it?
Q. Yes m'am? A. Reece Hilderbrand.
Q. When were you married to your husband, Reece Hilderbrand?
A. We have been married thirty-three years, you can count how long it has been.
Q. Was he a recognized citizen of the Cherokee Nation at the time you married him?
A. Yes sir.
Q. And was living in the Cherokee Nation, was he? A. Yes sir
Q. Were you his first wife? A. Yes sir.
Q. Was he your first husband? A. Yes sir.
Q. Since your marriage to your husband, Reece Hilderbrand, in about the year 1873, have you and he continuously lived together as husband and wife? A. Yes sir.
Q. And have lived in the Cherokee Nation all that time?
A. Yes sir.
Q. Who married you?
A. Judge Woodall.

Cherokee Intermarried White 1906
Volume VI

Q. Did he give you a certificate of your marriage?
A. No sir, we didn't have them in them days.
Q. Were there any witnesses to your marriage? A. None but Tom Woodall.
Q. Is he living? A. Yes sir; he was when we left home; He is not here.

The applicant, Lydia Hilderbrand, is identified on the Cherokee authenticated tribal roll of 1880 Cooweescoowee District, No. 879. Her husband, Reece Hilderbrand, in[sic] included in an approved partial roll of citizens by blood of the Cherokee Nation opposite No. 4458.

The undersigned, being first duly sworn, states that as stenographer to the Commissioner to the Five Civilized Tribes she correctly recorded the testimony taken in this case, and that the above and foregoing is a full, true and correct transcript of her stenographic notes thereof.

Lucy M Bowman

Subscribed and sworn to before me this 5th day of January, 1907.

John E. Tidwell
Notary Public.

◇◇◇◇◇

Cherokee 1672.

DEPARTMENT OF THE INTERIOR,
COMMISSIONER TO THE FIVE CIVILIZED TRIBES.
Muskogee, Indian Territory,
February 11, 1907.

In the matter of the application for the enrollment of LYDIA HILDERBRAND as a citizen by intermarriage of the Cherokee Nation.

Cherokee Nation represented by
W. W. Hastings, Atty.

THOMAS WOODALL, being first duly sworn by Walter W. Chapell[sic], a Notary Public, testifies as follows:

ON BEHALF OF THE COMMISSIONER:

Cherokee Intermarried White 1906
Volume VI

Q   What is your name?
A   Thomas Woodall.
Q   Your age?
A   47 in March.
Q   Your post-office address?
A   Warner, Indian Territory.
Q   You appear here for the purpose of giving testimony relative to the right of Lydia Hilderbrand to enrollment as a citizen by intermarriage of the Cherokee Nation.
A   Yes sir.
Q   How long have you known them?
A   I could'nt[sic] tell you exactly.
Q   Was your father a minister?
A   No sir, he was a judge.
Q   Do you remember when they were married?
A   No sir, I saw them married, but don't remember when it was.
Q   Has it been 35 years?
A   Something like that.

BY W.W. HASTINGS, ATTY. FOR CHEROKEE NATION.

Q   How old are you?
A   47 on the 8th of March.
Q   What you want to testify to today is to the effect that you saw them married, but you are not prepared, you say, to give any date?
A   It has been a long time, but I can't remember any date.

(Witness excused)

REECE HILDERBRAND, being first duly sworn by Walter W. Chapell[sic], a Notary Public, testifies as follows:

BY THE COMMISSIONER:

Q   What is your name?
A   Reece Hilderbrand.
Q   Your age?
A   About 56 years old.
Q   What is your post-office address?
A   Webbers Fall[sic], Indian Territory.
Q   Are you the husband of Lydia Hilderbrand, the applicant in this case?
A   Yes sir.
Q   When were you married?
A   Its[sic] been about 33 years.
Q   What year were you married in?
A   I don't know exactly, right at '73.

Cherokee Intermarried White 1906
Volume VI

Q   Are you a citizen by blood of the Cherokee Nation?
A   Yes sir.
Q   Were you born in the Cherokee Nation?
A   Yes sir.
Q   Never lived out of the Cherokee Nation?
A   No sir.
Q   Were you ever married before your marriage to Lydia Hilderbrand?
A   No sir.
Q   Was she ever married before?
A   No sir.
Q   You are her first husband and she is your first wife?
A   Yes sir.
Q   Have you ever been separated?
A   No sir.

BY W. W. HASTINGS, ATTY. FOR CHEROKEE NATION:

Q   You were married about 33 years ago?
A   Just about.
Q   How old is your oldest child?
A   I don't really know, about 30 years old.
Q   What is the name of your oldest child by this wife?
A   Mary Hilderbrand.
Q   Is she married?
A   Walters is her married name, Mary Walters.

    1880 Roll examined, Canadian District, Page 24, said applicant Lydia Hilderbrand is identified opposite No. 679, and Mary E. Hilderbrand, her daughter is enrolled opposite No. 680 as a native Cherokee four years old.

(Witness excused)

    This certifies that the undersigned, being duly sworn, states that as stenographer to the Commission to the Five Civilized Tribes she reported the proceedings had in the above entitled cause and that the above and foregoing is a full, true and correct transcript of her stenographic notes thereof.

Georgia Coberly
Stenographer.

Subscribed and sworn to before me this 12th day of February, 1907.

Walter W. Chappell
Notary Public.

Cherokee Intermarried White 1906
Volume VI

CERTIFIED COPY.

United States of America,)
)
Indian Territory,) ss
)
Western District)

BE IT KNOWN, That, on this 23rd. day of January, 1907, personally appeared before me, a Notary Public, within and for the Western District of the Indian Territory, Thomas F. Woodall, who, being sworn, said: That he has known Reece Hilderbrand and Lydia Hilderbrand, his wife, for about thirty-five years; that he was present and witnessed the marriage of Reece Hilderbrand to Lydia Latty about thirty three years ago; that he knows the present wife of Reece Hilderbrand, who is called Lydia Hilderbrand, to be the same identical person who was married to Reece Hilderbrand at the above mentioned ceremony; and that they have lived together continuously since said ceremony.

(Signed) H. C. Wynne,
Notary Public.

My commission expires Sept. 27. 09.

(SEAL)

This certifies that the undersigned, being duly sworn, states that as stenographer to the Commission to the Five Civilized Tribes she made the above and foregoing copy and that the same is a full, true and correct copy of the original instrument now on file in this office.

Georgia Coberly
Stenographer.

Subscribed and sworn to before me this 13th day of February, 1907.

Frances R Lane
Notary Public.

Cherokee Intermarried White 1906
Volume VI

E C M

Cherokee 1672.

DEPARTMENT OF THE INTERIOR,

COMMISSIONER TO THE FIVE CIVILIZED TRIBES.

In the matter of the application for the enrollment of LYDIA HILDERBRAND as a citizen by intermarriage of the Cherokee Nation.

D E C I S I O N

THE RECORDS OF THIS OFFICE SHOW: That at Fort Gibson, Indian Territory, August 20, 1900 application was received by the Commission to the Five Civilized Tribes for the enrollment of Lydia Hilderbrand as a citizen by intermarriage of the Cherokee Nation. Further proceedings in the matter of said application were had at Muskogee, Indian Territory, September 11, 1902, October 20, 1902, Tahlequah, Indian Territory, November 24, 1904 and at Muskogee, Indian Territory, January 4, 1907 and February 11, 1907.

THE EVIDENCE IN THIS CASE SHOWS: That the applicant herein, Lydia Hilderbrand, a white woman was married in 1873 to one Reece Hilderbrand, who was at the time of said marriage a recognized citizen by blood of the Cherokee Nation, who is identified on the Cherokee authenticated tribal roll of 1880, Canadian District No. 686, as a native Cherokee, and whose name is included on the approved partial roll of citizens by blood of the Cherokee Nation opposite No. 4458. It is further shown that from the time of said marriage the said Reece Hilderbrand and Lydia Hilderbrand resided together as husband and wife and continuously lived in the Cherokee Nation up to and including September 1, 1902. Said applicant is identified on the Cherokee authenticated tribal roll of 1880 and the Cherokee census roll of 1896 as an intermarried citizen of the Cherokee Nation.

IT IS, THEREFORE, ORDERED AND ADJUDGED: That in accordance with the decision of the Supreme Court of the United States dated November 5, 1906 in the cases of Daniel Red Bird, et al. vs. the United States, Nos. 125, 126, 127, and 128, the said applicant, Lydia Hilderbrand is entitled, under the provisions of Section Twenty-one of the Act of Congress approved June 28, 1898 (30 Stats. 495), to enrollment as a citizen by intermarriage of the Cherokee Nation, and her application for enrollment as such is accordingly granted.

Tams Bixby
Commissioner.

Dated at Muskogee, Indian Territory,
this   FEB 15 1907

Cherokee Intermarried White 1906
Volume VI

Cherokee 1672

Muskogee, Indian Territory, February 15, 1907.

W. W. Hastings,
    Attorney for the Cherokee Nation,
        Muskogee, Indian Territory.

Dear Sir:

    There is enclosed herewith a copy of the decision of the Commissioner to the Five Civilized Tribes, dated February 15, 1907, granting the application for the enrollment of Lydia Hilderbrand as a citizen by intermarriage of the Cherokee Nation.

        Respectfully,

Encl. H-2
JMH
        Commissioner.

◇◇◇◇◇

Cherokee 1672

Muskogee, Indian Territory, February 15, 1907.

The Commissioner to the Five Civilized Tribes,
    Muskogee, Indian Territory.

Sir:

    Receipt is acknowledged of the testimony and of your decision enrolling Lydia Hilderbrand as a citizen by intermarriage of the Cherokee Nation. Time for protesting said decision is waived and I consent that said person may be placed upon the schedule immediately.

        Respectfully,
        W. W. Hastings
        Attorney for Cherokee Nation.

◇◇◇◇◇

Cherokee Intermarried White 1906
Volume VI

Cherokee 1672

Muskogee, Indian Territory, February 15, 1907.

Lydia Hilderbrand,
Webbers Falls, Indian Territory.

Dear Madam:

There is enclosed herewith a copy of the decision of the Commissioner to the Five Civilized Tribes, dated February 15, 1907, granting the application for your enrollment as a citizen by intermarriage of the Cherokee Nation.

You will be advised when your name has been placed upon a schedule of citizens of the Cherokee Nation and approved by the Secretary of the Interior.

Respectfully,

Encl. H-3
JMH

Commissioner.

Cher IW 186

E.C.M.

DEPARTMENT OF THE INTERIOR,

COMMISSIONER TO THE FIVE CIVILIZED TRIBES.

In the matter of the application for the enrollment of

FRENCH MILLER

as a citizen by intermarriage of the Cherokee Nation.

CHEROKEE NO. 1742.

Cherokee Intermarried White 1906
Volume VI

DEPARTMENT OF THE INTERIOR.
COMMISSION TO THE FIVE CIVILIZED TRIBES.
FT. GIBSON, I. T., AUGUST 21st, 1900.

IN THE MATTER OF THE APPLICATION OF French Miller, wife and children for enrollment as citizens of the Cherokee Nation, and he being sworn by Commissioner, T. B. Needles, testified as follows:

Q What is your name? A French Miller.
Q What is your age? A Fifty two.
Q What is your Postoffice? A Ft. Gibson.
Q Are you a recognized citizen of the Cherokee Nation? A No sir; as an adopted citizen/[sic]
Q What district do you live in? A Illinois.
Q How long have you lived in Illinois? A Since 1870.
Q Whom do you apply for for[sic] enrollment? A For myself.
Q For any one else? A My wife.
Q Have you any children? A I got some children, but they are not mine; I have one, but two are not mine.
Q Do you want to enroll any one desides[sic] yourself and wife?
A Yes sir; two children.
Q Are you father and mother living? A No sir.
Q They were non citizens? A Yes sir.
Q What is the name of your wife? A Cora Miller.
Q Her maiden name was? A Runyan.
Q What is her age? A Twenty six years old.
Q Is she white or Indian? A Indian by blood.
Q What is her father's name? A Ross Runyan.
Q Is he living? A No sir.
Q When did he die; about what year? A About 1894 I believe.
Q Was he a Cherokee citizen by blood? A Yes sir.
Q What is the name of your wife's mother? A I do not know.
Q She died before 1880? A Yes sir.
Q What are the names of your children? A Chute Miller.
Q How old is Chute? A About four years old.
Q What is the name of the next one? A Charlie Miller.
Q How old? A Born on Decoration day[sic]; will be three months old.
Q Have you any marriage certificate? A Yes sir.
Q Have you been married before? A Yes sir.
Q Is your first wife living? A No sir; she is dead.
Q Did you live with her until she died? A Yes sir.
(Applicant's wife identified on the roll of 1880, Page 572, #1513, as Cora Runyan, Illinois District)
(On the roll of 1896, Page 898, #1644, Cora Runyan, Illinois)

Cherokee Intermarried White 1906
Volume VI

(Applicant identified on the roll of 1880, Page 552, #1092, French Miller, Illinois District)
(On the roll of 1896, Page 932, #139, French Miller, Illinois)
(1896 Roll, Page 844, #300, Jack Blythe, Illinois District)
Q What is the name of Jack Blythe's mother? A Cora Runyan.
Q Was she ever married to Blythe? A I can not say.
Q Are you sure that Jack Blythe is Cora Runyan's son? A Yes sir.
Q Is he living with you? A Yes sir.
Q Chute and Charley are both living with you? AA[sic] Yes sir.
Q Have you any proof of their birth? A Yes sir.

   The name of French Miller appears on the authenticated roll of 1880, and the census roll of 1896, and the name of his wife, Cora Runyan appears on the authenticated roll of 1880, and the census roll of 1896, as Cora Runyan, her maiden name, she having been married to said French Miller according to the Certificate he presents, on the 11th day of August, 1895. The name of Jack Blythe, the child of the said Cora Runyan, appears on the census roll of 1896. And the said French Miller will be duly listed for enrollment by this Commission as a citizen by intermarriage. His wife, Cora French, and her son, Jack Blythe will be listed for enrollment as citizens by blood.

And his sons, Charles and Chute Miller, whose names do not appear on any of the rolls of the Cherokee Nation, they having been born since said rolls were compiled, will be listed for enrollment by this Commission as citizens by blood, when proper certificates of birth are furnished the Commission.

   R. R. Cravens, being sworn, states that as stenographer to the Commission to the Five Civilized Tribes, he reported in full the foregoing testimony and proceedings, and that the foregoing is a true, full and correct transcript of his stenographic notes in said case.

                         R R Cravens

Sworn to and subscribed before
me this 28th day of August, 1900.
                   TB Needles
                   COMMISSIONER.

Cherokee Intermarried White 1906
Volume VI

Cherokee 1742.

Department of the Interior.
Commission to the Five Civilized Tribes.
Muskogee, I. T., October 14, 1902.

In the matter of the application of French Miller for the enrollment of himself as a citizen by intermarriage, and for the enrollment of his wife, Cora, and children, Chute, Charles and step-child, Jack Blythe, as citizens by blood of the Cherokee Nation: he being sworn and examined by the Commission, testified as follows:

Q What is your name? A French Miller.
Q How old are you? A Fifty-six.
Q What is your postoffice? A Fort Gibson.
Q Are you a white man? A Yes sir.
Q Your name appears on the roll of 1880 does it? A Yes sir.
Q What is your wife's name? A Katie Vann.
Q Was she your wife in 1880? A Yes sir.
Q When did she die? A In '91.
Q Did you live with your wife, Katie, from 1880 to 1891? A Yes sir.
Q Never was separated? A No sir.
Q Always lived in the Cherokee Nation? A Yes sir.
Q Have you married again? A Yes sir.
Q When did you marry Cora? A In '94 or '95.
Q Been living with her ever since you married her? A Yes sir.
Q Have you made your home in the Cherokee Nation from 1880 up to this time? A Yes sir.
Q How many children have you? A Four; one of them is not on the roll; it is just coming. It has already come, I only have three on the roll.
Q You applied for three children? A Yes sir.
Q They are living at home with you? A Yes sir.

The undersigned, being duly sworn, states that as stenographer to the Commission to the Five Civilized Tribes he correctly recorded the testimony and proceedings in this case, and the foregoing is a true and correct transcript of his stenographic notes thereof.

E.G. Rothenberger

Subscribed and sworn to before me this 10th day of November, 1902.

BC Jones
Notary Public.

Cherokee Intermarried White 1906
Volume VI

F.R.   Cherokee 1742.

DEPARTMENT OF THE INTERIOR,
COMMISSIONER TO THE FIVE CIVILIZED TRIBES.
Muskogee, I. T., February 2, 1907.

In the matter of the application for the enrollment of Franch[sic] Miller as a citizen by intermarriage of the Cherokee Nation.

Appearances:
For the Cherokee Nation. H. M. Vance.
For the applicant: Major Waldron of the firm of
                Waldron & Cramer,
                      Muskoge[sic], Indian Territory.
Cora Miller, being first duly sworn, testified as follows: Sworn by Frances R. Lane, a Notary Public for the Western District of Indian Territory.

By the Commissioner:
Q What is your name? A Cora Miller.
Q What is your age? A Thirty-three years.
Q And your postoffice address? A Fort Gibson, I. T.
Q You appear here for the purpose of giving testimony relative to the right of French Miller as a citizen of the Cherokee nation[sic] by intermarriage? A Yes sir.
Q What relation is French Miller to you? A My husband.
Q When were you married to French Miller? A In 1895, August.
Q Had French Miller been married before he married you? A Yes sir.
Q How many times? A Once that I know of.
Q What was the name of that wife? A Kate Vann.
Q French Miller was a white man, not possessed of any Indian blood? A Yes, he was a white man.
Q His first wife, Katie Van[sic], was she a recognized citizen by blood of the Cherokee Nation at the time of their marriage? A Yes sir.
Q What is your understanding as to the time of the marriage of French Miller and Kate Vann?
A All I know is from hearing the neighbors say when they were married.
Q Qhat[sic] is your understanding? What have you heard to be the date? A 1872.
Q Do you know in what district they were married? A No, I do not.
Q Kate Vann is dead, is she? A Yes sir.
Q Do you know when she died? A No, I don't; I don't know what year she died.
Q It is your understanding that she was dead at the time you married Mr. Miller?
A Yes sir.
Q Is it your understanding that French Miller and Kate Vann resided together as husband and wife from the time of their marriage until she died? A Yes sir.
Q And that they lived in the Cherokee Nation during all that time? A Yes sir.
Q Mr. Miller continued to reside in the Cherokee Nation until his marriage to you?
A Yes sir.

Cherokee Intermarried White 1906
Volume VI

Q And since his marriage to you you have lived together as husband and wife?
A Yes sir.
Q And have lived continuously in the Cherokee nation[sic], and were so living on September 2, 1902? A Yes sir.
Q At the time of your marriage to French Miller you were a recognized citizen by blood of the Cherokee Nation? A Yes sir.
Q Have you any documentary evidence showing that marriage of French Missler[sic] and Kate Vann? A I don't know whether I have.
Q You have no papers or certificates? A No, no certificate. There was a paper; it was a pension paper filled out with the name of his first wife and the death of his children.
Q You don't know the name of Kate Vann's father do you? A No.
Q You don't remember who was present at the marriage--you don't know who was present at the marriage of French Miller and Kate Vann, do you? A No sir.
Q Were there any children born to Mr. Miller and Kate Vann? A Yes sir.
Q What is the name of the oldest one? A Oscar Miller.
Q Is he living at this time? A No sir.
Q When did he die? A I don't know what year he died in.
Q You don't know what year he was born? A No, I don't.
Q What is the next child's name? A Leslie or Ida. I guess Ida Miller was the second child--yes, I know she was.
Q Have you any witnesses who would know anything about the marriage of Miller and Kate Vann? A I know of several that ought to know.
Q What are their names, some of them?
A Mr. Henry Eiffert.

Witness excused.

Henry Eiffert, being duly sworn by Frances R. Lane, testified as follows:
Q What is your name? A Henry Eiffert.
Q How old are you? A Fifty-seven years.
Q Your postoffice address? A Fort Gibson, I. T.
Q Did you ever know one French Miller in the Cherokee Nation? A Yes sir.
Q When did you first know him? A Got acquainted with him along in 1868.
Q Was he a married man at the time you first knew him?
A No, he belonged to the army.
Q Did you know one Kate Vann in the Cherokee Nation?
A Yesm[sic] she had two names, but I think she went by the name of Kate Vann; she was a full blood Cherokee woman. Her father's name was Rope Campbell.
Q When did you first know her? A I got acquainted with her along in 1868.
Q Were French Miller and Kate Vann ever married? A Yes sir.
Q Were you present at their marriage? A I can't say positively whether I was or nor, but it seems to me I was. I knew of the marriage taking place. I was in the town when they were married. I don't know for sure whether I was there or not.
Q What is your understanding as to the date of the marriage?
A I think along in 1873 or '74, as near as I can remember.
Q Where did it take place? A Fort Gibson.

Cherokee Intermarried White 1906
Volume VI

Q Was it your understanding that marriage was under a license of the Cherokee Nation?
A Yes sir.
Q Were you one of the signers to Mr. Miller's petition?
A I don't remember; it is the first time the question has been asked me; it is so long ago; probably might have been.
Q What is your understanding as to the person who performed the marriage ceremony?
A My recollection is it was a preacher by the name of Rev. Willey. I can't recall his given name. He has a son living at Fort Gibson now; Charley Willey.
Q How do you remember the date of their marriage as being about the year 1872?
A Well he was married either just before I was or right afterwards is why I remember the circumstance.
Q And you were married when? A I was married in 1872.
Q You don't think you could be mistaken as much as 2 or 3 years as to the date of his marriage? A No, it seems to me that he was married before I was.
Q They resided together as husband and wife and held themselves out as such in that country, and were so regarded in that neighborhood? A Yes, Miller lived with her until she died, and all his children died with consumption--the whole family. He never left them.
Q When did Kate Vann die? A I don't remember that.
Q About what year? A I wasn't living in Fort Gibson at the time. I was living in Vinita. I heard about the death of Mrs. Miller.
Q French Miller was married again, was he? A Yes sir.
Q What was the name of his second wife? A Cora Runyan. She had been married previous to a man named Creekmore.
Q At the time she married French Miller she was a citizen by blood of the Cherokee Nation? A Yes.
Q Is it your understanding that Mrs. Miller or Kate Vann was dead at the time French Miller married Mrs. Runyan? A Yes sir.
Q And that French Miller and his wife here, Mrs. Miller, resided together as husband and wife and continuously lived in the Cherokee nation[sic] until September 1, 1902?
A Mr. Miller died in 1896.
Q Well, up untill[sic] his death? A With this exception. He got so sick that they sent him to a soldier's home in Ft. Leavenworth, Kansas, and he died while there.
Q How long was he in Kansas prior to this death? A I don't know; he made two trips and the second time he was took sick under medical treatment and died.
Q Is it your understanding that he maintained his home in the Cherokee nation[sic]?
A Yes, he was temporarily out for his health. He left everything; I don't think Mr. Miller was ever out of the country until he went out to die.
Q What is the date of his death? A I think in January, 1906.
Q You said awhile ago you thought it was in 1896? You meant 1906 did you not? (referring to death affidavit)
A Yes sir.
Q You don't know do you, who was present at that marriage of Kate Vann at Fort Gibson in 1872? A No, only just by remembering people who lived there at that time. I don't know of my own knowledge anyone being present.

Cherokee Intermarried White 1906
Volume VI

Q But you have every reason to believe that they were lawfully married in accordance with the laws of the Cherokee Nation--that is, under license of the Cherokee Nation?
A Yes, I am qualified to say that they were lawfully married under the laws of the Cherokee nation[sic]. I never heard anything to the contrary, and judging from the way that the marriage took place, in those days they would have to have a regular marriage license before a marriage could be performed Before[sic] a man would perform the marriage ceremony.
Q I will ask you if French Miller and Kate Vann had any children?
A They had three I remember.
Q What is the name of the oldest child? A Oscar, Leslie and Ida were the names, but I don't know which was the oldest child.
Q Did they ever have a child named Susie? A I don't remember.
Witness excused.

Oscar Miller is identified on the Cherokee authenticated tribal roll of 1880, Illinois District, page 552, opposite No. 1094, as a native Cherokee. The age of Oscar Miller is given thereon as seven years.

French Miller id identified on the Cherokee authenticated tribal roll of 1880, Illinois District, opposite No 1092, and on the Cherokee Census roll of 1896, Illinois District, page 932, opposite No. 139, as an intermarried citizen of the Cherokee Nation.

Cora Miller, the second wife of French Miller, is identified on the Cherokee authenticated roll of 1880, Illinois District, opposite No. 1513 as Cora Runyan, and on the Cherokee census roll of 1896, Illinois District page 898, No. 1644, as Cora Runyan.
She is also included in the approved partial roll of citizens of the Cherokee Nation opposite No. 4619.

Frances R. Lane, upon oath states that as stenographer to the Commission to the Five Civilized Tribes she reported the testimony in the above entitled cause and that the foregoing is an accurate transcript of her stenographic notes thereof.

Frances R Lane

Subscribed and sworn to before me this February 4, 1907.

Walter W. Chappell
Notary Public.

Cherokee Intermarried White 1906
Volume VI

G.H.L.   Cherokee 1742.

In[sic]

DEPARTMENT OF THE INTERIOR,
COMMISSIONER TO THE FIVE CIVILIZED TRIBES.
Muskogee, I. T. February 5, 1907.

Appearances:
        For the Cherokee Nation: W. W. Hastings.
        For the applicant, Major Waldron of the firm of
                Waldron & Cramer,
                Muskogee, Indian Territory.

    William Hudson being first duly sworn by C. E. Webster, a Notary Public for the Western District, testified as follows:

By the Commissioner:
Q What is your name? A William Hudson.
Q What is your age? A Sixty years.
Q What is your postoffice address? A Fort Gibson, I. T.
Q Were you ever acquainted with a white man by the name of French Miller? A I was.
Q When did you first become acquainted with him? A In '70 I believe. As near as I can recollect in 1870.
Q Do you know whether he was ever married to a Cherokee by blood?
A Yes, he was married to a Cherokee by the name of Kate Vann.
Q Do you know when he and Kate Vann were married? A Married in 1872 as near as I can recollect.
Q Were you present at that marriage? A I was not present at the marriage but we was living right close together and I see them when they was going to the wedding. You know white folks don't ask--- (Witness is a freedman).
Q Was it your understanding that they were married in accordance with Cherokee laws?
A Yes, they was living together as man and wife right by me all the time.
Q How long did they live together as man and wife? A About 25 or 30 years I reckon, as near as I can recollect. We lived right there together.
Q Did they ever separate or did Kate Vann die? A Kate died. They had three children and they all died. Kate and the two boys and a girl.
Q Did this fellow French Miller remarry after the death of his wife, Kate? A Yes, he married Cora Runyan;- the called her Cora Runyan all the time.
Q Was his second wife, Cora Bunyan, a Cherokee by blood? A Yes sir.
Q Was Kate Vann a recognized Cherokee at the time of her marriage to French Miller?
A Yes sir.
Q They were considered as man and wife in the community where they lived?
A Yes sir.
Q In what district were they married? A In Illinois District.
Q Do you know the name of the children of French Miller and Kate Vann? A Yes sir.

Cherokee Intermarried White 1906
Volume VI

Q What is the name of the oldest? A The oldest one is Oscar.
Q What is the name of the next? A Ida.
Q And the next one? A Leslie.
Q That was all the children they had? A That was all they had
Q About how long after that marriage before Oscar was born?
A Well, I don't recollect exactly. I never kept no track of it;- they lived right by us too. I couldn't tell you how long.
Q Oscar was born after they were married? A Yes, I think he was as well as I can recollect. The lived right there adjoining us. The place I am living on now- I bought from him.

Frances R. Lane upon oath states that as stenographer to the Commissioner to the Five Civilized Tribes she reported the testimony in the above entitled cause and that the foregoing is an accurate transcript of her stenographic notes thereof.

Frances R Lane

Subscribed and sworn to before me this February 5, 1907.

Walter W. Chappell
Notary Public.

◇◇◇◇◇

E C M   Cherokee 1742.

DEPARTMENT OF THE INTERIOR,

COMMISSIONER TO THE FIVE CIVILIZED TRIBES.

In the matter of the application for the enrollment of FRENCH MILLER as a citizen by intermarriage of the Cherokee Nation.

D E C I S I O N

THE RECORDS OF THIS OFFICE SHOW: That at Fort Gibson, Indian Territory, August 21, 1900, application was received by the Commission to the Five Civilized Tribes for the enrollment of French Miller as a citizen by intermarriage of the Cherokee Nation. Further proceedings in the matter of said application were had at Muskogee, Indian Territory, October 14, 1902 and February 2, 1907 and February 5 1907.

THE EVIDENCE IN THIS CASE SHOWS: That the applicant herein, French Miller, a white man, was married in accordance with Cherokee law about the year 1872 to his wife, Katie Miller, nee Vann, since deceased, who was at the time of said marriage a recognized citizen by blood of the Cherokee Nation; who is identified on the Cherokee

Cherokee Intermarried White 1906
Volume VI

authenticated tribal roll of 1880, Illinois District No. 1093, as a native Cherokee marked "Dead"; that from the time of said marriage until the death of said Katie Miller, which occurred prior to 1895, the said French Miller and Katie Miller resided together as husband and wife and continuously lived in the Cherokee Nation. If it further shown that in 1895 said French Miller was married to one Cora Miller, nee Runyan, who was as the time of said marriage a recognized citizen by blood of the Cherokee Nation, who is identified on the Cherokee authenticated tribal roll of 1880, Illinois District No. 1513, as a native Cherokee, and whose name is included on the approved partial roll of citizens by blood of the Cherokee Nation opposite No. 4619; that from the time of said marriage the said French Miller and Cora Miller resided together as husband and wife and continuously lived in the Cherokee Nation up to and including September 1, 1902. Said applicant is identified on the Cherokee authenticated tribal roll of 1880 and the Cherokee census roll of 1896 as an intermarried citizen of the Cherokee Nation.

IT IS, THEREFORE, ORDERED AND ADJUDGED: That in accordance with the decision of the Supreme Court of the United States, dated November 5, 1906, in the cases of Daniel Red Bird, et al. vs. the United States, Nos. 125, 126, 127, and 128, the said applicant, French Miller, is entitled, under the provisions of Section Twenty-one of the Act of Congress approved June 28, 1898, (30 Stats. 495), to enrollment as a citizen by intermarriage of the Cherokee Nation, and his application for enrollment as such is accordingly granted.

Tams Bixby
Commissioner.

Dated at Muskogee, Indian Territory,
this   FEB 14 1907

◇◇◇◇◇

Cherokee 1742

Muskogee, Indian Territory, February 14, 1907.

W. W. Hastings,
    Attorney for the Cherokee Nation,
        Muskogee, Indian Territory.

Dear Sir:

    There is enclosed herewith a copy of the decision of the Commissioner to the Five Civilized Tribes, dated February 14, 1907, granting the application for the enrollment of French Miller as a citizen by intermarriage of the Cherokee Nation.

Respectfully,

Commissioner.

Encl. H-22
JMH

◇◇◇◇◇

Cherokee Intermarried White 1906
Volume VI

Cherokee 1742

Muskogee, Indian Territory, February 14, 1907.

The Commissioner to the Five Civilized Tribes,
Muskogee, Indian Territory.

Sir:

Receipt is acknowledged of the testimony and of your decision enrolling French Miller as a citizen by intermarriage of the Cherokee Nation. Time for protesting said decision is waived, and I consent that said person may be placed upon the schedule immediately.

Respectfully,
W. W. Hastings
Attorney for Cherokee Nation.

◇◇◇◇◇

Cherokee 1742

Muskogee, Indian Territory, February 14, 1907.

French Miller,
Fort Gibson, Indian Territory.

Dear Sir:

There is enclosed herewith a copy of the decision of the Commissioner to the Five Civilized Tribes, dated February 14, 1907, granting the application for your enrollment as a citizen by intermarriage of the Cherokee Nation.

You will be advised when your name has been placed upon a schedule of citizens of the Cherokee Nation and approved by the Secretary of the Interior.

Respectfully,

Encl. H-23
JMH

Commissioner.

Cher IW 187

◇◇◇◇◇

Cherokee Intermarried White 1906
Volume VI

T.W.L.

Cherokee 2209

DEPARTMENT OF THE INTERIOR

COMMISSIONER TO THE FIVE CIVILIZED TRIBES

In the matter of the application for the enrollment of Martha Kelley, formerly Crittenden, as a citizen by intermarriage of the Cherokee Nation.

DECISION

THE RECORDS OF THIS OFFICE SHOW: That at Fort Gibson, Indian Territory, August 29, 1900, application was received by the Commission to the Five Civilized Tribes for the enrollment of Martha Kelley, formerly Crittenden, as a citizen by intermarriage of the Cherokee Nation. Further proceedings in the matter of said application were had at Muskogee, Indian Territory, October 25, 1902, December 8, 1902 and January 8, 1907.

THE EVIDENCE IN THIS CASE SHOWS: That the applicant herein, Martha Kelley, formerly Crittenden, a white woman, was married under the laws of the State of Texas in the year 1869, to one James Crittenden, since deceased, an alleged Cherokee; that the said James Crittenden was admitted to citizenship in the Cherokee Nation by the duly constituted authorities thereof, November 27, 1874; that the said James Crittenden is identified upon the Cherokee authenticated tribal roll of 1880, Canadian District, Page 10, No. 282, as an adopted Cherokee; that from the time of said admission, the said James Crittenden and Martha Crittenden resided together as husband and wife and continuously lived in the Cherokee Nation until his death, which occurred about the year 1885; that subsequent to the death of the said James Crittenden, the said Martha Crittenden on June 10, 1889, was married to one John D. Kelley, who at the time of said marriage was a recognized citizen by blood of the Cherokee Nation and who is identified upon the Cherokee authenticated tribal roll of 1880, Going Snake District, Page 448, No. 1023, as a native Cherokee; that since the time of said marriage, the said John D. and Martha Kelley have resided together as husband and wife and have continuously lived in the Cherokee Nation; said applicant is identified upon the Cherokee authenticated tribal roll of 1880 and the Cherokee census roll of 1896, as an intermarried citizen of the Cherokee Nation.

IT IS THEREFORE ORDERED AND ADJUDGED: That in accordance with the decision of the Supreme Court of the United States, dated November 5, 1906, in the cases of Daniel Red Bird, et al., vs. the United States, Nos. 125, 126, 127, and 128, the said applicant, Martha Kelley is entitled under the provisions of Section 21 of the Act of Congress approved June 28, 1898 (30 Stats., 495), to enrollment as a citizen by

Cherokee Intermarried White 1906
Volume VI

intermarriage of the Cherokee Nation, and her application for enrollment as such is accordingly granted.

Tams Bixby
Commissioner.

Dated at Muskogee, Indian Territory, this FEB 15 1907

◇◇◇◇◇

Cherokee 2209

Muskogee, Indian Territory, February 15, 1907.

W. W. Hastings,
    Attorney for the Cherokee Nation,
        Muskogee, Indian Territory.

Dear Sir:

    There is inclosed herewith a copy of the decision of the Commissioner to the Five Civilized Tribes, dated February 15, 1907, granting the application for the enrollment of Martha Kelley as a citizen by intermarriage of the Cherokee Nation.

Respectfully,

SML Ecl. 1   Commissioner.

◇◇◇◇◇

Cherokee No. 2209.

Muskogee, Indian Territory, February 15, 1907.

Commissioner to the Five Civilized Tribes,
    Muskogee, Indian Territory.

Sir:

    Receipt is acknowledged of the testimony and of your decision, enrolling Martha Kelley as a citizen by intermarriage of the Cherokee Nation. Time for protesting said decision is waived and I consent that said person may be placed upon the schedule immediately.

Respectfully,
W. W. Hastings
Attorney for Cherokee Nation.

◇◇◇◇◇

Cherokee Intermarried White 1906
Volume VI

Cherokee 2209

Muskogee, Indian Territory, February 15, 1907.

Martha Kelley,
    Muskogee, Indian Territory.

Dear Madam:

    There is enclosed herewith a copy of the decision of the Commissioner to the Five Civilized Tribes, dated February 15, 1907, granting your application for enrollment as a citizen by intermarriage of the Cherokee Nation.

    You will be advised when your name has been placed upon a schedule of citizens of the Cherokee Nation and approved by the Secretary of the Interior.

                  Respectfully,

SML.Enc.1   Commissioner.

Cher IW 188

                                                                         E.C.M.

DEPARTMENT OF THE INTERIOR,

COMMISSIONER TO THE FIVE CIVILIZED TRIBES.

In the matter of the application for the enrollment of

PETER McELMEEL

As a citizen by intermarriage of the Cherokee Nation.

CHEROKEE NO. 7057.

Cherokee Intermarried White 1906
Volume VI

DEPARTMENT OF THE INTERIOR,
COMMISSION TO THE FIVE CIVILIZED TRIBES,
MUSKOGEE, I. T., JANUARY 15th, 1901.

In the matter of the application of Peter McElmeel for the enrollment of himself, wife and adopted child as citizens of the Cherokee Nation; said McElmeel being sworn and examined by Commissioner Breckinridge, testified as follows:

Q Give me your full name? A Peter McElmeel.
Q How old are you? A About 60.
Q What is your post office? A Muskogee.
Q In what district do you live? A Canadian.
Q You live in Canadian but get your mail at Muskogee? A Yes, sir.
Q Who is it you want to have enrolled? A Myself and wife and one adopted child.
Q Are you a Cherokee by blood? A No, sir.
Q You are a white man? (No response.)
Q What is your wife, Cherokee by blood? A Yes, sir.
Q When were you married to your wife? (Hands paper to COM'R.)
　　Com'r:--The applicant presents an official copy of the records of Illinois district showing that he was united in marriage on the 16th of March, 1874, in accordance with Cherokee law, to Elizabeth Spaniard. This is filed herewith.
Q Is your wife, Elizabeth Spaniard still living? A Yes, sir.
Q This is your present wife? A Yes, sir.
Q Have you and she lived in the Cherokee Nation ever since you were married in 1874?
A Pretty near, part of the time we lived here in Muskogee; I was railroading when we lived here in Town.
Q How long did you live here? A I come here with this railroad when it came in.
Q How long since you lived here and went back to Canadian district?
A About 17 years.
Q You had had a job here on the railroad? A Yes, sir; I worked in the roundhouse and afterwards was car inspector.
Q Did you continue to keep your interest in the Cherokee Nation?
A Yes, sir, soon after I married I got stock and took there.
Q Did you go back there and vote? A Yes, sir.
Q You did not vote in the Tribal elections here? A No, sir.
Q Was your wife born in the Cherokee Nation? A I think from the best, from what I heard, she was born on her way to this country.
Q Has she lived in the Cherokee Nation ever since you and she were married except this time you speak of? A Yes, sir, she was raised at Fort Gibson.
Q She has lived in the Cherokee Nation except the time you were here[sic]?
A Yes, sir.
Q You and she have lived together all the time? A Yes, sir.
Q How old is your wife? A She is about 60 years old I guess.
Q Give me the name of her father? A Her father he was a Field[sic].
Q You did not know his full name? A No, sir.

Cherokee Intermarried White 1906
Volume VI

Q You say yur[sic] wife was born wheil[sic] she was coming to this country, where was she coming from? A The old country, Georgia.
Q Her father is dead? A Yes, sir.
Q And her mother, she is dead too? A They both died when she was small and that's how she got her Spaniard name; her grandmother raised her.
Q Now, this adopted child, what is its name? A I call it Elizabeth McElmeel now, I give it my name.
Q How old is the child? A 11 years old.
Q What is the name of the father of this child? A William Martin.
Q White man or Cherokee? A Cherokee.
Q Is he dead? A No, sir, he is in Texas.
Q What is the name of the mother of this child? A Emma, she was a white woman.
Q Is she dead? A She is dead.
Q When did she die, how long? A It has been seven or eight years ago, I am not positive.
Q Now, William Martin, was he born in the Cherokee Nation? A Yes, sir; his proper name I guess you might find it on the roll as Buzzard Flopper.
Q When did William Martin go to Texas? A Last Spring was a year.
Q Was he born in the Cherokee Nation? A As I always understood it he was.
Q Did he live in the Cherokee Nation all his life until last Spring a year ago? A Yes, sir.
Q Was he ever married except to this woman, Emma? A Not previous, he has been since.
Q Was she ever married except to him? A We did not think so, she is quite a young woman.
Q How old is William Martin now? A He should be something over 30 years of age.
Q What proof have you got of their marriage? A They lived together; if Judge Lowery was her[sic] he could prove it, he married them.
Q Where were they married? A At Judge Lawery's[sic] place.
Q What knowledge have you of the marriage between Martin and his wife Emma? A Well, after they married they lived together.
Q You knew that? A Yes, sir, for after I raised him and they got married while he was working for me.
Q They got married while he was living at your place? A Yes, sir.
Q Did you see them married? A No, sir.
Q You understood that they were married by Judge Lowery? A Yes, sir.
Q Where were they married, here at Muskogee? A No, sir, at Goose Neck at his house.
Applicant:--I don't think you will find me on the 1880 roll, I was living here at Muskogee.
Q Why did not you have yourself put on that roll? A My wife started out to be enrolled there and got out to Bennet[sic] and told all the Cherokees that lived here in Town to go there, and when they got there they had left.
Q Who was his father (William Martin's)? A Martin Buzzard Flopper.
   1880 Roll; page 7, #185, Willie Buzzard Flopper, Canadian
   1896 Roll; page 90, #179, Peter McElmeel, Canadian.
   1896 Roll, page 48, #1321, Elizabeth McElmeel, Canadian.

Cherokee Intermarried White 1906
Volume VI

Q Is his (William Martin's) name William H? A Yes, sir.
  1896 Roll; page 54, #1475, William H. Martin, Canadian.
  1896 Roll; page 54, #1476, Elizabeth Martin, Canadian.
Q Now, this child is living now is she? A Yes, sir.
Q How did you acquire this child, did her father give her to you?
A Yes, sir, that is what these papers are. (Hands papers to COM'R)
Q Has your wife any brothers or sisters? A Not living she is the last one of the family.
Q She has had brothers and sisters? A Yes, sir.
Q How many brothers? A I can't tell you.
Q Do you remember any brothers or sisters? A Yes, sir, a sister and brother, Johnson Fields.
Q Was Johnson Fields her full brother? A No, sir, I think he was only a half.
Q Was he a brother on the mother's side of[sic] Father's side? A On her father's side.
Q She had no full brother or sister since you have been married? A No, sir.
Q Do you know whether her mother was a white woman or Cherokee? A Her mother was a Cherokee, or at least that is what I understand.
Q Was Johnson Fields older or younger than your wife? A Older.
Q Did he die here in the Cherokee Nation? A He died near Tahlequah
  1880 Roll; page 759, #719, Johnson Fields, Tahlequah.
Q You don't remember the name of your wife's father? A No. He was generally called Spaniard; he died before the roll of 1880 was made, he died when my wife was very young.
Q He come here? A Yes, sir, he lived down here on Spaniard Creek that is where the creek gets its name.
Q Was your wife's father a Cherokee or white man? A He was a Cherokee; old Dick Fielfs[sic] that used to represent the Cherokees in Washington up to the war and in fact he died in Washington, he was my wife's uncle.
Q A brother of her father? A Yes, sir.

  Com'r Breckinridge:--The applicant applies for the enrollment of himself, his wife and one adopted child: He is shown to have married his wife in accordance with Cherokee law in 1874, he being a white man and she a Cherokee by blood. They have lived together ever since their marriage. Part of the time they have lived at Muskogee in the Creek Nation, but not under ciscumstances[sic] and conditions that are considered to in any was invalidate their claim to Cherokee citizenship. They are identified as husband and wife on the roll of 1896. They are not identified on the roll of 1880 but the testimony disclosed that this was due to neglect and not to their right to be on their[sic] roll. Her half brother is identified on the roll of 1880 under conditions set forth in the testimony, which further show the right of the applicant's wife to have been upon that roll if her name had been presented at the time. The applicant was at that immediate time engaged on a railroad job at the town of Muskogee. They will both be listed for enrollment, the wife as a Cherokee by blood and the applicant as a Cherokee by intermarriage.
  The adopted child, Elizabeth McElmeel, is duly identified on the roll of 1896. This child's father is identified on the roll of 1880. He is now living in the State of Texas. Her mother was a white woman, but it appears conclusive from the testimony of the applicant and also from the documents which have been examed[sic] which are recorded in the

Cherokee Intermarried White 1906
Volume VI

United States Court conveying this child to the applicant, and that the marriage between the child's father and mother was a lawful marriage. This child is now living and will be listed for enrollment as a Cherokee by blood.

---oooOOOooo---

J. O. Rosson, being first duly sworn, states that as stenographer to the Commission to the Five Civilized Tribes, he correctly recorded the testimony and proceedings in this case, and the foregoing is a true and complete transcript of his stenographic notes thereof.

JO Rosson

Subscribed and sworn to before me this 17th day of January, 1901.

CR Breckinridge
Commissioner.

Cherokee 7057.

Notary Public the Interior,
Notary Public Five Civilized Tribes,
Notary Public I. T., September 25, 1902.

In the matter of the application of Peter McElmeel for the enrollment of himself as an intermarried citizen, and for the enrollment of his wife, Elizabeth, and adopted daughter Elizabeth McElmeel, as citizens of the Cherokee Nation; he being sworn and examined by the Commission, testified as follows:

Q What is your name? A Peter McElmeel.
Q What is your age? A I am about 67 or 68 somewhere along there. I was twenty-six when I went in the army during the war.
Q What is your postoffice address? A Muskogee.
Q Are you the identical Peter McElmeel that applied for enrollment to this Commission for yourself and your wife, Elizabeth, and an adopted daughter Elizabeth, on January 15, 1901? A I am.
Q What is your wife's name? A Elizabeth.
Q Were you ever married previous to your marriage to her? A No sir.
Q Was she ever married before? A Yes sir.
Q Was her husband dead when she married you? A Yes sir, he died during the war; he went in the war and she never heard from him anymore.
Q When did your wife and you marry? A In '74.
Q Where? A In the Cherokee Nation.
Q Have you and she lived together in the Cherokee Nation ever since your marriage?
A Pretty much, yes.

Cherokee Intermarried White 1906
Volume VI

Q Have you ever lived out of the Indian Territory since you marriage? A No sir, never lived out of the Indian Territory.
Q Your wife is a Cherokee by blood is she? A Yes sir.
Q Were you married under a Cherokee license? A I was.
Q You filed those with the Commission have you? A Yes sir.
Q Your wife and you have never separated or lived apart since you were married? A No sir.
Q You were living together on the first day of September, 1902? A Yes sir.
Q You have never married any other woman since your marriage to her? A No sir.
Q Is this wife and your stepdaughter, Elizabeth, living at this time?
A Yes sir, I live five miles from here on Coodys Creek.
Q In the Cherokee Nation? A Yes sir.
Q Whose child is this? A This child is a daughter of an adopted son. I will show you the paper.
Q What was the name of the father of this child? A His Indian name was Buzzard Flopper; when I had him he was a McElmeel; when he left me he took the name of William Martin.
Q Was he a Cherokee citizen by blood? A Yes, he was a fullblood.
Q Is this child, Elizabeth, his child? A His child by his wife Emma, she was a white woman.
Q Was he ever married to the mother of this child? A Notary Public[sic] sir.
Q How do you know? A I know from the fact that the man who married them said they were. Judge Lowrey[sic] married them; I wasn't present; they lived together up until her death.
Q They lived together as husband and wife? A Yes sir, and had three children previous to her death. This child we have is the oldest, is the first child.
Q Did William Martin always recognize this as his child during his lifetime? A Yes sir.

The undersigned, being duly sworn, states that as stenographer to the Notary Public Five Civilized Tribes he correctly recorded the testimony and proceedings in this case, and that the foregoing is a true and correct transcript of his stenographic notes thereof.

E.G. Rothenberger

Notary Public to before me this 13th day of October 1902.

BC Jones
Notary Public.

Cherokee Intermarried White 1906
Volume VI

Cherokee 7057

DEPARTMENT OF THE INTERIOR,
COMMISSION TO THE FIVE CIVILIZED TRIBES,
MUSKOGEE, IND. TER., OCT. 13, 1902.

In the matter of the application for the enrollment of Peter McElmeel et al. as citizens of the Cherokee Nation:

SUPPLEMENTAL STATEMENT.

An examination of the 1886 pay roll of the Cherokee Nation shows that Elizabeth McElmeel is identified on that roll, at page 56, #1118, Canadian District, as Betsie McElmeel.

An examination of the 1890 census roll of the Cherokee Nation shows that Peter McElmeel is identified on that roll at page 67, #1388, and that Elizabeth McElmeel is identified on that roll at page 67, #1389, Canadian District.

It is ordered that copies of this statement be filed with and made a part of the record of this case.

TB Needles
Commissioner.

◇◇◇◇◇

C O P Y .

Clerks Office Dist. Court.)
Illinois District C. N.)

To any regular minister of any regular evangelical denomination or Judge of a Cherokee Court, to whom these may come greeting:

The bearer McElmeal[sic] Peter, a citizen of the United States, having obtained such recommendation as is required by law, regulating intermarriage with white men and has presented the same to this office with an application for a license for marriage which is hereby granted - You are therefore authorized to solemnize the rites of matrimony between the said Peter McElmeal and Elizabeth Spaniard a Cherokee and citizen, according to the form and serimony[sic] usual

Cherokee Intermarried White 1906
Volume VI

and practised[sic] in your church or office and to attach a certificate of said marriage hereto and to return the same by bearer to this office for record.

Given from under my hand in office this 16th day of March 1874.

           (Signed) Geo. O. Sanders, Clerk,
                 Illinois Dist. Court, C.N.

Oath administered this the 16th March 1874.

           (Signed) Geo. O. Sanders, Clerk,
                 Illinois Dist. Court, C.N.

To whom it may concern.

  I hereby certify that I have this day solemnized the marriage of Peter McElmeal[sic] and Elizabeth Spaniard under a license from the clerk of the District Clerk of Illinois Dist. Cherokee Nation.

  This 16th day of March 1874   Signed, Saml M. Taylor,
                  Judge C. Court, C.N.

I certify the above to be a true copy of the original.

           (Signed) Geo. O. Sanders, Clk, I.D. Court.

Executive Office Cherokee Nation.
  Tahlequah I. T.

  I, B.W. Alberty, assistant Executive secretary of the Cherokee Nation do hereby certify that the foregoing is a true copy taken from the marriage record of Illinois District Cherokee Nation, now filed in this office by law and in my custody.

  Given under my hand and the seal of the Cherokee Nation this the 16th day of November 1900.

           (Signed) B. W. Alberty
                Assistant Executive Secretary,
                Cherokee Nation.

This certifies that the undersigned, being duly sworn, sates[sic] that as stenographer to the Commission to the Five Civilized Tribes she made the above and foregoing copy and the same is a full, true and correct copy of the original instrument now on file in this office.

Subscribed and sworn to before me this 24th day of January, 1907.

                Chas E Webster
                Notary Public

**Cherokee Intermarried White 1906
Volume VI**

E C M

Cherokee 7057.

DEPARTMENT OF THE INTERIOR,

COMMISSIONER TO THE FIVE CIVILIZED TRIBES.

In the matter of the application for the enrollment of PETER McELMEEL as a citizen by intermarriage of the Cherokee Nation.

D E C I S I O N

THE RECORDS OF THIS OFFICE SHOW: That on January 15th, 1900 application was received by the Commission to the Five Civilized Tribes for the enrollment of Peter McElmeel as a citizen by intermarriage of the Cherokee Nation. Further proceedings in the matter of said application were had at Muskogee, Indian Territory, September 26th, 1902 and October 13th, 1902.

THE EVIDENCE IN THIS CASE SHOWS: That the applicant herein, Peter McElmeel, a white man, was married in accordance with Cherokee law March 16th, 1874 to his wife, Elizabeth McElmeel, nee Fields, who was at the time of said marriage a recognized citizen by blood of the Cherokee Nation, who is identified on the 1886 Pay Roll of the Cherokee Nation at Page 56, No. 1118, Canadian District as Betsy McElmeel, and whose name appears upon the approved partial roll of citizens by blood of the Cherokee Nation opposite No. 16847. It is further shown that from the time of said marriage the said Peter McElmeel and Elizabeth McElmeel resided together as husband and wife and continuously lived in the Cherokee Nation up to and including September 1st, 1902. Said applicant is identified on the Cherokee census roll of 1896 as an intermarried citizen of the Cherokee Nation.

IT IS, THEREFORE, ORDERED AND ADJUDGED: That in accordance with the decision of the Supreme Court of the United States, dated November 5th, 1906 in the cases of Daniel Red Bird, et al. vs. the United States, Nos. 125, 126, 127, and 128, the said applicant, Peter McElmeel is entitled, under the provisions of Section Twenty-one of the Act of Congress approved June 28th, 1898 (30 Stats. 495), to enrollment as a citizen by intermarriage of the Cherokee Nation and his application for enrollment as such is accordingly granted.

Tams Bixby
Commissioner.

Dated at Muskogee, Indian Territory,
this   FEB 13 1907

◇◇◇◇◇

Cherokee Intermarried White 1906
Volume VI

Cherokee
7057.

Muskogee, Indian Territory, February 13, 1907.

W. W. Hastings,
   Attorney for the Cherokee Nation,
      Muskogee, Indian Territory.

Dear Sir:

    There is enclosed herewith a copy of the decision of the Commissioner to the Five Civilized Tribes, dated February 13, 1907, granting the application for the enrollment of Peter McElmeel, as a citizen by intermarriage of the Cherokee Nation.

Respectfully,

Encl. HJ-38.
HJC.
                      Commissioner.

◇◇◇◇◇

Cherokee 7057.

Muskogee, Indian Territory, February 13, 1907.

The Commissioner to the Five Civilized Tribes,
   Muskogee, Indian Territory.

Sir:

    Receipt is acknowledged of the testimony and of your decision enrolling Peter McElmeel as a citizen by intermarriage of the Cherokee Nation. Time for protesting said decision is waived and I consent that said person may be placed upon the schedule immediately.

Respectfully,
W. W. Hastings
Attorney for Cherokee Nation.

◇◇◇◇◇

Cherokee Intermarried White 1906
Volume VI

Cherokee
7057.

Muskogee, Indian Territory, February 13, 1907.

Peter McElmeel,
    Muskogee, Indian Territory.

Dear Sir:

    There is enclosed herewith a copy of the decision of the Commissioner to the Five Civilized Tribes, dated February 13, 1907, granting your application for enrollment as a citizen by intermarriage of the Cherokee Nation.

    You will be advised when your name has been placed upon a schedule of citizens of the Cherokee Nation and approved by the Secretary of the Interior.

    Respectfully,

Encl. HJ-47.
HJC   Commissioner.

Cher IW 189

◇◇◇◇◇

E.C.M.

DEPARTMENT OF THE INTERIOR,
COMMISSIONER TO THE FIVE CIVILIZED TRIBES.

In the matter of the application for the enrollment of

CHARLES W. KOLPIN

as a citizen by intermarriage of the Cherokee Nation.

CHEROKEE NO. 5871.

◇◇◇◇◇

Cherokee Intermarried White 1906
Volume VI

DEPARTMENT OF THE INTERIOR,
COMMISSION TO THE FIVE CIVILIZED TRIBES,
TAHLEQUAH, I.T., NOVEMBER 30th, 1900.

In the matter of the application of Charles Kolpin for the enrollment of himself, wife and children as citizens of the Cherokee Nation; said Kolpin being sworn and examined by Commissioner Needles, testified as follows:

Q What is your name? A Charles Kolpin.
Q How old are you, Mr. Kolpin? A 55 years old.
Q What is your post office address? A Tahlequah.
Q What district do you live in? A Tahlequah.
Q Are you a recognized citizen of the Cherokee Nation? A By adoption.
Q Whom do you want to enroll? A My wife and children.
Q Yourself too, don't you? A Yes, sir.
Q What is the name of your wife? A Eliza Kolpin.
Q How old is she? A 42 years old.
Q When did you marry her? A IN[sic] '75.
Q What is[sic] the names of your children? A Leon Kolpin.
Q How old is Leon? A 20 years old.
Q What is the next child, Mr. Kolpin? A Augusta.
Q How old is Augusta? A Three years old.
Q Is that all? A That is all.
   1880 Roll; page 776, #1220, Chas. W. Kolpin, Tahlequah.
   1880 Roll; page 776, #1221, Eliza Kolpin, Tahlequah.
   1896 Roll; page 1283, #153, Charles W. Kolpin, Tahlequah.
   1896 Roll; page 1198, #1851, Eliza Kolpin, Tahlequah.
   1896 Roll; page 1198, #1854, Leon, Kolpin, Tahlequah.
Q Have you always lived in the Cherokee Nation since you married? A Yes, sir.
Q Is Eliza your first wife? A Yes, sir.
Q Are you her first husband? A Yes, sir.
Q Are you living with her now? A Yes, sir.
Q Are these children both alive and living with you now? A Yes, sir.

   Com'r Needles:--The name of Charles Kolpin appears upon the authenticated roll of 1880 as Charles W. Kolpin as well as upon the census roll of 1896. The name of his wife, Eliza is found upon the authenticated roll of 1880 and the census roll of 1896 and he presents satisfactory proof of birth as to Augusta, a child whose name does not appear upon said roll, having been born since said roll was compiled. They all being duly identified and having made satisfactory proof as to their residence, the said Charles Kolpin will be duly listed for enrollment as a Cherokee citizen by intermarriage and his wife, Eliza, and children as enumerated herein, will be duly listed for enrollment as Cherokee citizens by blood.

---oooOOOooo---

Cherokee Intermarried White 1906
Volume VI

J. O. Rosson, being first duly sworn, states that as stenographer to the Commission to the Five Civilized Tribes, he correctly recorded the testimony and proceedings in this case, and the foregoing is a true and complete transcript of his stenographic notes thereof.

JO Rosson

Subscribed and sworn to before me this 30th day of November, 1900.

TB Needles
Commissioner.

◇◇◇◇◇

R.
Cher. 5871.

Department of the Interior.
Commission to the Five Civilized Tribes.
Tahlequah, I. T., October 1, 1902.

SUPPLEMENTAL TESTIMONY AND PROCEEDINGS in the matter of the application for the enrollment of CHARLES KOLPIN as a citizen by intermarriage of the Cherokee Nation.

CHARLES KOLPIN, being first duly sworn, and being examined, testified as follows:

BY COMMISSION: What is your name? A Charles W. Kolpin.
Q Is that your full name? A Yes sir.
Q Do you desire to be listed for enrollment under your full name?
A I don't remember what was,--something was said about that because my name had been once on the 1880 roll as Charles W.
Q You gave your name at the time you made application for enrollment as Charles Kolpin. Do you desire to be enrolled under the name of Charles W. Kolpin?
A Yes sir, that's right.
Q How old are you? A Fifty-seven.
Q What is your post office address? A Tahlequah.
Q You are a white man? A Yes sir.
Q What is the name of your wife? A Eliza.
Q Is she living? A Yes sir.
Q Is she a Cherokee by blood? A Yes sir.
Q Do you claim your right to enrollment by reason of your marriage to her? A Yes sir.
Q Have you and she lived together continuously ever since your marriage? A Yes sir.
Q You are living together now? A Yes sir.
Q Were you ever married before you married her? A No sir.
Q Was she ever married before she married you? A No sir.

Cherokee Intermarried White 1906
Volume VI

Q At the time you made application for enrollment, did you file with the Commission satisfactory proof of your marriage to your Cherokee wife according to Cherokee law? A Yes sir.

Q Have you lived in the Cherokee Nation continuously since the date of your application for enrollment? A Yes sir.

This testimony will be filed with and made a part of the record in the matter of the application for the enrollment of Charles Kolpin as a citizen by intermarriage of the Cherokee Nation, Cherokee straight card field No. 5871.

Wm. Hutchinson, being first duly sworn, states that as stenographer to the Commission to the Five Civilized Tribes he correctly recorded the testimony and proceedings in this case, and the foregoing is a true and complete transcript of the stenographic notes

Wm Hutchinson

Subscribed and sworn to before me this 1st day of October, 1902.

John O Rosson
Notary Public.

◇◇◇◇◇

C5891

DEPARTMENT OF THE INTERIOR,
COMMISSIONER TO THE FIVE CIVILIZED TRIBES.

Muskogee, Indian Territory. January 2, 1907.

In the matter of the application for the enrollment of Charles W. Kolpin as a citizen by intermarriage of the Cherokee Nation.

Charles W. Kolpin being first duly sworn by Edward Merrick, Notary Public, testifies as follows:

BY THE COMMISSIONER:

Q State your name, age and postoffice address. A Charles W. Kolpin, Talequah[sic], Cherokee Nation; 64.
Q You claim citizenship in the Cherokee Nation by intermarriage? A Yes, sir.
Q Through whom do you claim.[sic] A Through my wife Eliza Lillard, that is her maiden name.

Cherokee Intermarried White 1906
Volume VI

Q What is her citizenship? A Cherokee by blood.

The said Eliza Kolpin nee Lillard is identified on Cherokee Straight Card No. 5871 and is on the approved roll of citizens by blood of the Cherokee Nation opposite No. 14056. The applicant is also identified on the same Cherokee card as an intermarried white. The said Eliza Kolpin nee Lillard the applicant, Charles W. Kolpin, are also identified on the Cherokee authenticated tribal roll of 1880 and the Cherokee census roll of 1896.

Q Is your wife living at this time.[sic] A Yes, sir.
Q When were you married to here? A 18 and 75 in March.
Q Where were you married? A Talequah[sic], Cherokee Nation.
Q Were you married under a Cherokee license. A Yes, sir.
Q Have you that license with you? A No, sir.
Q Have you a copy of it ? A No, sir. I went to the executive office to obtain a copy of the license but Mr. Harris said the records had all been sent to this office.
Q Had you ever been married prior to your marriage to your present wife? A No, sir.
Q Has she been married prior to that time? A No, sir.
Q Have you lived together continuously since your marriage? A Yes, sir.
Q Where have you lived during that time? A In Talequah[sic] district, Cherokee Nation.
Q You say you were married under a Cherokee license? A Yes, sir.
Q Who was that license issued by? A O. C. Daniels, clerk of the District Court.
Q What district? A Tahlequah.
Q Who was the marriage ceremony performed by? A Judge James Hendricks, Judge of the District Court, Tahlequah district.
Q Are either of those two persons living? A No, sir.
Q Both dead? A Both dead.
Q What is the date of your marriage? A It is on or about the 20th of March.
Q What year? A 18 and 75.
Q Do you remember what procedure you followed in order to obtain a Cherokee license? A Yes, sir.
Q Just explain what you did? A The application was issued by the clerk-- I had to get signers to the effect of my getting married. I returned this application after getting the signers--I think it was ten signers Cherokees by blood. I returned these applications and then license was issued to marry. This license was returned after I married and put on record. I never received them back.
Q Did you receive a certificate of marriage.[sic] A No, sir.
Q You have no documentary evidence whatever to show that you were married under the Cherokee law? A No, sir. The reason I guess was that I was living close to Tahlequah and the records was kept there and I could get them any time. They was as safe in the office of the Cherokee Nation as they would be in my house.
Q You say Mr. Harris of the Cherokee Executive office told you that the court records were here at Muskogee did he? A Yes, sir
Q Did he tell you that after he had made an examination over there or did he just tell you that when you requested a certified copy. A No, sir. I made application on Saturday last for to get a copy of my marriage certificate and Mr. Harris said " I am

Cherokee Intermarried White 1906
Volume VI

sorry to say that a week ago that the records containing the names of intermarried citizens after November 1, 1875 was called for by the Commissioner's office at Muskogee. I ain't got anything in the office here that will help you."

The records of marriage licenses issued by the Cherokee Nation and furnished this office by said nation fail to cover the year 1875, hence no documentary evidence can be found showing the marriage of the applicant, Charles W. Kolpin, to the said Eliza Kolpin nee Lillard.

Q Mr. Kolpin the records furnished this office by the Cherokee Nation fail to cover the date that you allege you were married to your request wife. Can you again request the Cherokee Nation to furnish you with a certified copy of that license? A Yes, sir.
Q If the Cherokee Nation should be unable to furnish you with a certified copy of this record, have you any witnesses that you could introduce to show that you were married at the time that you allege and in accordance with the Cherokee law?
A Yes, sir. I could furnish witnesses to that effect, and then one witness is living who was present at the time of my marriage.
Q What is his name? [sic] Walter Lozier.
Q Where does he live.[sic] A Tahlequah.
Q You wife of course could also testify to this matter. A Yes, sir.
Q In case we are unable to get a certified copy of this record it will be necessary for you to introduce secondary evidence, that is, testimony of witnesses who saw you married and know you were married in accordance with Cherokee law, in order to establish your rights to citizenship by intermarriage of the Cherokee Nation. You will be notified if further evidence is required to establish your rights.

WITNESS EXCUSED.

F. Elma Lane upon oath states that she reported the proceedings in the above entitled cause and that the foregoing is a true and correct transcript of her stenographic notes therein.

F Elma Lane

Subscribed and sworn to before me this 2nd day of January 1907.

Walter W. Chappell
Notary Public.

Cherokee Intermarried White 1906
Volume VI

C. F. B.

Cherokee 5871.

DEPARTMENT OF THE INTERIOR,
COMMISSIONER TO THE FIVE CIVILIZED TRIBES.
Muskogee, Indian Territory, January 29, 1907.

In the matter of the application for the enrollment of Charles W. Kolpin as a citizen by intermarriage of the Cherokee Nation.

APPEARANCES:
Walter Loser[sic] for applicant.

Cherokee Nation represented by
W. W. Hastings, Attorney.

Walter Loser being first duly sworn by B. P. Rasmus, Notary Public, testified as follows:

ON BEHALF OF COMMISSIONER:

Q   What is your name?   A   Walter Loser.
Q   What is your age?   A   About 47.
Q   What is your post office address?
A   Tahlequah.
Q   Are you a citizen of the Cherokee Nation?
A   Yes sir.
Q   By blood?   A   Yes sir.
Q   Are you acquainted with a person in the Cherokee Nation by the name of Charles W. Kolpin?
A   Yes, I am acquainted with him.
Q   How long have you known him?
A   Something over 30 years.
Q   He has been recognized since you knew him as a citizen by intermarriage of the Cherokee Nation?
A   Yes sir.
Q   Are you acquainted with his wife?   A   Yes sir.
Q   Did you know her before her marriage to Charles W. Kolpin?
A   Yes sir.
Q   What was her maiden name?   A   Eliza Lillard.
Q   Do you know when they were married? A   Yes sir.
Q   In what year?   A   '75 in March.
Q   Were you present at the marriage ceremony?
A   Yes sir.
Q   Where were they married?   A   Judge Hendricks.
Q   In what district?   A   Tahlequah District.

Cherokee Intermarried White 1906
Volume VI

Q   Was she a recognized citizen of the Cherokee Nation at the time he married her?
A   Yes sir.
Q   citizen by blood?   A   Yes sir.
Q   Do you know of your own personal knowledge that Charles W. Kolpin secured a marriage license and married his wife in accordance with the law of the Cherokee Nation?
A   Yes sir.
Q   Did you see his license?
A   No, I didn't see his license, either; I was there at the marriage but I never looked at the license.
Q   You have every reason to believe though that he had one?
A   Yes sir.
Q   You didn't sign his petition?   A   No sir.
Q   You have known Charles W. Kolpin ever since his marriage, have you?
A   Yes sir.
Q   You know of your own personal knowledge that since that time he has been recognized as a citizen by intermarriage of the Cherokee Nation?
A   Yes sir.
Q   And enjoyed all the rights and privileges of a citizen by intermarriage?
A   Yes sir.
Q   He has voted at the elections?
A   Yes sir; he has voted.
Q   Has he ever held any office of any kind?
A   Not that I know of.
Q   Was his wife ever married to your knowledge, prior to her marriage to him?
A   Not that I know of.
Q   Was he ever married that you know of prior to his marriage to his wife?
A   Not that I know of.
Q   Since their marriage they have lived together continuously as husband and wife?
A   Yes sir.

BY MR. HASTINGS.

Q   Why do you think it was in March of 1875; do you remember it independently or is there any circumstance which makes you remember that date?
A   There is nothing in particular that causes me to remember it?[sic]
Q   You just remember that it was in March of '75?
A   Yes sir; somewhere in March of '75.

Dennis Hendricks being first duly sworn by B. P. Rasmus, Notary Public, testified as follows:

ON BEHALF OF COMMISSIONER.

Q   What is your name?   A   Dennis Hendricks.
Q   What is your age?   A   53.

Cherokee Intermarried White 1906
Volume VI

Q   What is your post office address?
A   Tahlequah
Q   You are a citizen by blood of the Cherokee Nation?
A   Yes sir.
Q   Are you acquainted with Charles W. Kolpin?
A   Yes sir.
Q   When did you first become acquainted with him?
A   Along sometime in '75, I think it was; along in March, '75.
Q   He is a married man?
A   He came to my father's house at that time and my father married him.
Q   Were you acquainted with his wife before he married her?
A   No sir.
Q   You say they came to your father's house and were married?
A   Yes sir.
Q   Was your father at that time an official of the Cherokee Nation?
A   Yes sir.
Q   What position did he hold?   A   District Judge.
Q   You were a witness to the marriage, were you?
A   Yes sir.
Q   When did you say it occurred?
A   I think it was sometime in March,- I don't know the date exactly but it was in March of '75.
Q   How long was your father Judge of the District?
A   Four years.
Q   When did his term begin?
A   I think he was elected in '72 and he was re-elected after that; served two years to the office.
Q   You have been personally acquainted with Charles W. Kolpin since that time?
A   Yes sir.
Q   To your own personal knowledge he has been recognized since then as a citizen by intermarriage of the Cherokee Nation?
A   Yes sir.
Q   He has exercised all the rights of a citizen by intermarriage?
A   Yes sir.
Q   Has he voted at the elections?
A   Yes sir; I think he did.
Q   Did you see his marriage license?
A   Well, I did at the time when father married him but I don't know what ever went with it.
Q   You have every reason then to believe that Charles W. Kolpin secured a license and married his wife in accordance with the law of the Cherokee Nation?
A   Yes sir.

Charles W. Kolpin being first duly sworn by B. P. Rasmus, Notary Public, testified as follows:

Cherokee Intermarried White 1906
Volume VI

ON BEHALF OF COMMISSIONER.

Q   State your name, age and post office address.
A   Charles W. Kolpin; 61; Tahlequah, Cheronee[sic] Nation.
Q   What is the name of your oldest child?
A   John P. Kolpin.

An examination of the Cherokee authenticated tribal roll of 1880, shows that the applicant in this case, Charles W. Kolpin, his wife Eliza, and the name of the child given by the applicant as his oldest child, John P. Kolpin, are identified on said roll, Tahlequah District, at No. 1220, 1221 and 1222 respectively, the age of said John P. Kolpin appearing on said roll as four years.

The undersigned being first duly sworn states that as stenographer to the Commissioner to the Five Civilized Tribes, she recorded the testimony taken in this case and that the foregoing is a true and correct transcript of her stenographic notes thereof.

Myrtle Hill

Subscribed and sworn to before me this the 1st day of February, 1907.

John E. Tidwell
Notary Public.

(The Marriage License below typed as given.)

Book "C" record of marriages Tahlequah District appears the following entry.

"# 61   License granted Charles Kolpin, a citizen of the United States to marry Miss Eliza Lilard a Cherokee March 29th 1875   Ceremony by judge James Hendericks March 30th A. D. 1875."

Homer J. Councilor being first duly sworn states that as stenographer to the Commission to the Five Civilized Tribes he made the above and foregoing from the original thereof and that the same is true and correct.

Homer J Councilor

Cherokee Intermarried White 1906
Volume VI

Subscribed and sworn to before me this February 6, 1907.

Notary Public.

◇◇◇◇◇

E C M   Cherokee 5871.

DEPARTMENT OF THE INTERIOR,

COMMISSIONER TO THE FIVE CIVILIZED TRIBES.

In the matter of the application for the enrollment of CHARLES W. KOLPIN as a citizen by intermarriage of the Cherokee Nation.

D E C I S I O N

THE RECORDS OF THIS OFFICE SHOW: That at Tahlequah, Indian Territory, November 30, 1900, application was received by the Commission to the Five Civilized Tribes for the enrollment of Charles W. Kolpin as a citizen by intermarriage of the Cherokee Nation. Further proceedings in the matter of said application were had at Tahlequah, Indian Territory, October 1, 1902 and Muskogee, Indian Territory, January 2, 1907, and January 29, 1907.

THE EVIDENCE IN THIS CASE SHOWS: That the applicant herein, Charles W. Kolpin, a white man, was married in accordance with Cherokee law March 30, 1875 to his wife Eliza Kolpin, nee Lillard, who was at the time of said marriage a recognized citizen by blood of the Cherokee Nation, who is identified on the Cherokee authenticated tribal roll of 1880, Tahlequah District No. 1221, and whose name is included on the approved partial roll of citizens by blood of the Cherokee Nation opposite No. 14056. It is further shown that from the time of said marriage the said Charles W. Kolpin and Eliza Kolpin resided together as husband and wife and continuously lived in the Cherokee Nation up to and including September 1, 1902. Said applicant is identified on the Cherokee authenticated tribal roll of 1880 and the Cherokee census roll of 1896 as an intermarried citizen of the Cherokee Nation.

IT IS, THEREFORE, ORDERED AND ADJUDGED: That in accordance with the decision of the Supreme Court of the United States, dated November 5, 1906 in the cases of Daniel Red Bird, et al. vs. the United States, Nos. 125, 126, 127, and 128, the said applicant, Charles W. Kolpin is entitled, under the provisions of Section Twenty-one of the Act of Congress approved June 28, 1898 (30 Stats., 495), to enrollment as a citizen by intermarriage of the Cherokee Nation, and his application for enrollment as such is accordingly granted.

Cherokee Intermarried White 1906
Volume VI

Tams Bixby
Commissioner.

Dated at Muskogee, Indian Territory,
this   FEB 13 1907

◇◇◇◇◇

Cherokee 6871

Muskogee, Indian Territory, February 13, 1907.

W. W. Hastings,
    Attorney for the Cherokee Nation,
        Muskogee, Indian Territory.

Dear Sir:

    There is enclosed herewith a copy of the decision of the Commissioner to the Five Civilized Tribes, dated February 13, 1907, granting the application for the enrollment of Charles W. Kolpin, as a citizen by intermarriage of the Cherokee Nation.

Respectfully,

Encl. HJ-44.
HJC
                          Commissioner.

◇◇◇◇◇

Cherokee 5871.

Muskogee, Indian Territory, February 13, 1907.

The Commissioner to the Five Civilized Tribes,
    Muskogee, Indian Territory.

Sir:

    Receipt is acknowledged of the testimony and of your decision enrolling Charles W. Kolpin, as a citizen by intermarriage of the Cherokee Nation. Time for protesting said decision is waived and I consent that said person may be placed upon the schedule immediately.

Respectfully,
W. W. Hastings
Attorney for Cherokee Nation.

◇◇◇◇◇

Cherokee Intermarried White 1906
Volume VI

Cherokee
5871.

Muskogee, Indian Territory, February 13, 1907.

Charles W. Kolpin,
    Tahlequah, Indian Territory.

Dear Sir:

    There is enclosed herewith a copy of the decision of the Commissioner to the Five Civilized Tribes, dated February 13, 1907, granting your application for enrollment as a citizen by intermarriage of the Cherokee Nation.

    You will be advised when your name has been placed upon a schedule of citizens of the Cherokee Nation and approved by the Secretary of the Interior.

                  Respectfully,

Encl. HJ-45.
HJC   Commissioner.

Cher IW 190

◇◇◇◇◇

                                                            E.C.M.

DEPARTMENT OF THE INTERIOR,

COMMISSIONER TO THE FIVE CIVILIZED TRIBES.

In the matter of the application for the enrollment of

WILLIAM H. STEVENS

as a citizen by intermarriage of the Cherokee Nation.

CHEROKEE NO. 6606.

◇◇◇◇◇

Cherokee Intermarried White 1906
Volume VI

DEPARTMENT OF THE INTERIOR.
COMMISSION TO THE FIVE CIVILIZED TRIBES.
TAHLEQUAH, I.T., DECEMBER 13th, 1900.

IN THE MATTER OF THE APPLICATION OF Elmira Stevens for the enrollment of herself, husband and children as citizens of the Cherokee Nation, and she being sworn and examined by Commissioner, T. B. Needles, testified as follows:

Q What is your name? A Elmira Stevens.
Q How old are you? A Forty three.
Q What is your Postoffice address? A ParkHill[sic].
Q What district do you live in? A Tahlequah.
Q Are you a recognized citizen of the Cherokee Nation? A Yes sir.
Q By blood? A Yes sir.
Q Is your name on the roll of 1880? A Yes sir.
Q Whom do you want to enroll? A My family.
Q Are you married? A Yes sir.
Q Is your husband living? A Yes sir.
Q Why is he not here? A He had a sick father he had to staw[sic] with
Q What is his name? A William Henderson Stevens.
Q Is he a white man? A Yes sir.
Q How old is he? A He is about fifty six.
Q What is his Postoffice? A ParkHill.
Q When were you married to him? A I can not tell you.
Q Have you a certificate of marriage? A No sir; we got out license destroyed.
Q Were you married before 1880? A Yes sir.
Q What are the names of your children? A Elizabeth.
Q How old is she? A She is eighteen.
Q Next one? A Stephen.
Q How old is he? A He is seventeen.
Q Next one? A Sarah.
Q How old is she? A Fifteen.
Q Next child? A Fanny.
Q How old is she? A Eleven.
Q Next child? A That is all.

(1880 Roll, Page 391, #1201, Henderson Stephens[sic], Flint D'st)
(1880 Roll, Page 391, #1202, Elmira Stephens, Flint D'st)
(1896 Roll, Page 1288, #231, Henderson Stephens, Tahlequah D'st)
(1896 Roll, Page 1238, #2895, Elmira Stephens, Tahlequah D'st)
(1896 Roll, Page 1238, #2897, Elizabeth Stephens, Tahlequah ")
(1896 Roll, Page 1238, #2898, Stephen Stephens, Tahlequah ")
(1896 Roll, Page 1238, #2899, Sarah Stephens, Tahlequah ")
(1896 Roll, Page 1238, #2900, Fannie Stephens, Tahlequah ")

Cherokee Intermarried White 1906
Volume VI

Q Have you and your husband lived together continuously since 1880?
A Yes sir.
Q He is living with you now? A Yes sir.
Q Never have been separated? A No sir.
Q Are these children all living? A Yes sir.

Com'r. T. B. Needles: The name of William Henderson Stevens appears upon the authenticated roll of 1880, as an intermarried white, and upon the census roll of 1896, as *Stephens:* The name of his wife, Elmira Stevens, appears upon the authenticated roll of 1880, as well as the census roll of 1896, she being identified as a Cherokee citizen by blood. The names of their children, Elizabeth, Stephen, Sarah and Fanny are found upon the census roll of 1896. They are all duly identified, and make satisfactory proof as to their residence; consequently, the said William Henderson Stephens will be duly listed for enrollment as a Cherokee citizen by intermarriage, and his wife, Elmira Stephens and children as enumerated herein as Cherokee citizens by blood.

The undersigned, being sworn, states that as stenographer to the Commission to the Five Civilized Tribes, he correctly recorded the testimony and proceedings in this case, and the foregoing is a true and correct transcript of his stenographic notes thereof.

R R Cravens

Subscribed and sworn to before me this 19th day of December, 1900.

T B Needles
COMMISSIONER.

JOR.
Cher. 6606.

Department of the Interior.
Commission to the Five Civilized Tribes.
Tahlequah, I. T., October 8, 1902.

SUPPLEMENTAL TESTIMONY AND PROCEEDINGS in the matter of the application for the enrollment of WILLIAM H. STEVENS as a citizen by intermarriage of the Cherokee Nation.

WILLIAM H. STEVENS, being first duly sworn, and being examijed[sic], testified as follows:

Cherokee Intermarried White 1906
Volume VI

BY COMMISSION: What is your name? A William Henderson Stevens.
Q Have you a child William H. Stevens? A No sir.
Q How old are you? A I am about fifty-seven.
Q What is your post office address? A Park Hill.
Q You are a white man, are you? A Yes sir.
Q Have you heretofore made application to this Commission for enrollment as a citizen by intermarriage of the Cherokee Nation?
A My wife did. She came, I didn't come.
Q What is the name of your wife? A Elmira Catherine before she was married. Elmira Stevens now.
Q Is she living? A Yes sir.
Q Is she a Cherokee by blood? A Yes sir.
Q Do you claim your right to enrollment by reason of your marriage to her? S[sic] Yes sir.
Q When were you and she married? A We have been married over twenty-nine years.
Q Were you married at that time under Cherokee law? A Yes sir.
Q Have you and she lived together continuously ever since that time[sic]
A Yes sir.
Q Are you living together now? A Yes sir.
Q Were you living together on the 1st day of September, 1902? A Yes sir.
Q Were you ever married before you married her? A No sir.
Q Was she ever married before she married you? A No sir.
Q You are her first husband and she is your first wife? A Yes sir.
Q Have you resided in the Cherokee Nation continuously since you and your wife were married? A Yes sir.
Q Has she? A Yes sir.
Q You have how many children? A I have got five living and one dead.
Q How long has that child been dead? A I don't know, it has been about a year. He was a grown man, married and had a family. He came here and enrolled himself.
Q You made application for the enrollment of how many children?
A I think three-four I reckon.
Q Are all those children living now? A Yes sir.

This testimony will be filed with and made a part of the record in the matter of the application for the enrollment of William H. Stevens as a citizen by intermarriage of the Cherokee Nation, Cherokee straight card field No. 6606.

Wm. Hutchinson, being first duly sworn, states that as stenographer to the Commission to the Five Civilized Tribes he correctly recorded the testimony and proceedings in this case, and the foregoing is a true and complete transcript of the stenographic notes thereof.

Wm Hutchinson

Cherokee Intermarried White 1906
Volume VI

Subscribed and sworn to before me this 14th day of October, 1902.

John O Rosson

◇◇◇◇◇

JOR

Cherokee 6606.

DEPARTMENT OF THE INTERIOR,
COMMISSION TO THE FIVE CIVILIZED TRIBES,
CHEROKEE LAND OFFICE.

Tahlequah, I. T., November 22, 1904.

In the matter of the application of William H. Stevens Sr. for the enrollment of himself and[sic] a citizen by intermarriage and of his wife Elmira Stevens and children Elizabeth and Stephen Stevens and Sarah James, Fannie Stevens and Jesse L. James, as citizens by blood of the Cherokee Nation.

SUPPLEMENTAL TESTIMONY:

ELIZABETH HAMILTON, being duly sworn and examined by the Commission, testified as follows:

Q What is your name? A Elizabeth Hamilton.
Q How old are you? A 22 years old.
Q What is your postoffice? A Park Hill.
Q Are you a Cherokee by blood? A Yes sir.
Q Are you a daughter of William H. Stevens and Elmira Stevens?
A Yes sir.
Q Have you married since you were enrolled? A Yes sir.
Q What is the name of your husband? A Joseph Hamilton.
Q Is he a citizen of the Cherokee Nation? A No sir.
Q Are you and he living together now? A Yes sir.
Q When were you married? A
    There is offered in evidence a marriage license that the applicant was married on May 17, 1902.
Q Is that the correct date of your marriage? A Yes sir.

Clinton W. Myers, being duly sworn, states that as stenographer to the Commission to the Five Civilized Tribes, he correctly recorded the supplemental testimony in this case and that the foregoing is a true and complete transcript of his stenographic notes therein.

Clinton Q Myers

Cherokee Intermarried White 1906
Volume VI

Subscribed and sworn to before me
this the 29 day of November, 1904.

            Samuel Foreman
            Notary Public.

◇◇◇◇◇

C. F. B.   Cherokee 6606.

DEPARTMENT OF THE INTERIOR,
COMMISSIONER TO THE FIVE CIVILIZED TRIBES.
Muskogee, Indian Territory, January 19, 1907.

In the matter of the application for the enrollment of William H. Stevens as a citizen by intermarriage of the Cherokee Nation.

William H. Stevens being first duly sworn by John E. Tidwell, Notary Public, testified as follows:

ON BEHALF OF COMMISSIONER.

Q What is your name?   [sic]William Henderson Stevens.
Q What is your age?   A 60.
Q What is your post office address?
A Park Hill.
Q You are an applicant for enrollment as a citizen by intermarriage of the Cherokee Nation?
A Yes sir.
Q You have no Cherokee blood?   A No sir.
Q Your only claim to the right to enrollment as a citizen of the Cherokee Nation is by virtue of your marriage to a citizen by blood?
A Yes sir.
Q What is the name of the citizen through whom you claim such right?
A Elmira Srevens[sic].
Q Is she living?   A Yes sir.
Q When were you married to Elmira Stevans[sic]?
A In '73.
Q Was she a recognized citizen of the Cherokee Nation at the time you married her?
A Yes sir.
Q Living in the Cherokee country?
A Yes sir.
Q Did you procure a marriage license and marry her in accordance with the law of the Cherokee Nation?
A Yes sir.

Cherokee Intermarried White 1906
Volume VI

Q In what district was the license issued?
A In Flint District.
Q By whom were you married? A Judge Christie.
Q He was Judge of Flint District at that time?
A Yes sir.
Q Since your marriage to your wife, Elmira Stevens, have you and she continuously lived together as husband and wife?
A Yes sir.
Q And lived all these years in the Cherokee Nation?
A Yes sir.
Q Was she your first wife? A Yes sir.
Q Were you her first husband? A Yes sir.

The applicant, William H. Stevens, is identified on the Cherokee authenticated tribal roll of 1880, Flint District, No. 1201. His wife, Elmira Stevens, is identified on said roll at No. 1202 and her name is included in the approved partial roll of citizens by blood of the Cherokee Nation, opposite No. 25, 287.

Q Have you any evidence of a documentary character to show your marriage to your wife?
A No sir; I got them misplaced.
Q Have you any witnesses here?
A Yes sir; I have two witnesses.
Q Since your marriage to your wife, Elmira Stevens, you have exercised all the rights and enjoyed all the privileges of a citizen of the Cherokee Nation? by intermarriage?
A Yes sir.
Q Did you ever hold any office? A No sir.
Q But you have voted at elections?
A Yes sir; and sat on the grand jury.

Elmira Stevens being first duly sworn by B. P. Rasmus, Notary Public, testified as follows:

Q What is your name? A Elmira Stevens.
Q What is your age? A 49.
Q What is your post office address?
A Park Hill.
Q You appear for the purpose of giving testimony relative to the right to enrollment of William H. Stevens as a citizen by intermarriage of the Cherokee Nation?
A Yes sir.
Q How long have you known William H. Stevens?
A About 36 or 37 years.
Q He is a white man? A Yes sir.
Q Are you acquainted with his wife, Elmira Stevens?
A I am his wife.

Cherokee Intermarried White 1906
Volume VI

Q   You are a citizen by blood of the Cherokee Nation?
A   Yes sir.
Q   And residing in the Cherokee country?
A   Yes sir.
Q   Where were you and he married?
A   Wauhilla, Flint District.
Q   Did your husband secure a license and marry you in accordance with the law of the Cherokee Nation?
A   Yes sir.
Q   Was William H. Stevens your first husband?
A   Yes sir.
Q   Are you his first wife?   A   Yes sir.
Q   Since your marriage, have you and he continuously lived together as husband and wife?
A   Yes sir.

Henry M. Brown being first duly sworn by B. P. Rasmus, Notary Public, testified as follows:

Q   What is your name?   A   Henry Marshall Brown.
Q   What is your age?   A   52.
Q   What is your post office address?
A   Chance, Indian Territory.
Q   Do you know a person in the Cherokee Nation by the name of William H. Stevens?
A   Yes sir; I always knew him by the name of Henderson Stevens.
Q   Are you related to him in any way?
A   No sir.
Q   How long have you known him?
A   34 or 35 years.
Q   Do you know his wife, Elmira Stevens?
A   Yes sir.
Q   She is a Cherokee by blood?
A   Yes sir; always claimed to be.
Q   He claims the right to enrollment as a citizen of the Cherokee Nation by virtue of his marriage to her?
A   Yes sir.
Q   He is recognized as a white man?
A   Yes sir.
Q   When were William H. and Elmira Stevens married?
A   In '73 or '74
Q   Were you present?   A   Yes sir.
Q   Where were they married?
A   On Hungry Mountain at Judge Christie's, in Flint District.
Q   Did you see his marriage license?
A   No sir; if I did, I don't recollect it.

Cherokee Intermarried White 1906
Volume VI

Q But it has always been your understanding and you believe that he secured a license and married his wife in accordance with the law of the Cherokee Nation?
A I guess he did; he was married by the Judge of the District.
Q Since his marriage he has been recognized as a citizen by intermarriage of the Cherokee Nation?
A Yes sir.
Q He has enjoyed all the rights and privileges of that class of citizens?
A Yes sir; so far as I know.
Q Have you known these parties continuously since their marriage
A Why, I haven't lived right near them; 20 to 30 miles distance.
Q You never have heard of any separation?
A No sir.

Mr. William H. Walker, being first duly sworn by John E. Tidwell, Notary Public, testified as follows:

Q What is your name?
A William H. Walker.
Q What is your age?
A 40.
Q What is your post office address?
A Tahlequah.
Q You are acquainted with a person in the Cherokee Nation by the name of William H. Stevens?
A Yes sir.
Q Do you know him as an intermarried citizen of the Cherokee Nation?
A Yes sir; he has always been recognized as such.
Q His wife is a recognized citizen by blood?
A Yes sir.
Q How long have you known William H. Stevens?
A I have known him for 30 years.
Q Since you became acquainted with him, he has to your own personal knowledge, been recognized as a citizen by intermarriage of the Cherokee Nation and has enjoyed all the rights and privileges of that class of citizens?
A Yes sir.

The undersigned being first duly sworn states that as stenographer to the Commission to the Five Civilized Tribes, she recorded the testimony taken in this case and that the foregoing is a full, true and correct transcript of her stenographic notes thereof.

Myrtle Hill

Subscribed and sworn to before me this the 24th day of January, 1907.

John E. Tidwell
Notary Public.

Cherokee Intermarried White 1906
Volume VI

C. F. B.   Cherokee 6606.

DEPARTMENT OF THE INTERIOR,
COMMISSIONER TO THE FIVE CIVILIZED TRIBES.
Muskogee, Indian Territory, January 29, 1907.

In the matter of the application for the enrollment of William H. Stevens as a citizen by intermarriage of the Cherokee Nation.

                           Applicant represented by Mr. Gorney in behalf of
APPEARANCES: Soper, Huckleberry & Owen.
                           Cherokee Nation represented by
                           W. W. Hastings, Attorney.

Wilson Rider being first duly sworn by B. P. Rasmus, Notary Public, testified as follows:

ON BEHALF OF COMMISSIONER.

Q What is your name?   A Wilson Rider.
Q What is your age?   A 67.
Q What is your post office address?
A Tahlequah.
Q You appear here today for the purpose of giving testimony relative to the right to enrollment of William H. Stevens, as a citizen by intermarriage of the Cherokee Nation?
A Yes sir.

BY MR. GORNEY.

Q How long have you known Mr. Stevens, Mr. Rider?
A I can't just exactly tell you how long but I have known him ever since before the war; me and him was little boys together; his father had a water mill up yonder,- belongs to Nancy Adair; this Henderson Stevens,-- his father put up a water mill for Nancy Adair, and we used to play at the mill.
Q You are a citizen of the Cherokee Nation?
A Yes sir; that's what they all said; I reckon I am.
Q Whereabouts did you reside Mr Rider, in the 70's,- between 70 and 80?
A I lived at what they called Park Hill.
Q In what district?   A In Tahlequah District.
Q Were you acquainted with the woman that Henderson Stevens married?
A Yes sir.
Q Was she a citizen of the Cherokee Nation or not?
A Yes sir; she was a citizen of the Cherokee Nation; Cherokee by blood.

Cherokee Intermarried White 1906
Volume VI

Q   What was her name before she was married?
A   We called her Miry,- Elmira Cabin I reckon.
Q   Do you know where she and Henderson Stevens were married?
A   They got married in Flint District. Jackson Christie who was District Judge, married them.
Q   Did you or didn't you sign the petition for the license of Henderson Stevens?
A   I signed the petition; old man Levi Keys,- he's dead though now,- was the first man signed the petition; William Keys signed the petition and Marshall Brown,- I think he's living,- he signed the petition.
Q   Did the people look upon Henderson Stevens as a citizen of the Cherokee Nation?
A   I reckon so; he was married under the Cherokee law because Judge Christie was a Cherokee.

BY MR. HASTINGS.

Q   Do you know when he was married?
A   I think it was in '73.
Q   What month?
A   I don't know what month it was.
Q   How old are you?   A   I am about 67.
Q   How far was you living from him when he was married?
A   I lived about half a mile from him.
Q   Had his wife ever been married before?
A   No sir; not as I know of.
Q   Had Stevens ever been married before:
A   No sir; not that I know of.
Q   Did you know them?   A   Of course I knew them.
Q   Then you know they hadn't been married, don't you?
A   No sir.
Q   They lived in the same community with you, didn't they?
A   I don't think the girl had ever been married before and I don't think Henderson was ever married before either.
Q   Is his wife a sister of John Cabin?   A   Yes sir.

ON BEHALF OF COMMISSIONER.

Q   You have known Henderson Stevens continuously since his marriage?
A   Yes sir.
Q   And he has always been recognized as a citizen by intermarriage of the Cherokee Nation?   A   Yes sir
Q   He has voted at the elections?   A   Yes sir.
Q   He has exercised all the rights of a citizen by intermarriage of the Cherokee Nation?
A   Yes sir; so far as I know he did.
Q   You never heard his right as an intermarried citizen questioned?
A   No sir.

Cherokee Intermarried White 1906
Volume VI

The undersigned being first duly sworn states that as stenographer to the Commission to the Five Civilized Tribes, she recorded the testimony taken in this case and that the foregoing is a true and correct transcript of her stenographic notes thereof.

Myrtle Hill

Subscribed and sworn to before me this the 1st day of February, 1907.

John E. Tidwell
Notary Public.

◇◇◇◇◇

E C M   Cherokee 6606.

DEPARTMENT OF THE INTERIOR,

COMMISSIONER TO THE FIVE CIVILIZED TRIBES.

In the matter of the application for the enrollment of WILLIAM H. STEVENS as a citizen by intermarriage of the Cherokee Nation.

D E C I S I O N

THE RECORDS OF THIS OFFICE SHOW: That at Tahlequah, Indian Territory, December 13, 1900 application was received by the Commission to the Five Civilized Tribes for the enrollment of William H. Stevens as a citizen by intermarriage of the Cherokee Nation. Further proceedings in the matter of said application were had at Tahlequah, Indian Territory, October 8, 1902 and November 22, 1904 and at Muskogee, Indian Territory, January 19, 1907 and January 29, 1907.

THE EVIDENCE IN THIS CASE SHOWS: That the applicant herein, William H. Stevens, a white man, was married in accordance with Cherokee law in 1873 to his wife, Elmira Stevens, nee Catron[sic], who was at the time of said marriage a recognized citizen by blood of the Cherokee Nation, who is identified on the Cherokee authenticated tribal roll of 1880, Flint District, No. 1202 as a native Cherokee and whose name is included on the approved partial roll of citizens by blood of the Cherokee Nation, opposite No. 25287. It is further shown that from the time of said marriage the said William H. Stevens and Elmira Stevens resided together as husband and wife and continuously lived in the Cherokee Nation up to and including September 1, 1902. Said applicant is identified on the Cherokee authenticated tribal roll of 1880 and the Cherokee census roll of 1896 as an intermarried citizen of the Cherokee Nation.

IT IS, THEREFORE, ORDERED AND ADJUDGED: That in accordance with the decision of the Supreme Court of the United States, dated November 5, 1906 in the cases of Daniel Red Bird et al. vs. the United States, Nos. 125, 126, 127, and 128, the said

Cherokee Intermarried White 1906
Volume VI

applicant, William H. Stevens is entitled, under the provisions of Section Twenty-one of the Act of Congress approved June 28, 1898, (30 Stats. 495), to enrollment as a citizen by intermarriage of the Cherokee Nation, and his application for enrollment as such is accordingly granted.

              Tams Bixby
               Commissioner.

Dated at Muskogee, Indian Territory,
this FEB 14 1907

◇◇◇◇◇

Cherokee 6606

        Muskogee, Indian Territory, February 14, 1907.

W. W. Hastings,
  Attorney for the Cherokee Nation,
    Muskogee, Indian Territory.

Dear Sir:

  There is enclosed herewith a copy of the decision of the Commissioner to the Five Civilized Tribes, dated February 14, 1907, granting the application for the enrollment of William H. Stevens as a citizen by intermarriage of the Cherokee Nation.

      Respectfully,

Encl. H-20   Commissioner.
JMH

◇◇◇◇◇

Cherokee 6606

        Muskogee, Indian Territory, February 14, 1907.

The Commissioner to the Five Civilized Tribes,
  Muskogee, Indian Territory.

Sir:

  Receipt is acknowledged of the testimony and of your decision enrolling William H. Stevens as a citizen by intermarriage of the Cherokee Nation. Time for protesting said decision is waived, and I consent that said person may be placed upon the schedule immediately.

      Respectfully,
        W. W. Hastings
        Attorney for Cherokee Nation.

Cherokee Intermarried White 1906
Volume VI

Cherokee 6606

Muskogee, Indian Territory, February 14, 1907.

William H. Stevens,
Park Hill, Indian Territory.

Dear Sir:

There is enclosed herewith a copy of the decision of the Commissioner to the Five Civilized Tribes, dated February 14, 1907, granting the application for your enrollment as a citizen by intermarriage of the Cherokee Nation.

You will be advised when your name has been placed upon a schedule of citizens of the Cherokee Nation and approved by the Secretary of the Interior.

Respectfully,

Encl. H-21
JMH

Commissioner.

Cher IW 191

E.C.M.

DEPARTMENT OF THE INTERIOR,

COMMISSIONER TO THE FIVE CIVILIZED TRIBES.

In the matter of the application for the enrollment of

CHARLES M. McCLELLAN

as a citizen by intermarriage of the Cherokee Nation.

CHEROKEE NO. 10152

Cherokee Intermarried White 1906
Volume VI

Department of the Interior,
Commission to the Five Civilized Tribes
Muskogee, I. T. February 12th 1901.

In the matter of the application of Charles M. McClellan for enrollment as a Cherokee citizen; he being sworn before Commissioner C. R. Breckinridge, testified as follows:-

Q What is your name? A. Charles M. McClellan.
Q How old are you? A. 55.
Q What is your post office? A. Claremore.
Q In what district do you live? A. Cooweescoowee.
Q Do you want to enroll yourself and family? A. ~~Yes~~ My family has been enrolled.
Q Just apply for yourself? A. Yes sir.
Q Your wife and children have been applied for? A. Yes sir.
Q What is your wife's name? A. Jennie L.
Q You claim as an inter-married citizen? A. Yes sir.
Q You are a white man? A. Yes sir.
Q Have you your marriage license and certificate? A. No sir.
Q When were you married? A. 8th of February, 1869.
Q What was your wife's name when you married her? A. Foreman.
Q Was that her maiden name? A. Yes sir.
Q Give me the name of her father? A. Stephen Foreman.
Q Is he dead? A. Yes sir.
Q Give me the name of her mother? A. Sallie.
Q Is her mother dead? A. Yes sir.
Q Has your wife lived in the Cherokee Nation all her life? A. Yes sir, excepting a year or two during the war.
Q She of course is a Cherokee by blood? A. Yes sir.
Q Was your wife never married except to you? A. No sir.
Q And you were never married except to her ? A. No sir.
Q Have you and she lived together since you were married in 1869? A. Yes sir.

> The 1880 authenticated rolls of the Cherokee Nation examined and on page 141, #1927 thereof appears the name of C. M. McClellan in Cooweescoowee district.

> The 1896 census rolls of the Cherokee Nation examined and on page 316, #~~1927~~ 751 thereof appears the name of Charles McClellan in Cooweescoowee district.

Q Did you ever take an allotment on the Cherokee Strip? A. Yes sir, myself and my family all taken allotments on the Strip.

By W. W. Hastings:-
" The Representatives of the Cherokee Nation protest against the enrollment of Charles M. McClellan as a citizen of the Cherokee Nation by

Cherokee Intermarried White 1906
Volume VI

adoption because of the fact that in September, 1893, he took allotment on what is known as the Cherokee strip, without any compensation to the Cherokee Nation, as did other allottees of the Cherokee Strip who were residents of the Cherokee Nation and citizens of the same by blood.

Examination of applicant continued by the Commission:

Q Did you take an allotment on what is known as the Cherokee Strip in 1893?
A Yes sir.
Q Did you live there prior to that time? A. Yes sir.
Q When it was a part of the Cherokee Nation? A. Yes sir.
Q How long did you live there after you took your allotment? A. I had a ranche[sic] there.
Q Have you that ranche yet? A. No sir.
Q How long did you have it? A. All cattle men were put out of there in '90.
Q When have you ceased to make your home in that section? A. I lived there in 1883; I staid there myself most of the time until we left for good; went there in '80 and staid until '90. My family did not live there long we had chills and fever and they went back home-I staid out there.
Q And your family were back at home near Claremore ? A. Yes sir in 1883.
Q Your family never did live there did they? A. Yes sir in 1883.
Q When did your family quit living there? A. Same year.
Q You haven't lived there yourself since 1890? A. No sir.
Q Do you still own a place there? A. Yes sir own an interest.
Q Your real home was back here in the Cherokee Nation? A. Yes sir.
Q How much land did you take in that allotment? A. Eighty acres.
Q You sold that did you? A. Yes sir.
Q When did you sell it? A. Think it was in 1894.
Q And you kept the proceeds of it? A. Never got anything out of it; started a town-site on it and I lost it.
Q But if any proceeds had arisen you would have gotten it individually
Q[sic] Yes sir I guess so, the Government issued me a patent to it; it was valued at $112.00[sic]
Q You have heard to protest made by the Representatives of the Cherokee Nation: your claim I presume is that you had under Cherokee Constitution and laws the same right as any other Cherokee citizen? A. Yes sir I think I have.
Q You didn't receive any Strip money in 1894 did you? A. No sir.
Q So there was no reduction made from the Strip money by reason of your allotment and no balance paid over to you in 1894? A. No sir.

Com'r Breckinridge,--
The applicant is identified on the 1880 and 1896 rolls as an adopted Cherokee. He is a white man and states that he has lived with his wife, a Cherokee woman, and in the Cherokee Nation ever since their marriage in 1869. The Cherokee Representatives present protest against the enrollment of this applicant upon the ground that he being an intermarried citizen, took an allotment in what is known as

Cherokee Intermarried White 1906
Volume VI

the Cherokee Strip in 1893. For the further consideration of this point the applicant will now be listed for enrollment as a Cherokee by intermarriage on a doubtful card, and the final decision of the Commission will be made known to him at his post office address.

= =

Chas. von Weise, being sworn states that as stenographer to the Commission to the Five Civilized Tribes he reported in full all the proceedings in the above cause and that the foregoing is a full, true and correct transcript of his stenographic notes therein.

Chas von Weise

Subscribed and sworn to before me this the 13th of February, 1901.

CR Breckinridge
Commissioner.

◇◇◇◇◇

Statement of Applicant Taken Under Oath.

Coo.

CHEROKEE BY BLOOD AND ADOPTION.

1551 Date **Feb. 12th** 1900. **1**
Name **Charles M. McClellan** **Claremore I.T.**
District **Coo.** Year **1880** Page **441** No. **1927**
Citizen by blood **No** Mother's citizenship
Intermarried citizen **Yes**
Married under what law Date of marriage
License Certificate
Wife's name
District Page No.
Citizen by blood Mother's citizenship
Intermarried citizen
Married under what law Date of marriage
License Certificate

Doubtful

Names of Children:

	Dist.	Year	Page	No.	Age
	Dist.	Year	Page	No.	Age
	Dist.	Year	Page	No.	Age
	Dist.	Year	Page	No.	Age
	Dist.	Year	Page	No.	Age

No. 1 on 1880 roll as C. M. McClellan

◇◇◇◇◇

Cherokee Intermarried White 1906
Volume VI

Supl.-C.D. #1189.

Department of the Interior,
Commission to the Five Civilized Tribes,
Muskogee, I. T., March 19?[sic] 1902.

SUPPLEMENTAL in the matter of the enrollment of CHARLES M. McCLELLAND[sic] as a citizen of the Cherokee Nation:

The applicant was notified by registered letter February 28, 1902, that his application for the enrollment of himself as a citizen of the Cherokee Nation would be taken up for final consideration by the Commission at its offices in Muskogee, Indian Territory, on the 19th day of March, 1902, and that on said date he might appear before the Commission either in person or by attorney when an opportunity would be given him to introduce any additional testimony affecting his application. The applicant having this day, to-wit: the 19th day of March, 1902, been called and failing to respond either in person or by attorney, the case is deemed completed and will be reported to the Commission for final decision based upon the evidence now of record.

---oooOOOooo---

I, J. O. Rosson, do hereby certify that as stenographer to the Commission to the Five Civilized Tribes I correctly recorded the proceedings has this day in the above application, and that the foregoing is a true and complete transcript of my stenographic notes thereof.

JO Rosson

Cherokee D-1089.

Department of the Interior,
Commission to the Five Civilized Tribes.
Muskogee, I. T., October 28, 1902.

In the matter of the application of Charles M. McClellan for the enrollment of himself as a citizen by intermarriage of the Cherokee Nation; he being sworn and examined by the Commission, testified as follows:

Q What is your name?   A Charles M. McClellan.
Q How old are you?   A I will be fifty-seven next birthday; fifty-six last March.
Q What is your postoffice address?   A Claremore.
Q Are you an applicant for enrollment as an intermarried citizen?   A Yes sir.
Q What is your wife's name?   A Jennie L.
Q Is she living?   A Yes sir.

Cherokee Intermarried White 1906
Volume VI

Q   Is she a Cherokee by blood?   A   Yes sir.
Q   When were you married to your wife, Jennie L.?   A   February, '69.
Q   Married under a Cherokee marriage license were you?   A   Yes sir.
Q   Have you filed your license with the Commission?   A   No sir, we couldn't find my license, it got misplaced some way.
Q   Did you make proof to the Commission?   A   Yes sir.
Q   Were you on the 1880 roll with your wife as an intermarried citizen?   A   Yes sir.
Q   Have you and your wife lived together from 1880 up to the present time?   A   All the time, yes sir.
Q   Never have been separated?   A   No sir.
Q   You never have been married to any other woman since 1880?   A   No sir.
Q   You and your wife were living together on the first day of September, 1902?   A   Yes sir.
Q   Have you lived in the Cherokee Nation all the time since 1880 up to the present time?   A   Yes sir.

The undersigned, being duly sworn, states that as stenographer to the Commission to the Five Civilized Tribes he correctly recorded the testimony and proceedings in this case, and the foregoing is a true and correct transcript of his stenographic notes thereof.

E.G. Rothenberger

Subscribed and sworn to before me this 29th day of November, 1902.

BC Jones
Notary Public.

◇◇◇◇◇

Tahlequah, Ind Terry March 14th" 1902.

$ 112.00

Receipt of Charles M. McClellan, One Hundred and twelve Dollars, ($112.00) the amount due the Cherokee Nation from him for his allotment taken on the Cherokee Strip.

Treasurer Cherokee Nat'n

◇◇◇◇◇

Cherokee Intermarried White 1906
Volume VI

Cherokee D-1089.

Department of the Interior,
Commission to the Five Civilized Tribes.

In the matter of the application for the enrollment of Charles M. McClellan as a citizen by intermarriage of the Cherokee Nation.

DECISION.

--oOo--

The record in this case shows that on February 12, 1901, Charles M. McClellan appeared before the Commission at Muskogee, Indian Territory and made personal application for the enrollment of himself as a citizen by intermarriage of the Cherokee Nation. Further proceedings in the matter of said application were had at Muskogee, Indian Territory, on March 19, 1902 and on October 28, 1902.

The evidence shows that the said Charles M. McClellan was married to Jennie L. Foreman, a Cherokee citizen by blood, in 1869. The said Charles M. McClellan is identified on the 1880 authenticated tribal roll of the Cherokee Nation, and on the 1896 Census roll of said nation.

It further appears that the said Charles M. McClellan took an allotment of eighty acres on the "Cherokee Strip", and received a patent therefor. It further appears that the said Charles M. McClellan on March 14, 1902 paid to the treasurer of the Cherokee Nation $112.00, the receipt therefor stating that the same was the amount due the Cherokee Nation from him for his allotment on the "Cherokee Strip."

The evidence further shows that the said Charles M. McClellan has lived in the Cherokee Nation with his said wife continuously since 1880, up to, and including September 1, 1902.

It is therefore, the opinion of this Commission that Charles M. McClellan should be enrolled as a citizen by intermarriage of the Cherokee Nation in accordance with the provisions of section twenty-one of the Act of Congress approved June 28, 1898 (30 Stats., 495), to enrollment as a citizen by intermarriage of the Cherokee Nation, and h application for enrollment as such is accordingly granted., approved June 28, 1898 (30 Stats., 495), and it is so ordered.

COMMISSION TO THE FIVE CIVILIZED TRIBES.

Tams Bixby
    Acting Chairman.

TB Needles
    Commissioner.

C. R. Breckinridge
    Commissioner.

Dated at Muskogee, Indian Territory,
this   FEB -2 1903

Cherokee Intermarried White 1906
Volume VI

Dup

DEPARTMENT OF THE INTERIOR THE INTERIOR.

COMMISSION TO THE FIVE CIVILIZED TRIBES.

CHEROKEE ENROLLMENT OFFICE.

Tahlequah, I. T.F. JUL 31 1903 A. D. 190___

To the Clerk in charge of the Cherokee Land Office :

This is to certify that the names of the following persons:

Card Number	NAME	Relationship to Person First Named	Age
10152	Charles M. McClellan		57

All appear upon the records of the Commission to the Five Civilized Tribes as applicants for enrollment as citizens of the Cherokee Nation.

In the event that said persons are finally enrolled as citizens of said Nation, a certificate of citizenship in the usual form will be issued.

THE COMMISSION TO THE FIVE CIVILIZED TRIBES.

Tams Bixby CHAIRMAN

_____
Chairman.

W.J. Cook
Enrollment Clerk.

JR

Cherokee Intermarried White 1906
Volume VI

F.R. Cherokee 10152

DEPARTMENT OF THE INTERIOR,
COMMISSIONER TO THE FIVE CIVILIZED TRIBES.
Muskogee, I. T., January 31, 1907.

In the matter of the application for the enrollment of Charles M. McClellan as a citizen by intermarriage of the Cherokee Nation.

Cheroke[sic] Nation represented by W. W. Hastings.

Charles M. McClellan being first duly sworn by B. P. Rasmus, a Notary Public, testified as follows:

By the Commissioner:
Q What is your name? A Charles M. McClellan.
Q Your age? A Sixty-one.
Q Your postoffice address? A Claremore, I. T.
Q You are a white man are you? A Yes sir.
Q You claim right to enrollment as a citizen by intermarriage of the Cherokee Nation? A Yes sir.
Q Your claim to such right is by virtue of your marriage to a citizen by blood of the Cherokee Nation? A Yes sir.
Q What is her name? A Jennie L. Foreman.
Q When were you married to Jennie L. Foreman? A Ninth of February, 1869.
Q Where were you married to her? A Park Hill.
Q What District? A Tahlequah.
Q Was your marriage under a license of the Cherokee Nation? A Yes sir.
Q Have you any documentary evidence showing that marriage? A No sir.
Q Who issued the license to you? A O. P. Brewer.
Q What office did he hold at that time? A Clerk of Canadian District.
Q Who were some of the signers of your petition? A Louis Downing, Rufus Ross, Roach Young.
Q Who married you? A Ballentine. He issued me a certificate and we had it framed and hung up at our house for I guess twenty years, and finally it fell down and broke the glass, and my wife put it away and now she can't find it.
Q Was the license ever returned so far as you know to the Clerk's office? A I don't know.
Q Is your wife living at this time? A Yes sir.
Q At the time you married her was she a recognized citizen by blood of the Cherokee nation? A Yes sir.
Q Have you resided together as husband and wife and lived continuously in the Cherokee Nation from the time of your marriage up until the present time? A Yes sir.
Q Had you ever been married before you married Miss Foreman? A No sir.
Q Had she ever been married before she married you? A No sir.

Cherokee Intermarried White 1906
Volume VI

Q Is there anyone here today who was present at that marriage?
A Yes, Mr. Foreman, her brother.

Witness excused.

John A. Foreman being first duly sworn by B. P. Rasmus, testified as follows:

By the Commissioner:
Q What is your name?   A John A. Foreman.
Q What is your age?   A Sixty-two.
Q And your postoffice address?   A Talala, I. T.
Q You appear here for the purpose of giving testimony as to the right to enrollment of Charles M. McClellan as a citizen by intermarriage of the Cherokee Nation?   A Yes sir.
Q How long have you known Charles M. McClellan?   A I have known him ever since about 1859 I think; we went to school together previous to the war.
Q Do you know his wife?   A Yes sir.
Q How long have you known her?   A Known her ever since her birth in 1850.
Q Are you related to her?   A Yes, I am her brother.
Q When were they married?   A Married in 1869, sometime during February.
Q Where?   [sic] At Park Hille[sic] at my father's house.
Q Was their marriage under a license of the Cherokee Nation?   A Yes sir.
Q You saw the license, did you?   A I don't remember whether I saw it or not. I am satisfied that a license was had.
Q And the marriage ceremony was under that license?   A Yes. I was well acquainted with the minister and I know he wouldn't have performed the marriage ceremony unless he had a license.
Q You have no reason to think that they were not married in accordance with the laws of the Cherokee nation?   A No sir.
Q They have resided together as husband and wife since that time?   A Yes sir.
Q Always held themselves out as such in the community where they resided?
A Yes sir.
Q And lived continuously in the Cherokee nation from the time of their marriage up to the present time?   A Yes, they have made little trips out--
Q The absences were only of a temporary nature?   A Yes.
Q Was you one of the signers to M. McClellan's petition?   A No sir.

>The applicant is identified on the Cherokee authenticated tribal roll of 1880, Cooweescoowee District as C. M. McClellan, No. 1927 as an intermarried citizen, and is identified on the Cherokee census roll of 1896, Cooseescoowee[sic] District, page 316, No. 731.

>Frances R. Lane upon oath states that as stenographer to the Commissioner to the Five Civilized Tribes she reported the testimony in the above entitled cause and that the foregoing is an accurate transcript of her stenographic notes thereof.

Frances R Lane

Cherokee Intermarried White 1906
Volume VI

Subscribed and sworn to before me this January 31, 1907.

Edward Merrick
Notary Public.

◇◇◇◇◇

E C M

Cherokee 10152.

DEPARTMENT OF THE INTERIOR,

COMMISSIONER TO THE FIVE CIVILIZED TRIBES.

In the matter of the application for the enrollment of CHARLES M. McCLELLAN as a citizen by intermarriage of the Cherokee Nation.

D E C I S I O N

THE RECORDS OF THIS OFFICE SHOW: That at Muskogee, Indian Territory, February 12, 1901 application was received by the Commission to the Five Civilized Tribes for the enrollment of Charles M. McClellan as a citizen by intermarriage of the Cherokee Nation. Further proceedings in the matter of said application were had at Muskogee, Indian Territory, March 19, 1902, October 28, 1902 and January 31, 1907. The records further show that on February 2, 1903 the Commission to the Five Civilized Tribes rendered its decision herein granting said applicant the right to enrollment as a citizen by intermarriage of the Cherokee Nation.

THE EVIDENCE IN THIS CASE SHOWS: That the applicant herein, Charles M. McClellan, a white man, was married in accordance with Cherokee law February 8, 1869 to his wife, Jennie L. McClellan, nee Foreman, who was at the time of said marriage a recognized citizen by blood of the Cherokee Nation, who is identified on the Cherokee authenticated tribal roll of 1880, Cooweescoowee District No. 1928 as a native Cherokee. It is further shown that from the time of said marriage the said Charles M. McClellan and Jennie L. McClellan resided together as husband and wife and continuously lived in the Cherokee Nation up to and including September 1, 1902. Said applicant is identified on the Cherokee authenticated tribal roll of 1880 and the Cherokee census roll of 1896 as an intermarried citizen of the Cherokee Nation.

IT IS, THEREFORE, ORDERED AND ADJUDGED: That the decision rendered by the Commission to the Five Civilized Tribes, February 2, 1903, granting the application for the enrollment of Charles M. McClellan as a citizen by intermarriage of be and is hereby affirmed, and that in accordance with the decision of the Supreme Court of the United States, dated November 5, 1906 in the cases of Daniel Red Bird, et al. vs. the United States, Nos. 125, 126, 127, and 128, the said applicant, Charles M. McClellan is entitled, under the provisions of Section Twenty-one of the Act of Congress approved

Cherokee Intermarried White 1906
Volume VI

June 28, 1898 (30 Stats. 495), to enrollment as a citizen by intermarriage of the Cherokee Nation, and his application for enrollment as such is accordingly granted.

Tams Bixby
Commissioner.

Dated at Muskogee, Indian Territory, this FEB 14 1907

◇◇◇◇◇

COMMISSIONERS:
HENRY L. DAWES,
TAMS BIXBY,
THOMAS B. NEEDLES,
C. R. BRECKINRIDGE.

DEPARTMENT OF THE INTERIOR,
COMMISSION TO THE FIVE CIVILIZED TRIBES.

REFER IN REPLY TO THE FOLLOWING:
Cherokee D-1089

ALLISON L. AYLESWORTH,
SECRETARY.

ADDRESS ONLY THE
COMMISSION TO THE FIVE CIVILIZED TRIBES.

Muskogee, Indian Territory, **February 28,** 1902

Mr. Charles M. McClellan,
Claremore, Indian Territory,

Sir:-

You are hereby notified that the application of **yourself**

for enrollment as ......citizen..... of the Cherokee Nation will be taken up for final consideration by the Commission to the Five Civilized Tribes, at its office in Muskogee, Indian Territory, on **the 19 day of March, 1902.**

On said date, you may, if you desire, appear before the Commission, in person or by attorney, when an opportunity will be given you to introduce any additional testimony affecting your application, **that you may deem necessary.**

You are further notified that the Representatives of the Cherokee Nation will also, at the same time, be afforded an opportunity to introduce testimony tending to disprove your right to enrollment, but said Representatives will be required to notify you of their intention to introduce such testimony before they will be permitted to do so.

Cherokee Intermarried White 1906
Volume VI

Register.   Yours truly,

Commissioner in Charge.
A̶c̶t̶i̶n̶g̶ ̶C̶h̶a̶i̶r̶m̶a̶n̶.

◇◇◇◇◇

COPY

Cherokee D-1089

Muskogee, Indian Territory, February 7, 1903.

W. W. Hastings,
      Attorney for the Cherokee Nation,
           Muskogee, Indian Territory.

Dear Sir:

    There is herewith enclosed a copy of the decision of the Commissioner to the Five Civilized Tribes, dated February 2, 1903, granting the application of Charles M. McClellan for the enrollment of himself as a citizen by intermarriage of the Cherokee Nation.

    You are hereby advised that you will be allowed fifteen days from date hereof, in which to file such protest as you may desire to make against the action of the Commission in this case, a copy of which protest you will be required to serve upon the applicant. If you fail to file protest within the time allowed, this decision will be considered final.

Respectfully,

Tams Bixby
Acting Chairman.

Enc. M-24

◇◇◇◇◇

Cherokee Intermarried White 1906
Volume VI

COPY

Cherokee D-1089.

Muskogee, Indian Territory, February 26, 1903.

Charles M. McClellan,
Claremore, Indian Territory.

Dear Sir:

There is herewith inclosed a copy of the decision of the Commissioner to the Five Civilized Tribes, dated February 2, 1903, granting your application for the enrollment of yourself as a citizen by intermarriage of the Cherokee Nation.

Respectfully,

Tams Bixby
Chairman.

Enc H-13.

Register.

◇◇◇◇◇

Cherokee
10152.

Muskogee, Indian Territory, December 27, 1906.

Charles M. McClellan,
Claremore, Indian Territory.

Dear Sir:

November 6, 1906, the United States Supreme Court held that white persons who intermarried with Cherokee citizens according to Cherokee law prior to November 1, 1875, are entitled to enrollment and allotments of land as citizens of the Cherokee Nation.

You are advised that to properly determine your right to enrollment as a citizen by intermarriage of the Cherokee Nation, it will be necessary for you to appear before the Commissioner for the purpose of giving testimony as to the date of your marriage and whether or not your wife, by reason of your marriage to whom you claim the right to enrollment as a citizen of the Cherokee Nation, was a recognized citizen of the Cherokee Nation at the time of your marriage to her, and whether or not you were married to her in accordance with Cherokee laws.

Cherokee Intermarried White 1906
Volume VI

You are therefore directed to appear before the Commissioner at Muskogee, Indian Territory, at 9 o'clock A. M., on Saturday, January 5, 1907, and give testimony as above indicated.

        Respectfully,

GHL   Acting Commissioner.

◇◇◇◇◇

Cherokee
10152

           Muskogee, Indian Territory, January 7, 1907

C. M. McClellan,
  Oak Ridge, Louisiana.

Dear Sir:

  This office is in receipt of your letter of January 1, 1907, in which you state that you are absent from the Territory on business, and it is therefore impossible for you to appear before the Commissioner in connection with your application for enrollment as a citizen by intermarriage of the Cherokee Nation. You ask information in the premises.

  In reply you are advised that the record in the matter of your application for enrollment will be examined, and if it is found necessary for further evidence to be introduced you will be advised thereof and given an opportunity to introduce the same.

  If you have a marriage license, or a certificate of marriage, you should forward same to this office by return mail to be used in connection with your case.

         Respectfully,

L M B   Commissioner

◇◇◇◇◇

Cherokee Intermarried White 1906
Volume VI

Cherokee 10152

Muskogee, Indian Territory, February 14, 1907.

W. W. Hastings,
    Attorney for the Cherokee Nation,
        Muskogee, Indian Territory.

Dear Sir:

    There is enclosed herewith a copy of the decision of the Commissioner to the Five Civilized Tribes, dated February 14, 1907, granting the application for the enrollment of Charles M. McClellan as a citizen by intermarriage of the Cherokee Nation.

        Respectfully,

Encl. H-26   Commissioner.
JMH

◇◇◇◇◇

Cherokee 10152

Muskogee, Indian Territory, February 14, 1907.

The Commissioner to the Five Civilized Tribes,
    Muskogee, Indian Territory.

Sir:

    Receipt is acknowledged of the testimony and of your decision enrolling Charles M. McClellan as a citizen by intermarriage of the Cherokee Nation. Time for protesting said decision is waived, and I consent that said person may be placed upon the schedule immediately.

        Respectfully,
           W. W. Hastings
           Attorney for Cherokee Nation.

◇◇◇◇◇

Cherokee Intermarried White 1906
Volume VI

Cherokee 10152

Muskogee, Indian Territory, February 14, 1907.

Charles M. McClellan,
 Claremore, Indian Territory.

Dear Sir:

There is enclosed herewith a copy of the decision of the Commissioner to the Five Civilized Tribes, dated February 14, 1907, granting the application for your enrollment as a citizen by intermarriage of the Cherokee Nation.

You will be advised when your name has been placed upon a schedule of citizens of the Cherokee Nation and approved by the Secretary of the Interior.

Respectfully,

Encl. H-27
JMH

Commissioner.

Cher IW 192

◇◇◇◇◇

E.C.M.

DEPARTMENT OF THE INTERIOR,

COMMISSIONER TO THE FIVE CIVILIZED TRIBES.

In the matter of the application for the enrollment of

THOMAS B. McDANIEL

as a citizen by intermarriage of the Cherokee Nation.

Cherokee 7029.

◇◇◇◇◇

Cherokee Intermarried White 1906
Volume VI

DEPARTMENT OF THE INTERIOR, COMMISSION TO THE FIVE CIVILIZED TRIBES, MUSKOGEE, I.T., JANUARY 12th, 1901

In the matter of the application of Thomas B. McDaniel for the enrollment of himself and wife as citizens of the Cherokee Nation; said McDaniel being sworn and examined by Commissioner Needles, testified as follows:

Q What is your name? A Thomas B. McDaniel.
Q What is your age, Mr. McDaniel? A 61.
Q What is your post office? A Muskogee.
Q What district do you live in? A Canadian district.
Q You are a recognized citizen of the Cherokee Nation? A Yes sir.
Q By blood? A No, sir.
Q By intermarriage? A By intermarriage.
Q Whom do you desire to enroll? A My wife and myself.
Q What is your wife's name? A Nancy McDaniel.
Q What is her age? A 66.
Q When were you married? A '74.
    1880 Roll; page 559, #1284, T. B. McDaniel, Illinois.
    1880 Roll; page 559, #1285, Nan McDaniel.
    1896 Roll; page 90, #178, Thomas B. McDaniel, Canadian.
    1896 Roll; page 48, #1319, Nan McDaniel, Canadian.
Q Have you and your wife been living together continuously since you married?
A Yes, sir.
Q How long have you lived in the Cherokee Nation? A Ever since '59.
Q Living in the Cherokee Nation now? A Yes, sir.
Q You are a non-citizen? A We are in Town now, but that is my home, out here in Canadian district.
Q You have never voter in the Creek Nation over here? A No, sir.
Q Recognized as a Cherokee citizen? A Yes, sir.
Q You are a white man are you? A Supposed to be.

    Com'r Needles:--The name of Thomas B. McDaniel appears upon the authenticated roll of 1880 as T. B. McDaniel, and the census roll of 1896 as Thomas B. The name of his wife, Nancy, also appears upon the authenticated roll of 1880 and the census roll of 1896 as a Cherokee citizen by blood; he having been enrolled as a Cherokee citizen by intermarriage. They are duly identified according to the page and number of the roll and makes satisfactory proof as to residence, consequently said Thomas B. McDaniel will be duly listed for enrollment as a Cherokee citizen by intermarriage, and his wife, Nancy, as a Cherokee citizen by blood.

---oooOOOooo---

Cherokee Intermarried White 1906
Volume VI

J. O. Rosson, being first duly sworn, states that as stenographer to the Commission to the Five Civilized Tribes, he correctly recorded the testimony and proceedings in this case, and the foregoing is a true and complete transcript of his stenographic notes thereof.

JO Rosson

Subscribed and sworn to before me this 14th day of January, 1901.

C R Breckinridge
Commissioner.

◇◇◇◇◇

Cherokee 7029.

DEPARTMENT OF THE INTERIOR,
COMMISSION TO THE FIVE CIVILIZED TRIBES.
Muskogee, I. T., October 16, 1902.

In the matter of the application of Thomas B. McDaniel for the enrollment of himself as a citizen by intermarriage, and for the enrollment of his wife, Nancy McDaniel, as a citizen by blood, of the Cherokee Nation.

SUPPLEMENTAL PROCEEDINGS.

THOMAS B. McDANIEL, being sworn, testified as follows:

By the Commission,

Q What is your name? A T. B. McDaniel.
Q Thomas? A Yes, sir.
Q How old are you? A Sixty-three years old.
Q What's your postoffice? A Muskogee.
Q You are a white man, are you? A Supposed to be.
Q You are on the roll of 1880 as a white man, as an intermarried white man?
A Yes, sir.
Q What is your wife's name? A Nancy.
Q Was she you wife in 1880? A Yes, sir.
Q She's the wife through whom you claim your citizenship? A Yes, sir.
Q Have you and your wife, Nancy, been living together in the Cherokee Nation ever since 1880? A We have not been living altogether in the Cherokee Nation; we have been living in town for a while.
Q You have not been living outside the Territory? A No, sir.
Q You have never been separated? A No, sir.
Q Living together now? A Yes, sir.
Q And have not lived out of the Indian Territory for the past twenty-two years?
A No, sir.

Cherokee Intermarried White 1906
Volume VI

Q Have no children? A No.

By Mr. Starr.

Q How long have you been living in Muskogee? A Six years. I always had a farm out there in the Cherokee Nation.

Retta Chick, being first duly sworn, states as stenographer to the Commission to the Five Civilized Tribes, she recorded the testimony and proceedings in the matter of the application foregoing, and that the above is a true and complete transcript of her stenographic notes thereof.

Retta Chick

Subscribed and sworn to before me this 12th day of November, 1902.

BC Jones
Notary Public.

◇◇◇◇◇

F.R. Cherokee 7029.

DEPARTMENT OF THE INTERIOR,
COMMISSIONER TO THE FIVE CIVILIZED TRIBES.
Muskogee, I. T. January 15, 1907.

In the matter of the application for the enrollment of Thomas B. McDaniel as a citizen by intermarriage of the Cherokee Nation.

Cherokee Nation represented by W. W. Hastings.
Applicant represented by W. C. Jackson.

Nancy McDaniel being first duly sworn by Frances R. Lane, a Notary Public for the Western District of Indian Territory, testified as follows:

By the Commissioner:
Q What is your name? A Nancy McDaniel
Q How old are you? A Seventy-two years.
Q Your postoffice address is Muskogee? A Yes sir.
Q How long have you lived in Muskogee? A We came here in October, 1894.
Q You have been married have you? A Yes sir.
Q What was your husband's name? A Thomas McDaniel.
Q Is Thomas B. McDaniel, living at this time? A No sir.
Q When did he die? A The last day of September, 1905.
Q Thomas B. McDaniel claimed the right to enrollment as a citizen by intermarriage of the Cherokee nation[sic], did he? A Yes sir.
Q You are a citizen of the Cherokee nation by blood? A Yes.

Cherokee Intermarried White 1906
Volume VI

Q When did you marry Thomas B. McDaniel?   A I don't remember exactly when it is, but in 1874, I think.
Q Where were you married to him?   A At Fort Gibson.
Q Was that marriage under a license of the Cherokee nation?
A Married according to the Cherokee laws.
Q Have you any documentary evidence of that marriage?   A No sir
Q Who performed the marriage ceremony?   A Judge Tim Walker, a Cherokee judge.
Q You say you have been living in Muskogee since 1894?   A Yes. October, 1894.
Q Did you come to Muskogee from the Cherokee nation?   A Yes sir.
Q From the time of your marriage to Thomas B. McDaniel in 1874, until your removal to Muskogee in 1894, did you reside together as husband and wife, and live continuously in the Cherokee nation?   A Yes sir.
Q At the time Thomas B. McDaniel married you I believe you said you were a recognized citizen by blood of the Cherokee Nation?   A Yes sir.
Q Do you know anyone who is living at this time who was present at that marriage?
A There was not anyone present but my uncle and he is dead. Uncle Richard Fields.
Q You don't know of your own personal knowledge, what record, if any was made of this marriage?   A No, I don't.
Q Were you married prior to the time you married Thomas B. McDaniels[sic]?
A Yes sir.
Q What was the name of your first husband?   A Ross.
Q When were you married to Mr. Ross?   A About 1850 I reckon.
Q Was Mr. Ross living at the time you married Mr. McDaniels[sic]?
A No, he was dead.
Q Was Mr. McDaniels married before he married you?   A No sir.

By Mr. Hastings:
Q Do you feel positive as to the date you were married to Mr. McDaniel?   A No, I aint[sic] positive about it, but it was along in 1873 or 1874 that I know of for certain.
Q Did you live in Fort Gibson then for awhile, immediately after your marriage?
A We lived there all the time, before and after. That was our home.
Q How long did you continue to live in Fort Gibson immediately after you were married to Mr. McDaniels[sic]?   A We lived there until 1880, and we moved to the Canadian District in 1880.
Q What time of the year were you married?   A Sometime in the winter; it was cold weather but I don't remember what day or what time of the year.
Q You don't remember whether it was the first part of the year or the last part?   A No, I don't.
Q You say Judge Tim Walker, who is now dead, married you?
A Yes sir.

By Mr. Jackson.
Q Where were you first married to Mr. McDaniels[sic]?   A In 1865 in the Choctaw Nation.
Q How long after that before you came back to the Cherokee Nation?   A Came here in about 1867 I think.

Cherokee Intermarried White 1906
Volume VI

Q Where did you go then? A To Fort Gibson.
Q You and Mr. McDaniels have lived together, and did at that time, as husband and wife? A Yes sir.
Q And in 1874 you were married under Cherokee law? A Yes sir.
Q How came you to be married in the Cherokee nation[sic]? A Because the Agent put the white man out; they was intruders if they didn't marry, and Richard Fields, he was my uncle, he told Mr. McDaniels he would have to re-marry me, and went and fixed up the papers for him; I didn't know anything about it until they came back.
Q He told you that you would have to re-marry under the Cheroke[sic] law?
A Yes, that is what uncle[sic] Dick Fields said, and we never were bothered after that.
Q He was recognized in the Cherokee nation as a citizen? A Yes sir.
Q And exercised the rights and priveleges[sic] of a Cherokee citizen? A Yes sir.
Q Voted and exercised other priveleges[sic]? A Yes sir.

By Mr. Hastings:
Q That is the reason that you were not right positive whether you were married in 1873 or 1874, because you had been previously married? A Yes, I thought it was all right until they got after the white men for marrying; they called them intruders and Uncle Dick got after him and said that he must marry according to the Cherokee law.

By the Commissioner:
A Mrs. McDaniel, from the time you moved from Fort Gibson in 1894 to Muskogee, Indian Territory did you and Mr. McDaniel continue to live together as husband and wife until his death? A Yes sir.

Witness excused.

William H. Barker, being first duly sworn by Frances R. Lane, a Notary Public for the Western District of Indian Territory, testified as follows:

By the Commissioner:
Q What is your name? A William H. Barker.
Q Your age? A Fifty-six.
Q Your postoffice address? A Muskogee, I. T.
Q Did you ever know Thomas B. McDaniel? A Yes sir.
Q When did you first know Mr. McDaniel? A My first recollection,- I got acquainted with Mr. McDaniel in the fall and winter of 1871, I think the first time I met him.
Q Was he married at that time? A I thought he was; he was living with Mrs. McDaniel at Fort Gibson.
Q You know Mrs. McDaniel? A Yes, before I knew Mr. McDaniel
Q Do you know anything with reference to Mr. Thomas B. McDaniel and his wife being married under Cherokee law in 1874? A No, I don't, only just what I have been told.
Q Was it generally understood on Fort Gibson at that time that Mr. McDaniel and his wife had been married according to Cherokee law? A It was my understanding. I can't say whether it was the general understanding or not.

Cherokee Intermarried White 1906
Volume VI

Q They resided together as husband and wife, and held themselves out to the community as such? A Yes, they lived there as husband and wife, and I come here and worked for him a great many years; they lived over here in my neighborhood two or three miles from here. Always been recognized and voted in the Cherokee nation as an adopted citizen.
Q Please state you reasons, if any, for thinking that Mr. McDaniel and his wife had been married under Cherokee law?
A I was making my home with Mr. McDaniel in the winter of (I think) 1871. Mr. McDaniel had a notice served on him by some of the United States officers from the Indian office to vacate the country. We went over into the Creek Nation to comply with the order, and we came back shortly. A few days later on he came to me and asked me if I wanted to go to Texas with him, and we went; we came back in five or six months and after we come back I staid here about Fort Gibson a good while and well, it was very unpleasant for me around Fort Gibson about that time. I then went to Webbers Falls and when I come back the old trouble commenced again and I got put on the police force where I could have police protection abd[sic] carry arms. I ate and slept at his house and staid with him all the time I was there. Went with him everywhere.
A In what year was this that you were appointed on the police force? A I was first put on there under the Chief in 1871, and after the trouble come up when they had disbanded the post, then I went across the river with Mr. McDaniel and lived with him on the farm. That was in the winter of 1871, is my recollection; in the spring I come back in 1872.
Q When did you go on the police force again? A I went to Webbers Falls; recollect I was gone about eight months; we had police regulation there. I got to work then and worked until the spring of 1875 when I was in town.
Q In your testimony awhile ago you referred to the time the white men were ordered out of the Nation as intruders. As I understand it Mr. McDaniel was included in that list?
A Yes sir.
Q You say you left Fort Gibson about that time? How long was it before you returned-- until you got back and saw Mr. McDaniel again? A I went with him.
Q I have reference to when you went to Webbers Falls. A That was in the fall of 1872 When I come to Webbers Falls was in the summer of 1874.
Q At that time did you understand that Mr. McDaniel and his wife had been married in accordance with the Cherokee laws? A Yes, that was my understanding.
Q They have resided together as husband and wife from that time until Mr. McDaniel's death? A Yes sir.
Q Mr. McDaniel was recognized as a citizen by intermarriage and permitted to vote at their elections? A Yes sir.
Q And serve on juries? A Yes sir.
Q Did he ever hold office in the Cherokee nation[sic], do you know? A No, not under Cherokee laws; they could hold certain offices but he never had any; but he went to the elections and voted for his friends

    The applicant is identified on the Cherokee authenticated tribal roll of 1880, Illinois District, opposite No. 1284.
    The applicant's wife, Nancy McDaniel appears upon the Cherokee authenticated roll of 1880, Illinois District, opposite No. 1285.

Cherokee Intermarried White 1906
Volume VI

Nancy McDaniel's name is also included in the approved partial roll of citizens of the Cherokee nation[sic], opposite No. 16787.
The applicant and his wife are also identified on the 1896 roll opposite Nos. 178 and 1319, respectively.

Frances R. Lane, upon oath states that as stenographer to the Commission to the Five Civilized Tribes she reported the testimony in the above entitled cause and that the foregoing is an accurate transcript of her shorthand notes thereof.

Frances R Lane

Subscribed and sworn to before me this January 17, 1907.

Edward Merrick
Notary Public.

◇◇◇◇◇

Cherokee 7029.

DEPARTMENT OF THE INTERIOR,
COMMISSIONER TO THE FIVE CIVILIZED TRIBES,
MUSKOGEE, I. T., JANUARY 22, 1907.

SUPPLEMENTAL PROCEEDINGS had in the matter of the application for the enrollment of THOMAS B. McDANIEL as a citizen by intermarriage of the Cherokee Nation:

FRANK SMITH, being first duly sworn by Edward Merrick, a Notary Public, testified as follows on behalf of applicant?

ON BEHALF OF THE COMMISSIONER:

Q What is your name?   A Frank Smith.
Q What is your age?   A 62.
Q What is your postoffice address?   A Keefton, Indian Territory.
Q Did you ever know a person in the Cherokee Nation by the name of Thomas B. McDaniel?   A Yes sir.
Q When did you first know Thomas B. McDaniel?   A About '73.
Q Was he a married man at that time?   A No sir.
Q Did you ever know a woman named Nancy McDaniel?   A Yes sir.
Q Who was she?   A A Shaw.
Q Was she a wife of Thomas B. McDaniel?   A Yes sir.

Cherokee Intermarried White 1906
Volume VI

Q State when Thomas B. McDaniel and Nancy McDaniel were married, if you know?
A Well I don't know exactly but it was somewhere in '74 sometime; I stayed with them there.
Q Where were they married?   A In Fort Gibson.
Q By whom were they married?   A My understanding was that Judge Tim Walker married them; I wasn't at the wedding.
Q You were no present at the wedding?   A No sir, I was not.
Q You were not present at the marriage ceremony but it was your understanding they were married under license of the Cherokee Nation?   A Yes sir.
Q You are a white man, are you?   A No sir.
Q You are a citizen of the Cherokee Nation by blood?   A Yes sir.
Q Were you one of the signers to Mr. McDaniel's petition?   A No sir.
Q Was the understanding in that community that Thomas B. McDaniel and Nancy McDaniel were lawfully married under license of the Cherokee Nation?   A Yes sir.
Q And they lived together as husband and wife?   A Yes sir.
Q Held themselves out as such and was so regarded in the community there by their neighbors?   A Yes sir.
Q At the time Thomas B. McDaniel married Nancy McDaniel, Nancy McDaniel was a recognized citizen by blood of the Cherokee Nation, was she?   A Yes sir.
Q They continued to live together as husband and wife until the death of Mr. McDaniel a short time ago?   A Yes sir.
Q How do you fix the date of their marriage as being in 1874, Mr. Smith?
A Well I went with him from there to Texas in '75, down to his father's, and I had been staying with them there about five or six months, living right there in the house with him, and we went in '75 down there and they had married the year before.
Q You went to Texas,---what time of the year did you go to Texas?   A In the fall, in September we left home, left Fort Gibson.
Q You remember positively they were married the year before?   A It was so understood they were married.
Q The marriage to which you refer took place the year before?   A Yes sir.
Q Was it your understanding that Thomas B. McDaniel and Nancy McDaniel had been married prior to that time?   A Yes sir.
Q Where and when were they first married?   A Married there in Fort Gibson at McDaniel's house.
Q Before 1874?   A No sir, not before, in '74; they were there but were not married, lived there as man and woman after '74.
Q Did you ever hear Mr. McDaniel say what disposition was made of the marriage certificate or the license?   A No sir.

(Witness excused).

---------------------------oOo--------------------------

Geo. H. Lessley, being first duly sworn, states that as stenographer to the Commissioner to the Five Civilized Tribes, he reported the proceedings had in the above

Cherokee Intermarried White 1906
Volume VI

entitled cause, and that the above and foregoing is a true and correct transcript of his stenographic notes thereof.

Geo H Lessley

Subscribed and sworn to before me this 22nd day of January, 1907.

John E. Tidwell
Notary Public.

◇◇◇◇◇

E.C.M. Cherokee 7029

DEPARTMENT OF THE INTERIOR,

COMMISSIONER TO THE FIVE CIVILIZED TRIBES.

In the matter of the application for the enrollment of Thomas B. McDaniel as a citizen by intermarriage of the Cherokee Nation.

DECISION.

THE RECORDS OF THIS OFFICE SHOW: That at Muskogee, Indian Territory, January 12, 1901, application was received by the Commission to the Five Civilized Tribes for the enrollment of Thomas B. McDaniel as a citizen by intermarriage of the Cherokee Nation. Further proceedings in the matter of said application were had at Muskogee, Indian Territory, October 16, 1902, and January 15, and 22, 1907.

THE EVIDENCE IN THIS CASE SHOWS: That the applicant herein, Thomas B. McDaniel, a white man, was married in accordance with Cherokee law in the year 1874, to one Nancy McDaniel, nee Stiff, who was, at the time of said marriage, a recognized citizen by blood of the Cherokee Nation; who is identified upon the Cherokee authenticated tribal roll of 1880, Illinois District, page 559, No. 1281, as a native Cherokee, and whose name is included in the approved partial roll of citizens by blood of the Cherokee Nation, opposite No. 16787; that since the time of said marriage the said Thomas B. McDaniel and Nancy McDaniel have resided together as husband and wife and continuously retained their citizenship in the Cherokee Nation up to and including September 1, 1902. Said applicant is identified upon the Cherokee authenticated tribal roll of 1880, and the Cherokee census roll of 1896, as an intermarried citizen of the Cherokee Nation.

IT IS, THEREFORE, ORDERED AND ADJUDGED: That in accordance with the decision of the Supreme Court of the United States, dated November 5, 1906, in the cases of Daniel Red Bird, et al., vs. the United States, Nos. 125, 126, 127, and 128, the applicant, Thomas B. McDaniel, is entitled, under the provisions of Section twenty-one of the Act of Congress approved June 28, 1898 (30 Stats. 495), to enrollment as a citizen

Cherokee Intermarried White 1906
Volume VI

by intermarriage of the Cherokee Nation, and his application for enrollment as such is accordingly granted.

Tams Bixby
Commissioner.

Dated at Muskogee, Indian Territory,
this   FEB 14 1907

◇◇◇◇◇

Cherokee 7029

Muskogee, Indian Territory, February 14, 1907.

W. W. Hastings,
    Attorney for the Cherokee Nation,
        Muskogee, Indian Territory.

Dear Sir:

    There is enclosed herewith a copy of the decision of the Commissioner to the Five Civilized Tribes, dated February 14, 1907, granting the application for the enrollment of Thomas B. McDaniel as a citizen by intermarriage of the Cherokee Nation.

Respectfully,

Encl. H-24   Commissioner.
JMH

◇◇◇◇◇

Cherokee 7029

Muskogee, Indian Territory, February 14, 1907.

The Commissioner to the Five Civilized Tribes,
        Muskogee, Indian Territory.

Sir:

    Receipt is acknowledged of the testimony and of your decision enrolling Thomas B. McDaniel as a citizen by intermarriage of the Cherokee Nation. Time for protesting said decision is waived, and I consent that said person may be placed upon the schedule immediately.

Respectfully,
W. W. Hastings
Attorney for Cherokee Nation.

◇◇◇◇◇

Cherokee Intermarried White 1906
Volume VI

Cherokee 7029

Muskogee, Indian Territory, February 14, 1907.

Nancy McDaniel,
 Muskogee, Indian Territory.

Dear Madam:

There is enclosed herewith a copy of the decision of the Commissioner to the Five Civilized Tribes, dated February 14, 1907, granting the application for the enrollment, as a citizen by intermarriage of the Cherokee Nation, of your deceased husband, Thomas B. McDaniel.

You will be advised when the name of your said husband has been placed upon a schedule of citizens of the Cherokee Nation and approved by the Secretary of the Interior.

Respectfully,

Encl. H-25
JMH

Commissioner.

Cher IW 193

◇◇◇◇◇

(Illegible)

DEPARTMENT OF THE INTERIOR

COMMISSIONER TO THE FIVE CIVILIZED TRIBES

In the matter of the application for the enrollment of

ABRAM MEEK

As a citizen by intermarriage of the Cherokee Nation.

No. D- 456

◇◇◇◇◇

Cherokee Intermarried White 1906
Volume VI

DOUBTFUL AS TO APPLICANT.

Cher. D. 456.

Department of the Interior,
Commission to the Five Civilized Tribes,
Vinita, I. T., September 27, 1900.

In the matter of the application of Abram Meek for the enrollment of himself and children as Cherokee citizens; being sworn and examined by Commissioner Breckinridge he testified as follows:

Q Give me your name?   A Abram Meek.
Q How old are you?   A 49.
Q What is your post-office?   A Vinita.
Q In what district do you live?   A Cooweescoowee.
Q Who is it you want to have put on the roll?   A Myself and children,
Q No wife?   A No sir.
Q How many children?   A 4 children.
Q Do you apply for yourself as a Cherokee by blood?   A Adoption.
Q Have you your marriage license and certificate?   A (produces certificate)
Q Where is your license?   A Burned up when my house burned.
Com'r Breckinridge: The applicant presents certificate showing that he was married to Miss Barilla Schrimsher on the 20th day of January 1874 by the Rev. Hamilton Balentine.
Q How long did you and your wife live together after your marriage in 1874?
A About 11 years.
Q Then did she die?   A Yes sir.
Q Was she a Cherokee?   A Yes sir.
Q Have you ever remarried since she died?   A Yes sir.
Q To whom did you marry the second time?   A Angeline Crowder.
Q What was her maiden name?   A Moore.
Q Is she a Cherokee or a white woman?   A I couldn't tell; she claims she was Cherokee, and some says she wasn't.
Q When did you marry her?   A 1887.
Q Is she living now?   A No sir.
Q How long did you and she live together?   A About three weeks.
Q Then you separated?   A She died.
Q Did she die in 1887?   A Yes sir.
Q How old was she when she died?   A She was about 19 I think.
Q Have you remarried since her death?   A Yes sir.
Q To whom did you marry the third time?   A Her name was Lillie Jones.
Q When did you marry her?   A 1889.
Q Are you and she living together now?   A No sir.
Q Is she dead or alive?   A She is living.
Q Is she a Cherokee or a white woman?   A She is Cherokee.
Q Have you ever been divorced from her?   A Yes sir.

Cherokee Intermarried White 1906
Volume VI

Q When were you divorced from her?   A 2 years ago.
Q Have you married since you were divorced from her?   A No sir.
Q Have you a copy of the decree of divorce?   A Yes sir. (Produces papers)
Com'r Breckinridge: The applicant presents an official copy of the records of divorce between himself and his last wife as stated by him granted in the October Term 1899 of the United States Court Northern District of the Indian Territory at Vinita, by Judge John R. Thomas in which he was granted a divorce from his wife and is given the custody of the minor children; this is returned to the applicant.
Q Now give me the names of these children please?   A William A.
Q How old is that child?   A 19.
Q The next child?   A Sabra E.
Q How old is she?   A She is 17.
Q The next child?   A Myrtle E.
Q How old is that child?   A 11.
Q Next child?   A Ethel Ray.
Q How old is that child?   A Six.
Q Which of these children are the children of the first wife?   A The two oldest.
Q Which are the children of the second wife?   A There isn't any.
Q The two youngest are the children of your third wife?   A Yes sir.
Q Your wife, Lillie Jones, was Jones her maiden name?   A No sir.
Q What was her maiden name?   A Dennie.
Q How old is she now?   A She is about 30.
Q Is she still alive?   A Yes sir.
Q She was a Dennie in 1880?   A Yes sir.
1880 roll page 136 #1797 Abe Meak[sic] Cooweescoowee Dist; Adopted white;
1880 roll page 136 #1798 Barilla Meak, Cooweescoowee, native Cher;
1880 roll examined for second wife, Angeline Moore, and name not found thereon.
Applicant: I think my other wife was on the roll as Stinger, that was her step-father's name.
1880 roll examined for present wife, and name not found.
1896 roll page 314 #629 Abram Meeks, Cooweescoowee District;
1896 roll page 215 #3273 Wm. A. Meeks,   "
1896 roll page 215 #3274 Sabra E. Meeks,   "
1896 roll examined for last two children, and their names not found thereon.
Q Why didn't they enroll these children in 1896?   A They wouldn't enroll them. And we applied to Council to have them enrolled.
Q Why wouldn't they enroll them?   A Because the mother of the childrens[sic] name was wrong on the roll of 1880; she was enrolled on the roll of 1880 as Mattie Stinger.
Q Where is the mother of these two latter children living now?
A She is living up near Edna, Kansas this side of the State line.
Q You didn't get a license when you were married the 3rd time?
A Never got any license only when I married the first time.
Q Have you any reason to believe that your second wife can be identified on the roll of 1880?   A I don't think she can only by that name.
Q I am talking about your second wife?   A I don't think--in fact I don't know anything about her; her mother is living; she was living at Catoosa not long ago.

Cherokee Intermarried White 1906
Volume VI

Com'r Breckinridge; You look like you married out when you married the second time, and the rejection by the authorities of the children of the third marriage strongly confirms that marriage; I will have to reject you, and if later you can get any evidence, of which there seems no earthly sign, show that your second wife is on the roll of 1880, you can bring it up.

Com'r Breckinridge: The applicant applies for the enrollment of himself and four children; he is identified on the roll of 1880 and 1896 as an intermarried white; his Cherokee wife to whom he was married in 1880 dies 11 years after he was married to her in 1874; he married a wife in 1887 who would be 32 years old at this time, who dies in three weeks after their marriage, and who cannot be identified upon the roll of 1880; it seems that at this point he married out of his Cherokee rights; after the death of this wife he married again in 1889; this wife cannot be identified upon the roll of 1880; they were divorced in two years after their marriage; her age at this time is said to be thirty years, and even if she be a Cherokee woman, he did not rehabilitate himself by procuring a Cherokee license for his last marriage; it is not seen that he really has any grounds for enrollment at this time; but for the present his application for his own enrollment will be placed upon a doubtful card.

Two of his children are the children of his first marriage, William A. and Sabra E. Meek; they are identified on the roll of 1896 and are living now, and they will be listed now for enrollment as Cherokees by blood. The two younger children, Myrtle E. and Ethel R., are the children of the third and last marriage; of the applicant; as their mother cannot be identified upon the roll of 1880, it is not seen that they can possess any rights; they are respectively 11 and 6 years of age; but neither of them are upon the roll of 1896; no ground is really seen upon which these children can be listed for enrollment, but to give them the benefit of any doubt whatever that may exist, they will for the present be listed upon a doubtful card.

M. D. Green, being first duly sworn, states that as stenographer to the Commission to the Five Civilized Tribes he correctly recorded the testimony and proceedings in this case and the foregoing is a true and complete transcript of his stenographic notes thereof.

(SIGNED) M. D. Green.

Subscribed and sworn to before me this 28 day of September 1900.

(SIGNED) T. B. Needles,
Commissioner.

Cherokee Intermarried White 1906
Volume VI

Department of the Interior,
Commission to the Five Civilized Tribes,
Muskogee, I. T., March 25, 1903.

The undersigned, Florine B. Hatch, being duly sworn, states that as stenographer to the Commission to the Five Civilized Tribes, she made the foregoing transcript, and that the same is a true and complete copy of the original now on file with said Commission.

Florine B. Hatch

Subscribed and sworn to before me this 27 day of March, 1903.

Edward Merrick
Notary Public.

◇◇◇◇◇

DEPARTMENT OF THE INTERIOR,
COMMISSION TO THE FIVE CIVILIZED TRIBES.
VINITA, I. T., OCTOBER 2nd, 1900.

IN THE MATTER OF THE APPLICATION OF LILLIE MILLER for the enrollment of her children, Ethel and Myrtle Meeks, as citizens of the Cherokee Nation, and she being sworn and examined by Commissioner, C. R. Breckinridge, testified as follows:

Q What is your full name?   A Lillie Miller.
Q How old are you?   A Thirty.
Q What is your postoffice?   A Edna, Kansas.
Q In what district do you live?   A Cooweescoowee.
Q Whos is it you want to have put on the roll: Two children?
A Yes sir / Ethel and Myrtle Meeks.
Q You, yourself, were enrolled just now by your husband, were you not?   A Yes sir.
Q When did you marry your husband Miller?   A In February of this year.
Q What was the name of your former husband?   A Abe Meeks.
Q When did you marry him?   A Twelve years ago.
Q How long did you live with him?   A Nine years.
Q Was he a Cherokee or white man?   A White man.
Q Have you ever had a divorce from him?   A Yes sir.
Q Was the divorce granted you, or him?   A Granted him.
Q Was the custody of the children given to you or given to him?   A Given to him.
Q Give me the names of the children?   A Myrtle L. Meeks.
Q How old is that child?   A Ten years old.
Q What is the name of the next one?   A Ethel R. Meeks.
Q How old is that child?   A Six years old.
Q Both living now, are they?   A Yes sir.
Q Give me the name of your mother?   A Louisa Stinger.
Q She is living now?   A Yes sir.

Cherokee Intermarried White 1906
Volume VI

Q She is a Cherokee, is she not?   A Yes sir.
Q She is on the roll of 1880, as a Stinger?   A Yes sir.
Q How are you on the roll of 1880?   A As a Stinger too.
Q Did they call you Mattie Stinger at that time?   A It was put in that way.
Q You were born in the Cherokee Nation?   A Yes sir.
Q You have lived here all your live?   A Yes sir.
Q Was your mother's husband in 1880 names David Stinger?   A Yes sir
   (1880 Roll, Page 178, #2725, Mrs. David Stinger, Cooweescoowee District)
   (1880 Roll, Page 178, #2726, Mattie Stinger, Cooweescoowee Dist)
Q Stinger was your step father?   A Yes sir.
Q Your own father was named what?   A Dinny.
Q You had no sister named Mattie?   A No sir.
Q They just put that name for you in 1880?   A Yes sir; they just put it down that way.

The applicant applies for the enrollment of two children. It is found that they have already been enrolled upon Care "D" 456. The testimony now given will be made supplementary to that accompanying "D" card 456, and it is shown in this testimony that the mother of these children is a native Cherokee, and she is identified on the roll of 1880 These are her children by a former marriage to a man named Meeks, from whom she has procured a divorce, as she states, after having lived with him from the time of their marriage some twelve years ago, about nine years.

The undersigned, being sworn, states that as stenographer to the Commission to the Five Civilized Tribes, he correctly recorded the testimony and proceedings in this case, and that the foregoing is a true and correct transcript of his stenographic notes thereof.

(SIGNED) R. R. Cravens.

Subscribed and sworn to before
me this 4th day of October, 1900.

C. R. Breckinridge,
Commissioner.

::::::::::::::::::::::::::::::::::::

Department of the Interior,
Commission to the Five Civilized Tribes,
Muskogee, I. T. March 26, 1903.

The undersigned, Florine B. Hatch, being duly sworn, states that as stenographer to the Commission to the Five Civilized Tribes she made the foregoing transcript, and that the same is a true and complete copy of the original now on file with said Commission.

Florine B. Hatch

Cherokee Intermarried White 1906
Volume VI

Subscribed and sworn to before me this 27 day of March, 1903.

Edward Merrick
Notary Public.

◇◇◇◇◇

Cher. D. 456.

Department of the Interior,
Commission to the Five Civilized Tribes,
Vinita, I. T. October 21st 1901.

SUPPLEMENTAL TESTIMONY in the matter of the application of Abraham[sic] Meeks, Cherokee Doubtful case #456.

Appearances:
    W. H. Karnegay for the applicant,
    J. L. Baugh for the Cherokee Nation.

NANCY MOORE, being first duly sworn by Commissioner T. B. Needles, testified as follows on the part of the applicant:
    (By Mr. Karnegay)
Q State your name?   A Nancy Moore.
Q How old are you?   A I am 71 the 10th of next January.
Q Where do you live and what is your post office?   A Catoosa.
Q Indian Territory?   A Yes sir.
Q How long have you lived there?   A A little over ten years.
Q Where did you live before you went to Catoosa?   A At Whiteoake[sic].
Q How far from town here?   A Eight or ten miles.
Q Do you know Abraham Meeks, the applicant?   A Yes sir.
Q Did you know his second wife?   A I know who they said she was.
Q Did you know Angeline Crowder?   A Yes sir.
Q What relation was she to you?   A I am her mother.
Q When did she die?   A She died in '87, I reckon it was.
Q Was she ever married?   A Yes sir.
Q How many times?   A She married twice before she married Meeks.
Q Was he a Cherokee?   A Yes sir.
Q By blood?   A Yes sir.
Q Where did he marry her?   A In Goingsnake district.
Q Where did she live at that time?   A There.
Q Where did you live then?   A With her.
Q Where did she live after she married Parris?   A We came west here and have lived here ever since.
Q What became of Parris?   A He got into trouble and skipped the country.
Q How long after he married your daughter before he left?   A Some two years.
Q What year did he marry your daughter?   A In '81.

Cherokee Intermarried White 1906
Volume VI

Q When, after that, did you daughter marry Crowder? A In March '86.
Q Had she lived with you all the time up to that time? A Yes sir.
Q Had she ever been divorced from Parris? A No sir.
Q How long did she live with Crowder? A They was married in March and lived together until the next August come a year.
Q What became of Crowder? A He went astray like a good many other men and afterwards got _drowned_ [sic] in the Virdigris[sic] river[sic].
Q When did the cease living together? A Eight days from the time her baby was born.
Q When was the child born? A In August '86.
Q What was the name of that child? A Her name?
Q Yes mam, the child's name? A Rosa Lee.
Q When did Crowder drown? A He was drownded I reckon the spring of '88, I believe it was '87 or '8, he was burried[sic] pretty close to where I live.
Q Where did your daughter live after Crowder left her? A With me.
Q When did she and Meeks get married? A They got married just before the baby was a year old.
Q Where had she been living from the time that Crowder left her until she married Meeks? A With me.
Q Was she ever divorced from Crowder? A No sir.
Q What became of her child by Crowder? A I have got her yet.
Q Have you kept her ever since your daughter died? A Yes sir.
Q State if she has ever drawn money from the Cherokee Nation at its payments? A Yes sir in '96.
Q What money was it she drew? A The grass money.
Q Did she draw the Strip money? A Yes sir.
Q Who was that money paid to originally by the Nation? A Bily[sic] Moore paid it to me, but Neilson was the man that drawed[sic] it.
Q Have you ever participated in any payment yourself? A Yes sir.
Q What one did you participate in? A The bread money in '73 or '4 and the grass money.
Q Did you, after the time that Abraham Meeks was married to your daughter, draw any money? A No sir.
Q When was the last time you drew any money? A The last payment before the Strip payment.
Q What year was that? A I reckon in '91, I never kept no ledger of anything and dont[sic] know the time exactly.
Q Were you drawing as an adopted citizen or as a citizen by blood? A By blood.
Q Was your daughter recognized as a citizen of the Nation? A She was as my child, same as any other Cherokee child.
  (By Mr. Baugh)
Q Does your name appear upon the authenticated roll of 1880? A Yes sir, I think it does.
Q Does your daughter's name appear on the roll? A On the '80 roll--no, let me see, I was not on the '80 roll, I was in Texas at that time on a visit.
Q When did you leave this country and go to Texas? A I disremember exactly, I think it was in seventy something, I disremember I reckon it was in '78 or '9.

Cherokee Intermarried White 1906
Volume VI

Q Had you lived in the Cherokee Nation all your life up to the time you moved out in '78 or '9?   A No sir I didn't move out then, I never have moved out of the Nation since I come in in '71.
Q What was you doing in Texas?   A I was there on a visit.
Q How long did you remain there?   A I dont[sic] remember exactly, I didn't move, I had some staock[sic] here.
Q Is your name on the roll of 1896?   A I guess it is.
Q Do you know if it is or not?   A Is that the roll that they drawed the money on?
A No, the one taken five years ago?   A I recollect now, no I am not on it because I wasn't on the '80 roll they wouldn't put me on that.
     (By the Commission)
Q Where were you born?   A Right close to the North Carolina line.
Q How old were you when you come to the Cherokee Nation?   A I left there in '56.
Q And come right on the the[sic] Cherokee Nation?   A No sir.
Q When[sic] did you come to first?   A Mississippi.
Q When did you come on to the Cherokee Nation?   A In '71.
Q Didn't you say you went to Texas?   A That was afterwards on a visit.
Q What year was that in?   A I went down there I think about '78 or '9 I disremember exactly.
Q How long did you stay in Texas?   A Well I staid on close to two years.
Q Where was Angeline born?   A In Texas.
Q You were living in Texas when she was born?   A Yes sir.
Q When did you come back to the Cherokee Nation after you lived in Texas that time?
A I guess I come back--I come back I think the same year I went in--I would have come back right away, would have come back sooner that I did if it had not been on account of sickness.
Q Now, did you come back before or after '80?   A I was in Texas in '80.
Q Were you re-admitted by the Cherokee Council after you come back?   A No sir.
Q You never have been re-admitted?   A Mr?[sic] Ross wrote to me about it and I wrote when I had moved out and when I came back and he wrote that it was no use for me to be re-admitted that I was all right.
Q What did I understand you to say about that money you drew from the Cherokee Nation-- did you draw the Strip money?   A No sir.
Q You didn't draw the Cherokee Strip money?   A No sir.
Q Did Angeline draw it?   A She was dead, Angeline's daughter drawed it.
     [sic]By Baugh)
Q You never was recognized by the Cherokee Nation--by the authorities were you?
A I thought I was, I carried evidence to the Council.
Q You moved from Mississippi to the Cherokee Nation and never was admitted to citizenship, were you?   A I thought I was, I carried evidence to the Council.
Q What did they[sic] Council do?   A They told me it was all right.
Q Did they ever give you a certificate?   A No sir they never, I didn't know anything about that, had no[sic] known that way.
     (By the Commission)
Q Did Abraham Meeks marry Angeline Crowder?   A Yes sir.
Q Where did they marry?   A At his house in the Cherokee Nation.

Cherokee Intermarried White 1906
Volume VI

Q Did you see them married? A No sir.
Q How long did they live together as man and wife? A Well it was but a short time, they wasn't married more that three weeks and the she died.
Q Were they regarded as man and wife? A Yes sir.
(By Baugh)
Q Was this Mr. Crowder dead when she married Meeks? A No sir.
Q She was never divorced from Crowder? A No sir.
Martin McDaniel, being first duly sworn by Com'r T. B. Needles testified as follows on the part of the applicant:
(By Mr. Karnegay)
Q State your name? A Martin McDaniel.
Q How old are you? A 36.
Q What is your post office? A Catoosa.
Q Are you a citizen of the Cherokee Nation? A Yes sir.
Q How? A By blood.
Q Do you know Meek's second wife, Angeline Crowder? A Yes sir.
Q Do you know the fact of her marriage to a man named Crowder? A Yes sir, she was married to Crowder, I saw them married.
Q When did they quit living together as man and wife, or did they quit? A Yes sir, he quit her I think.
Q Do you know when she married Abraham Meeks after that? A Yes sir about a year after.
Q Where was Crowder at the time she and Meeks married? A He was backward and forward from this country to the States.
Q Was he still living? A Yes sir.
Q How long after that was it before he drowned? A A year or more.
Q Were you living near where this Crowder woman was living up to the time she married Abraham Meeks? A Yes sir.
Q How close? A Half a mile apart.
Q Did you ever know of her getting a divorce from Crowder? A No sir.
Q Where was she living at that time? A She was at my house.
Q Where is that? A Whiteoak.
Q How far from here? A Ten miles.
Q In the Cherokee Nation? A Yes sir.
(No questions by the Cherokee Nation)

This will be filed with the papers in the case.

Chas. von Weise, being first duly sworn states that as stenographer to the Commission to the Five Civilized Tribes he reported in full all the proceedings in the above cause and that the foregoing is full, true and correct transcript of his stenographic notes therein.

(SIGNED) Chas. von Weise.

Subscribed and sworn to before me this 29th of October, 1901.

(SIGNED) T. B. Needles,
Commissioner.

Cherokee Intermarried White 1906
Volume VI

Department of the Interior,
Commission to the Five Civilized Tribes,
Muskogee, I. T., March 26, 1903.

The undersigned, Florine B. Hatch, being duly sworn, states that as stenographer to the Commission to the Five Civilized Tribes, she made the foregoing transcript, and that the same is a true and complete copy of the original now on file with said Commission.

Florine B. Hatch

Subscribed and sworn to before me this 27 day of March, 1903.

Edward Merrick
Notary Public

◇◇◇◇◇

"R"
D 456

Department of the Interior,
Commission to the Five Civilized Tribes,
Muskogee, I. T., February 27, 1902.

In the matter of the application of Abram Meek[sic], for the enrollment of himself and children as citizens of the Cherokee Nation:

Applicant and his attorney were notified by registered letter on February 11, 1902, that the application of Abram Meek for the enrollment of himself and children as citizens of the Cherokee Nation would be taken up for final consideration by the Commission on the 27th day of February, 1902.

Receipt has been acknowledged of the Commission's letter, and the applicant this day, to-wit: the 27th day of February, 1902, appears by his attorney W. D. Humphrey, representing W. H. Kornegay, of Vinita, I. T.

The Commission: Is there any statement you desire to make Mr. Humphrey?

Mr. Humphrey: The applicant was required to supply the Commission with a certified copy of his marriage license and certificate of marriage to his first wife Barrilla Schrimsher, and also a certified copy of the decree of divorce from said wife.

The Commission: There is offered in evidence a certificate signed by Hamilton Ballentine, a minister of the gospel, certifying that he did, on the 20th day of January, 1874 unite Abraham Meek in marriage to Miss Barrilla Schrimsher. The license and certificate are filed herewith. There is also offered in evidence a certified copy of the marriage record certifying that Abram Meek, a citizen of the United States was licensed to marry Miss Barrilla Schrimsher, a female citizen of the Cherokee Nation on the 10th day of January, 1874. This document is also filed. There is offered in evidence a certified copy of the decree of divorce between Lillie Meeks and Abram Meeks granted in the United States Court for the Indian Territory, Northern District, at Vinita, October term, 1899. The same is filed.

Cherokee Intermarried White 1906
Volume VI

Mr. Humphrey: In this case the applicant Abram Meek bases his right to enrollment upon the citizenship acquired by marriage to the said Lillie Schrimsher who was an Indian woman by blood, said marriage being entered into in accordance with the laws of the Cherokee Nation, and the applicant does not believe that he forfeited his citizenship by his marriage to the Mrs. Crowder referred to in the evidence in this case, for the reason that at the time of the marriage of this applicant to the said Mrs. Crowder Mrs. Crowder had a living husband from whom she had not been divorced. Such being the case the reputed marriage was a nullity.

Mr. Hastings: The Cherokee Nation contends that this man's marriage to his second wife forfeited his citizenship under section 666 of the Compiled Laws of the Cherokee Nation, (1892).

Mr. Humphrey: The contention of the attorney for the Cherokee Nation would be proper if the said marriage were valid, but as the said Mrs. Crowder had a living husband from whom she had not been divorced she could not contract with and enter into a valid marriage at that time.

Mr. Hastings: This man treated this marriage as a valid marriage; he recognized it as such; he held this woman out to the world as his wife, and treated her as such and never repudiated her as shown by the testimony.

Mr. Humphrey: If he did hold her out as his wife, if, under the law the marriage was invalid, such marriage could effect in no way the property rights of either party to such marriage. The marriage was a nullity--was absolutely void, and changed the statue of neither party to said marriage.

Mr. Hastings: This man had no property rights within the Cherokee Nation other than that acquired through his citizenship, and the moment his citizenship rights were forfeited, that moment his property rights vanished. He never had any per se.

Mr. Humphrey: But the marriage being invalid his rights to citizenship were never forfeited.

Mr. Hastings: He never recognized it as an invalid marriage, but continued to live with the woman and treated her as his wife.

Mr. Humphrey: What he did or did not do neither makes nor unmakes the law. Under the law a party having a spouse still living from which said party has had no divorce, such a party cannot enter into a valid marriage.

Mr. Hastings: This man did all he could to validate the marriage, and recognized it as such, and therefore he is estopped now from saying it is invalid.

Mr. Humphrey: The law of estoppel has no application to this case. The marriage was not only voidable, but was absolutely void, and can be attached either collaterally or directly anywhere and in any tribunal.

Mr. Hastings: The Cherokee Nation is not attacking this marriage, but simply recognizes the marriage. His testimony shows that it was entered into in good faith by this man, and that he forfeited his citizenship, and that if he lost his citizenship he cannot be heard now to complain.

Mr. Humphrey: The contention of the attorney for the Cherokee Nation is incorrect, being based upon the ground that the applicant herein really forfeited his citizenship, which was not the case.

Cherokee Intermarried White 1906
Volume VI

Mr. Hastings: It makes no difference whether this marriage was a legal marriage or not, he took up this woman and lived with her, and held her out as his wife, and it was a common law marriage, and one that would forfeit his citizenship.

Mr. Humphrey: Which the applicant denies.

The Commission: The attorney for the applicant and the representative of the Cherokee Nation present submit this case, and the ssame is ordered closed and reported to the Commission for final decision based upon the evidence now of record.

E. C. Bagwell, on oath states that, as stenographer to the Commission to the Five Civilized Tribes, he correctly recorded the testimony and proceedings had in the above entitled cause, and that the above and foregoing is an accurate transcript of his stenographic notes thereof.

(SIGNED) E. C. Bagwell.

Subscribed and sworn to before me this February 28, 1902.

(SIGNED) T. B. Needles.
Commissioner.

::::::::::::::::::::::::::::::::::::

Department of the Interior,
Commission to the Five Civilized Tribes,
Muskogee, I. T., March 26, 1903.

The undersigned, Florine B. Hatch, being duly sworn, states that as stenographer to the Commission to the Five Civilized Tribes, she made the foregoing transcript, and that the same is a true and complete copy of the original now on file with said Commission.

Florine B. Hatch

Subscribed and sworn to before me this 27 day of March, 1903.

Edward Merrick
Notary Public.

Cherokee Intermarried White 1906
Volume VI

R.

DEPARTMENT OF THE INTERIOR,
Commission to the Five Civilized Tribes,
Muskogee, Indian Territory, July 9th, 1902.

In the matter of the application of Abram Meek for the enrollment of himself as a citizen by intermarriage of the Cherokee nation[sic] and for the enrollment of his two children Myrtle E. Meek and Ethel R. Meek as citizens by blood of the Cherokee nation.

Appearances:
Applicant appears in person.
Cherokee nation by W. W. Hastings.

Supplemental to D-456.

ABRAM MEEK, being duly sworn, testified as follows:--
Examination by the Commission.
Q. What is your name?   A. Abram Meek.
Q. What is your post office address?   A. Vinita, Indian Territory.
Q. Are you an applicant before the Commission for enrollment as a citizen by intermarriage and for the enrollment of your children as citizens by blood of the Cherokee nation[sic]?   A Yes, sir.
Q. When did you come to the Cherokee nation the first time?   A. 1869.
Q. How long did you continue to reside there?   A. From then until the present.
Q. Have you been residing in the Cherokee nation continuously since 1869?
A. Yes, sir. That is I have been out a few times but I lived there; had my home there.
Q. How long and for what purpose were you out?   A. I was out once into Oklahoma about four weeks.
Q. How long ago was that?   A. That is about 10 years ago.
Q. When was the next time you were out?   A. I have never beem[sic] out only may be a day, I don't think a day at a time; may be accross[sic] the state line into Kansas. My family wasn't with me in Oklahoma, just myself.
Q. Where were your children born?   A. Born in the Cherokee nation[sic].
Q. Have they ever been out of the Cherokee nation for the purpose of making a home since their birth?   A. No, sir.
Q. Are they living here at the present time?   A. Yes, sir.
Q. Has your wife always live[sic] in the Cherokee nation since your marriage?
A. My last wife?
Q. Yes. Lillie Meek.   A. Yes, sir; she has never lived out any.
Q. When were you married to her?   A. 1889, I believe.

Cherokee Intermarried White 1906
Volume VI

This testimony will also be filed with and made a part of the record in Cherokee case #3632.

Jesse O. Carr, being first duly sworn, states that as stenographer to the Commission to the Five Civilized Tribes he correctly recorded the testimony and proceedings in this case and the foregoing is a true and correct transcript of his stenographic notes thereof.

(SIGNED) Jesse O. Carr.

(SEAL)
Subscribed and sworn to before me this 16 day of July, 1902.

(SIGNED) P. G. Reuter,
Notary Public.

◇◇◇◇◇

R.

DEPARTMENT OF THE INTERIOR.
Commission to the Five Civilized Tribes,
Muskogee, Indian Territory, September 30th, 1902.

In the matter of the application of Abram Meek for the enrollment of himself as a citizen by intermarriage of the Cherokee Nation and for the enrollment of his children Myrtle E. and Ethel R. Meek as citizens by blood of the Cherokee Nation.

Supplemental to D-456.

Appearances:
Applicant appears in person.
Cherokee Nation by J. C. Starr.

ABRAM MEEK, being duly sworn, testified as follows:
Examination by the Commission.
Q. What is your name?   A. Abram Meek.
Q. Got any middle name?   A. No, sir.
Q. What is your age at this time?   A. 51.
Q. Are you the same Abram Meek who applied to this Commission for enrollment as an intermarried citizen on September 22nd, 1900?   A. Yes, sir.
Q. What was your wife's name; your Cherokee wife?   A. Lillie. My first wife?
Q. I want your Cherokee wife first?   A. Alta Barrilla.

Cherokee Intermarried White 1906
Volume VI

Q. Was Alta Barrilla her maiden name?   A. Alta B. Schrimp[sic], was her maiden name.
Q. Was she your first wife?   A. Yes, sir.
Q. Were you her first husband?   A. Yes, sir.
Q. Neither one been married prior to your marriage to each other?   A. No, sir.
Q. When were you married to her?   A. 1874.
Q. Is she living or dead?   A. She is dead.
Q. When did she die?   A. In 1885, I think.
Q. Were you married to her under a Cherokee license?   A. Yes, sir.
Q. Have you filed it with the Commission--when you made the original application?   A. My attorney filed it. My license was destroyed when my house burned. He said he got a copy of it.
Q. Did you and she live together from the time of your marriage as husband and wife until her death?   A. Yes, sir.
Q. You never was separated during her life time?   A. No, sir.
Q. Since the death of your first wife have you married again?   A. Yes, sir.
Q. What is your second wife's name?   A. Her name was Angeline Crowder.
Q. Was she a Cherokee or white woman?   A. She claimed to be a Cherokee by blood.
Q. When were you married to her?   A. Married in 1887.
Q. Is she living or dead?   A. She is dead.
Q. When did she die?   A. In 1887.
Q. Died shortly after you were married?   A. Three weeks.
Q. What was her father's name?   A. I don't know?[sic]
Q. Do you know what her mother's name was?   A. I know what her mother's name was at that time. I don't know her maiden name. Her mother's name was Moore.
Q. Had your second wife been married before she married you?   A. Yes, sir.
Q. What was her husband's name?   A. She first married a man by the name of Parris. I don't know his given name.
Q. Then she married a man by the name of Crowder?   A. Yes, sir.
Q. Was Parris dead?   A. I don't know.
Q. Was Crowder dead?   A. No, sir.
Q. Had she been divorced from Crowder?   A. She said so.
Q. You don't know whether she was a recognized citizen of the Cherokee Nation or not, do you?   A. I don't.
Q. Do you know what her maiden name was, second wife's maiden name? Before she was ever married?   A. No, sir; I don't recollect that but I think it was Moore but I am not positive. Her mother's name was Moore at the time. I think that was her maiden name.
Q. After your second wife died did you marry again?   A. Yes, sir.
Q. What was your third wife's name?   A. Lillie Downing.
Q.. Is she living?   A. Yes, sir.
Q. When did you marry her?   A. Married her in 1889.
Q. Had she ever been married prior to her marriage to you?   A. No, sir.
Q. You are her first husband?   A. Yes, sir.
Q. She is your third wife, is she?   A. Yes, sir.

Cherokee Intermarried White 1906
Volume VI

Q. Have you and she lived together since your marriage in 1889 up to the present time?
A. No, sir.
Q. Separated? A.. Yes, sir.
Q.. When did you separate? A. About 5 years ago.
Q. Have you procured a divorce from her? A. Yes, sir.
Q. Who applied for the divorce, your[sic] or she? A. She did.
Q. What court? A. Federal court of the Cherokee Nation at Vinita.
Q. Do you know what grounds she obtained the divorce on? A. I got the divorce.
Q. I thought you said she applied? A. She applied and then I-----
Q. You went in and fought it and got the divorce? A. Yes, sir.
Q. What grounds did you get the divorce on? A. On her conduct.
Q. Where were you living when you separated? A. In Cooweescoowee on the head of Big creek[sic].
Q. In the country on a farm? A. Yes, sir.
Q. When you separated who stayed on the place, you or her? A. She left me on the place first and thin I left the place and went to another place.
Q. Did she go back to the place you were both living one[sic]? A. Yes, sir.
Q. Did you leave her in the first place? A. No, sir.
Q. She left you? A. Yes, sir.
Q. What did she do, just go without any cause? A. Not any cause that I know of.
Q. Never made any complaint to you about your treatment? A. Yes, sir; she had made complaints. She left some six or seven times before but stayed a week or two and come back. One time she stayed five or six months.
Q. But came back? A.. Yes, sir.
Q. Did you make any appeal to her to come back and live with you? A. Yes, sir.
Q. Wouldn't she come back? A. No, sir.
Q. Have you married any more since your marriage to your third wife? A. No, sir.
Q. Still a single man, are you? A. Yes, sir.
Q. Were you living as a single man on the first of September, 1902? A. Yes, sir.
Q. How long have you lived in the Cherokee Nation? A. I have lived in the Cherokee Nation since October, 1869.
Q. Never lived any where else since then? A. No, sir.
Q. Always lived in the Cherokee Nation since 1869 up to the present time?
A. Yes, sir.
Q. Are these your children, Myrtle E. and Ethel R.[sic] A. Yes, sir.
Q. What is their mother's name? A. Her name now?
A. No. A. Her name was Lillie Meek.
Q. These are your children by your last wife, are they? A. Yes, sir.
Q. Are they living with you? A. Yes, sir. Their home is with me. The oldest is at the Tahlequah school.
Q. They have always lived in the Cherokee Nation, have they? A. Yes, sir.
Q. Never lived any where else? A. No, sir.

Examination by Mr. Starr.
Q. Where were you living when this last separation took place?
A. Living on the head of Big creek.

Cherokee Intermarried White 1906
Volume VI

Q. Who were your neighbors? A. My nearest neighbor was a man by the name of Delp.
Q. Where did your wife go to? A. Edny[sic], Kansas.
Q. Whose place did she go to? A. Her mother's.
Q. Her mother lived at Edny, Kansas, at that time? A. Yes, sir.
Q. How long did she stay up there? A. The last time that she left me?
Q. Yes. A. About a month and a half.
Q. Then where did she go? A. She went back to the place. Same place where she left me.
Q. Were you living there when she came back? A. Yes, sir.
Q. Did she take possession of the place and control it? A. Yes, sir.

Examination by the Commission:

Q. Mr. Meek, your second wife you say you don't know whether she was a citizen or not?
A. I don't know positively whether she was or not.
Q. Have you got any witnesses that knew her as a girl before she was ever married?
A. I had her mother.
Q. Has her mother already testified in this case? A. Yes, sir; and her brother in law.
Q. They were people who identified her as a citizen by blood? A. I think so.

    Jesse O. Carr, being first duly sworn, states that as stenographer to the Commission to the Five Civilized Tribes he reported the above entitled case and that the foregoing is a true and complete transcript of his stenographic notes thereof.

                              (SIGNED) Jesse O. Carr.

Subscribed and sworn to before me this 14th day of October, 1902.

                              (SIGNED) B. C. Jones.
                                        Notary Public.

(SEAL)

Department of the Interior,
Commission to the Five Civilized Tribes,
Muskogee, I. T., March 26, 1903.

    The undersigned, Florine B. Hatch, being duly sworn, states that as stenographer to the Commission to the Five Civilized Tribes, she made the foregoing transcript, and that the same is a true and complete copy of the original now on file with said Commission.

                                        Florine B. Hatch
Subscribed and sworn to before me this __27__ day of March, 1903.
                                        Edward Merrick
                                            Notary Public.

Cherokee Intermarried White 1906
Volume VI

This is to certify that by me that Abram Meeks, a citizen of the U.S.A. was licensed to marry Berillar[sic] Scrimpsher[sic], a female Cherokee of this Nation. License issued Jan.'⁄ 10th 1874 licensed returned it being in accordance with an act passed by the Nation Council bearing date Oct 15th 1855 in regard to white men intermarriage in this Nation.

Given under my hand Jan'y 10th 1874.

S.N. Melton, clerk,
of District Court
in Del De C.N.

Executive Office Cherokee Nation,
    Tahlequah, Ind. Ter.

    I, B.W. Alberty, assistant Executive secretary of the Cherokee Nation do hereby certify that the foregoing is a true copy of all the marriage record of Delaware District show in reference to said marriage, and same is copied from said marriage record, now filed in this Office by law and is in my legal custody.

Given under my hand & the seal of the Cherokee Nation this the 22nd day of February 1902.

B. W. Alberty

Assistant Executive secretary,
Cherokee Nation.

(The Marriage Certificate below typed as given.)

Cherokee D 456.

    What, therefore, God hath joined together, let not

    man put asunder.

It is not good that man should be alone.

    Gen. 2-18

I will make him an help meet for him.

    Gen. 2-18.

THIS CERTIFIES

That Mr. Abram Meek and Miss Berilla Schrimsher,
of Vandalia Fayette County   of Cooweskoowe District
Illinois.   Cherokee Nation.

Cherokee Intermarried White 1906
Volume VI

Were united in HOLY MATRIMONY According to the Ordinance of God and the laws of the Cherokee Nation at Pleasant Hill on the Twentieth day of January in the year of Our Lord, One Thousand Eight hundred and Seventy four.

Witnesses (Anna H. Balentine.
     J.A.A. Balentine.

Hamilton Balentine
Officiating Clergyman.

Marriage is honorable in all.
Heb. 13.4

  I, the undersigned as stenographer to the Commission to the Five Civilized Tribes, do certify that the above is a full and correct copy of the certificate on file in this office.

(SIGNED) Ella Mielenz.

::::::::::::::::::::::::::::::::::::

Department of the Interior,
Commission to the Five Civilized Tribes,
Muskogee, I. T/, March 26, 1903.

  The undersigned, Florine b. Hatch, being duly sworn, states that as stenographer to the Commission to the Five Civilized Tribes, she made the foregoing transcript, and that the same is a true and complete copy of the original now on file with said Commission.

Florine B. Hatch

Subscribed and sworn to before me this 27 day of March, 1903.

Edward Merrick
Notary Public.

◇◇◇◇◇

Cherokee Intermarried White 1906
Volume VI

G   No_____ D 456

Lillie Meeks Pltf
- vs -
Abraham Meeks, Deft

Abraham Meeks Cross
Complaint, Pltf.
- vs -
Lillie Meeks Deft

Copy Decree

DEPARTMENT OF THE INTERIOR,
COMMISSION TO THE FIVE CIVILIZED TRIBES.
FILED
FEB 28 1902

 ACTING CHAIRMAN.

◇◇◇◇◇

(Below was originally typed with handwritten corrections as given on the microfilm. The transcribed copy immediately followed and is given below and typed as given.)

Cherokee D 456
Lillian Meeks, Plaintiff,

vs.

Abraham Meeks, Defendant,

Abrham Meeks Cross plaintiff
vs.
Lillie Meeks, Defendant.

In the United States
Court in the Indian Territory, Northern
District at Vinita, October Term, 1899.

Decree.

On this second day of November 1899 comes on for consideration and the rendition of a decree in this cause the same having been taken under advisement by the presiding judge at the last term of this court, named by the Hon. John R. Thomas, and the parties plaintiff by her solicitor Mr. J. S. Davenport and the defendant and cross complainant by his solicitor W. H. Kornegay, and after considering all the matters and things set forth in the pleadings, the evidence and the master's report, the court doth find that the facts are sufficient to entitle the cross complainant Abraham Meeks to a divorce from the plaintiff and that he is entitled to the custody of the minor children namely

Cherokee Intermarried White 1906
Volume VI

Myrtle Meeks and Ethel Meeks. It is therefore considered ordered decreed and adjudged that the bonds of matrimony heretofore existing between the cross complainant Abraham Meeks and the plaintiff Lilli Meeks be dissolved and that the custody of the minor children Myrtle Meeks and Ethel Meeks be awarded to Abraham Meeks the cross complainant. It is further ordered and decreed that the plaintiff Lilli Meeks shall be allowed to visit the said children at all proper times, and that Abraham Meeks permit her so to do. It is further ordered that neither party recover any costs herein of the other, and that one half the master's fee if not already paid be paid by each party.

John R. Thomas.

I hereby certify the above to be a true copy of the judgment made in the above entitled cause and entered of record in this court on Nov. 3, 1899.

Jas. A. Winston, Clerk.
By J. C. Anderson, De. C.

I, the undersigned, as stenographer to the Commission to the Five Civilized Tribes, do certify that the above is a full and correct copy of the copy on file in this office.

(SIGNED)   Ella Mielenz.

: :

Department of the Interior,
Commission to the Five Civilized Tribes,
Muskogee, I. T., March 26, 1903.

The undersigned, Florine B. Hatch, being duly sworn, states that as stenographer to the Commission to the Five Civilized Tribes she made the foregoing transcript, and that the same is a true and complete copy of the original now on file with said Commission.

Florine B. Hatch

Subscribed and sworn to before me this <u>27</u> day of March, 1903.

Edward Merrick
Notary Public.

Cherokee Intermarried White 1906
Volume VI

Cherokee D 456.

Department of the Interior,
Commission to the Five Civilized Tribes,
Muskogee, Indian Territory, January 6, 1903.

F.P.T.

--oOo--

In the matter of the application for the enrollment of Abram Meek et al as citizens of the Cherokee Nation.

SUPPLEMENTAL STATEMENT.

An examination of the 1894 Cherokee strip payment roll shows that the applicant, Myrtle E. Meek, is identified thereon at page 250, Cooweescoowee District, No. 2897, as Myrtle Meeks.

It is ordered that this statement be made a part of the record in this case.

(SIGNED) T. B. Needles.

Commissioner.

::::::::::::::::::::::::::::::::::::

Department of the Interior,
Commission to the Five Civilized Tribes,
Muskogee, I. T., March 26, 1903.

The undersigned, Florine B. Hatch, being duly sworn, states that as stenographer to the Commission to the Five Civilized Tribes, she made the foregoing transcript, and that the same is a true and complete copy of the original now on file with said Commission.

Florine B. Hatch

Subscribed and sworn to before me this 27 day of March, 1903.

Edward Merrick
Notary Public.

◇◇◇◇◇

Cherokee Intermarried White 1906
Volume VI

Cherokee D-456.

DEPARTMENT OF THE INTERIOR,
COMMISSION TO THE FIVE CIVILIZED TRIBES.

In the matter of the application for the enrollment of Myrtle E. Meek and Ethel R. Meek as citizens by blood of the Cherokee Nation.

DECISION.

The record in this case shows that on September 27, 1900, Abram Meek appeared before the Commission at Vinita, Indian Territory, and made personal application for the enrollment of his minor children, Myrtle E. Meek and Ethel R. Meek, as citizens by blood of the Cherokee Nation. Further proceedings in the matter of said application were had at Vinita, Indian Territory, on October 2, and October 21, 1900, and at Muskogee, Indian Territory, on February 27, July 9, and September 30, 1902. The application included other parties, but they are not embraced in this decision.

The evidence shows that the applicants herein are the children of Abram Meek, a white man, and his wife, Lillie Jones, a citizen by blood of the Cherokee Nation and identified on the Cherokee authenticated roll of 1880. Myrtle E. Meek is identified on the Cherokee strip payment roll of 1894; Ethel R. Meek is identified by a birth affidavit made a part of the record herein.

The evidence further shows that the said Myrtle E. and Ethel R. Meek were born and have always resided in the Cherokee Nation.

It is, therefore, the opinion of this Commission that Myrtle E. Meek and Ethel R. Meek should be enrolled as citizens by blood of the Cherokee Nation, in accordance with the provisions of section twenty-one of the Act of Congress approved June 28, 1898 (30 Stats., 495), and it is so ordered.

COMMISSION TO THE FIVE CIVILIZED TRIBES.

Tams Bixby
Chairman.

TB Needles
Commissioner.

C. R. Breckinridge
Commissioner.

W E Stanley
Commissioner.

Dated at Muskogee, I. T.,
this   JUN 1 - 1903

Cherokee Intermarried White 1906
Volume VI

C.F.B.	Cherokee D. 456

DEPARTMENT OF THE INTERIOR,
COMMISSIONER TO THE FIVE CIVILIZED TRIBES.
MUSKOGEE, IND. TER. JANUARY 5, 1907.

In the matter of the application for the enrollment of Abram Meek as a citizen by intermarriage of the Cherokee Nation.

APPEARANCES: Applicant appears in person.

Abram Meek, being first duly sworn by J. E. Tidwell, notary public, testified as follows:

Q. What is your name?   A. Abram Meek.
Q. What is your age?   A. Fifty-five.
Q. What is your postoffice address?   A. Vinita.
Q. You claim the right to enrollment as a citizen by intermarriage of the Cherokee Nation, do you?   A. Yes sir.
Q. You have no Cherokee blood?   A. No sir.
Q. Your only claim to the right to enrollment as a citizen of the Cherokee Nation is by virtue of your marriage to a citizen of the Cherokee Nation?   A. Yes sir.
Q. What is the name of the citizen through whom you claim that right?
A. Her maiden name was Alta Berrilla Schrimsher.
Q. Is she living or dead?   A. She is dead.
Q. When did you marry her?   A. I married her on the 20th of January, 1874.
Q. Was she a recognized citizen of the Cherokee Nation at the time you married her?
A. Yes sir.
Q. Living in the Cherokee country, was she?   A. Yes sir.
Q. Did you marry her in accordance with the law of the Cherokee Nation?
A. Yes sir.
Q. In what district did you secure your license?   A. Delaware District.
Q. The license, then, was issued in Delaware District in 1874 was it?
A. The license, I think, was issued in '73.
Q. Who married you?   A. James Valentine.
Q. Who was James Valentine?   A. He was the Missionary Minister
Q. When did your wife die?   A. She died 1884.
Q. Did you continuously live together as husband and wife from the time of your marriage until the time of her death?   A. Yes sir.
Q. And lived in the Cherokee Nation, did you?   A. Yes sir.
Q. Were you ever married prior to your marriage to her?   A. No sir.
Q. Was she ever married before she married you?   A. No sir.
Q. Since her death have you remarried?   A. Yes sir.
Q. When did you marry your second wife?   A. In '86.
Q. Is she living?   A. No sir.
Q. What was her name?   A. Her name was Angeline Crowder.

Cherokee Intermarried White 1906
Volume VI

Q. She is dead is she? A. Yes sir.
Q. Was she a Cherokee by blood? A. Yes sir, she was a Cherokee by blood.
Q. What was the name of her father? A. I do not know.
Q. What was her mother's name? A. Her name was Nancy Moore.
Q. When did you say your second wife died? A. She died in '86.
Q. '86? A. Yes sir.
Q. You and she continuously lived together as husband and wife from the time of your marriage to her until the time of her death, did you? A. Yes sir.
Q. Have you married since the death of your second wife? A. Yes sir.
Q. Is the woman that you married subsequent to the death of your second wife, living at this time? A. Yes sir, she is living.
Q. What is her name? A. Her first name?
Q. Yes, her name now? A. Her name is Miller, now, Lillie Miller.
Q. What was her maiden name? A. Lillie Deney.
Q. When did you marry her? A. 1887.
Q. Is she a Cherokee by blood? A. Yes sir.
Q. On the final roll is she? A. Yes sir.
Q. Are you and she living together as husband and wife at the present time?
A. No sir.
Q. When did you separate? A. Six or seven years ago, I think.
Q. You lived together from the time of your marriage until about seven years ago?
A. Yes sir.
Q. What was the cause of the separation? A. I can't tell now. She just got up and left.
Q. She left you did she? A. Yes sir.
Q. Did you own a home at the time she left you? A. Yes sir.
Q. And you lived in your home after she left did you? A. Yes sir.
Q. Did she give you a reason for leaving you? A. No particular reason. I had got broke and she thought I couldn't make money enough to keep her up.
Q. She became dissatisfied, did she and left you? A. Yes sir.
Q. Did you give her any cause for leaving you? A. No sir.
Q. Did you want her to leave you? A. No sir.
Q. She left of her own free will then? A. Yes sir.
Q. What did you say her name is at the present time? A. Miller, Lillie Miller.
Q. Do you know where she resides? A. Yes sir, she lives on Big Creek, ten miles south of Edna, Kansas.
Q. You have some children by her who are on the final roll, have you not?
A. Yes sir.
Q. Have you any documentary evidence showing your marriage to your first wife?
A. I haven's[sic] any in my possession, only what I have filed with the Commission.
Q. Have you filed with the Commission a marriage license and certificate showing your marriage to your first wife? A. Yes sir, I deposited a marriage certificate, and my license had been burned. Afterwards I had my attorney get a duplicate off of the clerk's book. He reported to me that he filed it with the Commission.

Cherokee Intermarried White 1906
Volume VI

BY MR. H. M. VANCE:

Q. Did you live with your first wife from the time of your marriage in '74 continuously as husband and wife until the time of her death in '84? A. Yes sir.
Q. Have you and your former wife, who is now Lillie Miller, been divorced?
A. Yes sir.
Q. Who applied for the divorce? A. She applied for it.
Q. On what grounds? A. I don't know that I can hardly say. She filed about four or five complaints, I think.
Q. She secured the divorce, did she? A. No sir, I secured the divorce.
Q. You say she applied for it? A. Yes sir she applied for it[sic]
Q. And the divorce was granted? A. Yes sir.
Q. In what court was the divorce granted? A. In the Federal Court at Vinita.
Q. Have you remarried since you and Lillie Miller were separated?
A. No sir.

ON BEHALF OF THE COMMISSIONER:

Q. Did you appear against your wife, Lillie Meek, when she applied for a divorce from you? A. Yes sir.
Q. What action did you take at the time.[sic] Did you attempt to prevent a divorce being granted? A. We did at the first time, my attorney did.
Q. What did you do after that? A. He filed an action against it. Then filed an action for the custody of the child.
Q. He filed an action on your behalf for a divorce from you wife, and for you to have the custody of the child? A. Yes sir.
Q. Was that granted by the court? A. Yes sir.
Q. So your petition for a divorce was granted, and not hers? A. It's pretty hard for me to answer that question as to how it was granted, because it was all carried on at one time in the court. The decision of the court, I recollect part of the time had her as plaintiff and he as defendant, and part of the time I was plaintiff and she was defendant, and so it's hard for me to tell that now. I filed that divorce with the Commission.
Q. That decree of divorce is on file at this office, is it? A. Yes sir.

BY MR. H. M. VANCE:

Q. Do you mean to swear under oath that your first wife had not been formerly married to a man by the name of James Duncan? A. Yes sir.
Q. She is not living with a man by the name of James Duncan as husband and wife?
A. No sir.
Q. Did either of your wives ever lived with James Duncan? A. Not to my knowledge.
Q. Did you wife have a sister by the name of Cynthia Ann?
A. No sir, She had three or four sisters.
Q. How old was Berrilla Schrimsher when you married her?
A. She was eighteen.

Cherokee Intermarried White 1906
Volume VI

ON BEHALF OF THE COMMISSIONER:

Q. Your residence has been continuously in the Cherokee Nation since your marriage to your first wife, has it? A. Yes sir.

The applicant, Abram Meek, is identified on the Cherokee authenticated tribal roll of 1880, Cooweescoowee District, No. 1797.

Mattie M. Pace, being first duly sworn, states that as stenographer to the Commission to the Five Civilized Tribes, she correctly reported the proceedings had in the above entitled cause, and that the same is a full, true and correct transcript of her stenographic notes thereof.

Mattie M Pace

Subscribed and sworn to before me this January 5, 1907.

John E. Tidwell
Notary Public.

◇◇◇◇◇

T.W.L. Cherokee D- 456

DEPARTMENT OF THE INTERIOR

COMMISSIONER TO THE FIVE CIVILIZED TRIBES

In the matter of the application for the enrollment of Abram Meek as a citizen by intermarriage of the Cherokee Nation.

D E C I S I O N

THE RECORDS OF THIS OFFICE SHOW: That at Vinita, Indian Territory, September 27, 1900, application was received by the Commission to the Five Civilized Tribes for the enrollment of Abram Meek as a citizen by intermarriage of the Cherokee Nation. Further proceedings in the matter of said application were had at Vinita, Indian Territory, February 27, 1902, July 9, 1902, September 30, 1902 and January 5, 1907.

THE EVIDENCE IN THIS CASE SHOWS: That the applicant herein, Abram Meek, a white man, was on January 20, 1874, in accordance with the tribal law of the Cherokee Nation, married to one Alta Barilla Meek, nee Shrimsher, since deceased, who was at the time of said marriage, a citizen by blood of the Cherokee Nation; that from the time of said marriage until the death of the said Alta Barilla Meek, which occurred in 1885 or 1886, the said Abram Meek and the said Alta Barilla Meek resided together as husband and wife and continuously lived together in the Cherokee Nation; that said

Cherokee Intermarried White 1906
Volume VI

applicant in 1886 married one Angeline Crowder, an alleged Cherokee, who had been married twice previous to said marriage; that one of her said husbands from whom she had not been divorced was living at the time of the marriage of the said Abram Meek and Angeline Crowder; that from the time of said marriage until the death of the said Angeline Crowder, which occurred about three weeks after her marriage to the said Abram Meek, the said Abram Meek and the said Angeline Crowder resided together as husband and wife and continuously lived in the Cherokee Nation.

In the matter of the application of Sarah Hines for enrollment as a citizen by intermarriage of the Cherokee Nation it was held by the Department that she did not, by reason of her marriage to one Joie Hines, an intermarried Cherokee applicant, while her Indian spouse was living, forfeit her right to enrollment. (I.T.D, 4017-1902).

THE EVIDENCE IN THIS CASE FURTHER SHOWS: That in 1889 said applicant was married to one Lillie Jones, nee Deney or Dennie, enrolled as Lillie Miller, her name being found opposite No. 9542 upon the approved partial roll of citizens by blood of the Cherokee Nation, with whom said applicant resided until said applicant was deserted by the said Lillie Miller; that on November 2, 1899, the said Abram Meek obtained a decree of divorce from the said Lillie Miller in the United States Court for the Northern Judicial District of Indian Territory; that since the separation of said Abram Meek and the said Lillie Meek, the said Abram Meek has remained unmarried and has continuously resided in the Cherokee Nation since 1869. Said applicant is identified on the Cherokee authenticated tribal roll of 1880 and the Cherokee census roll of 1896 as a citizen by intermarriage of the Cherokee Nation. The said Alta Barilla Meek and the said Lillie Miller are identified upon the Cherokee tribal roll of 1880, Cooweescoowee District, the former at page 136, No. 1798 as Barilla Meek, and the latter at page 178, No. 2726, as Mattie Stringer, each as a native Cherokee.

IT IS THEREFORE ORDERED AND ADJUDGED: That in accordance with the decision of the Supreme Court of the United States dated November 5, 1906, in the cases of Daniel Red Bird, et al., vs. the United States, Nos. 125, 126, 127, and 128, the said applicant Abram Meek, is entitled, under the provisions of Section twenty-one of the Act of Congress approved June 28, 1898 (30 Stats., 495) to enrollment as a citizen by intermarriage of the Cherokee Nation, and his application for enrollment as such is accordingly granted.

Tams Bixby
Commissioner.

Dated at Muskogee, Indian Territory,
this FEB 15 1907

Cherokee Intermarried White 1906
Volume VI

Department of the Interior.
COMMISSIONER TO THE FIVE CIVILIZED TRIBES.

In the matter of the death of **Abram Meek** a citizen of the **Cherokee** Nation, who formerly resided at or near **Vinita**, Ind. Ter., and died on the **16** day of **April**, **1907**

AFFIDAVIT OF RELATIVE.

Western District }
Ind. Ter.

I, **W. A. Meek**, on oath state that I am **26** years of age and a citizen by **blood**, of the **Cherokee** Nation; that my postoffice address is **Vinita**, Ind. Ter.; that I am **Son** of **Abram Meek** who was a citizen, by **intermarriage**, of the **Cherokee** Nation and that said **Abram Meek** died on the **16** day of **April**, **1907**

                        W.A. Meek

WITNESSES TO MARK:

Subscribed and sworn to before me this **13th** day of **June**, **1907**

                      Walter W. Chappell
                            Notary Public.

AFFIDAVIT OF ACQUAINTANCE.

Western District }
Ind. Ter.

I, **Henry J. Ward**, on oath state that I am **45** years of age, and a citizen by **blood** of the **Cherokee** Nation; that my postoffice address is **Muskogee**, Ind. Ter.; that I was personally acquainted with **Abram Meek** who was a citizen, by **intermarriage**, of the **Cherokee** Nation; and that said **Abram Meek** died on ~~the~~ or about **16** day of **April**, **1907**

                      Henry J. Ward

WITNESSES TO MARK:

Subscribed and sworn to before me this **13th** day of **June**, **1907**

                      Walter W. Chappell
                            Notary Public.

Cherokee Intermarried White 1906
Volume VI

COMMISSIONERS:
HENRY L. DAWES,
TAMS BIXBY,
THOMAS B. NEEDLES,
C. R. BRECKINRIDGE.

ALLISON L. AYLESWORTH,
SECRETARY.

DEPARTMENT OF THE INTERIOR,
COMMISSION TO THE FIVE CIVILIZED TRIBES.

Muskogee, Indian Territory, January 31, 1901.

Received of the Commission to the Five Civilized Tribes one copy of the testimony in the matter of the application of Abram Meek et al. for enrollment as citizens of the Cherokee Nation.

WH Kornegay
Attorney for applicant.

D - 456.

COMMISSIONERS:
HENRY L. DAWES,
TAMS BIXBY,
THOMAS B. NEEDLES,
C. R. BRECKINRIDGE.

ALLISON L. AYLESWORTH,
SECRETARY.

ADDRESS ONLY THE
COMMISSION TO THE FIVE CIVILIZED TRIBES.

DEPARTMENT OF THE INTERIOR,
COMMISSION TO THE FIVE CIVILIZED TRIBES.

Muskogee, Indian Territory, **February 11,** 1902

Mr. Abram Meek,
  Vinita, Indian Territory.

Sir:-

You are hereby notified that the application of **yourself and two minor children** for enrollment as citizen of the Cherokee Nation will be taken up for final consideration by the Commission to the Five Civilized Tribes, at its office in Muskogee, Indian Territory, on the **27th** day of **February**, 1902.

On said date, you may, if you desire, appear before the Commission, in person or by attorney, when an opportunity will be given you to introduce any additional testimony affecting your application.

You are further notified that the Representatives of the Cherokee Nation will also, at the same time, be afforded an opportunity to introduce testimony tending to disprove your

Cherokee Intermarried White 1906
Volume VI

right to enrollment, but said Representatives will be required to notify you of their intention to introduce such testimony before they will be permitted to do so.

You are required to supply the Commission with certified copy of marriage license and certificate to your first wife, Barilla Schrimsher; also certified copy of decree of divorce from your wife Lillie required.

Copy to W. H. Kornegay,
    Vinita, I. T.

                      Yours truly,

Cherokee D-456
Register.
                                        Acting Chairman.

◇◇◇◇◇

                                        Cherokee D 456

                  Muskogee, Indian Territory, June 24, 1902.

Mr. Abram Meek,
    Vinita, Indian Territory.

Sir:

    In the matter of the application for the enrollment of yourself and children, Myrtle E., and Ethel R. Meek, as citizens of the Cherokee Nation, further evidence regarding the residence of yourself and said children in the Cherokee Nation is important.

    You are required to appear before the Commission at its office in Muskogee, Indian Territory, on or before July 9, 1902, and submit evidence on this point.

                          Yours truly,

                                        Commissioner in Charge.

Register.

◇◇◇◇◇

Cherokee Intermarried White 1906
Volume VI

Muskogee, Indian Territory, November 14, 1902.

Abram Meek,
    Vinita, Indian Territory.

Dear Sir:-

When you applied to this Commission for the enrollment of yourself and your family as citizens of the Cherokee Nation, you were required to furnish the Commission with properly executed affidavit as to the birth of your child, Ethel R. Meek. Such affidavit has not yet been filed with the Commission.

You are requested to have same executed and forward to the Commission at the earliest possible date as until this affidavit is received, the application for the enrollment of yourself and family cannot receive further consideration.

    Respectfully,

    Acting Chairman.

◇◇◇◇◇

Cherokee D-456

Muskogee, Indian Territory, December 20, 1902.

Lillie Miller,
    Edna, Kansas.

Dear Madam:-

In further reply to your letter of November 25, relative to the enrollment, as citizens of the Cherokee Nation, of your two children, Myrtle E. and Ethel R. Meek, you are advised that the application for the enrollment of these children will not be complete until the Commission has been supplied with properly executed birth affidavits.

There are enclosed you herewith blank forms, which you are requested to have properly executed and forward to the Commission at the earliest possible date.

    Respectfully,

    Commissioner in Charge.

Enc. 2 B. C.

◇◇◇◇◇

Cherokee Intermarried White 1906
Volume VI

Cherokee 456

Vinita, Indian Territory, January 27, 1903.

Commission to the Five Civilized Tribes,
Muskogee, Indian Territory.

Gentlemen:

Referring to the list of Cherokee cases held for further testimony, transmitted to this office with the Commission's recent letter, the following note appears thereon as to case D 456, Abram Meek, et el., "Birth affidavit as to Ethel R., required."

On January 3, 1903, there was received at this office affidavits as to the births of Myrtle E. and Ethel R. Meek. These affidavits were forwarded to the Commission at Muskogee for approval and have not yet been returned to this office.

The record and decision forwarded to this office in Cherokee case D 456, are returned herewith and the affidavits in question will be forwarded to the Commission as soon as they are returned to this office.

Respectfully,

Clerk in Charge.

Encl-S-1

GRS

◇◇◇◇◇

Cherokee D-456.

Vinita, Indian Territory, February 6, 1903.

Commission to the Five Civilized Tribes,
Muskogee, Indian Territory.

Gentlemen:

There are enclosed herewith birth affidavits in the matter of the application for the enrollment of Myrtle E. and Ethel R. Meek, as citizens of the Cherokee Nation.

The original record in this case is in the office at Muskogee.

Cherokee Intermarried White 1906
Volume VI

Respectfully,

Clerk in Charge.

Encl. F-110.
HP

◇◇◇◇◇

Tahlequah, Indian Territory, September 10, 1903.

Commission to the Five Civilized Tribes,
 Muskogee, Indian Territory.

Gentlemen:

    I have the honor to transmit herewith the original cards and jackets in Cherokee cases:

D- 82	D- 648
D- 103	D- 786
D- 169	D-1029
D- 262	D-1049
D- 456	D-1146

    The Commission has heretofore rendered decisions granting the applications of some of the applicants in each case. The applicants embraced in the Commission's decisions have been transferred as shown by notes on the cards, and the original cards and jackets are returned herewith for the preparation of decisions as to the remaining applicants.

Respectfully,

Clerk in Charge,
Cherokee Land Office.

Encl-S-35
 GRS

◇◇◇◇◇

Cherokee Intermarried White 1906
Volume VI

Cherokee
D 456

Muskogee, Indian Territory, February 15, 1907.

W. W. Hastings,
    Attorney for the Cherokee Nation,
    Muskogee, Indian Territory.

Dear Sir:

    There is enclosed herewith a copy of the decision of the Commissioner to the Five Civilized Tribes, dated February 15, 1907, granting the application for the enrollment of Abram Meek as a citizen by intermarriage of the Cherokee Nation.

                      Respectfully,

Encl. H6   Commissioner.
JMH

◇◇◇◇◇

Cherokee D 456

                                   Muskogee, Indian Territory, February 15, 1907.

The Commissioner to the Five Civilized Tribes,
    Muskogee, Indian Territory.

Sir:

    Receipt is acknowledged of the testimony and of your decision enrolling Abram Meek as a citizen by intermarriage of the Cherokee Nation. Time for protesting said decision is waived, and I consent that said person may be placed upon the schedule immediately.

                        Respectfully,
                              W. W. Hastings
                            Attorney for Cherokee Nation.

◇◇◇◇◇

Cherokee Intermarried White 1906
Volume VI

10985
Cherokee D 456

Muskogee, Indian Territory, February 15, 1907.

Abram Meek,
    Vinita, Indian Territory.

Dear Sir:

    There is enclosed herewith a copy of the decision of the Commissioner to the Five Civilized Tribes, dated February 15, 1907, granting the application for your enrollment as a citizen by intermarriage of the Cherokee Nation.

    You will be advised when your name has been placed upon a schedule of citizens of the Cherokee Nation, and approved by the Secretary of the Interior.

                            Respectfully,

Encl. H-7   Commissioner.
JMH

<><><><><>

Cherokee
I.W. 193

Muskogee, Indian Territory, April 16, 1907.

Abram Meek,
    Vinita, Indian Territory.

Dear Sir:

    Your marriage license and certificate filed in connection with your application for enrollment as a citizen by intermarriage of the Cherokee Nation is returned to you herewith, copies of the same being retained in the files of this office.

                            Respectfully,

Encl. W-19   Commissioner.
S.W.

Index

(UNKNOWN), Cynthia Ann 336
ADAIR
   Hugh M 195,197,199
   James W 187
   Nancy 279
   Phebe A 195
   Phoeba A 199
   Phoebe 198
   R M 195
AGNEW
   Judge W S 148
   Mary E 156,163
   W S 155,167
ALBERTY, B W 255,328
ALEXANDER, Eliza 217
ANDERSON, J C 331
ARBUCKLE, Harriett E 118
ASHTON, Blanch 44
BAGWELL
   E C 3,5,61,85,124,160,162,
   176,187,215,216,322
   E G 105
BALENTINE
   Anna H 329
   Hamilton 329
   J A A 329
   Rev Hamilton 311
BALES, Mr 105
BALLENTINE
   (Unknown) 291
   Hamilton 320
BARKER, William H 304
BARTLES, Jacob A 57
BAUGH
   J L 50,316
   Mr 317,319
BEALL, Wm O 223
BEAN, Emily 192
BECK
   M J 128
   William B 128,137
BELL
   Hooley 102,107
   L B 60
BERTHOLF, I W 166
BIXBY, Tams 6,11,12,13,27,38,47,
50,53,57,67,76,89,98,110,119,130,139,
164,168,181,189,201,211,222,232,244,
247,256,269,282,289,290,294,295,296,
309,330,333,338
BLACKSTON, Josephine 222
BLACKSTONE
   Josephine 215,216,217,218,219,220
   Jospehine 217
   P N 166
   Rose 217,219,220
   Tom 217
BLYTHE, Jack 236,237
BOUDINOT, W P 115,117,118
BOWMAN, Lucy M 228
BRANSON, Eula Jeanes 126,166
BRECKINRIDGE
   C R 6,42,49,69,70,80,92,104,113,
   121,123,144,147,149,164,183,184,185
   ,214,252,284,286,289,301,314,315,
   333
   Clifton R 185
   Commissioner ... 18,40,92,101,112,148,
   203,249
   Com'r 18,50,92,203,251,285,
   311,312,313
BREEDLOVE
   Carrie 19
   Carrie W 18,19,21,23,24,26,27,29
   Cassie 18,19,21
   Charles W 18,19,21
   James W 19,27
   John C 18,19,21
   John D 18
   John W 17,18,19,20,21,23,24,25,
   26,27,28
   Mr 22
   Walton D 18,19,21
   Wharton 18,19,21
   William O 18,19,21
BREWER
   O P 291
   Thomas 166
BRIMMER, Andrew 110
BROWN
   Henry M 277
   Henry Marshall 277
   Marshall 280
BRUTON

Index

Carrie 25
Carrie W 21
BUFFINGTON
  Ellie 187
  Ellis 184
  Narcissa 186,187,188
BURSOM
  Eliza S 52
  H G 49
  Rebecca 49
BUTLER, Eli 45
BUZZARD FLOPPER 250,253
  Martin 250
  Willie 250
CABIN
  Elmira 280
  John 280
  Miry 280
CAMPBELL, Rope 239
CARLILE
  John 224
  Josephine 215,222
  Polly 213,214
  Rosa 222
  S L 213
  Stephen 213,221
  Stephen N 213,214,215,221, 222,223,224
  Thomas 214
CARLISLE
  John 216,225
  Mr 220
  Mrs 217
  Stephen 218,220
  Stephen N 216,217,218,219
CARR, Jesse O ... 94,135,159,175,324,327
CATHERINE, Elmira 273
CATRON, Elmira 281
CECIL
  Maver 75
  S W 75
  Samuel 71
  Samuel W 75
CHAPELL, Walter W 228,229
CHAPPELL
  W W 125
  Walter W .... 26,85,116,127,128, 166,197,198,200,205,207,241,243,263 ,339
CHICK, Retta 33,82,114,302
CHRISTIE
  Jackson 280
  Judge 276,277,280
CLEVELAND, J C 79
COBB
  (Maggie) 151
  (Unknown) 151
  Jack 142,153
  John 221
  Maggie 153,158,163,168
  Margaret 147,164,166
COBERLY
  Georgia 198,221,231
  Walter W 230
COMBS, J M 52
COOK, W J 290
COUNCILOR, Homer J 36,197,267
COUNTRYMAN
  John 41
  Malinda 46
  Malinda A 45
  Malinda Ann 45
  Patsy 41
COWSAR, Martha 34
CRAVENS, R R 123,185,214,236, 272,315
CREEKMORE, Cora 240
CRITTENDEN
  James 246
  Martha 246
CROWDER 317
  Angeline 311,316,318,319,325, 334,338
  Mr 319
  Mrs 321
  Rosa Lee 317
DANENBERGE, Mr B M 10
DANENBURG, Elvira 1
DANIEL
  Amanda J 58
  Eliza 102
  Eliza A 107
DANIELS
  Amanda 63,64

Index

E A 104
Eliza 108
Eliza A 106,109,110
O C 262
Tom 63
DANNEBERG, Elvira 9
DANNENBERG
  E B 2,4
  Elvira 3,12,13
  Elvira B 1,2,3,4,5,6,7,8,10,11,
  14,15,16,17
  J C 4,9,12,14,16,17
  John C 2,3,4,5,7,13
  Richard M 2,4,5,6,7,10,11
DAVENPORT, Mr J S 330
DELP 327
DENENBERGE
  B M 7,8
  Mr B M 9
DENEY, Lillie 335,338
DENNIE, Lillie 312,338
DERRICK, W S 25
DINNY, *(Unknown)* 315
DOWNING
  Lillie 325
  Louis 291
DUNCAN
  James 336
  W A 187
EATON
  G W 92,93
  George W 91,92,93,94,95,96,97,
  98,99,100
  Nancy 94
  Nancy E 98
EIFFERT
  Henry 239
  Margaret 30
ELDRIDGE
  Emma 206
  Jesse 203,204,206
  Mary J 203,211
  Mr 207
  Nancy J 203,209,210,211
  Nancy Jane 208
  Simeon 202,203,204,205,208,
  209,210,211,212
  Simon 203
  William B 203
  William J 203,204
  Wm J 206
ELDRIGE
  Jessie 203
  William J 203
ELLIOTT
  Annie 151
  George W 154
FARGO, C A 208
FERGUSON, Elder T R 9
FIELD, *(Unknown)* 249
FIELDS
  Dick 304
  Elizabeth 256
  Johnson 251
  Richard 166,303,304
FIELFS, Dick 251
FOREMAN
  Jennie L 284,289,291,293
  Jesse 218,219
  John A 292
  Sallie 284
  Samuel 85,275
  Stephen 284
FRAZIER, Edward B 108
GARLAND, Sim 151
GORNEY, Mr 279
GOSS
  B F 191
  Benj F 191,195
  Benjamin F .. 191,192,194,197,199,200
  Damaris 199
  Demaris 191,192,193,194,196,
  197,198,200,201,202
  Mary 191
  Mitie 191
  Thomas 191
  W P 196
  William P 193
  Wm P 196
GRANIS, Flora 63
GREEN, M D 19,92,155,173,204,313
GRIMES, W Morris 115,118
GUINN, Jane 203
GULAGER

Index

F W 114,117
Frederick W 112,113,114,115,
116,117,118,119,120
Henry C 113
Henry G 113,114
John D 113,114
Martha 114
Martha L 112,113,114,115,116,119
Mary E 112,113,114
William M 115
GULEGAR
  F W 113
  Henry G 113
  John D 113
  Martha L 113
  Mary E 113
HAMILTON
  Elizabeth 274
  Joseph 274
HANKS
  Bettie Jane 33
  C J 221
HANNA, Gertrude 8,207
HARLAND, E J 221
HARRIS, Mr 262
HASTINGS
  Mr 2,151,152,265,280,304,321,322
  W W 13,15,16,28,29,38,47,48,
54,57,67,77,90,94,99,100,110,111,119
,120,130,131,140,150,155,169,170,
181,182,189,193,201,211,212,223,224
,227,229,230,233,242,244,245,247,
257,264,269,279,282,284,291,295,298
,302,303,309,323,345
HATCH, Florine B 314,315,320,322,
327,329,331,332
HAWKINS, W S 44
HELDERBRAND, Susan C 81
HENDERSON, Sarah 122
HENDRERICKS, James 267
HENDRICKS
  Dennis 265
  James 262
  Judge 264
HENRY
  Anna B 86,87,89
  Annie B 81,84,85

HICKS, Stephen P 220
HILDEBRAND
  Susan 86,87
  Susan C 86,88
HILDERBRAND
  Annie 226
  J M 158
  John 226
  Johny 226
  Lelia 226
  Lydia 225,226,227,228,229,230,
231,232,233,234
  Mary 230
  Mary E 230
  R M 226
  Reece 225,226,227,228,229,231,232
  Thomas 226
  William 226
HILL, Myrtle 24,35,97,138,195,
210,267,278,281
HINES, Sarah 338
HINKLE, Oliver C 221
HIX, J C 52
HOGAN
  J H 86,87
HORN
  Martha J 79,80,84
  Martha L 79
  Mattie 80
HORNE, Martha J 87,89
HOWELL, *(Unknown)* 136
HUDSON, William 242
HUMPHREY
  Mr 321,322
  W D 320
HUTCHINSON, Wm 71,193,261,273
JACKSON
  Mr 303
  W C 302
JAMES
  Jesse L 274
  Sarah 274
JOHNS, Lena 148,167
JONES
  B C5,21,23,43,51,60,61,94,106,125,160,162,17:
  Bruce C 31,103
  Lena 148

Index

Lena J 147,163
Lillie 311,312,333,338
KARNEGAY
  Mr 316,319
  W H 316
KARNES, Joseph N 10
KAUFMAN, M S 167
KELLEY
  John D 246
  Margaret E 178
  Martha 246,247,248
KELLY, Thomas 9
KETCHUM, James 107
KEYES, *(Mr)* 105
KEYS
  James 108
  James M 64
  Jim 102
  Levi 280
  William 280
KIEFER, Henry 174,176
KOLPIN
  Augusta 259
  Charles 259,260,261,267
  Charles W 258,259,260,261,262, 263,264,265,266,267,268,269,270
  Chas W 259
  Eliza 259,260,262,263,267,268
  John P 267
  Leon 259
KORNEGAY, W H 320,330,340,341
LAMAR
  Frank 172,174,175,177,178,179, 180,181
  Frankie 173,174,175
  Franklin 175,176
  Jennie 176
  Jesse 173
  Jessie 173,174,175
  Lucius 173,174,175
  Mabel 173,174,175
  Mary 171,172,173,174,175,176, 177,178,179,180,181,182
  Maud 173,174,175
  Mildred 173,174,175
  Nettie 173,174,175
LAMAT, Mary 177

LANE
  F Elma 116,263
  Frances R26,45,71,73,74,108,109,118,137,
LATTA, Lydia 225
LATTY, Lydia 231
LAWERY, Judge 250
LEAMASTER
  Alice May 184
  Curtis 184
  Elizabeth 184
  Jessie 184
  John 183,184
  Narcissa 184
  Nellie 184
LEMASTER
  Alice May 186
  Curtis 186
  Elizbeth 186
  Jessie 186
  Joe 190
  John 183,185,186,187,188,189,190
  Narcissa 185,186,188
  Nellie 186
  William 186
LESSLEY, Geo H 307,308
LILARD, Eliza 267
LILLARD, Eliza 261,262,263,264,268
LINDFSAY, R W 65
LINDS(E)Y, Harvy 32
LINDSAT, Elizabeth Jane 31
LINDSAY
  Bettie 31
  Bettie J 31
  Elizabeth Jane 30,31
  Harry 31
  Harvey 30,31
LINDSEY
  Bettie Jane 32
  Dr H 36
  Dr Harvey 35
  Dr Harvy 35
  Elizabeth J 32,34,35
  H 221
  Harvey 32,33,35
  Harvy 32
LINDSY
  Elizabeth J 31,37

Index

Harvy 30,31,37,38,39
Harvy W 39
LINSDAY
   Elizabeth Jane 31
   Harvey 31
LOSER, Walter 264
LOWERY, Judge 250
LOWREY, Judge 253
LOZIER, Walter 263
LYNCH, Susan 218
MALL, Jonathan 63
MALLORY, Mary Tabor 59,188
MARTIN
   Elizabeth 251
   Emma 250
   William 250,253
   William H 251
MCCARKLE, J L 158
MCCARKLEY, W F 165
MCCARTEY, Mrs E J 36
MCCARTY
   Bettie J 35
   Bettie Jane 33
MCCARTY, Elizabeth J 37
MCCLELLAN
   C M 284,286,292,297
   Charles 284
   Charles M 283,284,286,287,288,
   289,290,291,292,293,294,295,296,298
   ,299
   Jennie L 284,287,288,293
   M 292
MCCLELLAND, Charles M 287
MCCORKLE
   (Mr) 153
   J L 36
MCCOY, J O 221
MCCRARY
   Amanda J 66
   Rev John W 102
MCCRONE, Hiram 59
MCDANIEL
   Martin 319
   Mr 304,305
   Mrs 304
   Nan 300
   Nancy 300,301,302,305,306,
   307,308,310
   T B 300,301
   Thomas 302
   Thomas B 299,300,301,302,303,
   304,306,307,308,309,310
MCDANIELS
   Mr 304
   Thomas B 303
MCDONALD
   B 41
   Brown 191,192,226
MCELMEAL, Peter 254,255
MCELMEEL
   Betsie 254
   Elizabeth 250,251,252,253,254,256
   Peter 248,249,250,252,254,256,
   257,258
MCGHEE
   T J 46
   Z M 52
MCKENNON, *(Mr)* 22
MCMURRAY, Mrs 218
MCSPADDEN
   Clem M 103,104
   Eliza 108
   Eliza A 109
   Helen 104
   Herbert T 103,104
   John T 101,103,104,106,107,
   108,109,110,111
   Maud I 103,104
   May 103,104
   Pauline 104
   Sallie 103,105
   Sallie C 103,104,105,107,109
   Thomas 103
   Thomas J 103
MEAK
   Abe 312
   Barilla 312
MEEK
   Abraham 320
   Abram 310,311,320,321,323,324,
   332,333,334,337,338,339,340,341,342
   ,343,345,346
   Abrasm 328
   Alta Barilla 337,338

Index

Alta Barrilla 324
Barilla 338
Ethel R 313,323,324,326,333,
341,342,343
Ethel Ray 312
Lillie 323,324,326,336,341
Mr 327
Myrtle 332
Myrtle E 312,313,323,324,326,
333,341,342,343
Sabra E 312,313
W A 339
William A 312,313
MEEKS 315
Abe 314
Abraham 316,317,318,319,330,331
Abram 312,320,328
Ethel 314,331
Ethel R 314
Lilli 331
Lillian 330
Lillie 320,330
Myrtle 314,331,332
Myrtle L 314
Sabra E 312
Wm A 312
MELTON, A N 328
MERRICK, Edward 45,65,74,88,
109,126,137,178,180,220,293,306,314,
316,320,322,327,329,331,332
MIELENZ, Ella 149,331,329
MILLER
Charles 236,237
Charley 236
Charlie 235
Chute 235,236,237
Cora 235,236,237,238,241,244
Franch 238
French 234,235,236,237,238,239,
240,241,242,243,244,245
Ida 239,241,243
Katie 243,244
Leslie 239,241,243
Lillie 314,335,336,338,342
Oscar 239,241,243
Susie 241
MITCHELL

Anna B 89
Beulah 84
Beulah B 80
Beulah V 80,83
Beulah W 79
Bulah V 79
Claud S 79,80,83
Claud Stevens 87
Claude S 87
Clay 84
Clay A 79,80,83
George 79,80,84
George W 78,79,80,81,82,83,85,
86,87,88,89,90,91
George W, Jr 79,80,83
Joseph 84
Joseph F 79,80,83
Lee 81,84
Lee R 79,80,83
Levia L 83
Martha J 79,80,81,83,84,87,89
Mattie J 79,80
Mr 85
Robert 81
Robert L 83
Ross 84
Ross B 80,83
Ross Benge 81
Sabola L 87
Savola L 79,80,82,83
Sivolie 79
Susan 80,83
Susan C 81,83,87,88,89
MONROE, T R 166
MOORE 325
Angeline 311,312
Bily 317
Nancy 316,335
MORRIS
D M 195,199
Rev D M 195
MYERS, Clinton W 274
NEEDLES
Commissioner 30,151,152,153,154,
155,191,259,300
Com'r 59,80,173,259,300
T B 6,19,31,50,58,59,79,82,

353

Index

133,144,146,149,164,173,192,204,225,226,235,236,254,260,271,272,289, 313,316,319,322,332,333
NEILSON 317
NICHOLSON, T A 75
PACE
   Demaris 195
   Mattie M 337
PARRIS 325
   (Unknown) 316
PERRY
   Earnest B 51
   Earnest Bursom 49
   Earnest V 50
   Effie D 49,51
   Eliver V 49
   Eliza 50
   Eliza A 50
   Ella D 50
   Merthe 50
   Myrtle 49,51
   O V 52,55
   Oliver B 51
   Oliver H 49,50,51
   Oliver V 53,55
   Stacy E 51,53,54,55,56,57
   Stacy Eliza 49
   Susan J 53,55,56
PETIT, Amanda 65
PETITT
   Bill 63,64
   Frank 63,64
   Minerva 64
PETTIT, Lottie 217
PHILIPPS, Elmo 122
PHILIPS
   Nancy 136,138
   Nancy J 135
   Sarah 122
PHILLIPPS, Dock 122
PHILLIPS
   Dock 122
   Elijah 122
   Elmer D 122
   Elmer L 122,123,124
   Elmer Lee 122
   Elmer R 123

Frank 126
Henry 122
Henry C 122,123,124
Henry P 121,122,123,124,125, 126,127,128,129,130
J Frank 127
Nancy J 139
Roie E 122
Roxie 123
Roxie E 123,124
Sarah 121,122,123,124,125,127, 128,129,130,131
Sarah A 126
Sidney 122
RASMUS, B P 25,33,62,65,95,96,106, 135,227,264,265,266,276,279,291,292
RAYMOND
   Alford C 59
   Alfred C 58,60,61,62,64,65,66,67,68
   Amanda 61
   Amanda J 58,59,60,61,66
   A C 59
   Minerva 66
RAYMONG
   Alford C 59
   Amanda J 59
   A C 59
RED BIRD, Daniel ......11,26,37,47,53,55, 66,76,89,98,110,119,130,139,168,181,188 ,200,211,222,232,244,246,256,268,281, 293,308,338
REUTER, P G ...3,33,82,114,135,159,324
RIDER, Wilson 279
RIDGE
   Eneas 70
   Widow 73
ROGERS
   Clem Mayes 103
   Clem V 103
   Helen 103
   Herbert Thomas 103
   Mary 103
   Maud Irene 103
   Sallie 103
   Sallie C 107,109
   W B 166
ROSS

Index

(Unknown) 303
Joshua 150,166
Mr 153,318
Rufus 291
ROSSON
   J O 50,59,69,70,80,133,146,
   157,252,260,287,301
   John O 71,261,274
ROTHENBERGER, E G 21,23,43,51,
60,144,146,148,205,237,253,288
RUNYAN
   Cora 235,236,240,241,242,244
   Ross 235
RUSSELL, Minerva 62,66
SANDERS
   (Mr) 69
   Elizabeth 69
   Geo O 255
SCALES, I A 220,221
SCHRIMP, Alta B 325
SCHRIMPSCHER
   Elizabeth 112
   Martin 112
SCHRIMPSHER
   Martha 117
   Martha L 118,119
SCHRIMSHER
   Alta Berrilla 334
   Barilla 311,341
   Barrilla 320
   Berilla 328
   Berrilla 336
   Lillie 321
   Martha L 115
SCRIMPSHER, Berillar 328
SHAW, Nancy 306
SHRIMSHER, Alta Barilla 337
SMITH
   Frank 306
   J L L 166
   Mr 307
SNYDER
   Anna B 87
   Anna H 86
   Hiram 86,87
   Hiram R 85,87
SOPER, HUCKLEBERRY & OWEN 279

SPANIARD 251
   Elizabeth 249,250,254,255
SREVENS, Elmira 275
STANBERRY
   (Unknown) 172
   Jane 172
STANLEY, W E 333
STANSBERG, Mary 177
STARR
   J C 20,174,324
   Mr 302,326
STEPHENS
   Elizabeth 271
   Elmira 271
   Fannie 271
   Henderson 271
   Sarah 271
   Stephen 271
STEVANS, Elmira 275
STEVENS
   Elizabeth 271,272,274
   Elmira ... 271,272,273,274,276,277,281
   Fannie 274
   Fanny 271,272
   Henderson 277,279,280
   Sarah 271,272
   Stephen 271,272,274
   William H 270,272,273,274,275,
   276,277,278,279,281,282,283
   William H, Sr 274
   William Henderson 271,272,273,275
STIFF, Nancy 308
STINGER
   David 315
   Louisa 314,315
   Mattie 312,315
   Mrs David 315
STOAKS
   Elizabeth 43
   James R 43
   Martin L 43
   Mattie L 43,44
STRINGER, Mattie 338
STROUT 108
   Eliza 102
   Eliza A 107
   F W 105

Index

Frederick W 102
STUBBLEFIELD, Demie T 65
TAYLOR
   Judge 152,153
   Mr Judge 152
   R R 25
   Sam 165
   Saml M 255
   Saml U 36
   Samuel 35
THOMAS
   John R 312,330,331
   Malinda A 45
THOMPSON
   (Mr) 105
   J F 177,179
   Joe L 108
   Mr 178
THORN, Mary 72
THORNTON
   John 136,138
   Judge 136
   Nancy J 204,211
   Nancy Jane 203,206
TIDWELL
   J E 334
   J R 176,178
   John E 23,97,129,164,169,210, 228,275,278,281,308,337
VALENTINE, James 334
VAN, Katie 238
VANCE, H M 94,166,179,227,238,336
VANN
   Kate 238,239,240,241,242
   Katie 237,243
VESTAL
   Doctor 2
   Mary J 2,3
   Miss E B 7,9,10
VICKORY, Lucy 153
VICTORY, Lucy 142
VON WEISE, Chas 113,286,319
VORE, Frank 219
WALDRON, Major 238,242
WALDRON & CRAMER 238,242
WALKER
   Judge Tim 303,307

W H 115
William H 278
WALTERS, Mary 230
WARD
   Henry J 339
   Laura 169
   T F 96
WATERS, Sarah 129
WEBSTER
   C E 242
   Chas E 8,36,37,59,138,188,195, 197,255
WHISENHUNT
   Fred 133
   Frederick 132,133,134,135
   Nancy 133,134,135
   Nancy J 132,133,134,135,136,137, 138,139
   Noah 132,133,134,135,136,137,138, 139,140,141
WHISSENHUNT, Noah 132
WILLEY
   Charley 240
   Rev 240
WILLIAM, George W 45
WILLIAMS
   Allie B 41,42,43
   Ally 41
   Andre W M 42
   Andrew W M 41,43
   Arthur R 41,42,43
   Auther 41
   Charlotte C 42,43
   George W 40,42,43,45,46,47,48
   Geroge 41
   John D 40
   Malid 44
   Malind 41
   Malinda 42,43
   Malinda N 41,42,46,47
   Mattie L 41,42,43
   Nan 97
   Nancy E 92
   Nancy Elizabeth 95
   Nancy M 41
   Narcissa 40
   Watie M 41

Index

WILSON
  Charles B 199
  Rory 209
WINSTON, Jas A 331
WOODALL
  Abe 221
  J P 69
  John F 73
  John P 69,71,73,74,76
  John Peter 70
  Judge 159,227
  M (Maud) 69
  M M 69
  Margaret M 68,71,72,73,74,76,77,78
  Margaret Maver 70
  Maver M 69,70,71
  Thomas 228,229
  Thomas F 231
  Tom 228
  William C 73
WOODSON, C R 1,2,12
WRIGHT, S T 88
WYNNE, H C 231
YOUNG, Roach 291
ZUFALL
  Benjaimin 143
  Benjamin H 142,159,161,162,163
  Eva 163
  George .... 141,143,144,145,147, 150,152,154,155,156,158,159,160,161 ,162,163,164,165,166,167,168,169, 170
  George, Jr 146,162,163
  George, Sr 156
  Grace 143
  Grace A 142,159,161,162,163
  Herbert 142,143,159,161,162,163
  Lena 167
  Lena J 147
  Lewis 148
  Lewis E 147,149,157,162,163,167
  Louia 167
  Maggie .... 142,143,145,146,152,153, 154,156,157,159,161,162,163,168,169 ,170
  Maggie, Jr 143
  Margaret 156,161,164,171

Marion B 148
Marion R 147,163
Marion Raymond 149
Mr 151
Mrs 150,151
Oscar O 142,159,161,162,163
Otto 143
Pearl 143,154,160
Pearl E 142,159,161,162,163
Pearl Elizabeth 159
Warren E 147,148,163,164

www.ingramcontent.com/pod-product-compliance
Lightning Source LLC
Chambersburg PA
CBHW020240030426
42336CB00010B/550